Exam Ref SC-300 Microsoft Identity and Access Administrator

Razi Rais
Ilya Lushnikov
Jeevan Bisht
Padma Chilakapati
Vinayak Shenoy

Exam Ref SC-300 Microsoft Identity and Access Administrator

Published with the authorization of Microsoft Corporation by: Pearson Education, Inc.

ISBN-13: 978-0-13-788652-4
ISBN-10: 0-13-788652-7

Library of Congress Control Number: 2022949358

1 2022

TRADEMARKS

Microsoft and the trademarks listed at http://www.microsoft.com on the "Trademarks" webpage are trademarks of the Microsoft group of companies. All other marks are property of their respective owners.

WARNING AND DISCLAIMER

Every effort has been made to make this book as complete and as accurate as possible, but no warranty or fitness is implied. The information provided is on an "as is" basis. The author, the publisher, and Microsoft Corporation shall have neither liability nor responsibility to any person or entity with respect to any loss or damages arising from the information contained in this book or from the use of the programs accompanying it.

SPECIAL SALES

For information about buying this title in bulk quantities, or for special sales opportunities (which may include electronic versions; custom cover designs; and content particular to your business, training goals, marketing focus, or branding interests), please contact our corporate sales department at corpsales@pearsoned.com or (800) 382-3419.

For government sales inquiries, please contact governmentsales@pearsoned.com.

For questions about sales outside the U.S., please contact intlcs@pearson.com.

EDITOR-IN-CHIEF
Brett Bartow

EXECUTIVE EDITOR
Loretta Yates

ASSOCIATE EDITOR
Charvi Arora

DEVELOPMENT EDITOR
Songlin Qi

MANAGING EDITOR
Sandra Schroeder

SENIOR PROJECT EDITOR
Tracey Croom

COPY EDITOR
Dan Foster

INDEXER
Valerie Haynes Perry

PROOFREADER
Scout Festa

TECHNICAL EDITOR
Jesse Spangenberger

EDITORIAL ASSISTANT
Cindy Teeters

COVER DESIGNER
Twist Creative, Seattle

COMPOSITOR
Danielle Foster

GRAPHICS
Vived Graphics

Pearson's Commitment to Diversity, Equity, and Inclusion

Pearson is dedicated to creating bias-free content that reflects the diversity of all learners. We embrace the many dimensions of diversity, including but not limited to race, ethnicity, gender, socioeconomic status, ability, age, sexual orientation, and religious or political beliefs.

Education is a powerful force for equity and change in our world. It has the potential to deliver opportunities that improve lives and enable economic mobility. As we work with authors to create content for every product and service, we acknowledge our responsibility to demonstrate inclusivity and incorporate diverse scholarship so that everyone can achieve their potential through learning. As the world's leading learning company, we have a duty to help drive change and live up to our purpose to help more people create a better life for themselves and to create a better world.

Our ambition is to purposefully contribute to a world where:

- Everyone has an equitable and lifelong opportunity to succeed through learning.
- Our educational products and services are inclusive and represent the rich diversity of learners.
- Our educational content accurately reflects the histories and experiences of the learners we serve.
- Our educational content prompts deeper discussions with learners and motivates them to expand their own learning (and worldview).

While we work hard to present unbiased content, we want to hear from you about any concerns or needs with this Pearson product so that we can investigate and address them.

Please contact us with concerns about any potential bias at
https://www.pearson.com/report-bias.html.

I would like to dedicate this book to my mother, Zahida, my lovely wife, Javeria, and my sister, Khaizran. Their love knows no bounds, and their encouragement has inspired me to believe that I can achieve anything.

—RAZI RAIS

To all dreamers who started small like me

—JEEVAN BISHT

Contents

Introduction   **xiii**

Organization of this book. xiii

Preparing for the exam xiv

Microsoft certifications xiv

Quick access to online references. xiv

Errata, updates, & book support. xv

Stay in touch xv

Chapter 1   **Implement identities in Azure AD**   **1**

Skill 1.1: Configure and manage an Azure AD tenant 3

    Configure and manage Azure AD roles   3

    Configure delegation by using administrative units   11

    Analyze Azure AD role permissions   14

    Configure and manage custom domains   16

    Configure tenant-wide settings   20

Skill 1.2: Create, configure, and manage Azure AD identities. 22

    Create, configure, and manage users   23

    Create, configure, and manage groups   26

    Configure and manage device joins and registrations,
including writeback   33

    Assign, modify, and report on licenses   37

Skill 1.3: Implement and manage external identities 40

    Manage external collaboration settings in Azure AD   41

    Invite external users, individually or in bulk (collectively)   45

Manage external user accounts in Azure AD   51

Configure identity providers, including SAML and WS-Fed   54

Skill 1.4: Implement and manage hybrid identity 56

Implement and manage Azure Active Directory Connect   57

Implement and manage Azure AD Connect cloud sync   66

Implement and manage Password Hash Synchronization (PHS)   74

Implement and manage Pass-Through Authentication (PTA)   77

Implement and manage Seamless Single Sign-On
(Seamless SSO)   81

Implement and manage Federation, excluding manual
ADFS deployment   82

Implement and manage Azure AD Connect Health   91

Troubleshoot synchronization errors   99

Chapter summary 102

Thought experiment. 103

Thought experiment answers 104

Chapter 2   **Implement an authentication and access
management solution**   **105**

Skill 2.1: Plan, implement, and manage Azure Multifactor
Authentication (MFA) and self-service password reset 106

Plan Azure MFA deployment, excluding MFA Server   106

Configure and deploy self-service password reset   108

Implement and manage Azure MFA settings   115

Manage MFA settings for users   119

Extend Azure AD MFA to third-party and on-premises devices   122

Monitor Azure AD MFA activity   123

Skill 2.2: Plan, implement, and manage Azure AD user authentication. . . . 123

Plan for authentication   124

Implement and manage authentication methods 125

Implement and manage Windows Hello for Business 132

Implement and manage password protection and
smart lockout 135

Implement certificate-based authentication in Azure AD 144

Configure Azure AD user authentication for Windows
and Linux virtual machines on Azure 146

Skill 2.3: Plan, implement, and manage Azure AD conditional access . . . 147

Plan conditional access policies 147

Implement conditional access policy assignments 152

Implement conditional access policy controls 159

Test and troubleshoot conditional access policies 161

Implement session management 165

Implement device-enforcement restrictions 165

Implement continuous access evaluation 167

Create a conditional access policy from a template 167

Skill 2.4: Manage Azure AD Identity Protection 168

Implement and manage a user risk policy 168

Implement and manage sign-in risk policy 172

Implement and manage MFA registration policy 175

Monitor, investigate, and remediate elevated risky users 176

Implement security for workload identities 187

Skill 2.5: Implement access management for Azure resources 190

Assign Azure roles 190

Configure custom Azure roles 191

Create and configure managed identities 193

Use managed identities to access Azure resources 194

Analyze Azure role permissions 195

Configure Azure Key Vault RBAC and policies 196

Chapter summary 198

Thought experiment. 199

Thought experiment answers 200

Chapter 3   Implement Access Management for Apps   201

Skill 3.1: Plan, implement, and monitor the integration of
Enterprise apps for SSO 202

Discover apps by using Microsoft Defender for Cloud Apps
or an ADFS application activity report   202

Design and implement app management roles   208

Understand and plan various built-in roles for application
management   212

Configure pre-integrated gallery SaaS apps for SSO and
implement access management   216

Integrate custom SaaS apps for SSO   220

Implement Application User Provisioning   225

Integrate on-premises apps by using the Azure AD
Application Proxy   229

Monitor and audit access/sign-ons to an Azure AD
integrated Enterprise application   234

Implement and configure consent settings   238

Skill 3.2: Implement app registrations. 240

Plan your line-of-business application registration strategy   240

Implement application registrations   244

Configure application permissions and implement
application authorization   250

Skill 3.3: Manage and monitor application access by using
Microsoft Defender for Cloud Apps. 261

Implement application-enforced restrictions   261

Configure connectors to apps   264

Deploy Conditional Access App Control for apps using

Azure Active Directory   266

Create access and session policies in Microsoft Defender
for Cloud Apps   270

Implement and manage policies for OAuth apps   275

Chapter summary 278

Thought experiment. 280

Thought experiment answers 281

Chapter 4 **Plan and implement an Identity
Governance strategy**   **283**

Skill 4.1: Plan and implement entitlement management. 284

Plan entitlements   284

Create and configure catalogs   286

Create and configure access packages   288

Manage access requests   293

Implement and manage Terms of Use   295

Manage the lifecycle of external users in Azure AD
Identity Governance settings   297

Configure and manage connected organizations   298

Review per-user entitlement by using Azure AD
entitlement management   299

Configure separation of duties checks for an access package   300

Skill 4.2: Plan, implement, and manage access reviews. 301

Plan for access reviews   302

Create and configure access reviews for groups and apps   306

Create and configure access reviews for access packages   311

Create and configure access reviews for Azure AD and
Azure resource roles   313

Create and configure access review programs   314

Monitor access review activity   315

Manage licenses for access reviews 318

Respond to access review activity, including automated
and manual responses 319

Skill 4.3: Plan and implement privileged access 320

Plan and manage Azure roles in Privileged Identity
Management (PIM), including settings and assignments 320

Plan and manage Azure resources in PIM, including settings
and assignments 328

Plan and configure privileged access groups 329

Analyze PIM audit history and reports 330

Create and manage break-glass accounts 334

Skill 4.4: Monitor Azure AD 335

Design a strategy for monitoring Azure AD 336

Review and analyze sign-in, audit, and provisioning logs
by using the Azure AD admin center 336

Configure diagnostic settings, including Log Analytics,
storage accounts, and Event Hub 345

Export sign-in and audit logs to a third-party SIEM 347

Monitor Azure AD by using Log Analytics, including
KQL queries 348

Analyze Azure AD by using workbooks and reporting
in the Azure Active Directory admin center 352

Configure notifications 356

Monitor and improve the security posture by using the
Identity Secure Score 357

Chapter summary 358

Thought experiment 359

Thought experiment answers 360

Index   361

Acknowledgments

The authors would like to thank Charvi and Loretta from the Pearson team for their unwavering support throughout this book's journey. They have been extremely helpful throughout the process. Finally, special thanks go to the editors and the entire Pearson team for going over the content with a fine-tooth comb and sharing their findings.

Razi Rais would like to thank: First and foremost, I would like to express my gratitude to my family, which includes three wonderful women in my life, especially my mother, Zahida, for her unquestioning support and encouragement. I would also like to thank Javeria, my wonderful and supportive wife, for putting up with my crazy schedule and allowing me to devote many weekends and evenings to this book. Finally, I'd like to thank my sister, Khaizran, for always instilling confidence and motivating me.

Ilya Lushnikov would like to thank: My son for his endless energy, hugs, and making me proud every day. I would like to thank my parents for their love and support. I would also like to thank Microsoft founders and employees for creating the company of my dreams.

Jeevan Bisht would like to thank: My whole Microsoft IDNA CXP team who never ceases to amaze me, my first professional certification mentor, Amar Kant, and first manager, Piyush Mittal of Asset Infotech, who supported me in my early career days. Of course, my wife, Indu Bisht, my kids, Lakshita and Reyansh, who always supported me and lend time slices from our family time.

Padma Chilakapati would like to thank: My husband and daughters for always being my strength and supporting me in all my endeavors, and my selfless and loving mom who's always been my rock. Thanks to all my coworkers over the years who have spent time to help me improve in my career.

Vinayak Shenoy would like to thank: The entire feature PM, data-scientist, and engineering crew at Microsoft, who work tirelessly every day to make this peerless feature a success! I hope I've done your incredible work justice, and all the credit goes to you!

S,S,K,P: You've always supported and believed in me and have been my inspiration! This one is for you!

To our customers and the identity–security community at large, you challenge us to make better products and to make the cloud safer and more secure!

About the Authors

RAZI RAIS has over two decades of experience designing and developing highly scalable and secure enterprise software and cloud services. He has been working at Microsoft for over ten years, serving in various roles such as software engineer, architect, and product manager. His current focus at Microsoft is on helping businesses strengthen their cybersecurity posture by protecting workloads at scale against the most sophisticated cyberattacks. Razi is also the lead author of several books, including *Zero Trust Networks, 2nd Edition* by O'Reilly Media and *Programming Microsoft's Clouds: Windows Azure and Office 365* by Wrox Press. He is also a member of the IEEE Computer Society, ACM, SANS advisory board, as well as a frequent speaker at international conferences and an instructor who provides security-related training all over the world. You can get in touch with him via LinkedIn at *linkedin.com/in/razirais* or through his website, *razibinrais.com*. His GitHub profile is *github.com/razi-rais*.

ILYA LUSHNIKOV is a Senior Product Manager in the Identity and Network Access division at Microsoft, where he works on new Azure AD features. Ilya has been working for Microsoft since 2010 in various positions, including six years as a Premier Field Engineer. He delivered Identity workshops, deployment projects, risk assessments, and health checks for customers in 10 countries and 25 U.S. states. Before joining Microsoft, he was a systems administrator for various companies.

JEEVAN BISHT has a Master of Science degree in computer science and is Principal PM Manager in the Microsoft Identity and Network Access division, where he leads a team of deep technical experts around the world to help enterprise customers plan and deploy their hybrid cloud identity strategies. Jeevan has been working for Microsoft since 2005 in different positions including being a senior support escalation engineer in CSS, Microsoft Consulting, helping design and implement some of the largest implementations on Identity and Management solutions across industry verticals. He has been a Microsoft Certified Professional since 1999 among other industry certifications from Cisco, Sun, and others, and has delivered training on various platforms. He has also been featured in conferences like Microsoft Ready, TechMentor, Identiverse, and many others. He is open to helping professionals grow: *linkedin.com/in/jeevan-bisht-a2a2634b/*

PADMA CHILAKAPATI is a Senior Product Manager in the Microsoft Identity and Network Access division. She acts as a trusted advisor to Fortune 500 enterprises in the Identity and Security space. She held multiple positions as an engineer and later program manager. She delivered Identity workshops and has spoken about Azure AD features and security recommendations at various conferences.

VINAYAK SHENOY is a Senior Product Manager focused on Microsoft Identity Security. As an engineer and later as product manager, he has more than a decade of experience across Identity/Access Management, wired/wireless networking, security, SDN, and datacenter/cloud provisioning.

Introduction

The goal of this book is help you prepare for the SC-300 Exam: Microsoft Identity and Access Administrator certification. This exam targets IT professionals who design, implement, and operate an organization's identity and access management systems by using Microsoft Azure Active Directory (Azure AD). This exam focuses on topics such as the planning and implementing of identity governance, self-service management capabilities, secure authentication and authorization, monitoring, troubleshooting, and reporting across the organization. This book provides comprehensive coverage of exam domain objectives, including hands-on exercises, explanations, exam tips, and demonstrations of real-world design scenarios. While we've made every effort possible to make the information in this book accurate, Azure is rapidly evolving, and it's possible that some parts of the Azure portal interface might be slightly different now than they were when this book was written, which might result in some figures in this book looking different than what you see on your screen. It's also possible that other minor interface changes have taken place, such as feature name changes and so on.

This book covers every major topic found on the exam, but it does not cover every specific exam question. Only the Microsoft exam team has access to the exam questions, and Microsoft regularly adds new questions to the exam, making it impossible to cover specific questions. You should consider this book a supplement to your relevant real-world experience and other study materials. If you encounter a topic in this book that you do not feel completely comfortable with, use the "Need More Review?" links that you'll find in the text to find more information and take the time to research and study the topic. Great information is available on MSDN, TechNet, and in blogs and forums.

Organization of this book

This book is organized by the "Skills measured" list published for the exam. The "Skills measured" list is available for each exam on the Microsoft Learn website: https://learn.microsoft.com/microsoft.com/learn. Each chapter in this book corresponds to a major topic in the list, and the technical tasks in each topic determine a chapter's organization. If an exam covers six major topic areas, for example, the book will contain six chapters.

Preparing for the exam

Microsoft certification exams are a great way to build your résumé and let the world know about your level of expertise. Certification exams validate your on-the-job experience and product knowledge. Although there is no substitute for on-the-job experience, preparation through study and hands-on practice can help you prepare for the exam. This book is *not* designed to teach you new skills.

We recommend that you augment your exam preparation plan by using a combination of available study materials and courses. For example, you might use this Exam Ref and another study guide for your "at home" preparation and take a Microsoft Official Curriculum course for the classroom experience. Choose the combination that you think works best for you. Learn more about available classroom training, find free online courses and live events, and take the Microsoft Official Practice Tests that are available for many exams at *microsoft.com/learn*.

Note that this *Exam Ref* is based on publicly available information about the exam and the author's experience. To safeguard the integrity of the exam, authors do not have access to the live exam.

Microsoft certifications

Microsoft certifications distinguish you by proving your command of a broad set of skills and experience with current Microsoft products and technologies. The exams and corresponding certifications are developed to validate your mastery of critical competencies as you design and develop, or implement and support, solutions with Microsoft products and technologies both on-premises and in the cloud. Certification brings a variety of benefits to the individual and to employers and organizations.

> **NEED MORE REVIEW?** **ALL MICROSOFT CERTIFICATIONS**
>
> For information about Microsoft certifications, including a full list of available certifications, go to *microsoft.com/learn*. Check back often to see what is new!

Quick access to online references

Throughout this book are addresses to webpages that the authors have recommended you visit for more information. Some of these links can be very long and painstaking to type, so we've shortened them for you to make them easier to visit. We've also compiled them into a single list that readers of the print edition can refer to while they read.

Download the list at *MicrosoftPressStore.com/ExamRefSC300/downloads*.

The URLs are organized by chapter and heading. Every time you come across a URL in the book, you can find the hyperlink in the list to go directly to the webpage.

Errata, updates, & book support

We've made every effort to ensure the accuracy of this book and its companion content. You can access updates to this book—in the form of a list of submitted errata and their related corrections—at:

MicrosoftPressStore.com/ExamRefSC300/errata.

If you discover an error that is not already listed, please submit it to us at the same page.

For additional book support and information, please visit *MicrosoftPressStore.com/Support*.

Please note that product support for Microsoft software and hardware is not offered through the previous addresses. For help with Microsoft software or hardware, go to *support. microsoft.com*.

Stay in touch

Let's keep the conversation going! We're on Twitter: *twitter.com/MicrosoftPress*.

CHAPTER 1

Implement identities in Azure AD

Azure Active Directory (Azure AD) is a cloud-based identity provider. It provides single sign-on access to Microsoft 365 and Azure clouds, thousands of pre-integrated Software as a Service (SaaS) applications, line-of-business applications, and platform as a service (PaaS) solutions. It provides seamless access for people located on site and remotely so that they can stay productive from anywhere. With Azure AD, you can collaborate with customers and partners using Azure AD B2B and Azure AD B2C technologies. With the Zero Trust approach, Multi-Factor Authentication (MFA), and passwordless authentication, you can provide secure access to your organization's applications and resources. Governance features help you ensure that employees and guests have the right level of access to the data when they need it.

In this chapter, we will cover initial configuration steps after you have created or inherited an Azure Active Directory (Azure AD) tenant: configuring roles for administrators, domain names, creating users and groups, managing hybrid configuration with on-premises Active Directory Domain Services (ADDS). We will also cover external identities—managing guest user access with Azure AD B2B.

Skills covered in this chapter:

- Skill 1.1: Configure and manage an Azure AD tenant
- Skill 1.2: Create, configure, and manage Azure AD identities
- Skill 1.3: Implement and manage external identities
- Skill 1.4: Implement and manage hybrid identity

New tenant setup—before you start

Setting up a new Azure AD tenant is beyond the scope of this book. There are multiple ways to create a new tenant:

- Sign up for Microsoft 365.
- Create an Azure AD tenant using the Azure portal.
- Sometimes Microsoft creates a tenant for your domain name, and you can later take over an unmanaged directory as an administrator.

Review the following documentation and create your own test tenant:

- *https://docs.microsoft.com/en-us/azure/active-directory/fundamentals/active-directory-access-create-new-tenant*
- *https://docs.microsoft.com/en-us/azure/active-directory/enterprise-users/domains-admin-takeover*

Azure AD tenant is an instance of Azure Active Directory that represents an organization. Most organizations need only one Azure AD tenant, but there are valid scenarios for which an organization may need more than one Azure AD tenant:

- National cloud deployments (Microsoft Cloud for US Government, Microsoft Cloud Germany, Azure and Microsoft 365 operated by 21ViaNet in China)
- Requirements driven by government or industry regulations
- SaaS provider scenario
- Merge and Acquisition (M&A) scenarios

For the purposes of this book, we will assume that one Azure AD tenant belongs to one organization unless stated otherwise.

Azure AD tenant can be one of two types:

- Azure Active Directory
- Azure Active Directory B2C

Azure Active Directory B2C tenants serve the purpose of hosting customer-facing applications. The type of the tenant cannot be changed after creation. For the purposes of this book and the SC-300 exam, we will cover only Azure Active Directory tenants.

Skill 1.1: Configure and manage an Azure AD tenant

With a new Azure AD tenant, you must take several steps for initial setup. In this section, we review the skills you need to manage role assignments—both tenant-wide and scoped to administrative units. Many organizations choose to configure custom domain names in their Azure AD tenant; in this section, we review reasons for this configuration and the steps for implementation.

> **This skill covers how to:**
> - Configure and manage Azure AD roles
> - Configure delegation by using administrative units
> - Analyze Azure AD role permissions
> - Configure and manage custom domains
> - Configure tenant-wide settings

Configure and manage Azure AD roles

Azure and Microsoft 365 have multiple Role-Based Access Control (RBAC) models, such as:

- Azure AD roles (also known as Azure AD directory roles)
- Azure resource roles
- Exchange Online roles
- Intune roles
- Other product-specific role models

To pass the exam, you must understand which roles will or will not be covered by the Azure AD RBAC model.

Azure AD roles can have:

- Azure AD specific permissions (such as Application Administrator or Authentication Administrator)
- Permissions across the Microsoft 365 stack covering multiple products (such as Global Administrator or Global Reader)
- High-level permissions for a specific product (such as Intune Administrator or Exchange Administrator)

Azure AD roles do not have:

- Permissions for Azure resources hosted in Azure subscriptions (such as VMs, websites, etc.)
- Granular permissions within the RBAC model of Microsoft 365 products such as Exchange, Intune, etc.

Azure AD roles can be:

- Built-in roles.

  The list of Azure AD roles is constantly expanding. You can find up-to-date information at *https://docs.microsoft.com/en-us/azure/active-directory/roles/permissions-reference*.

  Find least privileged roles by task at *https://docs.microsoft.com/en-us/azure/active-directory/roles/delegate-by-task*.

- Custom roles.

To assign a role, you need to create a *Role assignment*. A role assignment consists of the following elements:

- A security principal—a user, group, or service principal that will receive permissions
- Role information
- *Scope*
- *Type of assignment*

Scope defines which objects the security principal will have control over. Possible options are:

- Directory (Azure AD tenant)
- Administrative unit
- Azure AD resource (Azure AD group, Enterprise application, application registration)

Type of assignment defines when permissions will be available. Possible options are:

- Permanent eligible
- Permanent active
- Time-bound eligible
- Time-bound active

With eligible assignment, the security principal can get permissions just-in-time, when they need them. With active assignment, the security principal has permissions 24/7.

Time-bound assignments are typically used when a user is assigned to some project with specified start and end dates. Otherwise, permanent assignments are used.

We recommend having all Azure AD role assignments as eligible assignments with exceptions only for emergency access accounts (also known as "break glass" accounts).

To create an Azure AD role assignment using the Azure portal:

1. Open **Azure Active Directory** > **Roles and administrators** and select the role.
    See Figure 1-1. You must select the actual role name (**Application developer** in this
    example), not the checkbox on the left.

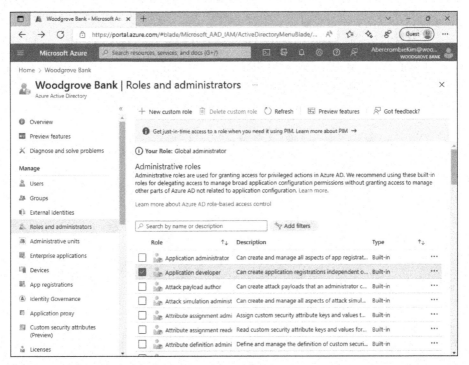

FIGURE 1-1 Roles and administrators page.

2. The next steps depend on the licensing level of your tenant—i.e., whether or not your
    license includes Azure AD Privileged Identity Management. In this book, we will assume
    that you have all necessary licenses. If you don't, you still can assign roles, but you won't
    have just-in-time capabilities or Custom roles functionality.

3. Select **Add assignments** in the Privileged Identity Management interface. See Figure 1-2.

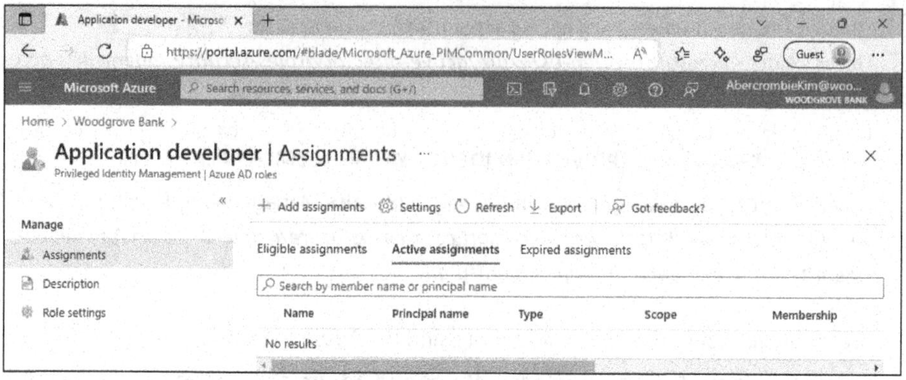

FIGURE 1-2 Assignments page for the Application developer role.

4. On the **Membership** tab of the **Add assignments** page, you specify security principals (members that should have roles assigned) and scope information. Available scope types depend on the role selected—for example, the User administrator role can be scoped to the administrative unit, since users can be included in an administrative unit, while the Application administrator role can be scoped to the Application or Service principal. Any role can be scoped to the Directory (tenant). Click **Next**. See Figure 1-3.

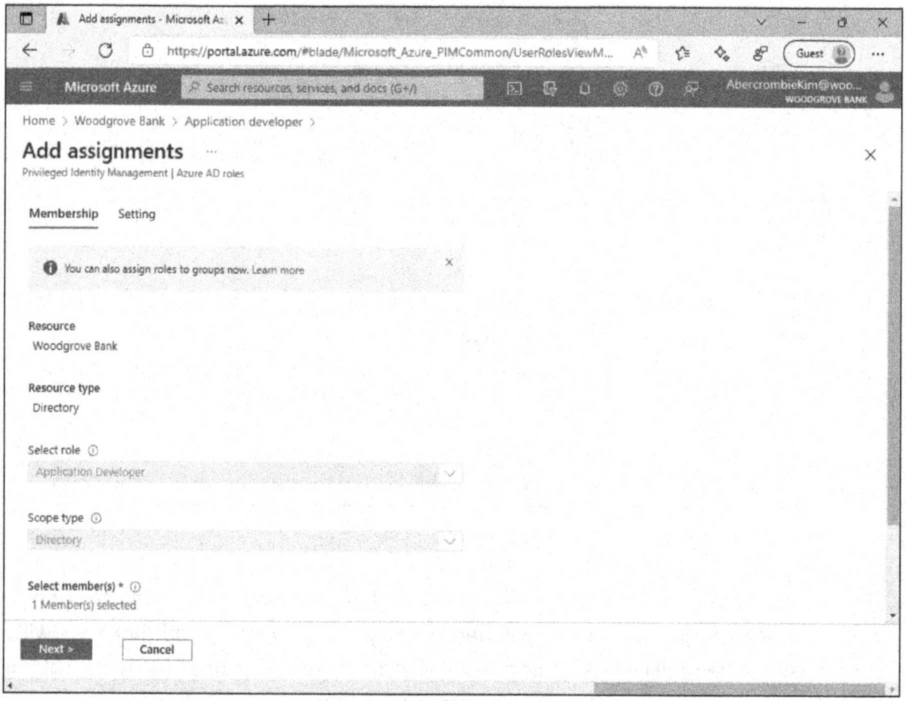

FIGURE 1-3 Add Assignments page for the Application developer role, Membership tab.

5. On the **Setting** tab of **Add assignments** page, specify the **Assignment type** (Eligible vs Active) and start/end dates if necessary. Select **Assign**. See Figure 1-4.

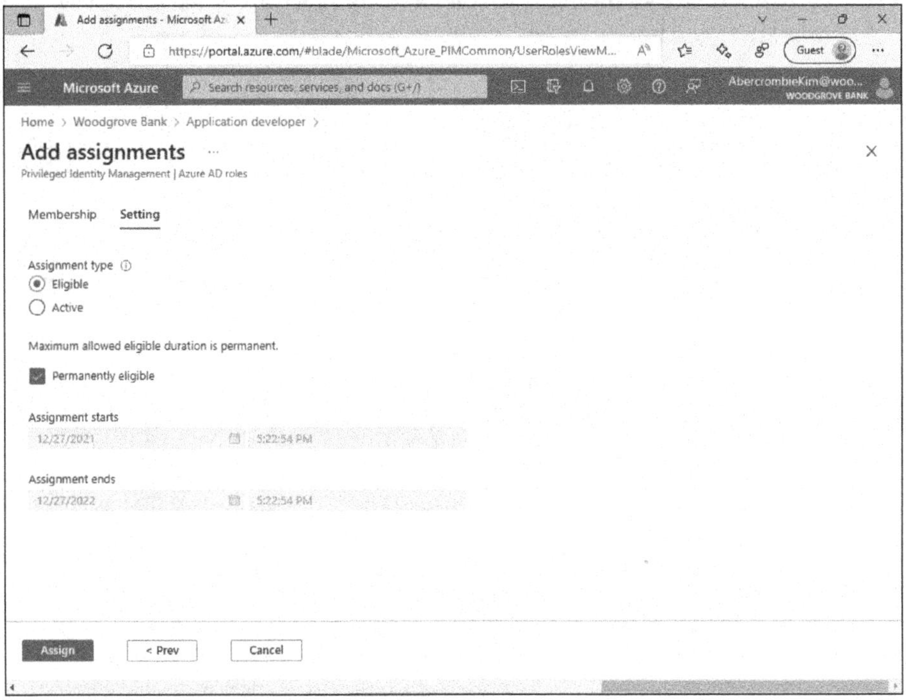

FIGURE 1-4 Add Assignments page for the Application developer role, Setting tab.

6. After an assignment is created, you can find it on the **Assignments** page on either the **Eligible assignments** or **Active assignments** tab. See Figure 1-5.

7. Use this page to remove the assignment or update assignment type if necessary.

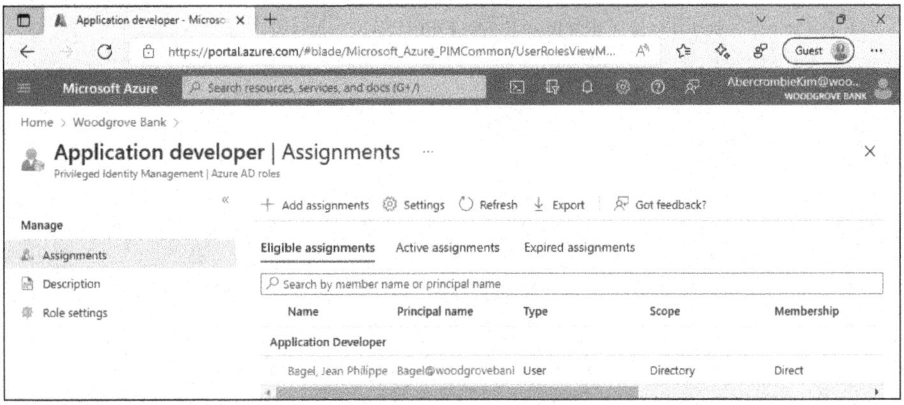

FIGURE 1-5 Add Assignments page for the Application developer role.

In the example above, we used the built-in Azure AD role. You can create your own Azure AD custom roles if you want to specify permissions granularly.

1. Open **Azure Active Directory** > **Roles and administrators** and select **New custom role**. See Figure 1-6.

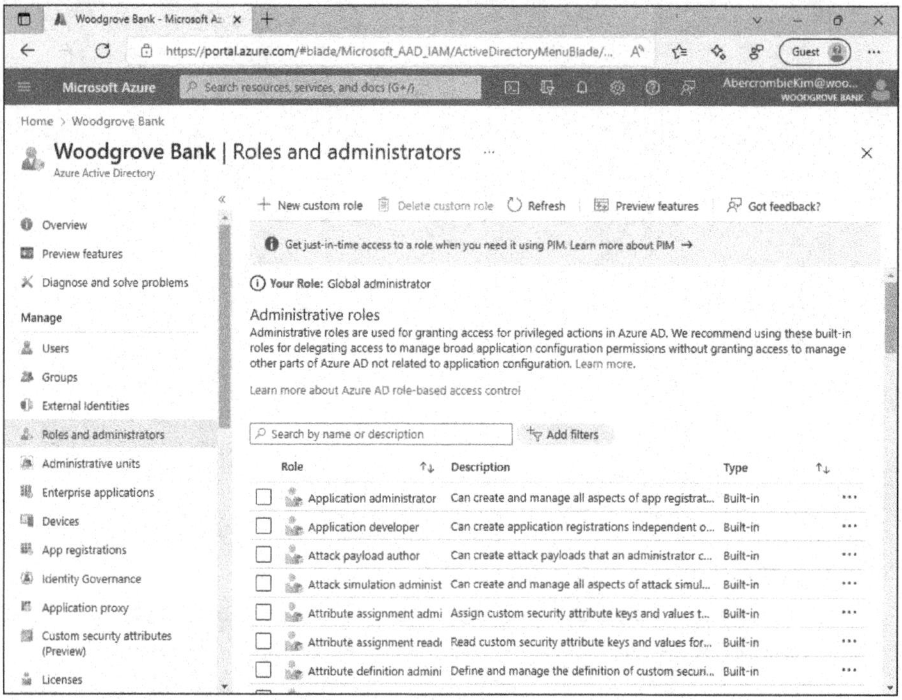

FIGURE 1-6   Roles and administrators page.

2. On the **Basics** tab of the **New custom role** page, specify the **Name** and **Description** and choose whether you want to start from scratch or clone a permissions list from an existing custom role. Click **Next**. See Figure 1-7.

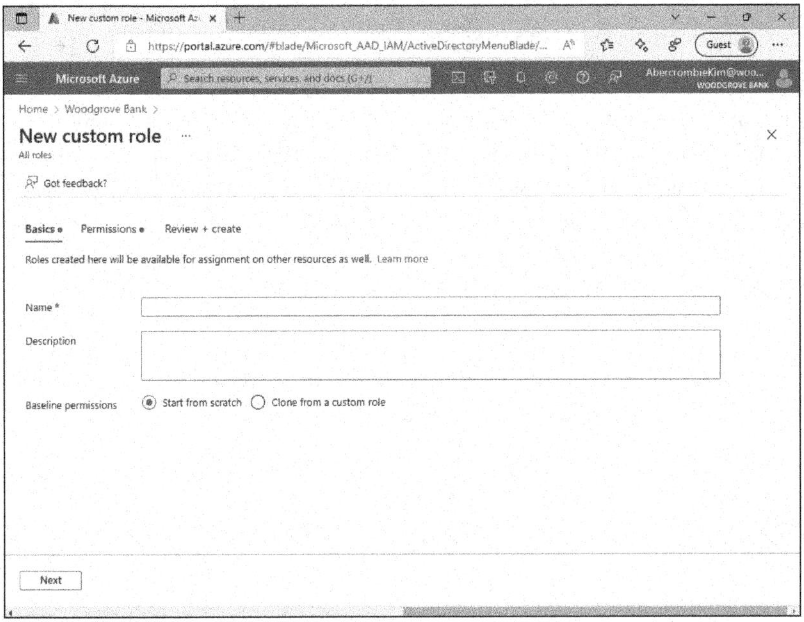

FIGURE 1-7 New custom role page, Basics tab.

3. On the **Permissions** tab of the **New custom role** page, select which permissions the new role will have. Click **Next**. See Figure 1-8.

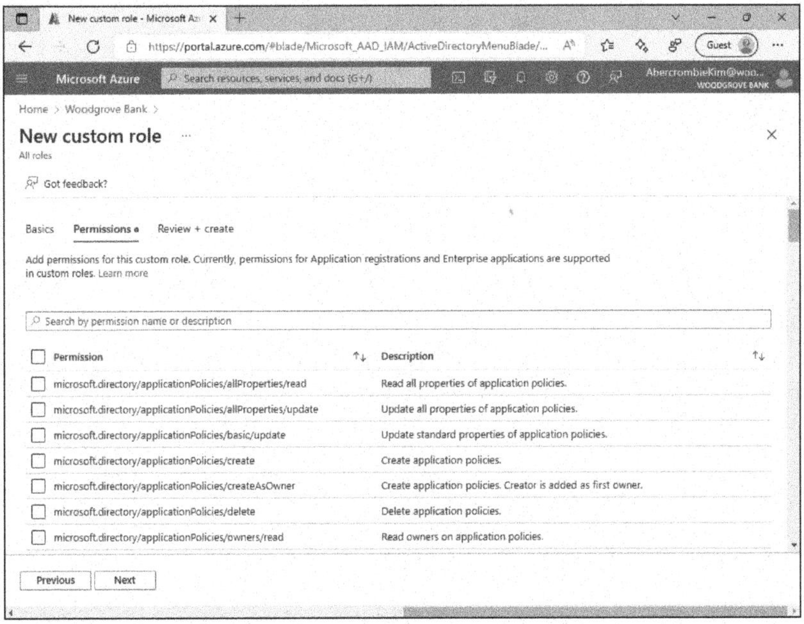

FIGURE 1-8 New custom role page, Permissions tab.

> ***NOTE*** **PERMISSIONS IN CUSTOM ROLES**
>
> Microsoft is constantly expanding its list of permissions available for custom roles. At the time of writing, custom role permissions are available for app registrations, enterprise applications, app consent, devices, and group management—some of them Generally Available and some in Public Preview. You can find an up-to-date list of available permissions on the Azure portal. Descriptions are available in the documentation—for example, for App registration permissions, see: ***https://docs.microsoft.com/en-us/azure/active-directory/roles/custom-available-permissions.***

4. On the **Review + create** tab of the **New custom role** page, review the definition of a new Azure AD custom role, and select **Create**. See Figure 1-9.

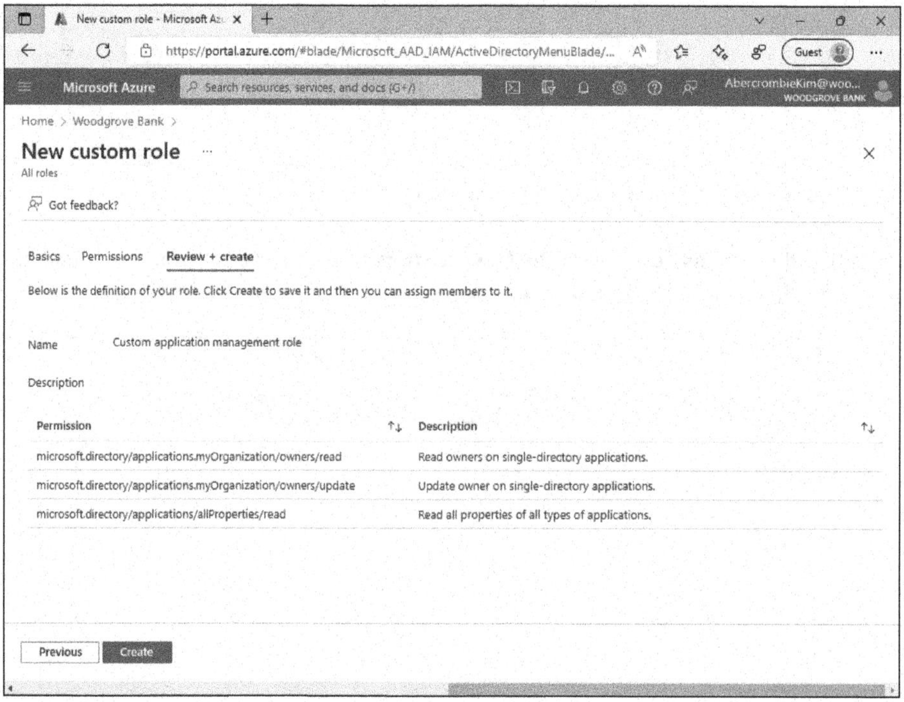

FIGURE 1-9 New custom role page, Review + create tab.

After an Azure AD custom role is created, assignments for this role can be managed the same way you'd manage them for Azure AD built-in roles.

> **NEED MORE REVIEW?** **MANAGING AZURE AD ROLES WITH GRAPH API**
>
> In the example above, we managed Azure AD roles with the Azure portal. Learn more about managing Azure AD roles with Graph API here:
>
> *https://docs.microsoft.com/en-us/graph/api/resources/directoryrole?view=graph-rest-1.0*
>
> *https://docs.microsoft.com/en-us/graph/api/resources/unifiedroledefinition?view=graph-rest-1.0*
>
> *https://docs.microsoft.com/en-us/graph/api/resources/unifiedroleassignment?view=graph-rest-1.0*

> **NEED MORE REVIEW?** **AZURE AD ROLES**
>
> Learn more about Azure AD roles from Azure AD roles documentation here:
> *https://docs.microsoft.com/en-us/azure/active-directory/roles/*

Configure delegation by using administrative units

An *administrative unit* is a container in an Azure AD tenant that can include other resources for the purpose of delegating permissions. At the time of writing, administrative units can contain only users and groups.

If you are familiar with Active Directory Domain Services (ADDS), you can compare an Azure AD administrative unit to an organizational unit in on-premises Active Directory Domain Services. Still, there are several differences between these technologies: in on-premises Active Directory Domain Services, organizational units were used both for Group Policies targeting and Role-Based Access Control. In Azure AD, administrative units are used for Role-Based Access Control only.

To list administrative units for the tenant, select **Azure portal** > **Azure Active Directory** > **Administrative units**. A new tenant doesn't have any administrative units. See Figure 1-10.

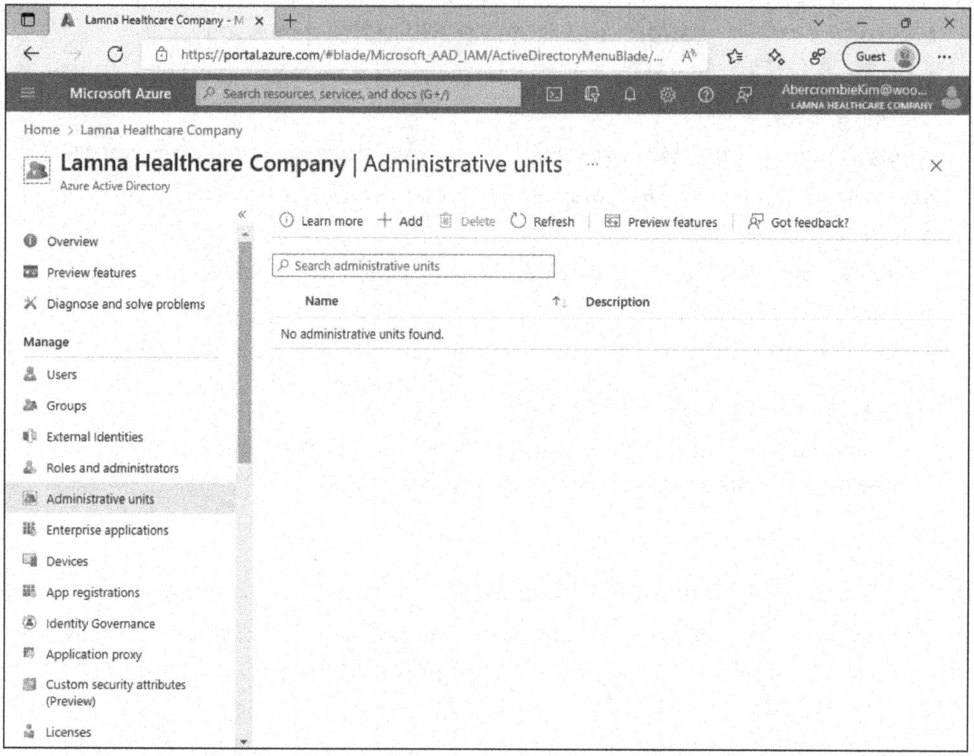

FIGURE 1-10 Administrative units page for new tenant.

To create an administrative unit:

1. Select **Azure portal** > **Azure Active Directory** > **Administrative units** > **Add**.

2. Specify a **Name** and **Description** (optional).

3. Create an administrative unit by clicking **Review + create** or click **Next: Assign roles** to add a role assignment.

4. If you chose to Assign roles, you will see a list of roles that can be assigned to administrative units. As discussed earlier, at the time of writing, administrative units can contain only users and groups. Therefore, only roles applicable to users and groups are shown on this screen. See Figure 1-11.

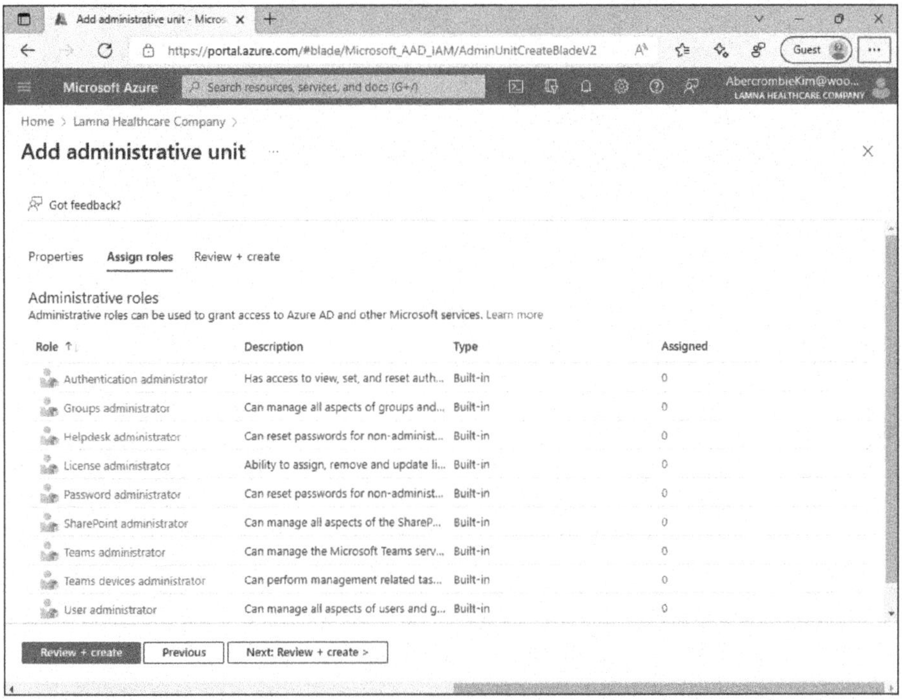

FIGURE 1-11 Custom domain names page with a verified custom domain name listed.

5. Select roles you want to assign security principals to and add security principals as delegated administrators. Select **Next: Review + create**.

6. Review the properties of the administrative unit and select **Create**.

Use the Administrative unit page to:

- Modify the **Display name** and **Description** of the administrative unit.

- Add/remove objects to/from an administrative unit. At the time of writing, this applies to users and groups.

- Assign roles to security principals that will manage objects from this administrative unit.

See Figure 1-12.

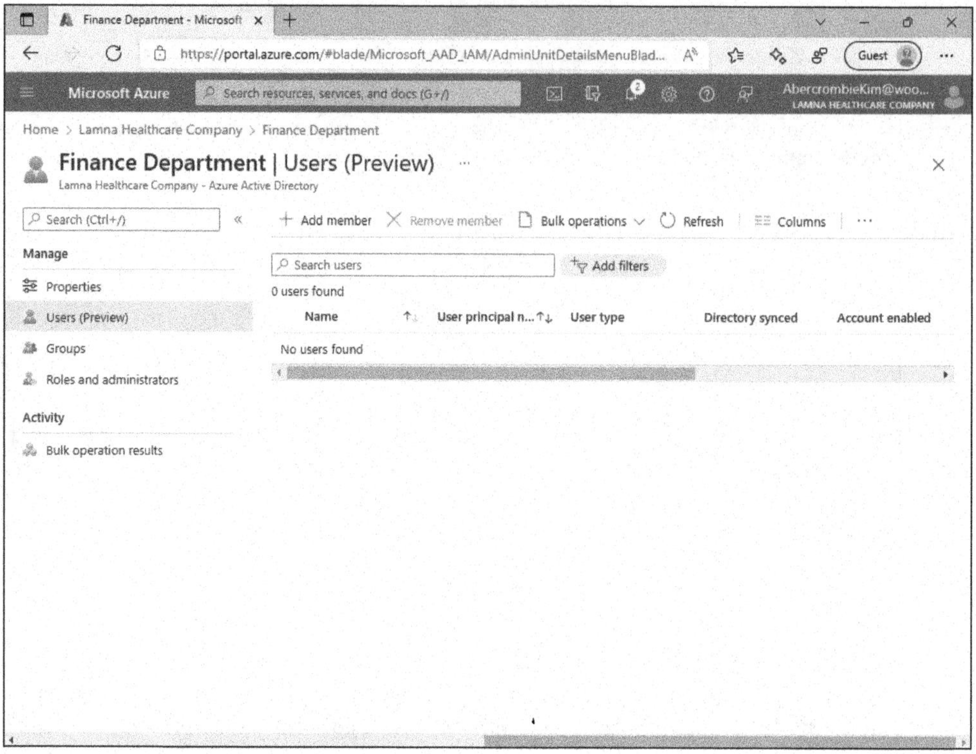

FIGURE 1-12 Administrative unit page.

> ***NEED MORE REVIEW?*** **ADMINISTRATIVE UNITS**
>
> **Read more about administrative units:**
> ***https://docs.microsoft.com/en-us/azure/active-directory/roles/administrative-units***
>
> **In the preceding examples, we managed administrative units through the Azure portal. Read more about managing administrative units with Graph API here:**
> ***https://docs.microsoft.com/en-us/graph/api/resources/administrativeunit?view=graph-rest-1.0***

Analyze Azure AD role permissions

Earlier in the "Configure and manage Azure AD roles" section, we discussed the management of role assignments and custom Azure AD roles.

In the SC-300 exam, you may be asked questions for which you need to identify permissions and roles necessary for a certain task. Documentation (*https://docs.microsoft.com/en-us/azure/active-directory/roles/permissions-reference*) includes information about Azure AD built-in roles and actions they can perform (permissions they have). Note that most Azure AD built-in roles have some actions listed that start with *microsoft.directory/*. These permissions allow the roles to create, update, or remove objects in Azure AD. Some roles also have permissions in other Azure and Microsoft 365 services and systems. At the moment of writing, these include:

- microsoft.azure.advancedThreatProtection/ - Azure Advanced Threat Protection
- microsoft.azure.devOps/ - Azure DevOps
- microsoft.azure.informationProtection/ - Azure Information Protection
- microsoft.azure.print/ - Microsoft Print
- microsoft.azure.serviceHealth/ - Azure Service Health
- microsoft.azure.supportTickets/ - Azure support tickets
- microsoft.cloudPC/ - Windows 365
- microsoft.commerce.billing/ - Microsoft 365 billing
- microsoft.commerce.volumeLicenseServiceCenter/ - Volume Licensing Service Center
- microsoft.dynamics365/ - Dynamics 365
- microsoft.edge/ - Microsoft Edge
- microsoft.insights/ - Microsoft Viva Insights
- microsoft.intune/ - Microsoft Intune
- microsoft.flow/ - Microsoft Power Automate
- microsoft.office365.complianceManager/ - Microsoft Purview Compliance Manager
- microsoft.office365.desktopAnalytics/ - Desktop Analytics
- microsoft.office365.exchange/ - Exchange Online
- microsoft.office365.knowledge/ - Microsoft 365 knowledge management
- microsoft.office365.lockbox/ - Microsoft Purview Customer Lockbox
- microsoft.office365.messageCenter/ - Message Center in Microsoft 365 admin center
- microsoft.office365.network/ - network locations
- microsoft.office365.usageReports/ - Office 365 usage reports
- microsoft.office365.protectionCenter/ - Microsoft 365 Defender
- microsoft.office365.search/ - Microsoft Search
- microsoft.office365.securityComplianceCenter/ - Security & Compliance Center
- microsoft.office365.serviceHealth/ - Service Health in Microsoft 365 admin center
- microsoft.office365.skypeForBusiness/ - Skype for Business Online
- microsoft.office365.sharePoint/ - SharePoint Online
- microsoft.office365.supportTickets/ - Microsoft 365 service requests
- microsoft.office365.usageReports/ - Office 365 usage reports
- microsoft.office365.userCommunication/ - user communication, including "What's New" messages

- microsoft.office365.webPortal/ - Microsoft 365 admin center
- microsoft.office365.yammer/ - Yammer
- microsoft.powerApps/ - Power Apps
- microsoft.powerApps.powerBI/ - Power BI
- microsoft.teams/ - Teams
- microsoft.virtualVisits/ - Virtual Visits app
- microsoft.windows.defenderAdvancedThreatProtection/ - Microsoft Defender for Endpoint
- microsoft.windows.updatesDeployments/ - Windows Update service

Some roles can have restrictions that prohibit them from managing certain objects in an Azure AD tenant. For example, Exchange Administrator can manage Microsoft 365 group membership because they have *microsoft.directory/groups.unified/members/update* permission. But this permission won't apply to Role-Assignable Groups.

Configure and manage custom domains

Every user in Azure AD has a User Principal Name (UPN). This attribute uniquely identifies the user. The UPN consists of a UPN prefix (user account name) and UPN suffix (domain name) divided by the @ symbol. For example, *alice@contoso.com* has a UPN prefix of *alice* and a UPN suffix of *contoso.com*.

A new Azure AD tenant has the initial domain name *<companyname>.onmicrosoft.com*. This means that your first user account(s) will have a UPN formatted as *<useraccountname>@<companyname>.onmicrosoft.com*.

After a custom domain name is added to the tenant, it is possible to have UPNs formatted as *<useraccountname>@<customdomain>*. For example, *alice@contoso.com*.

In addition to UPNs customization, custom domain names are also used to configure association with third-party identity providers, for Application Proxy configuration, and for groups in Exchange Online.

A key part of the custom domain name configuration process is verification: during verification, Microsoft ensures that you are the one who owns or manages the custom domain. Verification is completed through DNS records: you add requested DNS records to the public DNS servers, and Microsoft uses this as a confirmation that it is indeed your domain.

To list custom domain names for the tenant, select **Azure portal** > **Azure Active Directory** > **Custom domain names**. For the new tenant, only the initial domain name is listed. See Figure 1-13.

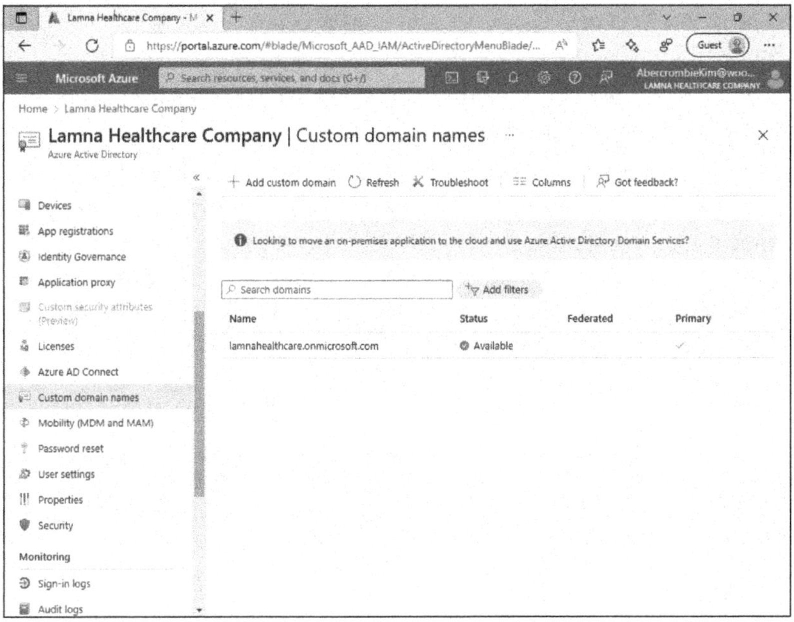

FIGURE 1-13 Custom domain names page for the new tenant.

To add a new custom domain name:

1.   Select **Add custom domain**, provide the custom domain name that you have control over, and select **Add domain**. See Figure 1-14.

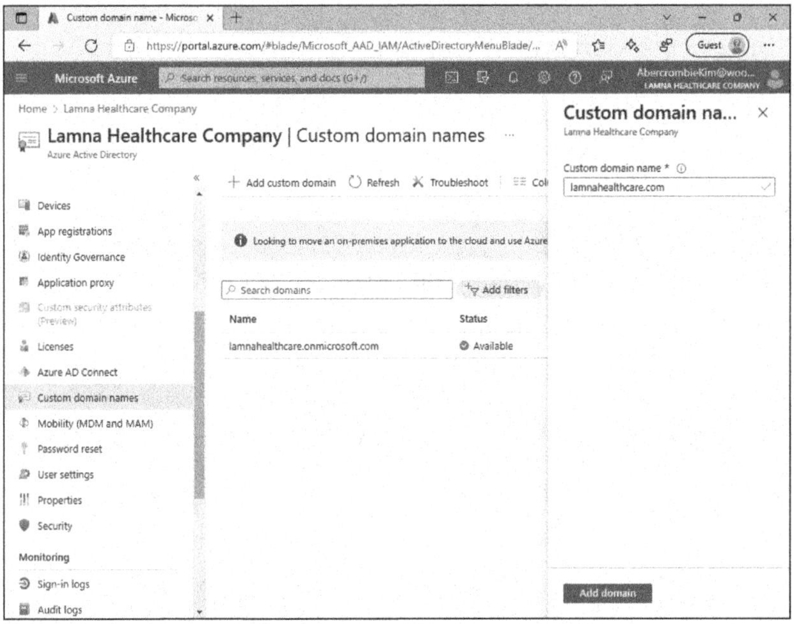

FIGURE 1-14 Add custom domain dialog.

2. On the next page, you will see DNS records. Microsoft asks you to add to the public DNS zone. See Figure 1-15.

   Either a TXT or MX record will work to verify a domain in Azure AD, but if you want to forward email for that domain you need an MX record.

3. You can add a DNS record and click **Verify**. Adding a DNS record might take significant time—you may need to contact the DNS administrator of your company, go through internal change management processes for DNS records, wait for replication, and so on. For now, you can select the ⊠ button in the top-right corner. A custom domain name is already added in the tenant; it is just not yet verified. See Figure 1-16 for an example of an added but not yet verified custom domain name.

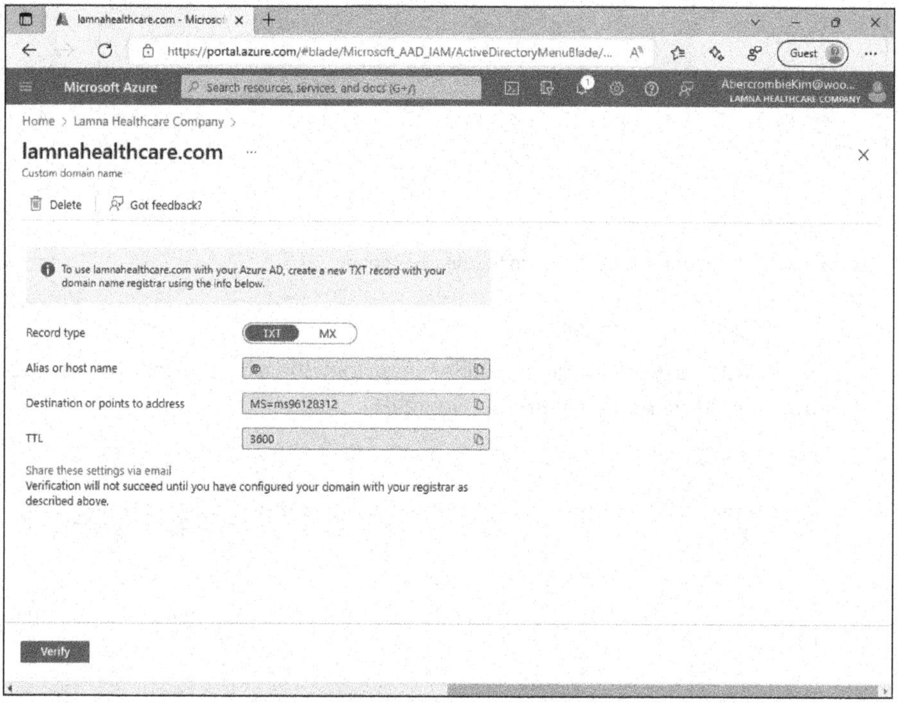

FIGURE 1-15 Add custom domain dialog with DNS records for verification.

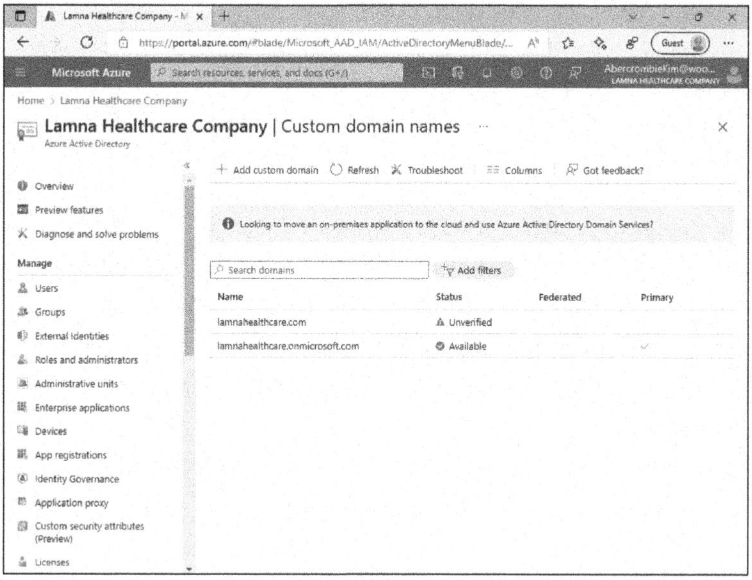

FIGURE 1-16 Custom domain names page with an unverified domain name listed.

4. After DNS records have been successfully added and verification has completed, successfully verified domain names will be shown in Azure AD as such. See Figure 1-17.

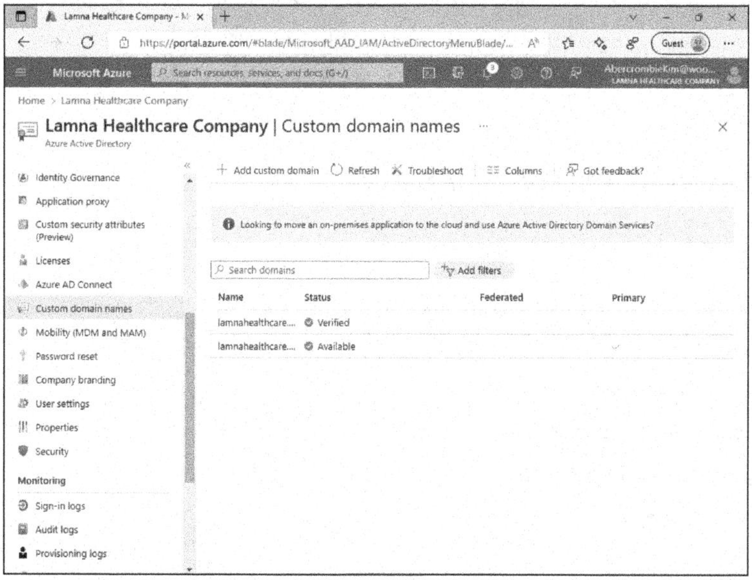

FIGURE 1-17 Custom domain names page with the verified custom domain name listed.

A custom domain name can be selected as primary. The primary domain is the default domain for new users. To make a domain name primary, select it and then select **Make primary**.

It is possible to add subdomains of existing custom domains. If a domain is already verified in the tenant and you add a subdomain, the subdomain will be verified automatically.

To delete a domain, select **Delete** on the domain's page. It is recommended to remove all references to that domain in your tenant first: any users, email addresses, proxy addresses, app ID URIs that mention the custom domain you are going to delete. Alternatively, you can use the ForceDelete option—in which case the custom domain will be deleted even if there are objects referencing it, and references will be updated to the initial domain name, such as *<company-name>.onmicrosoft.com*. The following conditions should be met for the ForceDelete option:

- There should be fewer than 1000 references to the custom domain name.
- Any references where Exchange is the provisioning service must be updated or removed.
- The domain name shouldn't be purchased through Microsoft 365 domain subscription services.
- You are not a partner administering on behalf of another organization.
- No multi-tenant apps should have app ID URIs mentioning the domain subject for removal.

> **NEED MORE REVIEW?** **CUSTOM DOMAINS**
>
> Read more about managing custom domains at:
> *https://docs.microsoft.com/en-us/azure/active-directory/enterprise-users/domains-manage*
>
> In the preceding examples, we managed custom domain names through Azure portal.
>
> Read more about managing custom domain names with Graph API at:
> *https://docs.microsoft.com/en-us/graph/api/resources/domain?view=graph-rest-1.0*

Configure tenant-wide settings

In this section, we will discuss tenant-wide settings shown from the tenant's Properties page and User Settings page.

The tenant Properties page (see Figure 1-18) allows you to modify:

- Tenant **Name**
- **Notification language**
- **Technical contact** information
- **Global privacy contact** information
- **Privacy statement URL**

> **NEED MORE REVIEW?** **PRIVACY INFORMATION IN AZURE AD TENANT PROPERTIES**
>
> Read more about your organization's privacy information in Azure AD:
> *https://docs.microsoft.com/en-us/azure/active-directory/fundamentals/active-directory-properties-area*

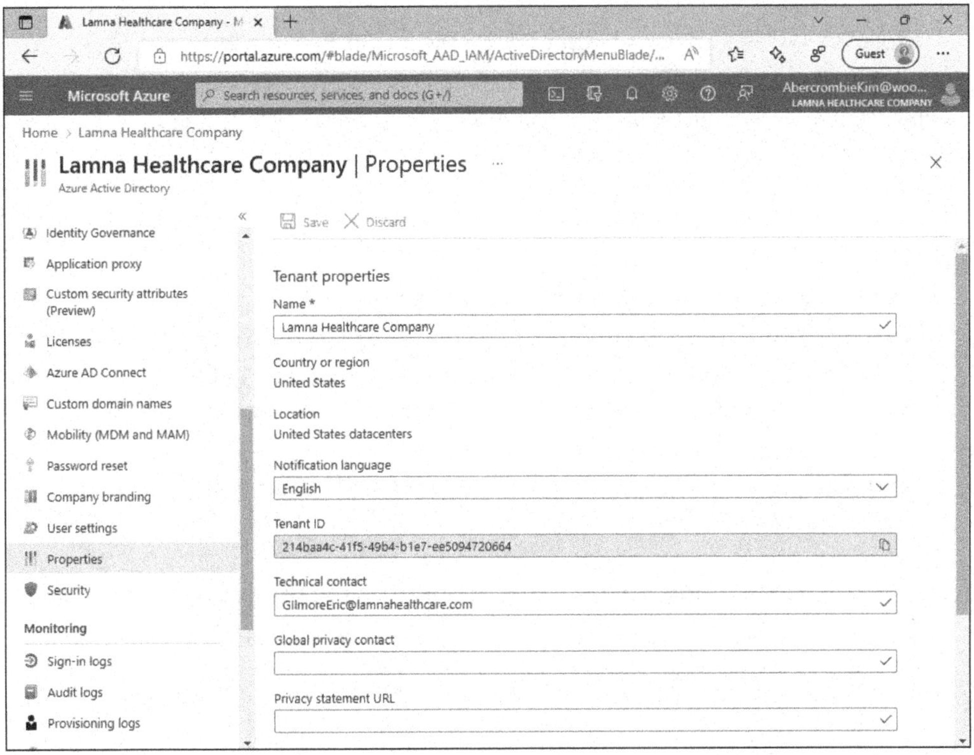

FIGURE 1-18 Tenant Properties page.

During Azure AD tenant creation, you specify a **Country/Region**. Based on the country/region information, the **Datacenter location** is determined. You cannot change the country, region, or datacenter location after the tenant is created.

> **NEED MORE REVIEW?** **AZURE AD DATA LOCATION**
>
> Read more about Azure AD data locations in this **Azure Active Directory Data Security Considerations** white paper: *https://azure.microsoft.com/en-us/resources/azure-active-directory-data-security-considerations/*

Users with Azure AD roles, including Global Administrators, don't generally have permissions to manage Azure subscriptions associated with tenant or resources in Azure subscriptions. There still may be scenarios when a Global Administrator needs access to an Azure subscription—for example, to recover access if the original subscription owner has left the organization. The **Access management for Azure resources** toggle allows the Global Administrator to elevate access and obtain a User access administrator role in Azure subscriptions associated with the tenant. It is recommended to use this option to recover access when needed and to disable the option again after the operation is completed.

Use the **Azure portal** > **Azure Active Directory** > **User Settings** page to control tenant-wide settings such as:

- Restricting users from registering applications in the tenant.
- Restricting users' access to the Azure AD administration portal (Azure Active Directory on Azure portal). This doesn't restrict users from doing anything through the API/PowerShell, so it shouldn't be considered a way to protect from a dedicated attacker.
- Sharing LinkedIn account connections: data sharing between Microsoft and LinkedIn that allows users to have information and insights from LinkedIn available in some Microsoft apps and services.

Skill 1.2: Create, configure, and manage Azure AD identities

An Azure AD tenant typically includes user objects and group objects (among other object types). In this section, we cover management of user and group objects in an Azure AD tenant—directly, not through synchronization from an on-premises environment. In this section, we also cover Microsoft 365 licenses assignment. An Azure AD tenant can have devices registered in it—in this section, we also cover device registration options (Azure AD Registration, Azure AD Join, Hybrid Azure AD Join), related controls, and implementation steps.

This skill covers how to:
- Create, configure, and manage users
- Create, configure, and manage groups
- Configure and manage device joins and registrations, including writeback
- Assign, modify, and report on licenses

Create, configure, and manage users

Most Azure AD tenants include user objects that represent the organization's employees or associates. There are multiple ways that the user object can be created in Azure AD:

- The user object can be created directly in Azure AD (via Azure portal, API, PowerShell, or Azure CLI).

- The user object can be synchronized from on-premises Active Directory Domain Services with Azure AD Connect or Azure AD Connect cloud sync.

For the rest of this section, we will focus on user objects created directly in Azure AD. Synchronization from on-premises environment will be covered in Skill 1.4: "Implement and manage hybrid identity."

To create a new user in the Azure portal:

1. Open **Azure portal** > **Azure Active Directory** > **Users** > **New user**. See Figure 1-19.

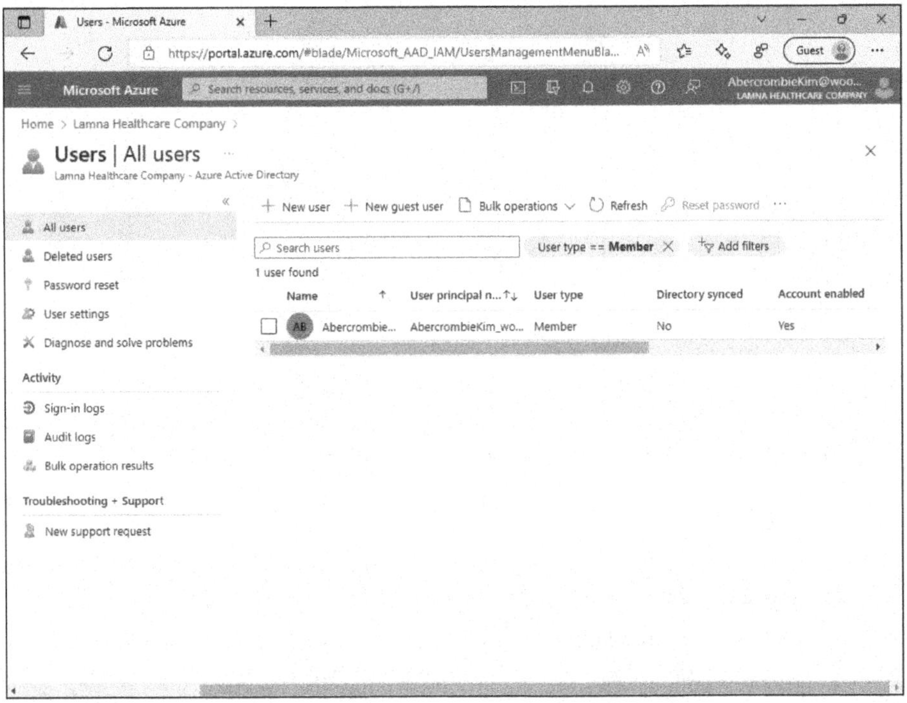

FIGURE 1-19 The custom domain names page with a verified custom domain name listed.

2. Keep **Create user** selected. See Figure 1-20. Specify a **User name** and **name**. Optionally, you can:

- Set a **First name**.

- Set a **Last name**.

- Add the user to groups.

- Assign roles to the user.
- **Block sign in**.
- Set **Usage location**. You must set **Usage location** if the user will have a Microsoft 365 license assigned directly.
- Set **Job info** (**Job title**, **Department**, **Company name**, **Manager**).

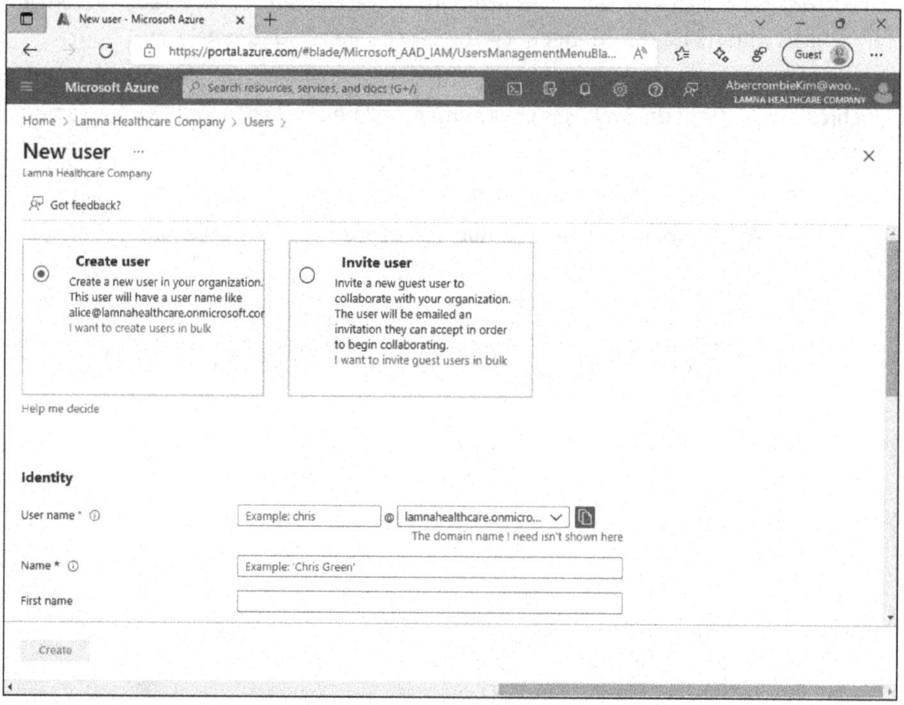

FIGURE 1-20 New user creation dialog.

3. Select **Create**.

4. In the preceding example, we discuss creating a user with the Azure portal **New user** dialog. Other ways to create users include:

   - Upload a CSV file with user information to the Azure portal. Read more at: *https://docs.microsoft.com/en-us/azure/active-directory/enterprise-users/users-bulk-add*

   - Use Graph API calls: *https://docs.microsoft.com/en-us/graph/api/resources/ user?view=graph-rest-1.0*

   - Use PowerShell: *https://docs.microsoft.com/en-us/powershell/module/microsoft. graph.users/?view=graph-powershell-1.0*

   - Use Microsoft School Data Sync: *https://docs.microsoft.com/en-us/schooldatasync/ overview-of-school-data-sync*

Once the user object is created, you can use the user profile page shown in Figure 1-21 to:

- Modify the user's attributes, such as Name, User Principal Name, Job info, Contact information, and so on.
- Manage Authentication methods available to users: email, phone number, Temporary Access Pass.
- Manage Custom security attributes.
- Assign roles to the user.
- Assign applications to the user.
- Add the user to administrative units.
- Manage devices associated with the user.
- Manage the user's licenses.
- View sign-in logs and audit logs information for a user.
- Revoke a user's sessions.
- Delete a user.

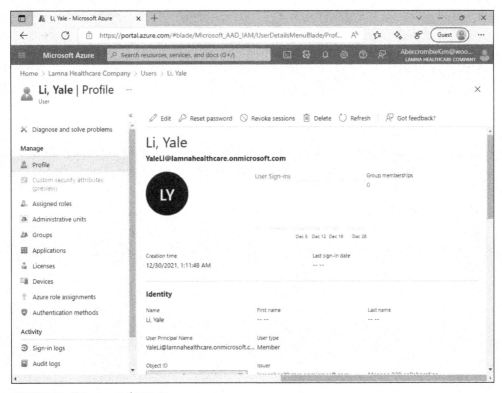

FIGURE 1-21 User properties page.

Create, configure, and manage groups

Group objects in an Azure AD tenant can be used in many scenarios, such as:

- Managing access to applications
- Assigning Azure AD roles
- Assigning Azure roles
- Assigning roles and permissions across various Microsoft 365 products such as Intune, Exchange Online, Cloud App Security, and others
- Managing group-based licensing
- Targeting Conditional Access policies
- Managing Authentication methods
- Managing Self-Service Password Reset

As with user objects, there are multiple ways that group objects can be created in Azure AD:

- Group objects can be created directly in Azure AD (via Azure portal, API, PowerShell, Azure CLI).
- Group objects can be synchronized from on-premises Active Directory Domain Services with Azure AD Connect or Azure AD Connect cloud sync.

Groups synchronized from on-premises environments are managed in on-premises environments; you can't modify them in Azure AD.

In Azure AD, you can create two types of groups:

- Security groups
- Microsoft 365 groups

Additionally, Microsoft 365 has concepts of Distribution groups and Mail-Enabled Security groups that are represented in Azure AD as read-only objects and are beyond the scope of this book.

Security groups are used for granting access to resources.

Microsoft 365 groups are used for collaboration between users, as well as between users and guests.

To create a group using the Azure portal:

1. Open **Azure portal** > **Azure Active Directory** > **Groups**. Select **New group**. See Figure 1-22.

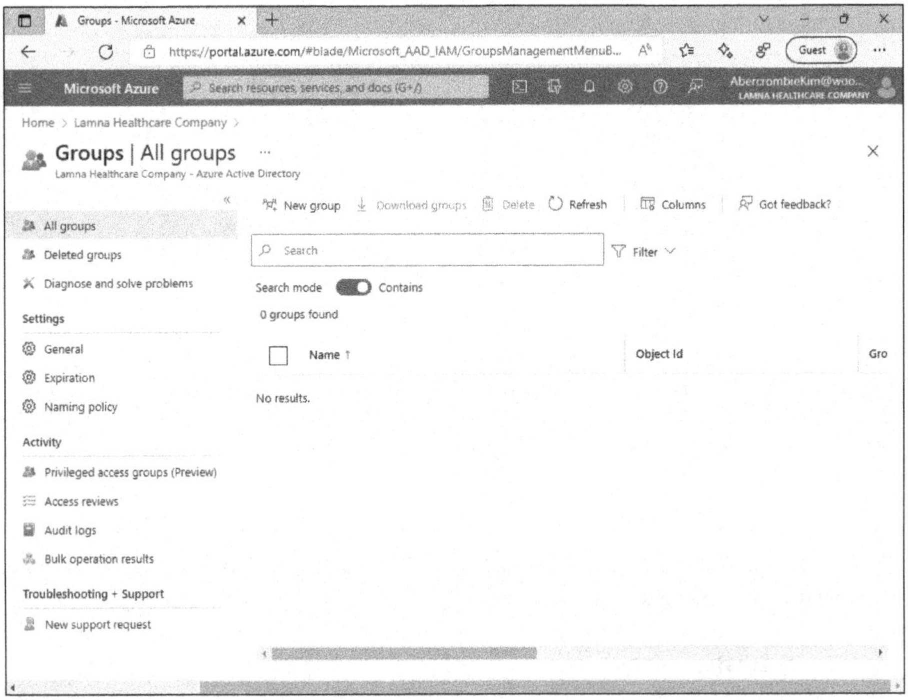

FIGURE 1-22 All groups page for the new tenant.

2. Specify the properties of the group you are creating, as shown in Figure 1-23:

    - **Group type**—Security or Microsoft 365
    - **Group name**
    - **Group email address** (for Microsoft 365 groups only)
    - **Group description** (optional)
    - **Azure AD roles can be assigned to the group**—if the group will be role-assignable. This setting can't be changed later.
    - **Membership type**—if the group should be dynamic. You will find more information about dynamic groups later in this section.
    - **Owners** (optional)
    - **Members** (optional, for non-dynamic groups only)
    - **Dynamic query** (for dynamic groups only)

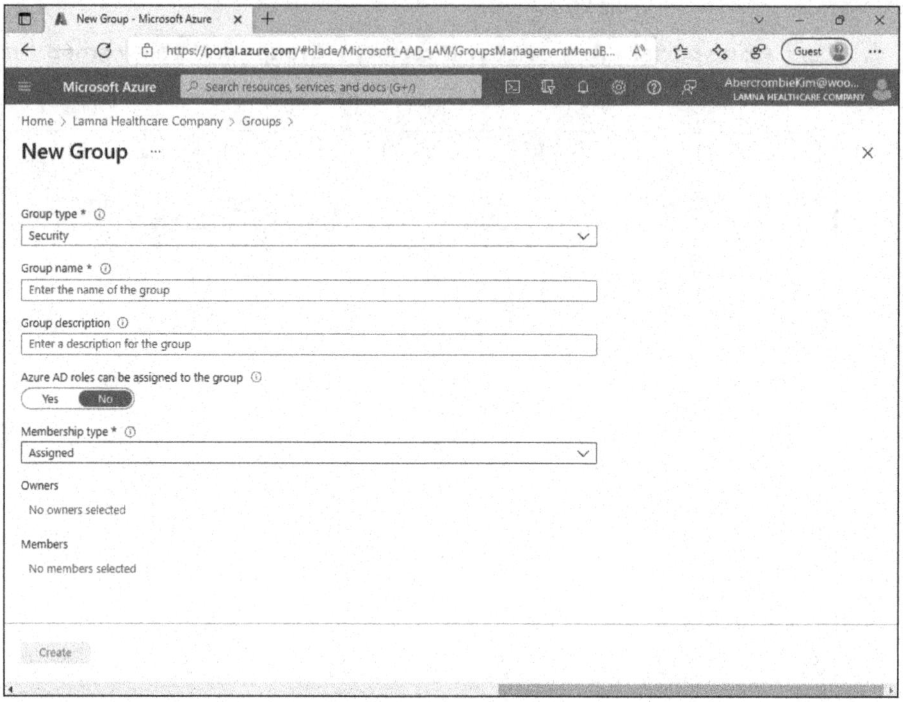

FIGURE 1-23 New group dialog.

3. Select **Create**.

   In the preceding examples, we managed a group through the Azure portal. Read more about managing groups with Graph API at: *https://docs.microsoft.com/en-us/graph/api/resources/group?view=graph-rest-1.0*

   Group nesting is supported only between Security groups. The Microsoft 365 group can't be added to any group, and no group can be added to the Microsoft 365 group.

> **NEED MORE REVIEW? GROUP NESTING**
>
> Read more about group nesting limitations at: *https://docs.microsoft.com/en-us/azure/active-directory/fundamentals/active-directory-groups-membership-azure-portal*

Even though nesting is supported between security groups, not every feature within Azure AD recognizes nested membership. Read Azure AD service limits documentation for up-to-date information on scenarios supported and not supported for nested groups: *https://docs.microsoft.com/en-us/azure/active-directory/enterprise-users/directory-service-limits-restrictions*.

Both Security and Microsoft 365 groups can be **dynamic groups**. This feature allows you to configure complex attribute-based rules to populate group membership automatically. A dynamic group can include users or devices but not at the same time.

Here is an example of a dynamic group membership rule (expression):

```
user.department -eq "Finance"
```

Here, the group will include all users from the Finance department.

Dynamic groups support expression operators (such as Equals, Starts With, Match, etc.), logical operators (And, Or, etc.), strings, numbers, Boolean and array properties.

> *NEED MORE REVIEW?* **DYNAMIC GROUPS**
>
> Find more examples of dynamic group membership rules, operators usage, and supported properties in this documentation: *https://docs.microsoft.com/en-us/azure/active-directory/enterprise-users/groups-dynamic-membership*

Azure AD Self-Service Group Management allows users to create and manage their groups. Self-Service Group Management is supported for security groups and Microsoft 365 groups but not mail-enabled security groups or distribution lists.

By default, users can create Security and Microsoft 365 groups using the Access panel page *https://account.activedirectory.windowsazure.com/r#/groups*, API calls, or PowerShell commands. See Figure 1-24 for an Access Panel user interface example. After the group is created, the creator becomes the first owner and first member of the group. Later, an owner or administrator can add additional owners and members to the group. For an owner to manage groups, they must use the Access Panel shown in Figure 1-24. For administrators to manage groups, they will need to use the Azure portal shown in Figure 1-22.

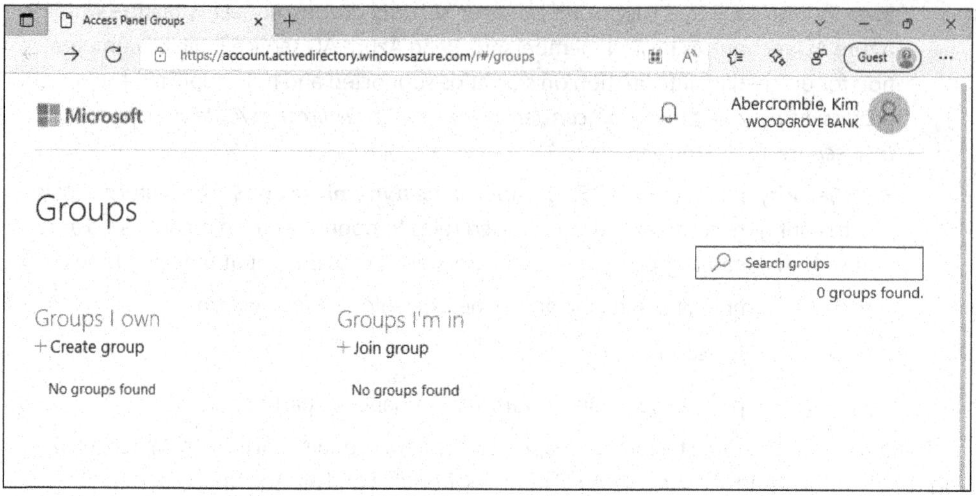

FIGURE 1-24   Access Panel, group management page.

Users can request membership in groups that may be granted automatically or under the owner's discretion. This is controlled by the Join policy of the group. Groups have a Join policy with one of the following values:

- This group is open to join for all users.
- Only the owner of this group can add members.
- This group requires owner approval.

The Join policy is managed by the group owner, as shown in Figure 1-25.

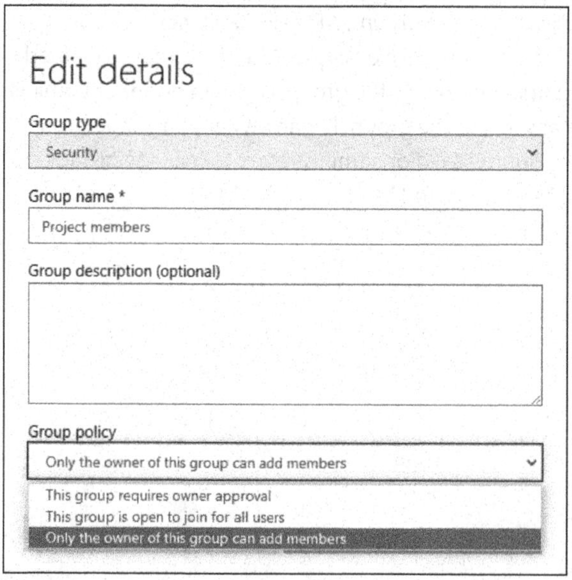

FIGURE 1-25   Access Panel, group properties.

The first two options are available for group owners in the tenant by default. The third option is available to group owners only if an administrator enables it by setting "Owners can manage group membership requests in the Access Panel" to "Yes." See Figure 1-26.

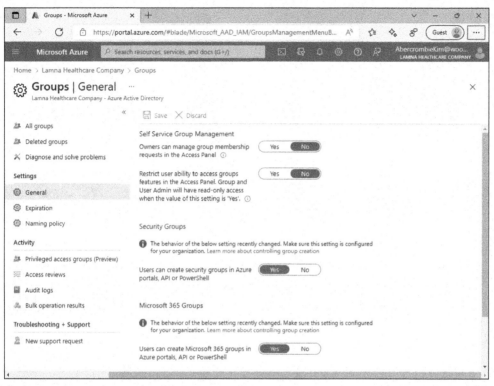

FIGURE 1-26 Group management settings, default values.

To join a group:

1. As a requestor (a user who needs to join a group), open the **Access Panel**, **Groups** page: *https://account.activedirectory.windowsazure.com/r#/groups*.

2. Select **Join group**.

3. Select the group you want to join and select **Join group**. See Figure 1-27.

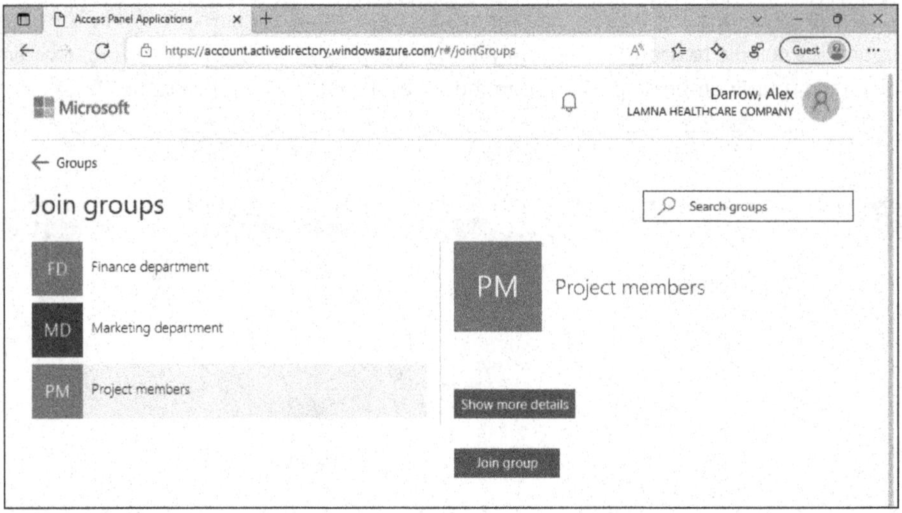

FIGURE 1-27 Access panel, Join groups dialog.

4. Provide business justification.

5. On the page **Your request has been sent to the owner of the group** select **OK**.

For the group owner to approve the request, they need to:

1. Open the **Access Panel**, **Groups** page: *https://account.activedirectory.windowsazure.com/r#/groups*.

2. Select the notification button and review the request. See Figure 1-28.

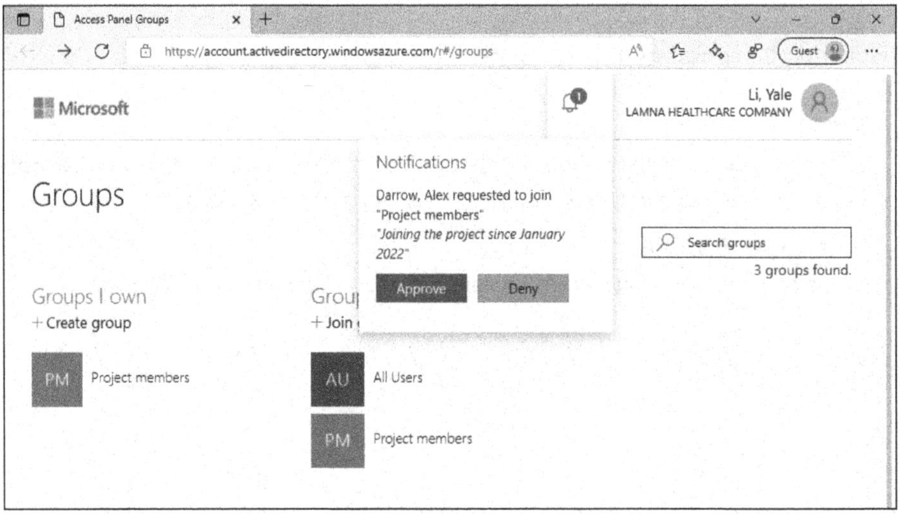

FIGURE 1-28 The Access panel, Groups page shows a group join notification for the group owner.

3. Select **Approve** or **Deny**.

Groups Expiration policy allows you to automatically remove Microsoft 365 groups that are no longer in use. When group expiration policy is enabled, all groups with user activity (such as document uploads, emails delivered) are renewed automatically, while for groups without user activity, owners should confirm if the group should be renewed and not deleted. Example settings for group expiration are shown in Figure 1-29.

Group Expiration policy is not applicable to Security groups.

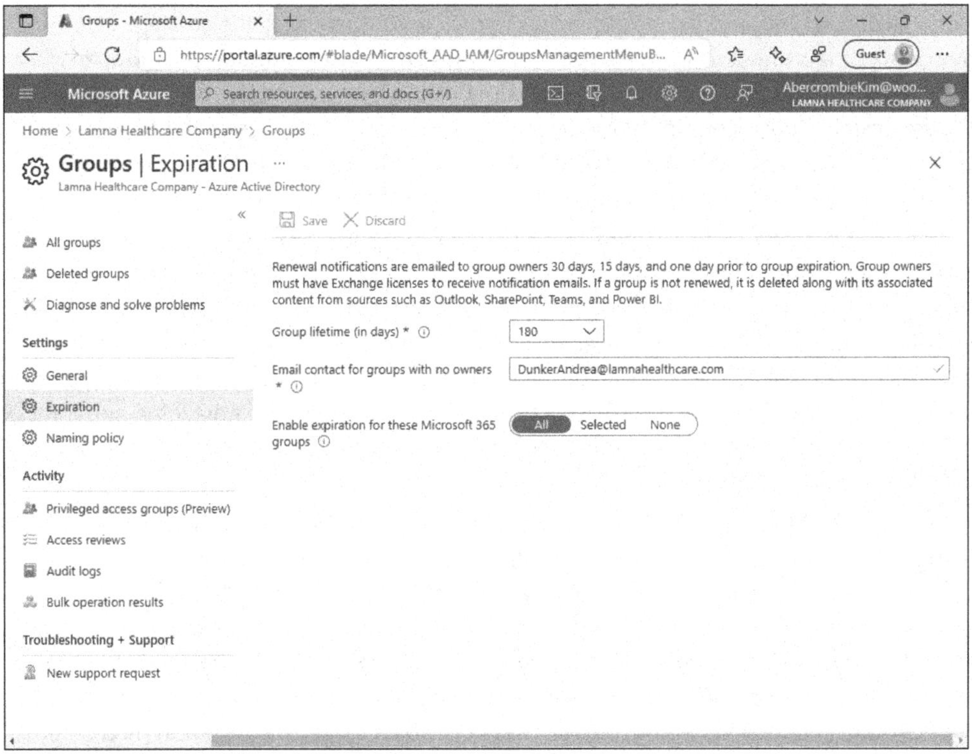

FIGURE 1-29 Group Expiration settings.

Configure and manage device joins and registrations, including writeback

Devices are represented in Azure AD in the form of device objects. You don't generally need your device to be represented in Azure AD to sign in, but in certain scenarios having device objects is a prerequisite or significantly improves the user experience. These scenarios include:

- Sign in to the device with Azure AD credentials
- Single Sign-On to Azure AD
- Device-based Conditional Access policies
- Mobile Device Management enrollment

There are three join types that can be used to register a device in Azure AD:

- Azure AD Registration
- Azure AD Join
- Hybrid Azure AD Join

Azure AD Registration (previously known as *Workplace Join*) is for personal (BYOD—Bring Your Own Device) scenarios. It works for Windows 10 and above, iOS, Android, and macOS. During *Azure AD Registration*, the user adds their Azure AD account to the device, and the device will be represented in Azure AD. In some cases, *Azure AD Registration* can happen when the user installs a Microsoft app and signs in with their Azure AD account—for example, when the user installs Outlook on a personal device and signs in with their (corporate) Azure AD account. *Azure AD Registration* doesn't affect how the user signs in to the device itself; they will continue to sign in the same way they did before *Azure AD registration* occurred.

Azure AD Join is for corporate devices with Windows 10 and above. A device is joined to an Azure AD tenant, and Azure AD users from that tenant can sign in to the device. *Azure AD Joined* devices are typically managed through Mobile Device Management (MDM) solutions, such as Intune. *Azure AD Joined* devices are not part of the on-premises Active Directory Domain Services domain. It is possible to get Single Sign-On from an *Azure AD Joined* device not only to Azure AD but also to on-premises resources. *Azure AD Join* works great for corporate computers, especially for remote workforce, if you are OK with managing devices with MDM solutions rather than Group Policy.

Hybrid Azure AD Join is for corporate devices running Windows 7 and above, Windows Server 2008 and above. Before *Hybrid Azure AD Join* process can be triggered, the device must be joined to the on-premises Active Directory Domain Services domain. After that, the device identity can be synchronized to Azure AD with Azure AD Connect and the device can complete the *Hybrid Azure AD Join* process. When a device is joined to Azure AD through the *Hybrid Azure AD Join* process, the device becomes represented in Azure AD tenant and the user gets Single Sign-On to Azure AD. Users will use on-premises Active Directory Domain Services mechanisms to sign in to a *Hybrid Azure AD Joined* device, which means line of sight to domain controllers will be required for certain scenarios, such as device password changes, user password changes, and TPM resets. Since the device is part of the on-premises Active Directory Domain Services domain, the device can be managed with Group Policy, but MDM is also an option.

For new implementations, we recommend deploying *Azure AD Joined* machines (*not Hybrid Azure AD Joined*), as they don't require line of sight to domain controllers or have other dependencies on on-premises Active Directory Domain Services.

All three options mentioned above (*Azure AD Registration, Azure AD Join, Hybrid Azure AD Join*) will provide you Single Sign-On to Azure AD. For Windows 10 and newer, in all three implementations it will be achieved by using a *Primary Refresh Token (PRT)*. Read more about PRT at *https://docs.microsoft.com/en-us/azure/active-directory/devices/concept-primary-refresh-token*.

An administrator can control device registration:

- For *Azure AD Registered* devices: An administrator can select whether users can register devices on the **Azure AD** > **Devices** > **Device settings** page. Azure AD Registration must be enabled if enrollment with Intune or MDM for Office 365 is enabled. See Figure 1-30.

- For *Azure AD Joined* devices: An administrator can select which users can join devices on the **Azure AD** > **Devices** > **Device settings** page. See Figure 1-30.

- For *Hybrid Azure AD Joined* devices: Service Connection Point (SCP) entry is required for a device to complete the Hybrid Azure AD Join process. SCP can be located in on-premises Active Directory Domain Services domain or in the form of registry settings on the client machine. An administrator can remove SCP from the domain and add client-side registry settings on desired machines.

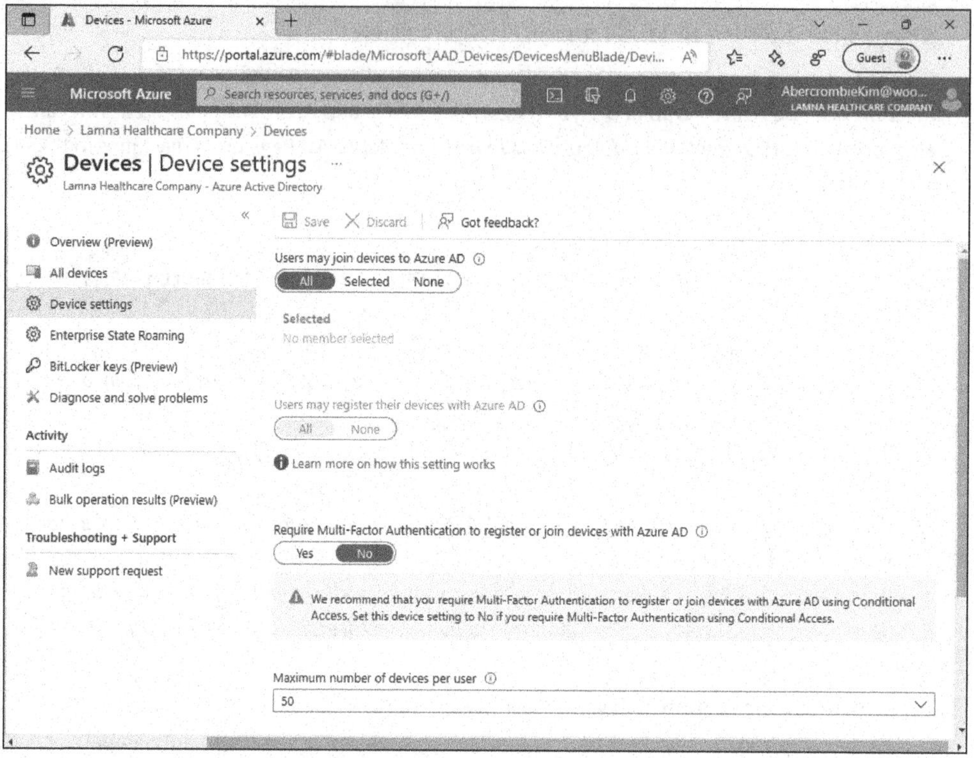

FIGURE 1-30 Device settings—default configuration.

> **NOTE** **SEAMLESS SINGLE SIGN-ON VS HYBRID AZURE AD JOIN**
>
> One more way to implement Single Sign-On to Azure AD from a Windows machine is to use *Seamless Single Sign-On (Seamless SSO, SSSO, Desktop SSO)*. This method will not use PRT, and you generally don't need SSSO if you have PRT through an *Azure AD Registered*, *Azure AD Joined*, or *Hybrid Azure AD Joined* devices implementation. If you have Windows 7, Windows 8.1, or for some reason you don't have PRT—Seamless SSO is the option you may consider. Seamless SSO will be covered in detail in the section "Implement and manage Seamless Single Sign-On (Seamless SSO)" under Skill 1.4: "Implement and manage hybrid identity."

> **NEED MORE REVIEW?** **DEVICE IDENTITIES IN AZURE AD OVERVIEW**
>
> Read more about device identities in Azure AD at:
> *https://docs.microsoft.com/en-us/azure/active-directory/devices/*

As discussed above, the Hybrid Azure AD Join process includes synchronization of device identity from on-premises Active Directory Domain Services to Azure AD.

There are also scenarios when information about a device must be synchronized in another direction—from Azure AD to on-premises Active Directory Domain Services. This is called *Device writeback*. Device writeback is used when you need to:

- Enable Windows Hello for Business with hybrid certificate trust deployment (for Hybrid Azure AD Joined machines only)

- Enable Conditional Access based on devices on ADFS 2012 R2 and higher (for environments with Active Directory Federation Services—ADFS)

Device writeback must be configured in Azure AD Connect. See Figure 1-78 for the **Optional features** page of Azure AD Connect in Skill 1.4: "Implement and manage hybrid identity."

When you enable device writeback in Azure AD Connect, it provides you with PowerShell script that performs the following operations in your on-premises environment:

- Creates containers and objects for the device registration configuration under CN=Device Registration Configuration,CN=Services,CN=Configuration,[forest-dn]

- Creates containers and objects for devices under CN=RegisteredDevices,[domain-dn]

- Gives Azure AD Connect necessary permissions to manage devices in on-premises Active Directory Domain Services

> **NEED MORE REVIEW?**   **DEVICE WRITEBACK**
>
> Read more about device writeback configuration in Azure AD Connect at:
> *https://docs.microsoft.com/en-us/azure/active-directory/hybrid/how-to-connect-device-writeback/*

Assign, modify, and report on licenses

Many Microsoft 365 services are available through licensing plans such as:

- Azure Active Directory Premium P1/P2

- Microsoft 365 E3/E5

- Office 365 E1/E3/E5

- Enterprise Mobility + Security E3/E5

Some of these plans include other plans: for example, Enterprise Mobility + Security E3 includes Azure Active Directory Premium P1, and Enterprise Mobility + Security E5 includes Azure Active Directory Premium P2, etc.

> **NEED MORE REVIEW?**   **MICROSOFT 365 LICENSING**
>
> Find more information about available licensing plans on the Microsoft 365 licensing page:
> *https://www.microsoft.com/en-us/licensing/product-licensing/microsoft-365*

Before a user can have a Microsoft 365 service license assigned, they need to set the **Usage-Location** attribute to the value representing their country or region. Usage location is important because not all Microsoft services are available in all regions.

- Cloud-only users can update their Usage location on the **Azure portal > Azure Active Directory > Users > [Name] > Manage > Profile** page.

- For user accounts synchronized from on-premises Active Directory Domain Services, you can manage the **msExchUsageLocation** attribute on-premises (if you have on-premises Active Directory Domain Services schema extended for Microsoft Exchange) or use another attribute of your choice and synchronize it to **UsageLocation** by modifying synchronization rules.

UsageLocation must be set before a license can be assigned to a user individually. If you assign a license to a group and one or more of the group's members doesn't have the **Usage-Location** attribute set, the location of the Azure AD tenant will be inherited.

To view licenses available in your tenant, open **Azure portal > Azure Active Directory > Licenses > All products**. See Figure 1-31.

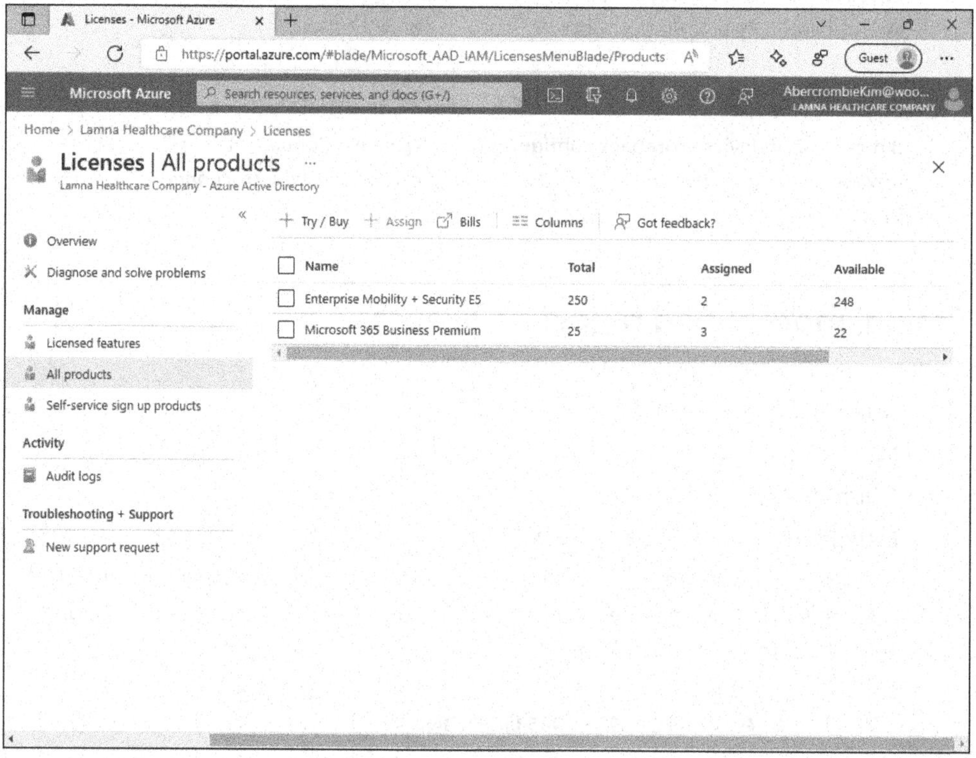

FIGURE 1-31 Manage licenses.

To assign a license:

1. Ensure that users you need to assign a license to have the **Usage location** attribute set to their country or region.

2. Select the checkbox near the license name and select **Assign**.

3. On the **Users and groups** tab of the **Assign license** page, select **Add users and groups** and add those who will be licensed. See Figure 1-32.

4. Select **Next: Assignment Options**.

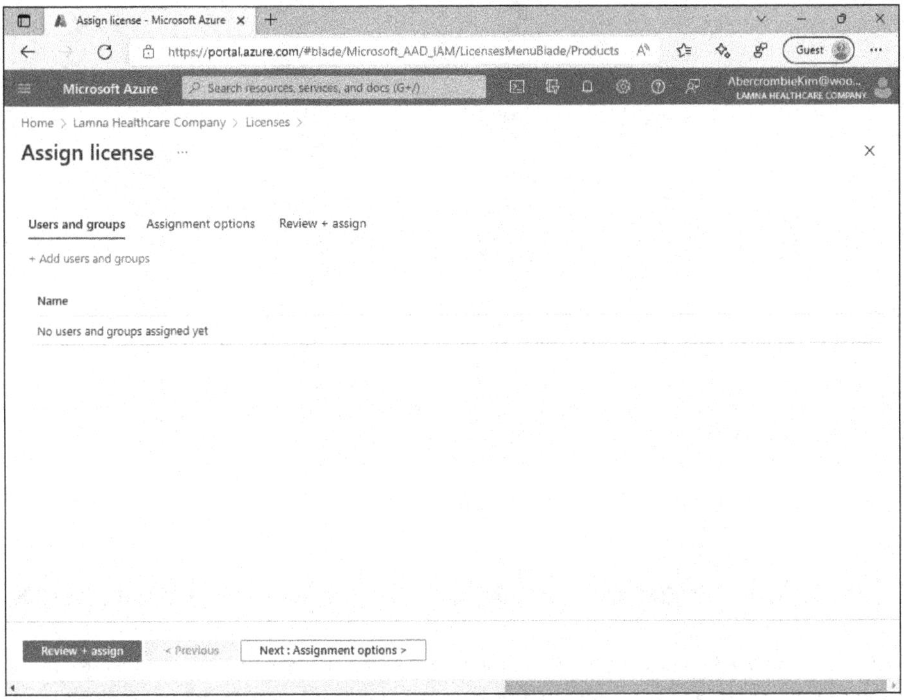

FIGURE 1-32   Assign license page, Users and groups tab.

5. On the **Assignment options** tab of **Assign license** page, you can turn specific products **On** or **Off** for licenses that include multiple products. See Figure 1-33. Select **Next: Review + Assign**.

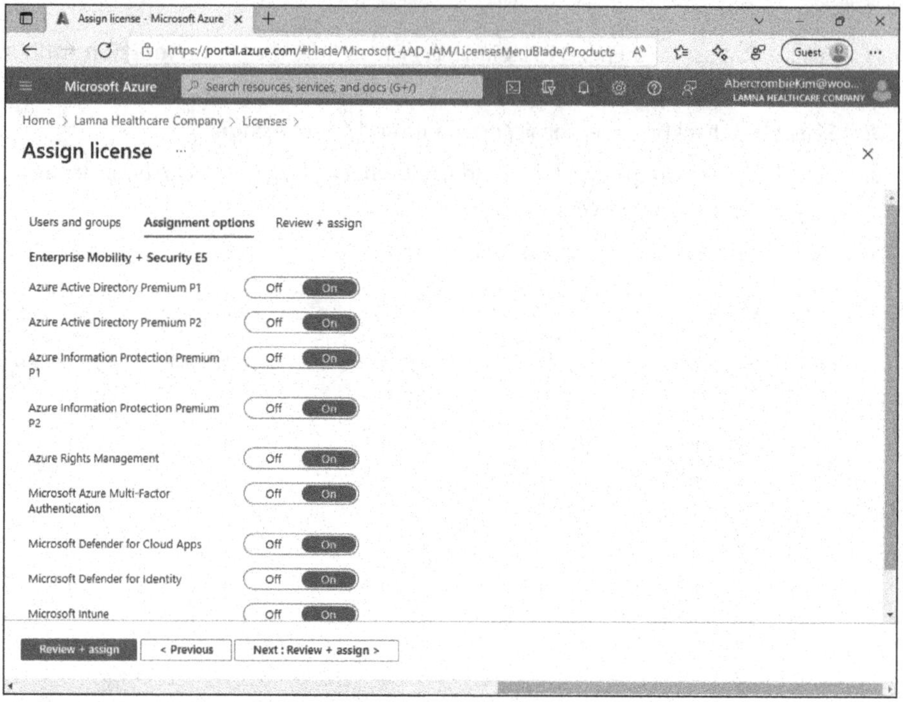

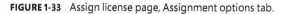

FIGURE 1-33 Assign license page, Assignment options tab.

6. Review the options and select **Assign**.

Skill 1.3: Implement and manage external identities

With Azure Active Directory, you can provide business partners and consumers seamless access to applications and resources. In this section we cover Azure AD B2B. We discuss authentication options available for guests—many guests can get single sign-on to resource tenants using their existing accounts such as Azure AD accounts, Microsoft accounts, Google federation, federated identity providers, etc. We discuss the process of inviting and re-inviting guests to your tenant. We cover collaboration settings applicable to guests. Also, we cover federation with identity providers.

> **This skill covers how to:**
> - Manage external collaboration settings in Azure AD
> - Invite external users, individually or in bulk (collectively)
> - Manage external user accounts in Azure AD
> - Configure identity providers, including SAML or WS-Fed

Manage external collaboration settings in Azure AD

With Azure AD, you can provide business partners and consumers seamless access to applications and resources. Seamless authentication allows external users to "bring their own identity" and get access without the need to set up new credentials such as new passwords. Collaboration is protected with security features such as Conditional Access and Identity Protection.

Azure AD B2B allows you to invite business partners to your tenant and provide them access to applications and resources. In Azure AD B2B, the invited party is called a *Guest* and the tenant they access as a guest is called a *Resource tenant*. To differentiate from a Guest, a regular user account is called a *Member* in this context.

When you invite a guest, the only required field is an email address—everything else (name information, job title, personal message) is optional. After a guest is invited, they need to accept the invite by following the redemption link and providing consent to access your tenant. The redemption link is already included in the invitation email, or you can provide it to a guest through other means.

After a guest accepts an invite, the *Identity issuer type* will be identified based on the guest's email address:

- Azure AD users will get the Single Sign-On experience. In this case, the tenant user account location is called *Home tenant*.
- A user with an email address matching the domain of a SAML/WS-Fed provider federated with a resource tenant will get the Single Sign-On experience. This option is used when resource tenant administrator needs to provide Single Sign-On to guests from a domain that is not Azure AD verified.
- A user with the domain suffix of gmail.com or googlemail.com will get the Single Sign-On experience if the resource tenant admin configured Google federation.
- A user with a personal Microsoft account will get the Single Sign-On experience.
- If none of the options above are applicable to a guest based on their email address:
    - If a one-time passcode is enabled in the tenant—for example, a passcode is sent to the guest over email—the guest can use the one-time passcode from email to sign in.
    - If a one-time passcode is disabled in the tenant, the guest will be prompted to create an Azure AD self-service account or personal Microsoft account.

> *NEED MORE REVIEW?*   **AZURE AD B2B INVITE REDEMPTION**
>
> **Read more about Azure AD B2B redemption flow in the documentation:**
> *https://docs.microsoft.com/en-us/azure/active-directory/external-identities/*
> *redemption-experience*

After a guest is invited, it is one more user account in the resource tenant. The difference with a regular user account will be that the regular user account has a **User type** of **Member**, while a guest has a **User type** of **Guest**. Like any other user account, Guest can have applications assigned to it, can have Azure AD roles or roles in other RBAC systems, can be a member of groups, and can have permissions for various resources, etc.

Use the **Azure portal** > **Azure Active Directory** > **External Identities** > **External collaboration settings** page to manage tenant-wide settings of the Azure AD B2B collaboration. See Figure 1-34 and Figure 1-35.

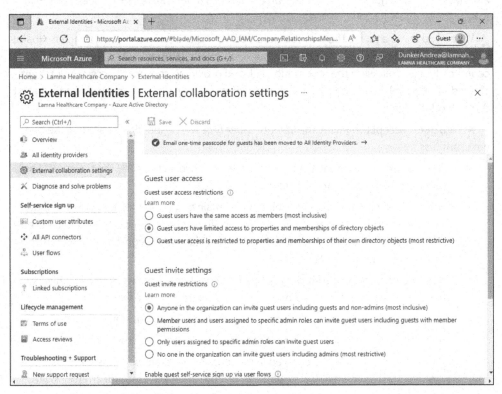

FIGURE 1-34 External collaboration settings.

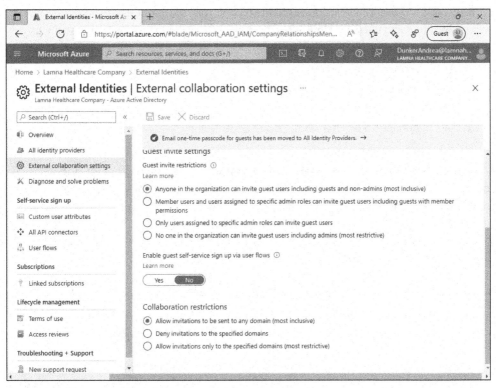

FIGURE 1-35 External collaboration settings (continued).

By default, guest users have limited permissions in the resource tenant—less than a member of the tenant—but their permissions can still be considered too broad, depending on the business scenario. For example, by default, guests can read properties of groups in the tenant (including membership and ownership) and read certain properties of other users, including guests, in the tenant: display name, email, sign-in name, photo, etc. To limit information guest users can read in your tenant, you can change the **Guest user access restrictions** setting by setting it to **Guest user access is restricted to properties and memberships of their own directory objects (most restrictive)**.

> **NEED MORE REVIEW?** **PERMISSIONS FOR USERS AND GUESTS**
>
> Read more about restricting guest access at: *https://docs.microsoft.com/en-us/azure/active-directory/enterprise-users/users-restrict-guest-permissions*
>
> Read more about default user permissions at: *https://docs.microsoft.com/en-us/azure/active-directory/fundamentals/users-default-permissions*

By default, any user can invite guests to the tenant. This means guests can invite new guests as well. By modifying the **Guest invite restrictions** setting you can control who can invite new guests:

- Any existing user (member or guest)
- Any member, and guests with specific administrative roles (Global Administrator, User Administrator, Guest Inviter)
- Global Administrator, User Administrator, or Guest Inviter
- No one can invite new guests

Azure AD External Identities self-service sign-up allows guests to use social identity providers (e.g., Azure AD, Microsoft Account, Email one-time passcode, Google, Facebook) to sign up to the application. Self-service sign-up works for applications built by resource tenant organizations and doesn't work for Microsoft's first-party applications. Self-service sign-ups must be enabled on the External collaboration setting. After it is enabled, you need to create user flows and API connectors.

> *NEED MORE REVIEW?* **AZURE AD B2B SELF-SERVICE SIGN-UP**
>
> Read more about Azure AD self-service sign-up at: *https://docs.microsoft.com/en-us/azure/active-directory/external-identities/self-service-sign-up-overview*

As discussed earlier, the most important attribute of a guest in the invite process is their email address. By default, users that have permissions to invite guests can invite guests from any email domain. You can change that with the **Collaboration restrictions** setting—you can configure a list of domains that invites cannot be sent to or allow invites to be sent only to the specified domains.

EXAM TIP

External identities need licenses when it comes to Azure AD Premium features such as Conditional Access. Review documentation on the Monthly Active Users (MAU) model for External Identities pricing at *https://azure.microsoft.com/en-us/pricing/details/active-directory/external-identities/.*

Invite external users, individually or in bulk (collectively)

There are multiple ways that a user can be invited as an Azure AD B2B guest to the resource tenant:

- Individually with Azure portal
- As part of a bulk invite with Azure portal
- Individually with PowerShell
- As part of a bulk invite with PowerShell
- Using Graph API

In addition to these methods, various applications may call Graph API to invite guests when they need to establish collaboration with external users. Examples are SharePoint Online, One-Drive for Business, or Teams: when you share a file with OneDrive or invite an external user to a Teams channel, this may lead to the creation of an Azure AD B2B guest account.

To invite an Azure AD B2B guest individually using the Azure portal:

1. Open **Azure portal** > **Azure Active Directory** > **Users**. See Figure 1-36.

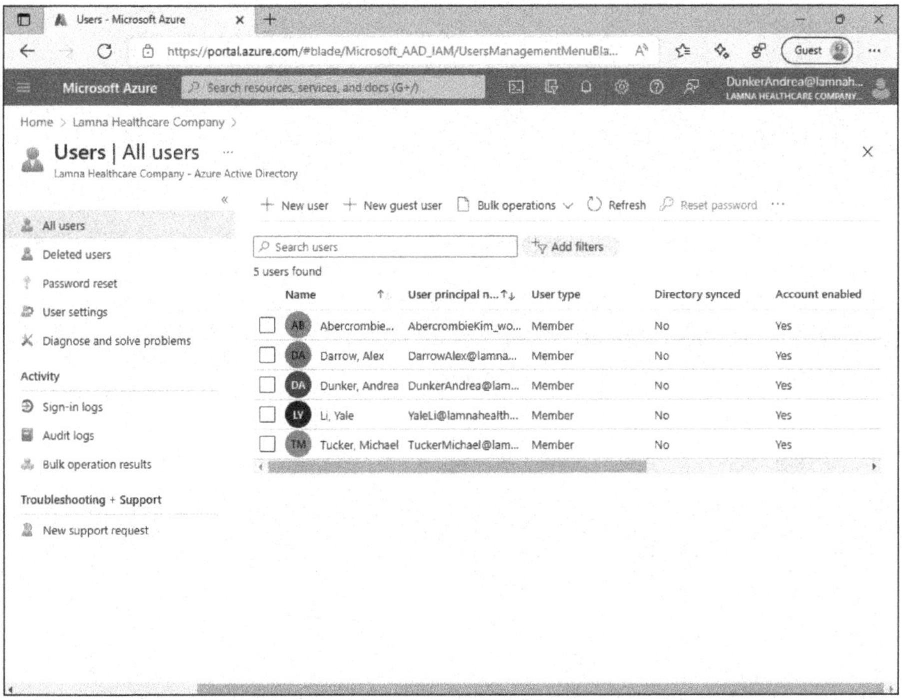

FIGURE 1-36   All users page.

2. Select **New guest user**.

3. On the **New user** page, keep the **Invite user** option selected. See Figure 1-37.

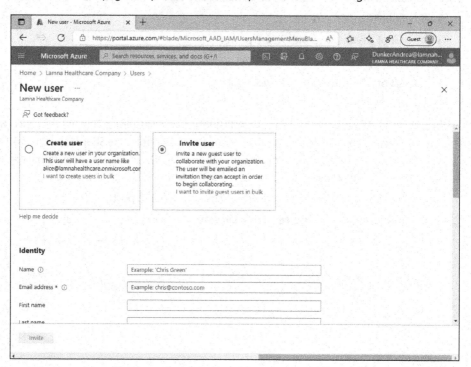

FIGURE 1-37 New user dialog.

4. Provide an **Email address** of the new guest.

5. Optionally, provide any of the following:

   - Name
   - First name
   - Last name
   - Personal message
   - Groups
   - Roles
   - Block sign in
   - Usage location
   - Job title
   - Department
   - Company name
   - Manager

6. Select **Invite**.

   After the preceding steps are completed, the invited person will receive an email. See Figure 1-38.

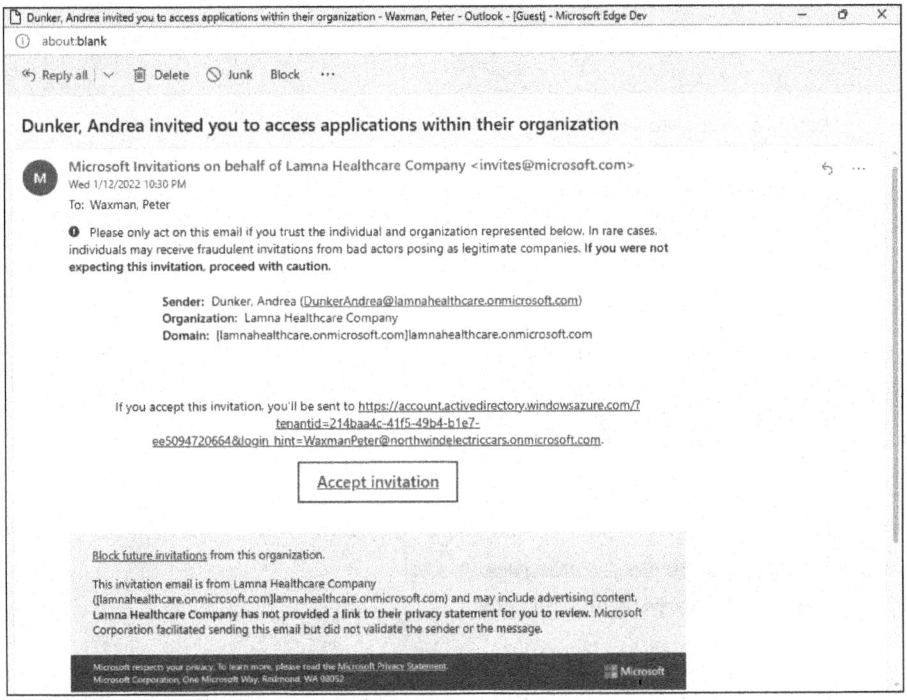

FIGURE 1-38 Azure AD B2B guest invite email.

At this time (before the invite is accepted by a guest), the guest user object already exists in the resource tenant. The resource tenant administrator can add that user object to groups, assign permissions, add the user to roles, and perform other management tasks. But nobody can sign in with that user account yet because the invite hasn't yet been accepted.

7. When the guest-to-be selects the **Accept invitation** link in the email, Azure AD identifies the Issuer type as described previously. If the guest-to-be is an Azure AD user, they are redirected to the consent page, where they can review the permissions that the resource tenant will have over their account if they accept an invite. See Figure 1-39.

FIGURE 1-39 Review permissions page.

8. After the guest selects **Accept**, they will be redirected to the **My Apps** portal, where they can see applications available to them in the resource tenant. The My Apps portal will open in the context of a guest account in the resource tenant. See Figure 1-40, where the user from the home tenant northwindelectriccars.onmicrosoft.com signed in to the resource tenant lamnahealthcare.onmicrosoft.com as a guest.

FIGURE 1-40 My apps page.

To bulk invite guests using the Azure portal:

1. Open the **Azure portal** > **Azure Active Directory** > **Users** page, as shown in Figure 1-36.

2. Select **Bulk operations** > **Bulk invite**. See Figure 1-41.

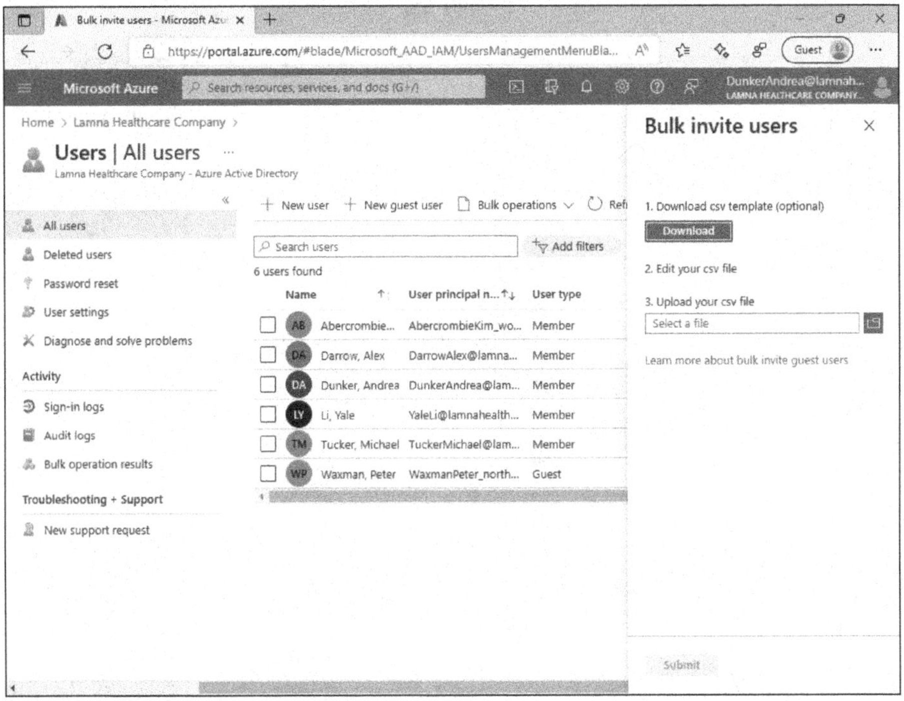

FIGURE 1-41 All users page, Bulk invite users dialog.

3. Download the csv file template.

4. Edit the csv file:

   ▪ Provide the email addresses of invitees (guests).

   ▪ Provide the redirection URL. The template provides the URL *https://myapplications. microsoft.com*. You can keep this one, and the guests' invite redemption experience will be like the one described earlier in this section. But in many cases, in a bulk invite scenario, you may want to redirect guests to some application after they accept the invite.

   ▪ Specify whether you want to send guests invites. The template includes a *TRUE* flag. You can keep this one, and the guests' invite redemption experience will be like the one described earlier in this section. Optionally, you can provide end users a redemption URL through other means: publish it on a custom portal, include it as part of custom email communication you have to them, and so on.

   ▪ Provide a customized invitation message.

5. Upload the csv file back to the Azure portal. You will see a **File uploaded successfully** message if there are no issues found with the file format.

6. Select **Submit**.

7. After processing is completed, select the **File is ready! Click here to download** link, as shown in Figure 1-42.

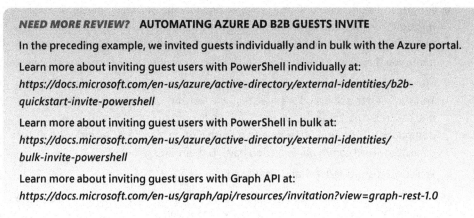

FIGURE 1-42 All users page, Bulk invite users dialog, after the CSV file has been uploaded and processed.

8. Download the CSV file from the portal: it will be mostly the same file you previously uploaded. A key difference is that it will now have a **Status** column where you can see whether the invite was sent successfully.

> **NEED MORE REVIEW? AUTOMATING AZURE AD B2B GUESTS INVITE**
>
> In the preceding example, we invited guests individually and in bulk with the Azure portal.
>
> Learn more about inviting guest users with PowerShell individually at:
> *https://docs.microsoft.com/en-us/azure/active-directory/external-identities/b2b-quickstart-invite-powershell*
>
> Learn more about inviting guest users with PowerShell in bulk at:
> *https://docs.microsoft.com/en-us/azure/active-directory/external-identities/bulk-invite-powershell*
>
> Learn more about inviting guest users with Graph API at:
> *https://docs.microsoft.com/en-us/graph/api/resources/invitation?view=graph-rest-1.0*

Manage external user accounts in Azure AD

In most scenarios, guest accounts in Azure AD can be used equivalently to member user accounts. You can assign applications to them, assign them Azure AD roles, assign permissions in various applications, include them in groups, etc. The guest account can be targeted in policies such as Conditional Access policies, and the guest account can be assigned a license in the resource tenant—all using the same mechanisms that member accounts are managed with.

A few principles are still unique to guest accounts and will be covered in this section.

If a guest user has not yet redeemed their invitation, in some cases you may need to resend the invitation email—for example, if the user mistakenly removed the original invite email.

To resend an invitation email:

1. Open **Azure portal** > **Azure Active Directory** > **Users**.
2. Open the properties of the guest account you need to resend the invitation email to.
3. In the **Identity** section, note that **Invitation accepted** is set to **No**. Select **(manage)**. See Figure 1-43.

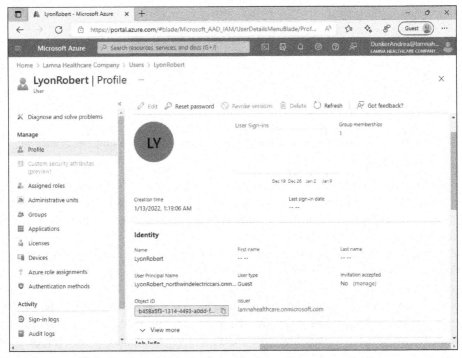

FIGURE 1-43 Profile of a guest user that hasn't yet redeemed their invite.

4. Set **Resend invite?** To **Yes**. See Figure 1-44.

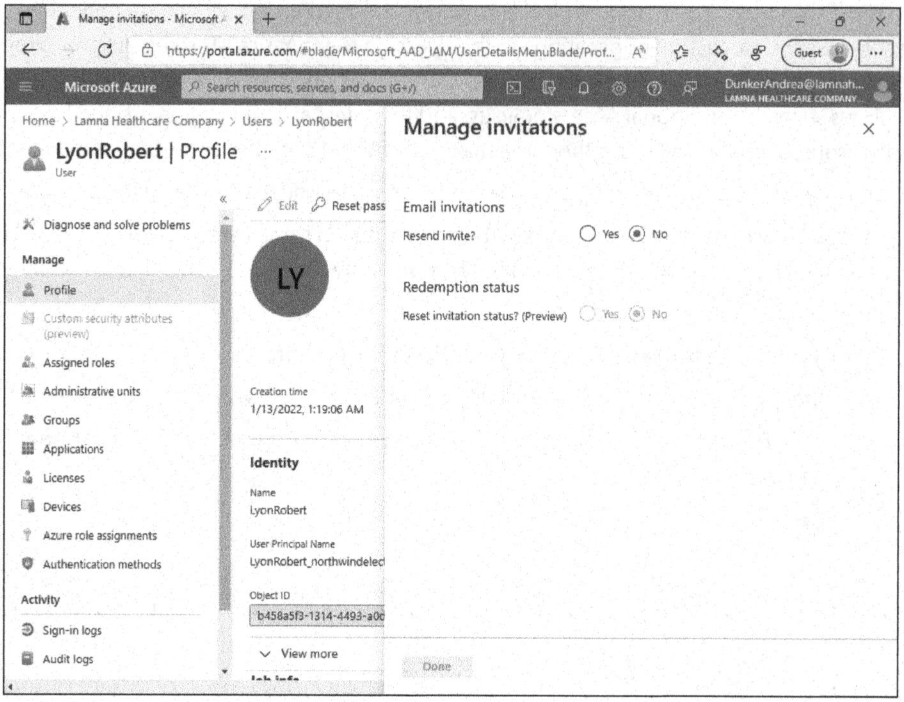

FIGURE 1-44 Profile of a guest user that hasn't yet redeemed their invite, Manage invitations tab.

5. In the **Are you sure you want to resend an invitation?** dialog, select **Yes**.
6. Select **Done**.

As discussed earlier, Azure AD B2B allows users with a variety of credentials (Azure AD accounts, Microsoft accounts, Google accounts, accounts from federated SAML/WS-Fed identity provider) to get Single Sign-On to a resource tenant. There still may be a situation when an invited guest has an email address that doesn't correspond to any of the account types above. In that case, depending on the resource tenant configuration, the guest can sign in with a one-time passcode delivered over email or be prompted to create a Microsoft account or Azure AD self-service account. We recommend the email one-time passcode option in these business scenarios; this will help you validate that the user has continuous access to the email address they were invited from before they access the resource tenant. With the Microsoft account/ Azure AD self-service account option, the guest will create a password of their choice, and you may not be notified if they leave their organization, so there will be no technical way to ensure that user still works for their employer at a later time.

To enable an email one-time passcode:

1. Open **Azure portal** > **Azure Active Directory** > **External identities** > **All identity providers**. See Figure 1-45.

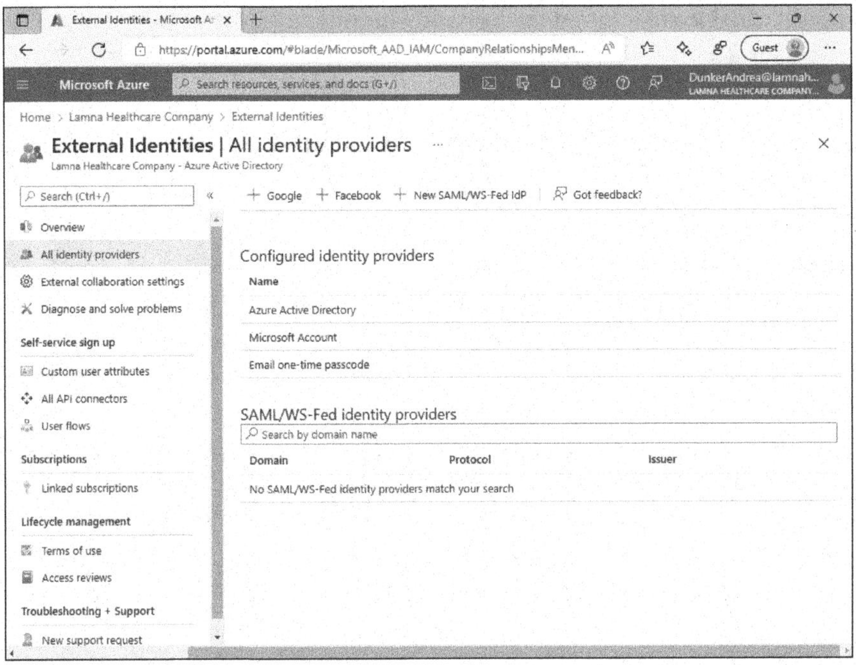

FIGURE 1-45 All identity providers page.

2. Select **Email one-time passcode**. See Figure 1-46.

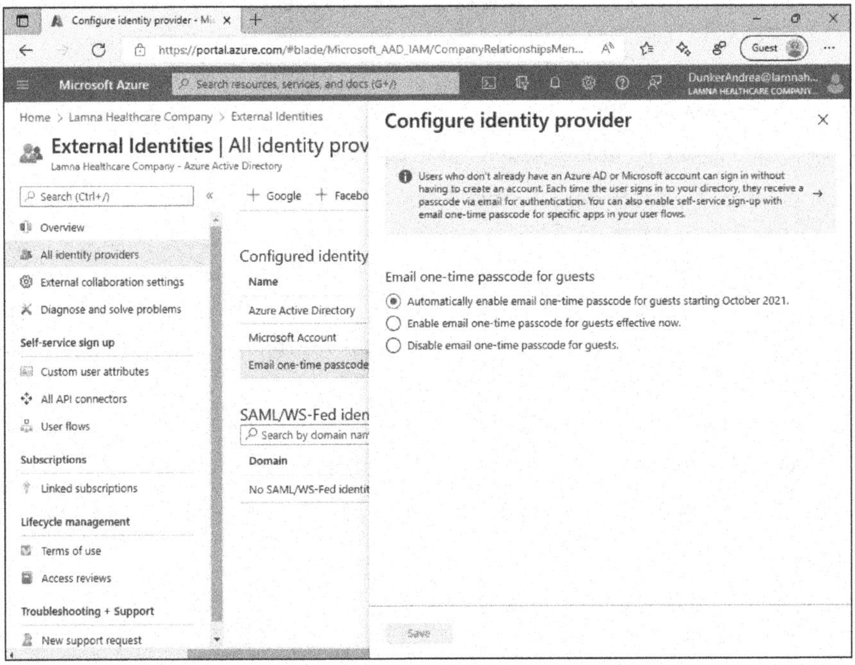

FIGURE 1-46 Configure identity provider—Email one-time passcode for guests.

3. Select **Enable email one-time passcode for guests effective now**.

4. Select **Save**.

Configure identity providers, including SAML and WS-Fed

With Azure AD B2B, you can configure federation with social providers (Google, Facebook) or SAML/WS-Fed identity providers.

Google federation with Azure AD External identities allows Gmail users to get Single Sign-On to a resource tenant they are invited to. Read more about Google federation at *https://docs.microsoft.com/en-us/azure/active-directory/external-identities/google-federation*. Google federation isn't applicable to Google Workspace domains—for Google Workspace domains, see the SAML/WS-Fed section below.

Facebook federation shares the same idea as Google federation: it allows Facebook users to sign in as Azure AD B2B guests to your tenant. Follow the article for details, here: *https://docs.microsoft.com/en-us/azure/active-directory/external-identities/facebook-federation*.

SAML/WS-Fed identity provider federation (previously known as **Direct federation**) is a Public Preview feature at the time of writing. This option is used when a resource tenant administrator needs to provide the Single Sign-On experience to guests from a domain that is not Azure AD verified.

To set up SAML/WS-Fed identity provider federation:

1. Determine if the guest company DNS administrator will need to update their DNS settings:

   - DNS changes are needed if the target domain does not match the identity provider's passive domain URL.

   - DNS changes are not needed if the target domain matches the identity provider's passive domain URL.

   For example, when setting up federation with *fabrikam.com*:

   - If the identity provider's authentication URL is *https://fabrikam.com* or *https://sts.fabrikam.com/adfs*, no DNS changes are necessary.

   - If the identity provider's authentication URL is *https://fabrikamhq.com* or *https://sts.fabrikamhq.com/adfs*, DNS changes are necessary to confirm that the company that owns the *fabrikam.com* domain name uses the identity provider with the authentication URL in the *fabrikamhq.com* domain.

   The following Identity Provider (IdP) domain names do not require DNS changes:

   - *accounts.google.com*
   - *pingidentity.com*
   - *login.pingone.com*
   - *okta.com*
   - *oktapreview.com*
   - *okta-emea.com*
   - *my.salesforce.com*
   - *federation.exostar.com*
   - *federation.exostartest.com*
   - *idaptive.app*
   - *idaptive.qa*

2. If DNS changes are necessary, add a DNS record:

<*domainname*> IN TXT DirectFedAuthUrl=<*IdP authentication URL*>

Taking the example from the previous step, a DNS record may look like this:

fabrikam.com IN TXT DirectFedAuthUrl=https://sts.fabrikamhq.com/adfs

3. If you choose to federate with SAML, ensure that the IdP includes the following attributes (as shown in Table 1-1 and Table 1-2) in the SAML 2.0 response:

TABLE 1-1   Required attributes for the SAML 2.0 response from the IdP

Attribute	value
AssertionConsumerService	*https://login.microsoftonline.com/login.srf*
Audience	urn:federation:MicrosoftOnline
Issuer	Issuer URI of the IdP

TABLE 1-2   Required claims for the SAML 2.0 token issued by the IdP

Attribute	value
NameID Format	urn:oasis:names:tc:SAML:2.0:nameid-format:persistent
Emailaddress	*http://schemas.xmlsoap.org/ws/2005/05/identity/claims/emailaddress*

4. If you choose to federate with WS-Fed, ensure that the IdP includes the following attributes (as shown in Table 1-3 and Table 1-4) in the WS-Fed message:

TABLE 1-3   Required attributes in the WS-Fed message from the IdP

Attribute	value
PassiveRequestorEndpoint	*https://login.microsoftonline.com/login.srf*
Audience	urn:federation:MicrosoftOnline
Issuer	Issuer URI of the IdP

TABLE 1-4   Required claims for WS-Fed token issued by the IdP

Attribute	value
ImmutableID	*http://schemas.microsoft.com/LiveID/Federation/2008/05/ImmutableID*
Emailaddress	*http://schemas.xmlsoap.org/ws/2005/05/identity/claims/emailaddress*

5. Go to **Azure portal** > **Azure Active Directory** > **External Identities** > **All identity providers**.

6. Select **+ new SAML/WS-Fed IdP**.

7. Under **Identity provider protocol**, select **SAML** or **WS-Fed**.

8. Provide **Domain name of federating IdP**.

9. Upload a metadata file or provide the following information manually:

   - Issuer URI

   - Passive authentication endpoint

   - Certificate

   - Metadata URL (Optional. We recommend allowing Azure AD to renew the signing certificate automatically when it expires).

10. Select **Save**.

> ***NEED MORE REVIEW?*** **SAML/WS-FED IDENTITY PROVIDER INTEGRATION**
>
> Learn more about configuring ADFS as SAML/WS-Fed identity provider at: *https://docs.microsoft.com/en-us/azure/active-directory/external-identities/ direct-federation-adfs*
>
> In the preceding example, we covered configuring the SAML/WS-Fed identity provider federation using the Azure portal.
>
> Learn more about configuring the SAML/WS-Fed identity provider using PowerShell at: *https://docs.microsoft.com/en-us/azure/active-directory/external-identities/ direct-federation*

Skill 1.4: Implement and manage hybrid identity

Many organizations have on-premises environments that include on-premises Active Directory Domain Services. In this section, we cover tools that synchronize on-premises identities to Azure AD: Azure AD Connect and Azure AD Connect Cloud Sync. We cover authentication methods that are applicable to on-premises users: Password Hash Synchronization, Pass-Through Authentication, and Federation. We discuss the configuration of Azure AD Connect with each of these methods. We also discuss Azure AD Connect Health—a tool that can be used to monitor the health of on-premises components of your environment such as Azure AD Connect synchronization engine, Active Directory Domain Services (AD DS), and Active Directory Federation Services (AD FS).

Implement and manage Azure Active Directory Connect

Many enterprises have existing on-premises infrastructures before they start their cloud journey. On-premises infrastructure often has identity providers including Active Directory Domain Services. Microsoft offers a set of hybrid capabilities that allows customers to use on-premises identities in the cloud. Two products currently offered are **Azure AD Connect** and **Azure AD Connect cloud sync**.

Azure AD Connect is an on-premises application that provides the following capabilities:

- Synchronization—based on on-premises users, groups, and devices information, this creates users, groups, and devices in Azure AD. For certain scenarios, writeback synchronization (creating/updating on-premises objects based on Azure AD object information) is also supported.

- Authentication—Azure AD Connect configures authentication of on-premises users using one of the following options:

  - Password Hash Synchronization
  - Pass-Through Authentication
  - Federation

- Health monitoring—Azure AD Connect Health provides monitoring for:

  - Azure AD Connect synchronization
  - Active Directory Domain Services
  - Active Directory Federation Services

Think about Azure AD Connect as a wizard that configures all the things mentioned above: Synchronization engine, Federation settings, Active Directory Domain Services monitoring, etc. And most of them are separate pieces of software—different agents, synchronization engines, and so on.

The Synchronization engine (also known as Azure AD Connect Sync) is a central part of Azure AD Connect. Authentication-related components may or may not be implemented, but the

Synchronization engine is always deployed in any Azure AD Connect installation. In this part, we will focus on basic Azure AD Connect implementation and the Synchronization engine.

The Azure AD Connect Synchronization engine can be used for synchronization between on-premises Active Directory Domain Services or LDAP directory on one side and Azure AD on another side. But for the purposes of this book, we will focus on synchronization between Active Directory and Azure AD.

Single tenant topologies:

The simplest Azure AD Connect topology consists of one on-premises Active Directory Domain Services forest, one Azure AD tenant and one Azure AD Connect that synchronize information between them See Figure 1-47.

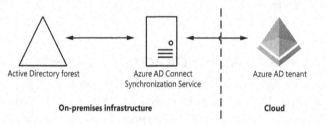

FIGURE 1-47 Azure AD Connect topology for one Active Directory forest and one Azure AD tenant.

Another possible situation is when you have multiple on-premises Active Directory Domain Services forests and need to synchronize information from each of them to a single Azure AD tenant. This is possible with one Azure AD Connect instance that should have network connectivity to domain controllers of all involved Active Directory domains. See Figure 1-48.

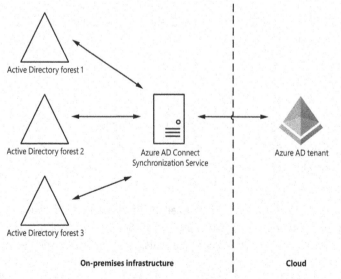

FIGURE 1-48 Azure AD Connect topology for multiple Active Directory forests and one Azure AD tenant.

Multiple tenant topologies:

In the common multi-tenant topology, one on-premises object (user, group, device) is synchronized to only one Azure AD tenant. This can be implemented using filtering mechanisms—for example, one organizational unit can be synchronized to one Azure AD tenant, and another organizational unit can be synchronized to another Azure AD tenant. See Figure 1-49. Filtering based on groups or custom rules will achieve the same result if one on-premises object is synchronized to only one Azure AD tenant.

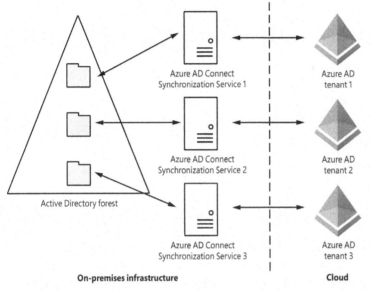

FIGURE 1-49 Azure AD Connect topology for one forest and multiple Azure AD tenants, where each object is synchronized to one tenant only.

In some situations, one on-premises object (user, device, group) needs to be synchronized to multiple Azure AD tenants. This topology is in Public Preview at the time of writing. In this configuration, synchronization from an on-premises environment can be configured to multiple Azure AD tenants, but only one Azure AD tenant can be configured to write back to the on-premises environment for the same object. See Figure 1-50.

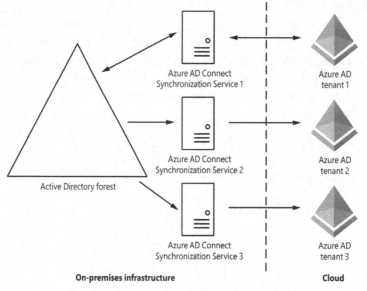

FIGURE 1-50 Azure AD Connect topology for one forest and multiple Azure AD tenants, where an object is synchronized to multiple tenants.

EXAM TIP

Note that in Figures 1-47 through 1-50 there is one Azure AD Connect Synchronization Service per Azure AD tenant. At no point in time can one Azure AD tenant have multiple **active servers**—i.e., Azure AD Connect Synchronization Service instances synchronizing to it. Having said that, it is possible to have one active Azure AD Connect server and one (or, potentially, more than one) staging Azure AD Connect server. A **staging server** reads data from connected directories to have up-to-date copy of the data but doesn't write to any directories. A staging server can be used to test a new configuration. An administrator can make a staging server active if the current active server becomes unavailable.

NEED MORE REVIEW? **TOPOLOGIES FOR AZURE AD CONNECT**

Read more about supported and unsupported topologies for Azure AD Connect at: *https://docs.microsoft.com/en-us/azure/active-directory/hybrid/plan-connect-topologies*

NOTE **AZURE AD CONNECT PREREQUISITES**

To deploy Azure AD Connect, you need a domain-joined server with Windows Server 2016 or later and with full GUI (not Server Core).

Read the full list of Azure AD Connect prerequisites here: *https://docs.microsoft.com/en-us/ azure/active-directory/hybrid/how-to-connect-install-prerequisites*

Choosing the right authentication method in a hybrid environment:

A key decision that must be made is the authentication method for user accounts that will be synchronized from an on-premises environment. Three options to choose from are:

- Password Hash Synchronization (PHS)
- Pass-Through Authentication (PTA)
- Federation

Each of these methods will be covered in detail in later sections.

We recommend using the Password Hash Synchronization authentication method unless you need to enforce user-level Active Directory security policies during sign-in or have a sign-in requirement not supported natively by Azure AD—such as Certificate-Based Authentication.

***NEED MORE REVIEW?* AUTHENTICATION METHODS FOR HYBRID ENVIRONMENT**

Read more about choosing the right authentication method at:
https://docs.microsoft.com/en-us/azure/active-directory/hybrid/choose-ad-authn

---

If PTA or Federation are chosen as the authentication method, we still recommend enabling Password Hash Synchronization in addition. That will allow you to switch to cloud authentication if something goes wrong with the on-premises Active Directory Domain Services environment or the federated identity provider and also will allow leaked credentials detection through Azure AD Identity Protection.

Prior to Azure AD Connect installation, it is recommended to use the IdFix tool to identify any potential issues with source data in on-premises Active Directory—such as duplicates or unsupported characters in attribute values. Follow the next steps to identify and resolve issues:

1. Download the IdFix tool from *https://github.com/Microsoft/idfix*.
2. Install the IdFix tool by launching an installation file and selecting **Install**.
3. Review the privacy statement.
4. Select **Query** to analyze Active Directory Domain Services domain data.
5. If you get a **Schema Warning** message, review it and select **Yes**.
6. Review identified issues as shown in Figure 1-51. An empty list indicates that there were no issues identified.

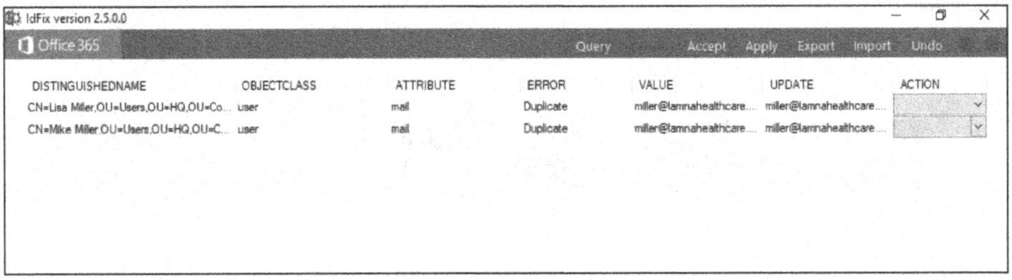

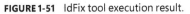

FIGURE 1-51 IdFix tool execution result.

7. Solve identified issues manually outside of the IdFix tool or select an applicable action in the right column and select **Accept**.

Azure AD Connect can be installed in one of two modes: **Express settings** or **Custom settings**. Choose Express settings if all of the following are true:

- You need to synchronize identities from one on-premises Active Directory Domain Services forest.

- Azure AD Connect server is a member of the same forest you will synchronize to Azure AD.

- Your authentication method of choice is Password Hash Synchronization.

- You are fine with synchronization of all attributes (eligible for synchronization) to Azure AD.

- You don't need to configure custom groups to manage Azure AD Connect Synchronization Engine.

To install Azure AD Connect:

1. Download Azure AD Connect from *https://go.microsoft.com/fwlink/?LinkId=615771*.

2. Run the installation file.

3. On the **Welcome to Azure AD Connect** screen, review the license terms and privacy notice and select **Continue**.

4. On the **Express Settings** page, select **Customize** or **Use express settings**. See Figure 1-52.

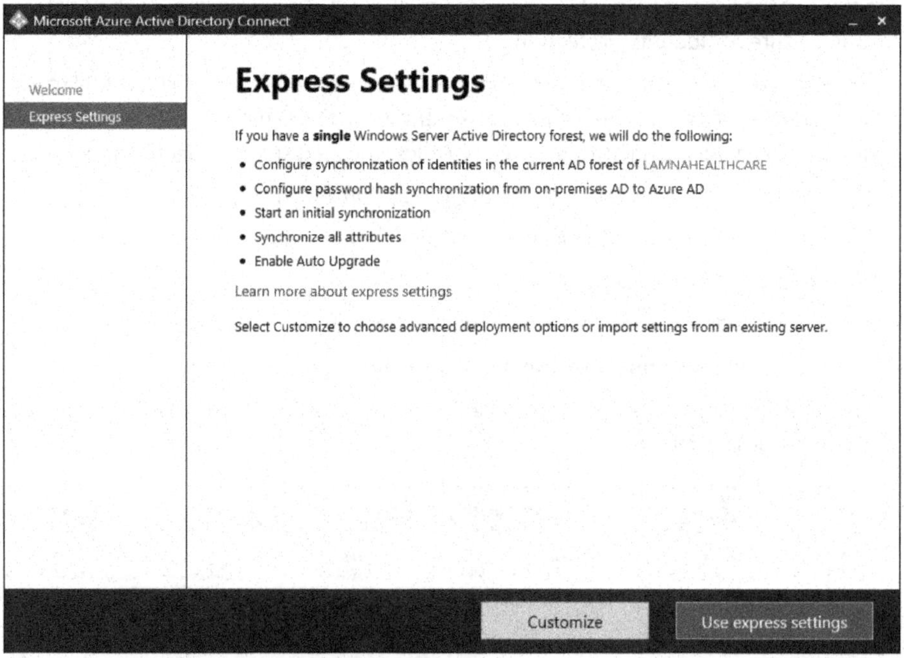

FIGURE 1-52 Azure AD Connect, Express Settings page.

For the rest of this exercise, we will assume that the **Use express settings** option was selected.

5. On the **Connect to Azure AD** page (shown in Figure 1-53), provide the credentials for the Azure AD Global Administrator or Hybrid Identity Administrator. You may also be asked to provide a second factor of authentication, depending on tenant settings.

> **NOTE   CREDENTIALS SUPPLIED TO AZURE AD CONNECT WIZARD**
>
> These credentials will be used for configuration and creating another user account for synchronization purposes (service account). There is no need to manually create a service account in Azure AD. It is safe to disable the Global Administrator or Hybrid Identity Administrator account at a later point—for example, if the administrator that made the Azure AD Connect configuration has left the company.

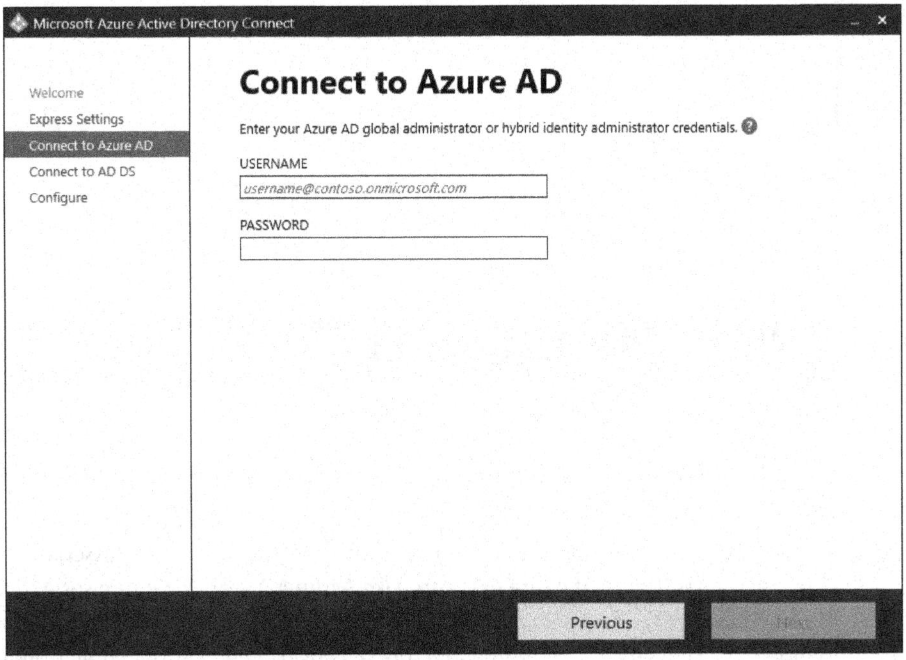

FIGURE 1-53   Azure AD Connect, Connect to Azure AD page.

6. On the **Connect to AD DS** page (shown in Figure 1-54), provide the enterprise administrator credentials for the Active Directory forest. Similar to the previous step, the enterprise administrator's credentials will be used to create the service account. There is no need to manually create a service account in Active Directory. It is safe to disable the enterprise administrator account used during installation at a later point—for example, if the administrator that made the Azure AD Connect configuration has left the company.

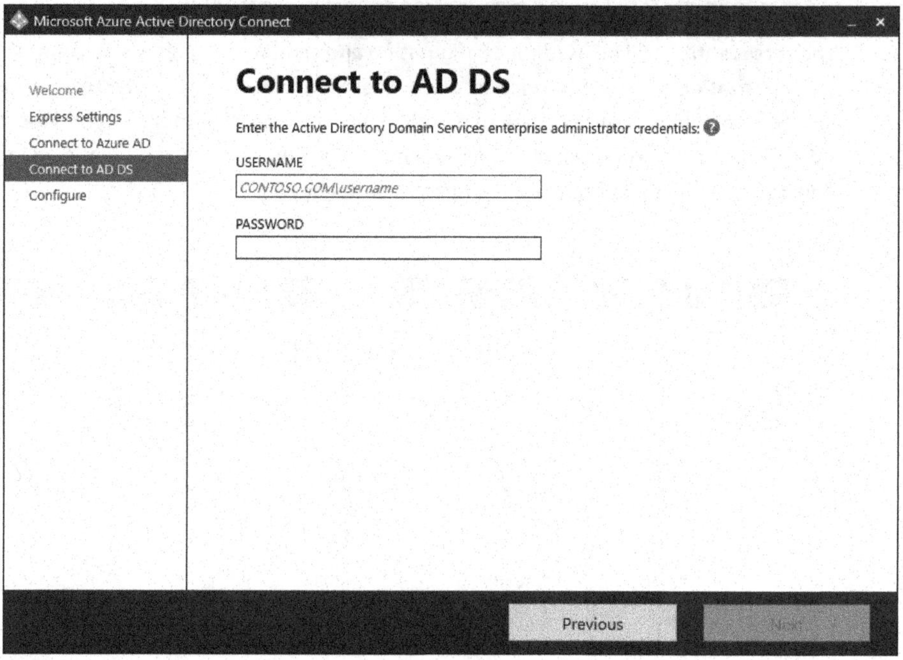

FIGURE 1-54 Azure AD Connect, Connect to AD DS page.

7. On the **Azure AD sign-in configuration** page, review the list of UPN suffixes configured in the Active Directory forest.

8. In the earlier section "Configure and manage custom domains," we discussed User Principal Names (UPNs) of Azure AD users. Like Azure AD users, on-premises Active Directory Domain Services users also have UPNs. For the best user experience, it is recommended that UPNs in on-premises and Azure AD environments should match. Review the UPN suffixes to ensure that UPN suffixes used on-premises are verified in Azure AD.

9. On the **Ready to configure** page, review the settings and proposed changes and select **Install**. See Figure 1-55.

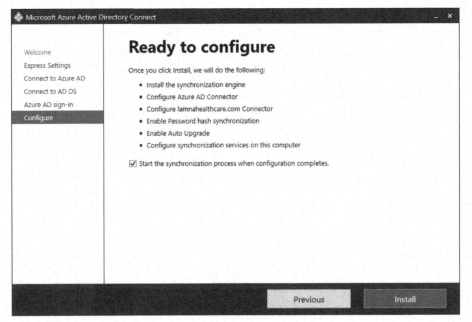

FIGURE 1-55   Azure AD Connect, Ready to configure page.

10. On the **Configuration complete** page, review the configuration summary and recommendations. Select **Exit**. See Figure 1-56.

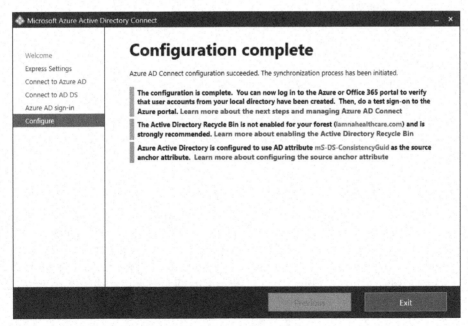

FIGURE 1-56   Azure AD Connect, Configuration complete page.

11. After configuration is completed, open the Azure AD Connect wizard (using a desktop or start menu shortcut) to perform the following actions:

- Review privacy settings: enable or disable application telemetry.
- View or export Azure AD Connect configuration.
- Customize synchronization options:
  - Configure Exchange Hybrid deployment.
  - Add/remove Active Directory forests for synchronization.
  - Implement domain/OU filtering.
  - Configure Azure AD app and attribute filtering.
  - Enable/disable Password Hash Synchronization.
  - Enable/disable password writeback.
  - Enable/disable group writeback.
  - Configure device writeback.
  - Configure directory extension attribute sync.
- Configure Hybrid Azure AD Join.
- Refresh schema to enable synchronization of new attributes.
- Enable/disable staging mode.
- Change user sign-in options.
- Manage federation settings.
- Launch AADConnect Troubleshooting tool (PowerShell-based).

EXAM TIP

The default synchronization cycle for Azure AD Connect server is 30 minutes. The default synchronization cycle for Azure AD Connect Cloud Sync (covered in the next section) is 2 minutes.

Read more about Azure AD Connect scheduler configuration at: *https://docs.microsoft.com/en-us/azure/active-directory/hybrid/how-to-connect-sync-feature-scheduler*

Implement and manage Azure AD Connect cloud sync

Azure AD Connect cloud sync is a new synchronization service for hybrid environments. It can be used by itself or with Azure AD Connect. Similar to Azure AD Connect, it provides synchronization between on-premises Active Directory and Azure AD. A key difference compared to Azure AD Connect is that Azure AD Connect runs its synchronization engine on an on-premises server, while Azure AD Connect cloud sync utilizes lightweight agents on-premises and a synchronization engine in the cloud.

Azure AD Connect cloud sync provides the following benefits, compared to Azure AD Connect:

- Simplified installation with lightweight provisioning agents.
- Synchronization from a multi-forest disconnected Active Directory environment. As discussed earlier, to synchronize from multiple forests with Azure AD Connect, you must establish network connectivity between Azure AD Connect and each involved domain. With Azure AD Connect cloud sync, you can deploy multiple provisioning agents—each in its own forest—without direct network connectivity between them.
- Multiple provisioning agents can be used to simplify high-availability deployments.

At the same time, Azure AD Connect cloud sync lacks the following functionality available in Azure AD Connect at the time of writing:

- Synchronization from LDAP directories
- Synchronization of device objects (required for Hybrid Azure AD Join)
- Synchronization of directory extension attributes
- Pass-Through Authentication support
- Filtering based on attribute values
- Advanced customization of attribute flows
- Device writeback
- Group writeback
- Azure AD Domain Services support
- Exchange Hybrid writeback
- Cross-domain references

Also, Azure AD Connect currently supports groups with up to 250K members, while Azure AD Connect cloud sync supports groups with up to 50K members only.

Azure AD Connect and Azure AD Connect cloud sync may coexist for the same tenant. This is typically used in Merges & Acquisitions scenarios: a company may have Azure AD Connect deployed for the main forest, and the forest of the acquired company may be synchronized with Azure AD Connect cloud sync agents. This may be done without establishing network connectivity between forests, which may be a challenging task if IP addresses overlap.

To deploy Azure AD Connect cloud sync:

1. Prepare the domain-joined server, Windows Server 2016 or later.
2. Select **Azure portal** > **Azure AD Connect** > **Manage Azure AD cloud sync** > **Review all agents**. See Figure 1-57.

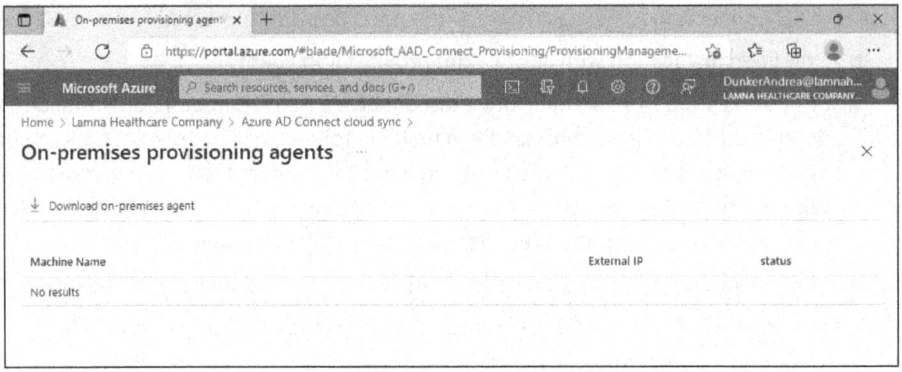

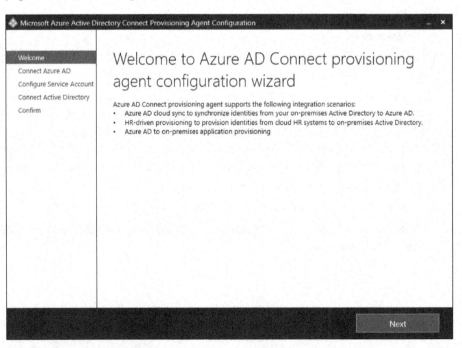

FIGURE 1-57 Azure portal, On-premises provisioning agents page.

3. Select **Download on-premises agent**.

4. Review the **Terms of Service** and select **Accept terms & download**.

5. Open the installation file.

6. Review the **License terms** and **Privacy notice**, and select **I agree to the license terms and conditions**.

7. Select **Install**.

8. On the **Welcome to Azure AD Connect provisioning agent configuration wizard** page, select **Next**. See Figure 1-58.

FIGURE 1-58 Azure AD Connect Provisioning Agent Configuration, Welcome page.

9. Sign in with Global Administrator or Hybrid Identity Administrator credentials.

10. On the **Configure Service Account** page (shown in Figure 1-59), provide Domain Admin credentials and select **Next**. The credentials will be used to create a group-managed service account (gMSA) in an on-premises Active Directory. It is safe to change the password or disable the Doman Admin account later if necessary—for example, if the Domain Admin leaves the organization.

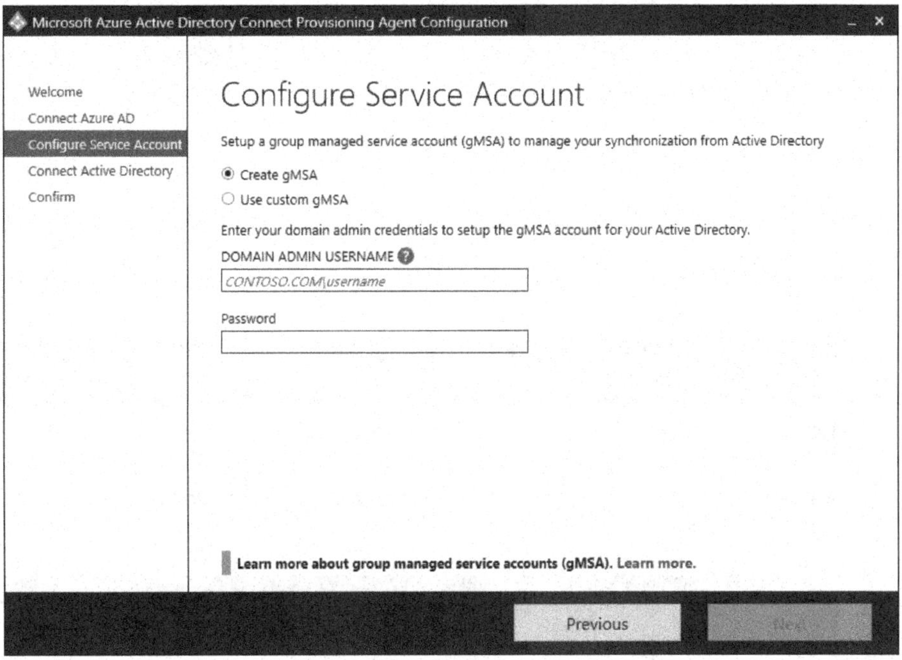

FIGURE 1-59   Azure AD Connect Provisioning Agent Configuration, Configure Service Account page.

11. On the **Connect Active Directory** page (shown in Figure 1-60), you can add additional on-premises Active Directory domains to the synchronization. If Azure AD Connect cloud sync is being configured on the member server of the same domain that will be synchronized, select **Next**.

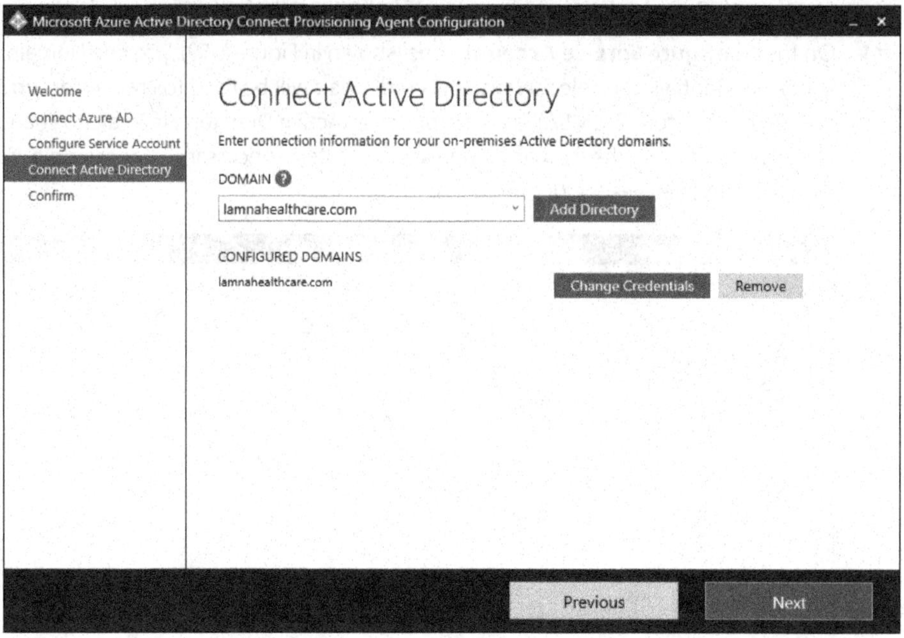

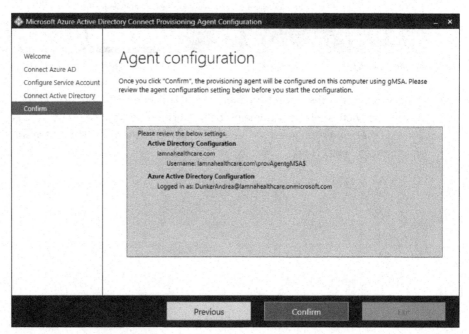

FIGURE 1-60   Azure AD Connect Provisioning Agent Configuration, Connect Active Directory page.

12. Review the proposed changes on the **Agent configuration** page and select **Confirm**.
See Figure 1-61.

FIGURE 1-61   Azure AD Connect Provisioning Agent Configuration, Agent configuration page.

13. After receiving the **Your agent installation and configuration is complete** message, select **Exit**.

14. Open **Azure portal** > **Azure Active Directory** > **Azure AD Connect** > **Manage Azure AD cloud sync** > **Review all agents**.

15. Notice that you now have an on-premises agent listed. See Figure 1-62.

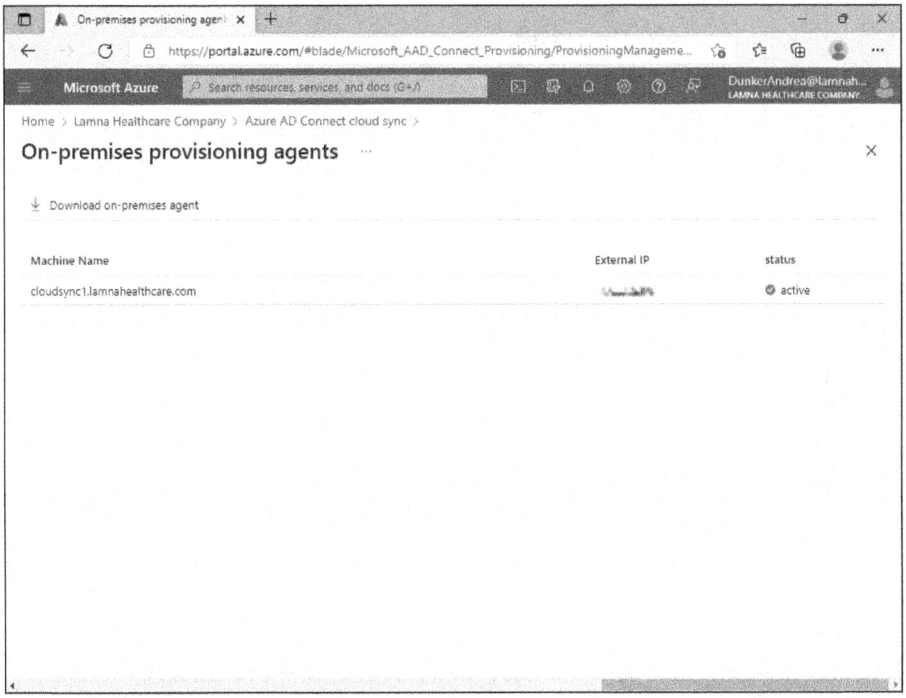

FIGURE 1-62 On-premises provisioning agents page.

16. Open **Azure portal** > **Azure Active Directory** > **Azure AD Connect** > **Manage Azure AD cloud sync**.

17. Select **New configuration**.

18. Ensure that the correct domain is selected and keep **Enable password hash sync enabled** as desired. Select **Create**. See Figure 1-63.

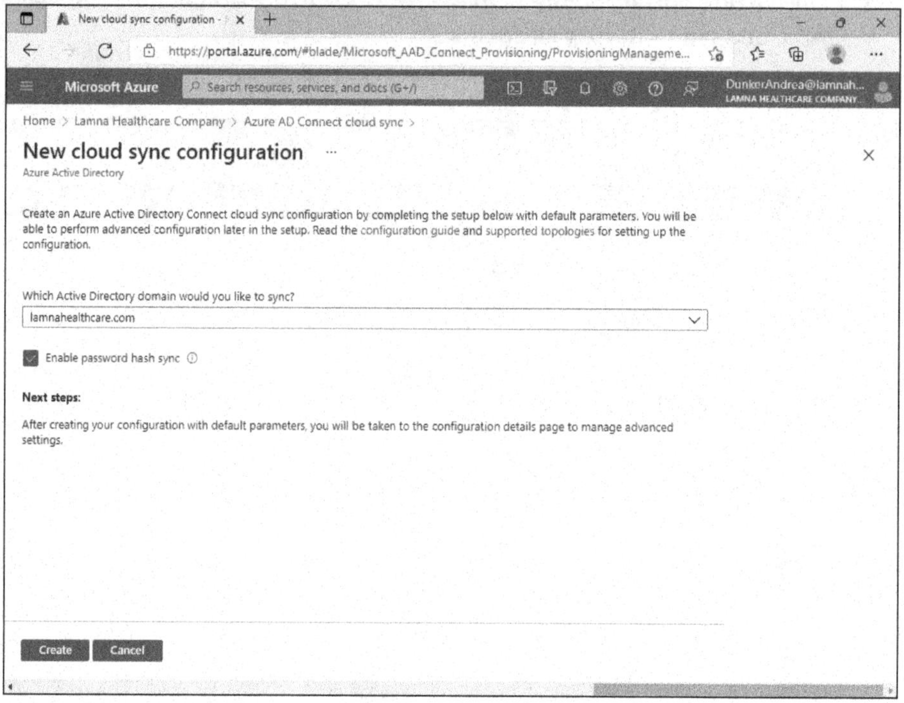

FIGURE 1-63 New cloud sync configuration page.

19. On the **Edit cloud sync configuration** page, adjust the following if necessary:
    - Scope—which users will be synchronized to Azure AD, based on OU or group
    - Attribute mapping
    - Notification email
    - Accidental deletion prevention
    - Accidental deletion threshold

    See Figure 1-64 and Figure 1-65.

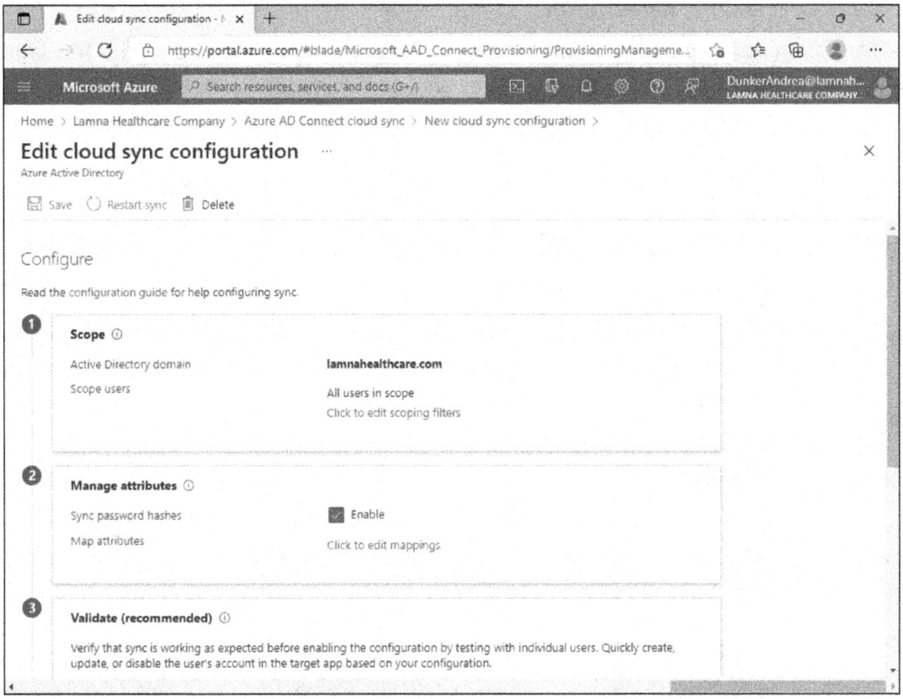

FIGURE 1-64 Edit cloud sync configuration page, part 1.

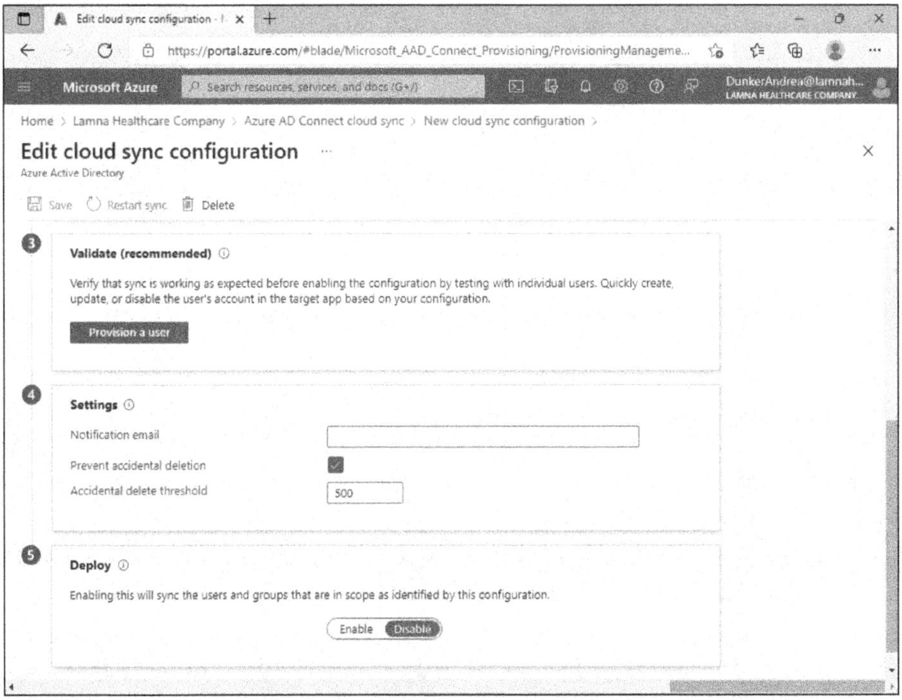

FIGURE 1-65 Edit cloud sync configuration page, part 2.

20. Select **Enable**, **Save** and **Yes**.

21. Open **Azure portal** > **Azure Active Directory** > **Azure AD Connect** > **Manage Azure AD cloud sync** and ensure that the configuration is now listed with the status **Healthy**.

22. To edit the settings of the configuration, select a domain name and adjust the settings accordingly.

Implement and manage Password Hash Synchronization (PHS)

Password Hash Synchronization serves two goals:

- PHS is one of the three main authentication mechanisms in hybrid environments and allows users to sign in to Azure AD with the same password they use in on-premises Active Directory Domain Services. See Figure 1-66.

- PHS allows Azure AD Identity Protection to check for leaked credentials and protect user accounts.

Even if your chosen authentication mechanism is Pass-Through Authentication (PTA) or Federation, we still recommend enabling Password Hash Synchronization for the purposes of detecting leaked credentials.

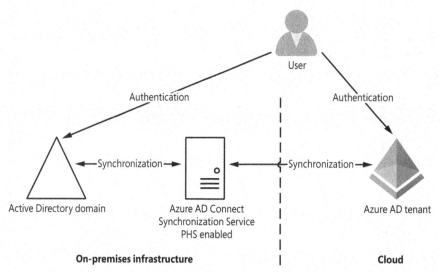

FIGURE 1-66 Password Hash Synchronization (PHS).

We recommend using Password Hash Synchronization as your authentication mechanism because it provides the following benefits:

- Business continuity. Authentication to Azure AD doesn't depend on the availability of an on-premises environment over the internet or on-premises components.

- Simple deployment. Implementation doesn't require any agents or federated identity providers to be deployed on-premises, which makes PHS the easiest authentication mechanism to implement.

At the same time, Password Hash Synchronization comes with the following limitations:

- Since on-premises Active Directory doesn't participate in the authentication process, recent changes to the account (such as the account being recently disabled) must be synchronized from the on-premises environment to Azure AD to take effect. This usually takes up to 30 minutes for Azure AD Connect and up to 2 minutes for Azure AD Connect cloud sync.

- Information about a password being expired or account being locked out in an on-premises Active Directory is not synchronized to Azure AD. Therefore, it will not be considered during the Azure AD sign-in.

- Information about logon hours configured in an on-premises Active Directory is not synchronized to Azure AD. Therefore, it will not be considered during the Azure AD sign-in.

- Sign-in features not natively supported by Azure AD, such as smartcards or certificates, can't be used.

NEED MORE REVIEW? **PASSWORD HASH SYNCHRONIZATION**

Read more about how password hash synchronization works from an encryption standpoint and how it coexists with password policies at: *https://docs.microsoft.com/en-us/azure/active-directory/hybrid/how-to-connect-password-hash-synchronization*

To enable Password Hash Synchronization in an existing Azure AD Connect installation:

1. Open the **Azure AD Connect wizard** using the desktop or Start menu shortcut.

2. On the **Welcome to Azure AD Connect** page, select **Configure**. See Figure 1-67.

FIGURE 1-67 Welcome to Azure AD Connect page.

3. On the **Additional tasks** page, select **Customize synchronization options**.
   See Figure 1-68.

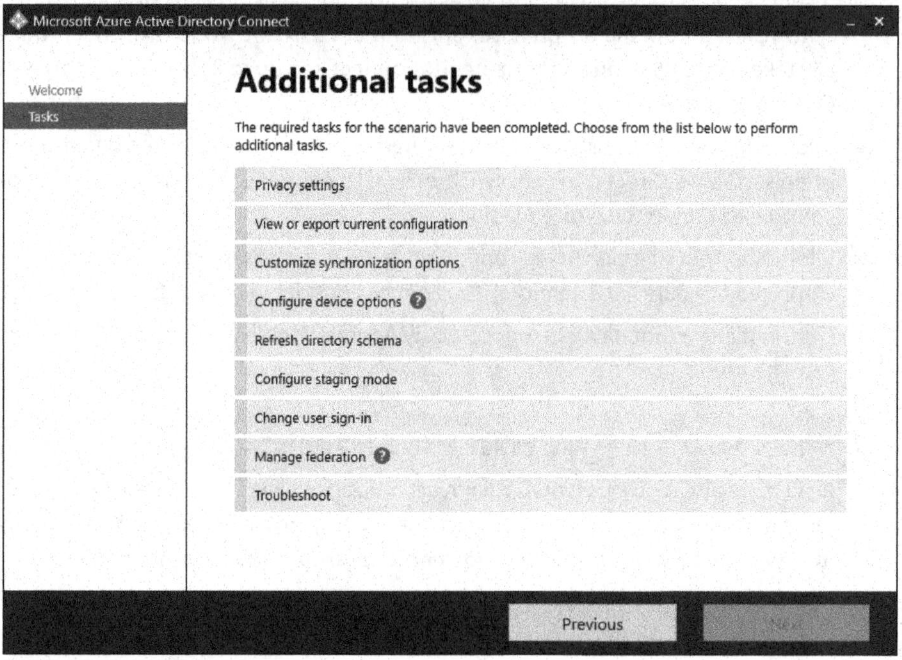

FIGURE 1-68   Additional tasks page.

4. On **Connect to Azure AD** page, provide the credentials of the Global Administrator or Hybrid Identity Administrator.

5. On the **Connect your directories** page, review the list of on-premises Active Directory domains that password hash synchronization will occur on and then select **Next**.

6. On the **Domain and OU filtering** page, review the OUs that will participate in synchronization and select **Next**.

7. On the **Optional features** page, select the **Password hash synchronization** checkbox and select **Next**. See Figure 1-69.

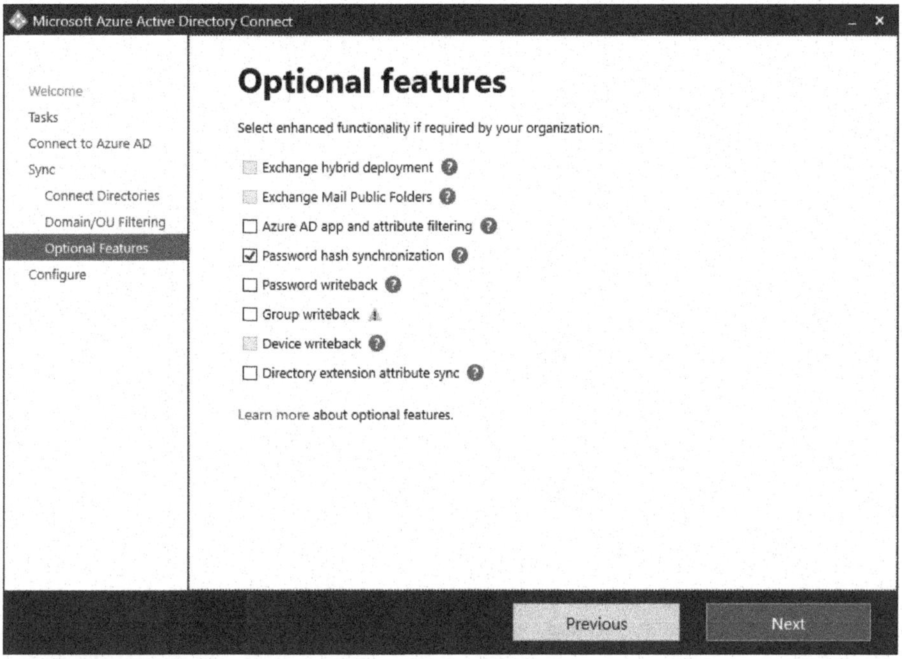

FIGURE 1-69 Optional features page.

8. On the **Ready to configure** page, select **Configure**.

9. On the **Configuration complete** page, select **Exit**.

To enable Password Hash Synchronization in an existing Azure AD Connect cloud sync installation:

1. Open **Azure portal** > **Azure Active Directory** > **Azure AD Connect** > **Manage Azure AD cloud sync**.

2. Select the configuration (the domain that is being synchronized).

3. Under **2, Manage attributes**, select **Sync password hashes, Enable**.

4. Select **Save**.

Implement and manage Pass-Through Authentication (PTA)

Pass-Through Authentication (PTA) is one of the three authentication mechanisms available in the hybrid deployment of Azure AD (the other two mechanisms are Password Hash Synchronization and Federation, covered in other sections).

When PTA is deployed, the user provides a password on the Azure AD login page, and Azure AD validates the password with on-premises Active Directory with the help of the PTA agent deployed on-premises. See Figure 1-70.

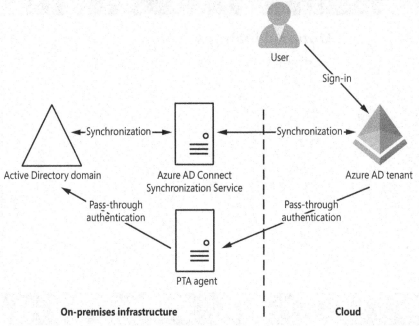

User

Sign-in

←Synchronization→   ←————Synchronization→

Active Directory domain   Azure AD Connect   Azure AD tenant
                            Synchronization Service

Pass-through   Pass-through
authentication   authentication

PTA agent

On-premises infrastructure   **Cloud**

FIGURE 1-70   Pass-Through Authentication (PTA).

A PTA agent can be enabled as part of the Azure AD Connect installation, on the same machine. In a production environment, for availability reasons, we recommend additionally installing two standalone PTA agents.

There is no need to publish any ports to the internet for the PTA agent to work. When the PTA agent service starts, it establishes a TCP session to Azure AD, which is an outbound connection. Previously established TCP session(s) will be used for pass-through authentication requests.

Pass-Through Authentication provides following benefits:

- Simple deployment. Implementation doesn't require complex network configuration, certificate management, or manually configured federation.

- High availability. It is possible to deploy multiple PTA agents on-premises.

- No synchronization-driven latency for existing accounts. Because each authentication request is validated with on-premises domain controllers, password changes or account status changes (enabled/disabled) are honored immediately. There is no need to wait for synchronization with Azure AD Connect.

- Security. On-premises policies such as logon hours configured in on-premises Active Directory are honored.

At the same time, Pass-Through Authentication comes with the following limitations:

- Sign-in features not natively supported by Azure AD, such as smartcards or certificates, can't be used.

- Sign-in to Azure AD Joined devices with expired passwords is not supported. If an on-premises password has expired, the user will need to sign in through a browser, get a password update, and then sign in to the Azure AD Joined device.

Pass-Through Authentication is only supported for Azure AD Connect installations (additional standalone agents may be installed as well, as discussed earlier) and isn't supported for Azure AD Connect cloud sync installations.

You can select the Pass-Through Authentication option during Azure AD Connect installation or enable it in an existing Azure AD Connect deployment.

To enable Pass-Through Authentication in an existing Azure AD Connect installation:

1. Open the **Azure AD Connect wizard** using the desktop or Start menu shortcut.

2. On the **Welcome to Azure AD Connect** page, select **Configure**.

3. On the **Additional tasks** page, select **Change user sign-in**.

4. On the **Connect to Azure AD** page, provide credentials of the Global Administrator or Hybrid Identity Administrator.

5. On the **User sign-in** page, select **Pass-through authentication**. Keep **Enable single sign-on** selected for Seamless SSO (covered in the following section). Select **Next**. See Figure 1-71.

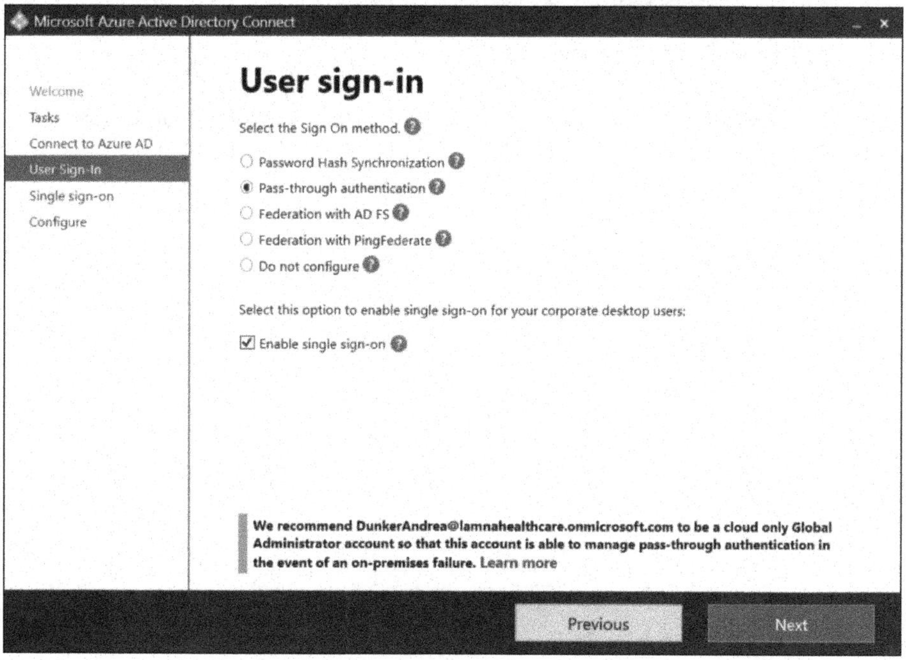

FIGURE 1-71 User sign-in page.

6. On the **Enable single sign-on** page, provide the credentials for the Domain Administrator account to enable Seamless SSO (covered in the following section) and select **Next**.

7. On the **Ready to configure** page, review the proposed changes and select **Configure**. See Figure 1-72.

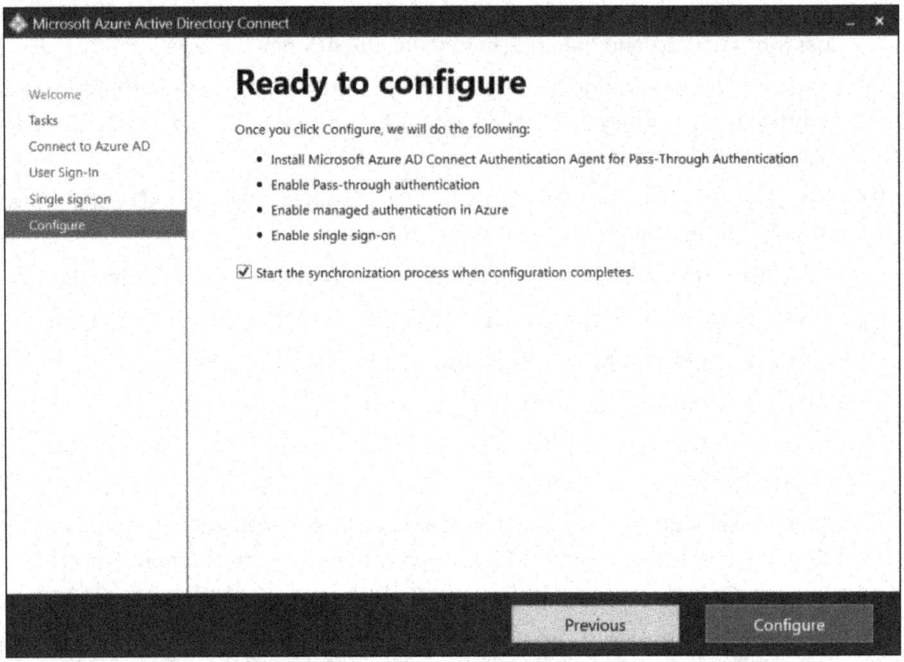

FIGURE 1-72 Ready to configure page.

8. On the **Configuration complete** page, review the completed changes and select **Exit**. See Figure 1-73.

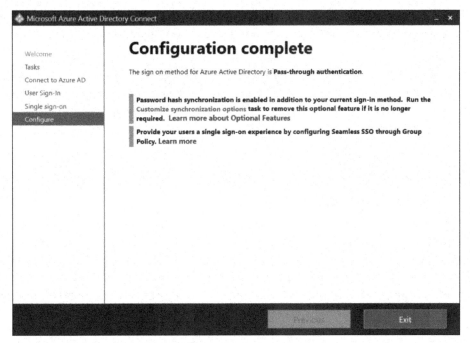

FIGURE 1-73 Configuration complete page.

Implement and manage Seamless Single Sign-On (Seamless SSO)

Password Hash Synchronization (PHS) or Pass-Through Authentication (PTA) allow a user to sign in to Azure AD with the same password they use in an on-premises Active Directory. But the mere implementation of PHS or PTA does not provide Single Sign-On from an on-premises environment. Single Sign-On can be accomplished in one of two ways:

- Primary Refresh Token (PRT)
- Seamless Single Sign-on (Seamless SSO)

Primary Refresh Token is available on Windows 10, Windows Server 2016, and later versions if the machine is Azure AD Registered, Azure AD Joined, or Hybrid Azure AD Joined.

Seamless SSO (also known as Desktop SSO or SSSO) is available on Windows 7 and later. The device must be domain joined.

We recommend using Primary Refresh Token when possible.

NEED MORE REVIEW? **SEAMLESS SSO AND PRT DOCUMENTATION**

Read more about how Seamless SSO works at: *https://docs.microsoft.com/en-us/azure/active-directory/hybrid/how-to-connect-sso-how-it-works*

Read about how Primary Refresh Token works at: *https://docs.microsoft.com/en-us/azure/active-directory/devices/concept-primary-refresh-token*

To enable Seamless SSO in an Azure AD Connect environment, select the checkbox **Enable single sign-on in Azure AD Connect configuration**. See Figure 1-71.

> *NOTE* **SEAMLESS SSO WITH AZURE AD CONNECT CLOUD SYNC**
>
> To enable Seamless SSO in an Azure AD Connect cloud sync environment, follow the steps as described in this article: *https://docs.microsoft.com/en-us/azure/active-directory/cloud-sync/how-to-sso*

Implement and manage Federation, excluding manual ADFS deployment

Federation is one of three main authentication mechanisms that provide single sign-on in an Azure AD hybrid environment (the other two mechanisms are Password Hash Synchronization and Pass-Through Authentication, as described earlier). Azure AD can be federated with various identity providers. For the purposes of this book, we will use Active Directory Federation Services (ADFS) as an example identity provider installed on-premises that can be federated with Azure AD, for two reasons: first, ADFS is an identity provider created by Microsoft; second, the Azure AD Connect installation wizard can configure an ADFS environment for you.

You may already have an ADFS environment with a number of relying party trusts configured. In that case, Azure AD will become one more relying party trust in that existing ADFS environment. Configuring Azure AD federation in existing ADFS environment is out of scope of this book. Manual ADFS deployment is out of scope as well. We will only cover configuring new ADFS environment with Azure AD Connect installation wizard.

When Federation is configured, Azure AD redirects users to the federated identity provider for authentication. While in the case of Password Hash Synchronization or Pass-Through Authentication, the user submits a password to an Azure AD page (login.microsoftonline.com), with Federation, a user submits a password or another credential to the federated identity provider. Because of that, the federated identity provider page should be exposed to the internet to allow users to authenticate externally. With ADFS, Web Application Proxy should be published to allow external connections from the internet.

Before installation, you will need to prepare. The prerequisites include:

- An Active Directory Domain Services environment.
- A machine that will become an Azure AD Connect server.
- A machine(s) that will become an ADFS server(s).
- A machine(s) that will become a Web Application Proxy server(s) and have port 443 published to the internet.

> *NOTE* **DOMAIN MEMBERSHIP FOR SERVERS**
>
> Azure AD Connect Server and ADFS Servers will be domain members, while Web Application Proxy servers won't.

- A PFX file with certificate for your future federation service name—for example, *sts.northwindeletriccars.com*. We recommend that the certificate should be publicly trusted.

- External clients should be able to resolve the federation service name—for example, sts.northwindelectriccars.com—to public IP address(es) of Web Application Server(s).

- Internal clients and Web Application Server(s) should be able to resolve the federation service name—for example, *sts.northwindelectriccars.com*—to IP address(es) of ADFS server(s).

- Ensure that remote management of the future Web Application Proxy servers from the future Azure AD Connect server is enabled:

  - On Azure AD Connect server, run *Set-Item WSMan:\localhost\Client\TrustedHosts – Value <DMZServerFQDN> -Force -Concatenate*

  - On Web Application Proxy servers, run *Enable-PSRemoting -force.*

> **NOTE   AZURE AD CONNECT PREREQUISITES**
>
> **Read the full list of Azure AD Connect installation prerequisites at:** *https://docs.microsoft.com/en-us/azure/active-directory/hybrid/how-to-connect-install-prerequisites*

See Figure 1-74 for the topology diagram.

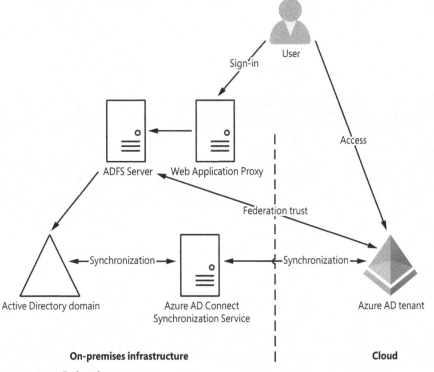

On-premises infrastructure   **Cloud**

FIGURE 1-74   Federation.

To install Azure AD Connect and configure ADFS:

1. Download Azure AD Connect from *https://go.microsoft.com/fwlink/?LinkId=615771*.

2. Run the installation file.

3. On the **Welcome to Azure AD Connect** screen, review the license terms and privacy notice, and select **Continue**.

4. On the **Express Settings** page (shown in Figure 1-52), select **Customize**.

5. On the **Install required components** page, select **Install**. See Figure 1-75 for other customization options available at this step.

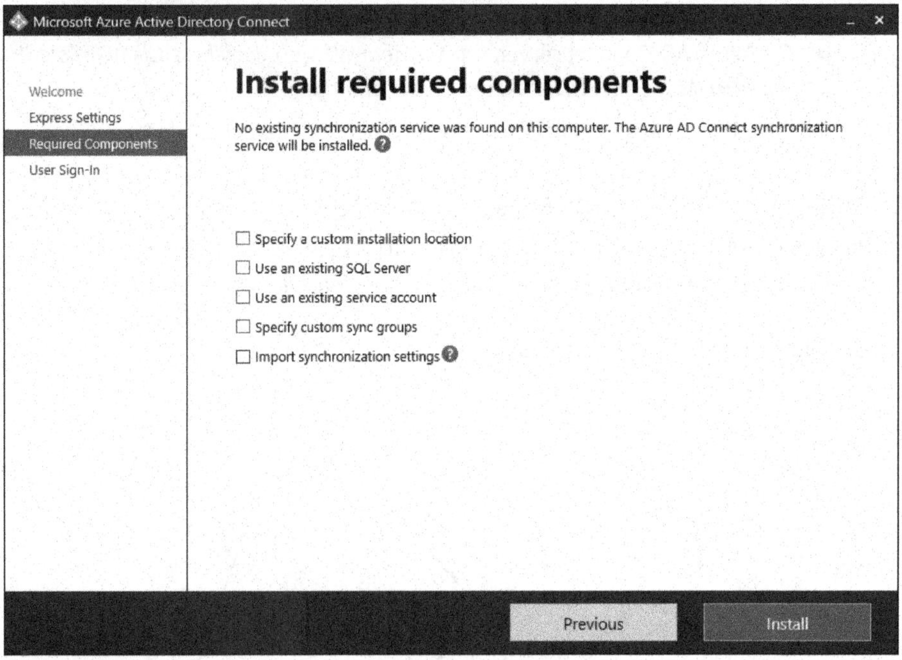

FIGURE 1-75   Install required components page.

6. On the **User sign-in** page, select **Federation with AD FS**. See Figure 1-76.

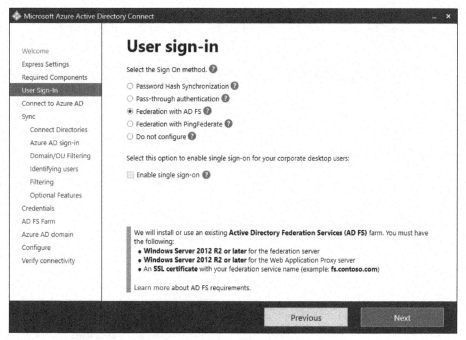

FIGURE 1-76   User sign-in page.

7. On the **Connect to Azure AD** page, provide the credentials of the Global Administrator or Hybrid Identity Administrator. You may also be asked to provide a second factor of authentication, depending on tenant settings.

8. These credentials will be used for configuration and creating another user account for synchronization purposes (service account). There is no need to manually create a service account in Azure AD. It is safe to disable the Global Administrator or Hybrid Identity Administrator account at a later point—for example, if an administrator that configured Azure AD Connect leaves the company.

9. On the **Connect your directories** page, select **Add Directory** to add the current directory to the synchronization. Provide the credentials of the enterprise administrator that will be used to configure the account for synchronization. Similar to the step above, it is safe to change the credentials or remove the enterprise administrator account later if needed. Select **Next**.

10. On the **Azure AD sign-in configuration** page, review the list of Active Directory UPN suffixes provided and the corresponding Azure AD domains. Select **Next**.

11. On the **Domain and OU filtering** page, include or exclude certain OUs from synchronization if required, and select **Next**.

12. Review the settings on the **Uniquely identifying your users** page. If you have only one Active Directory forest to synchronize from, and users from that forest are synchronized to only one Azure AD tenant, you can typically select **Next**. See Figure 1-77.

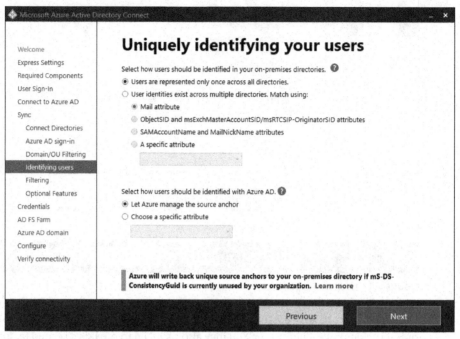

FIGURE 1-77 Uniquely identifying your users page.

13. On the **Filter users and devices** page, select the group of users and devices that should be synchronized. This option is supported only for pilot deployments. For production deployments, select **Next**.

14. On the **Optional features** page, review the options. We recommend enabling Password hash synchronization even if the selected authentication mechanism is Federation with ADFS. See Figure 1-78 for the available options.

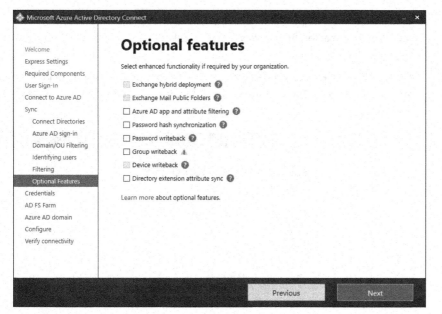

FIGURE 1-78 Optional features page.

15. On the **Domain Administrator credentials** page, provide the Domain Administrator credentials for the domain where the ADFS server will be installed.

16. On the **AD FS farm** page (shown in Figure 1-79), provide the PFX file with the certificate described in the prerequisites section.

FIGURE 1-79 ADFS farm page.

17. On the **AD FS Server** page, add the names of future ADFS servers and select **Next**.

18. On the **Web Application Proxy server** page, add the names of future Web Application Proxy servers and select **Next**.

19. On the **AD FS service account** page, keep **Create a group Managed Service Account** selected, provide the credentials of the Enterprise Administrator, and select **Next**. See Figure 1-80.

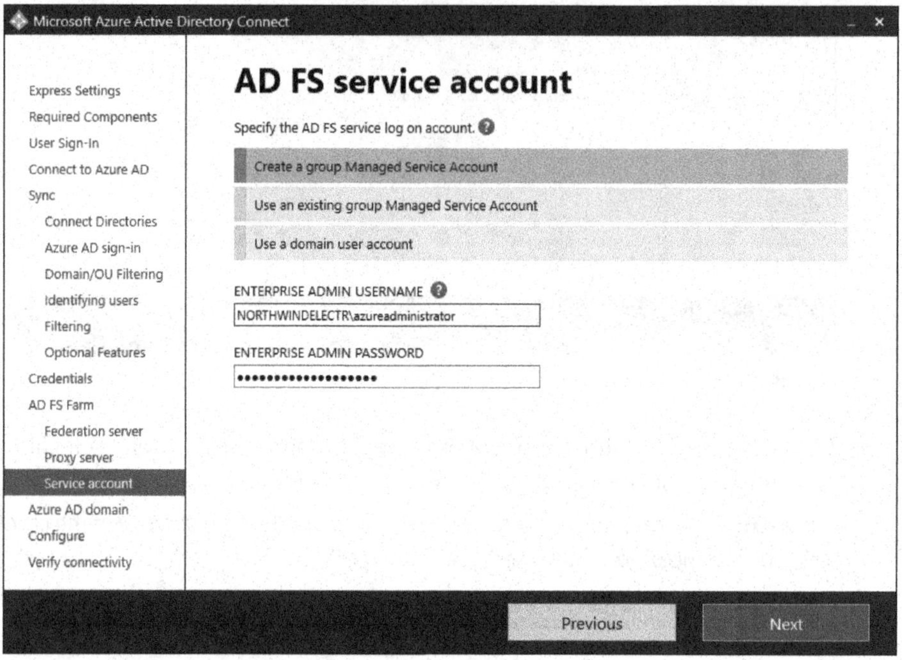

FIGURE 1-80 AD FS service account page.

20. On the **Azure AD domain** page, select a custom domain name that will be converted from Managed to Federated state. Select **Next**. See Figure 1-81.

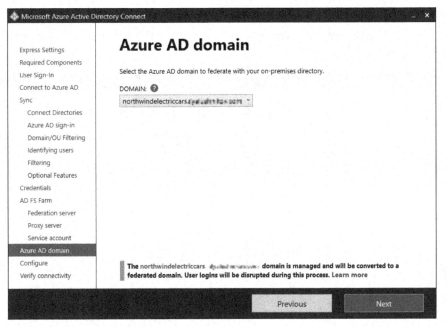

FIGURE 1-81   Azure AD domain page.

21. On the **Ready to configure** page, review the proposed changes and select **Install**. See Figure 1-82.

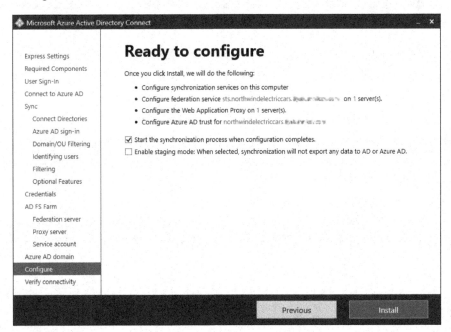

FIGURE 1-82   Ready to configure page.

22. On the **Configuration complete** page, select **Next**.

23. On the **Verify federation connectivity** page, select both checkboxes and select **Verify**. See Figure 1-83.

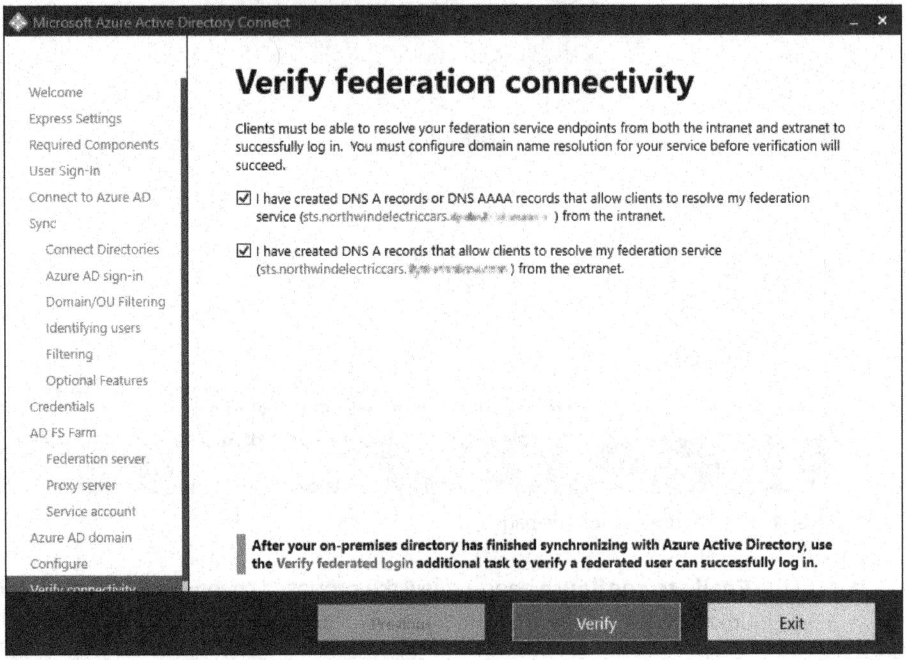

FIGURE 1-83 Verify federation connectivity page.

24. Ensure that verification was successful and select **Exit**.

25. Open Azure AD Connect using the desktop shortcut.

26. On the **Welcome to Azure AD Connect** page, select **Configure**.

27. On the **Additional tasks** page, select **Manage federation**.

28. On the **Manage federation** page, select **Verify federated login**.

29. On the **Connect to Azure AD** page, provide the credentials of the Global Administrator or Hybrid Identity Administrator.

30. Provide credentials of the synchronized user.

31. Ensure that you see the message **Successfully logged into Microsoft Online using a security token from AD FS with the provided user credentials** and select **Exit**.

32. Disable WS-Trust endpoints for the extranet usage by running the following commands on the primary ADFS server:

```
Set-AdfsEndpoint -TargetAddressPath /adfs/services/trust/2005/windowstransport
-Proxy $false
Set-AdfsEndpoint -TargetAddressPath /adfs/services/trust/13/windowstransport
-Proxy $false
```

> **NEED MORE REVIEW?   SECURITY BEST PRACTICES FOR ADFS**
>
> Read more about security reasons for this configuration at: *https://docs.microsoft.com/en-us/windows-server/identity/ad-fs/deployment/best-practices-securing-ad-fs*

33. Enable Extranet Lockout Protection to protect your users from brute force password attacks from the internet by running the following command on the primary ADFS server:
Set-AdfsProperties -EnableExtranetLockout $true

> **NEED MORE REVIEW?   ADFS EXTRANET LOCKOUT PROTECTION**
>
> Read more about ADFS Extranet Lockout Protection at: *https://docs.microsoft.com/en-us/windows-server/identity/ad-fs/operations/configure-ad-fs-extranet-soft-lockout-protection*

Implement and manage Azure AD Connect Health

Azure AD Connect Health helps to monitor on-premises components of your hybrid environment:

- Azure AD Connect Health Synchronization Engine
- Active Directory Domain Services (ADDS)
- Active Directory Federation Services (ADFS)

Azure AD Connect Health relies on agents that work on respective servers in an on-premises environment: Azure AD Connect servers, domain controllers, and ADFS servers. Azure AD Connect Health agents need outbound connectivity to Azure AD Connect Health service endpoints in the cloud. Installation procedures vary depending on the agent used—for the synchronization engine, domain controllers, or ADFS.

The Azure AD Connect Health agent for Synchronization Engine is installed automatically when you install Azure AD Connect. No manual installation steps are required.

To monitor the status of your Azure AD Connect Synchronization Engine, open **Azure portal** > **Azure AD Connect Health** > **Sync services**. You will see a list of Azure AD Connect servers with health agents installed. See Figure 1-84.

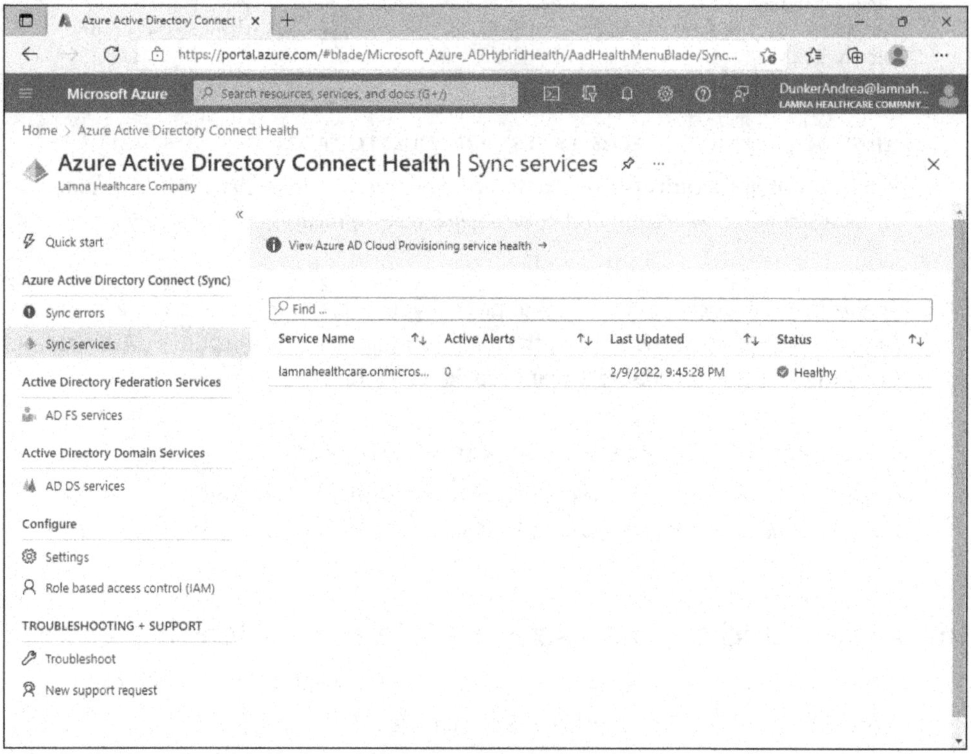

FIGURE 1-84 Azure Active Directory Connect Health, Sync services page.

Select a service name to view the run profile latency chart for the last 24 hours.

To view individual synchronization errors, open **Azure portal** > **Azure AD Connect Health** > **Sync** errors. See Figure 1-85.

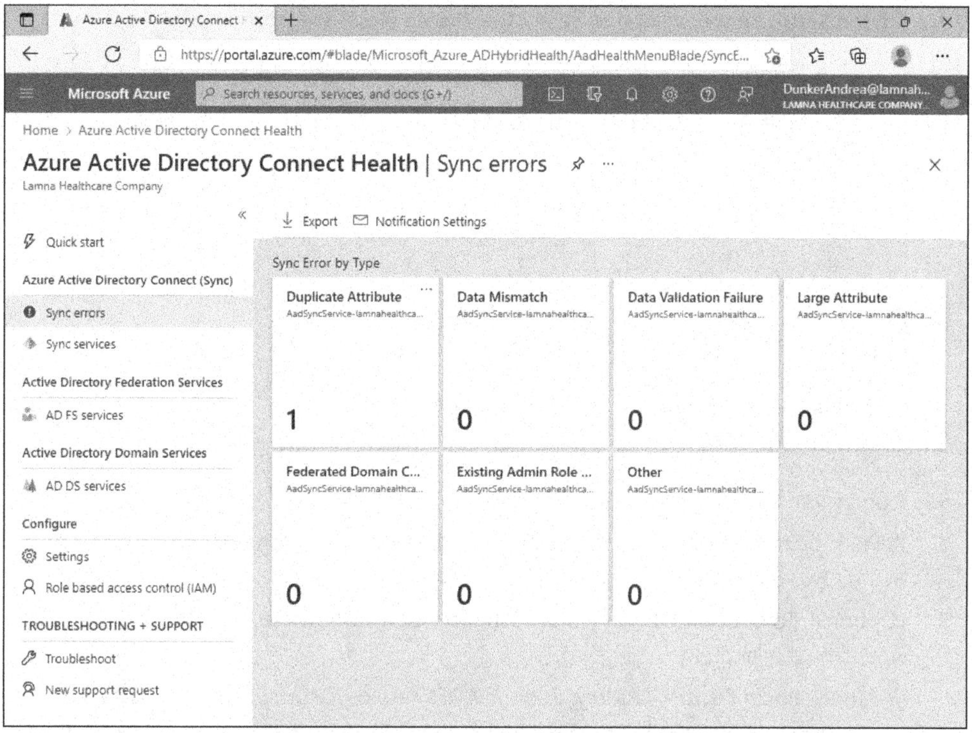

FIGURE 1-85   Azure Active Directory Connect Health, Sync errors page.

The Azure AD Connect Health agent for ADFS should be installed manually. To install the Azure AD Connect Health agent on ADFS servers:

1. Download the Azure AD Connect Health agent for ADFS from *https://go.microsoft.com/ fwlink/?LinkID=518973*.

2. Run the installation file.

3. On the first screen, review the **Microsoft Azure Subscription Agreement** and select **Install**. See Figure 1-86.

FIGURE 1-86   Azure AD Connect Health AD FS Agent Setup page.

4. On the **Setup Successful** page, select **Configure Now**. See Figure 1-87.

FIGURE 1-87 Azure AD Connect Health ADFS Agent Setup Successful page.

5. Sign in with a Global Administrator account.

6. Review the result of script execution. You may receive a warning that auditing isn't enabled (this will be covered below).

7. (Optional) To get Usage Analytics collected by the Azure AD Connect Health AD FS Agent, enable auditing:

   A. In the **Local Security Policy**, add the ADFS service account to the **Security Settings\Local Policies\User right assignment\Generate security audit** policy. The ADFS service account name is typically ***DOMAIN\aadcsvc$***.

   B. Run the following command in an elevated command prompt: `auditpol.exe /set /subcategory:{0CCE9222-69AE-11D9-BED3-505054503030} /failure:enable /success:enable`

   C. Run the PowerShell command `Set-AdfsProperties -AuditLevel Verbose`

   D. If agent registration previously completed with warnings, restart agent registration by running the PowerShell command `Register-AzureADConnectHealthADFSAgent`

8. Repeat steps 1-6 on Web Application Proxy servers. There is no need to enable auditing on them.

Once Azure AD Connect Health Agents for ADFS are installed and configured, they will start reporting health data. You can view their status at **Azure portal** > **Azure AD Connect Health** > **AD FS services**. See an example in Figure 1-88.

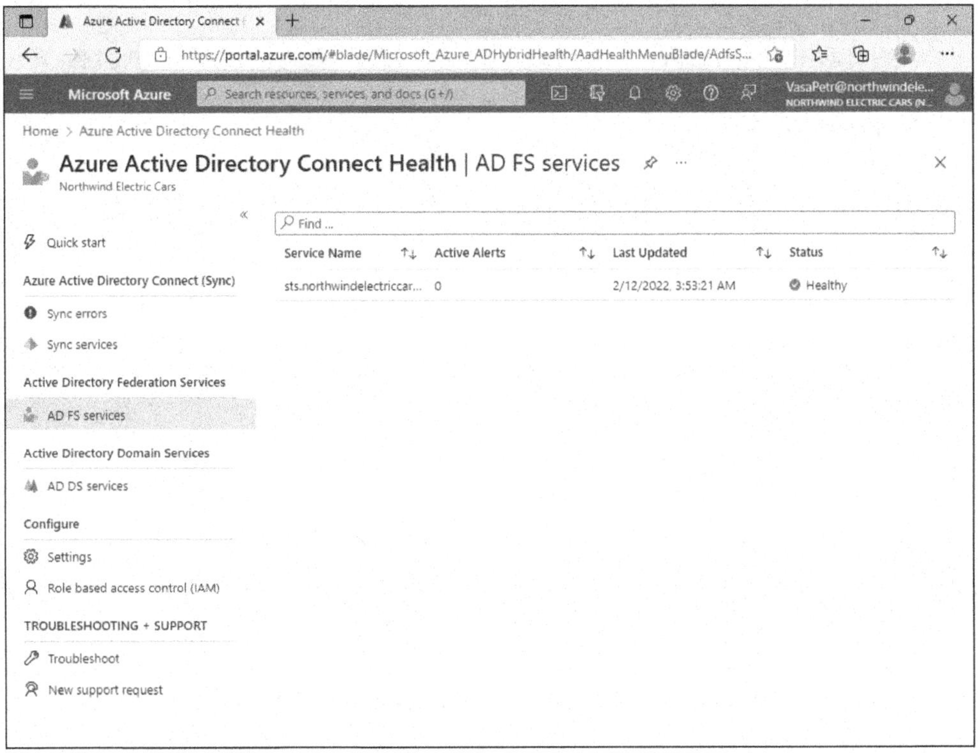

FIGURE 1-88 Azure Active Directory Connect Health | AD FS services page.

Use Azure AD Connect Health for ADFS to:

- View Properties of your ADFS configuration. See Figure 1-89.

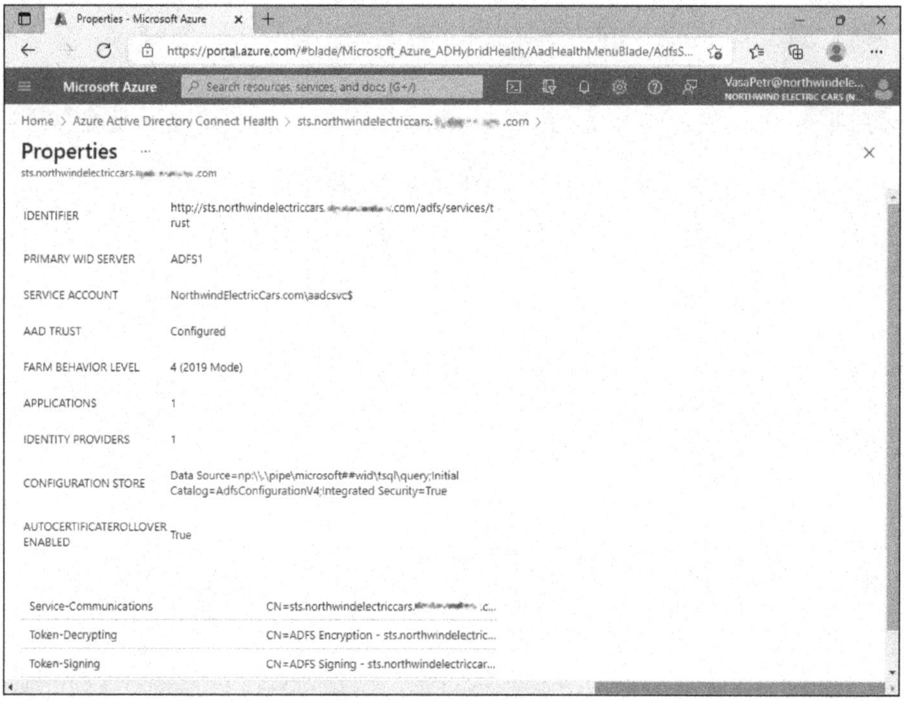

FIGURE 1-89 Azure Active Directory Connect Health for ADFS, Properties page.

- View alerts such as **Extranet Lockout Protection Disabled for ADFS** or **The Windows Transport endpoint is enabled. It is recommended that the endpoint be disabled from the extranet due to a known security vulnerability**.
- Configure notification settings.
- Monitor the number of token requests per second on ADFS servers and Web Application Proxies. See Figure 1-90.

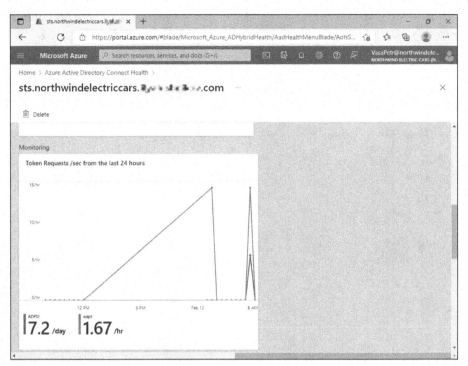

FIGURE 1-90 Azure Active Directory Connect Health for ADFS, Monitoring section.

- Monitor bad password attempts.

NEED MORE REVIEW? **AZURE AD CONNECT HEALTH FOR ADFS**

Read more about Azure AD Connect Health for ADFS at:

https://docs.microsoft.com/en-us/azure/active-directory/hybrid/how-to-connect-health-adfs

A third component of Azure AD Connect Health (along with Azure AD Connect Health for Sync and Azure AD Connect Health for ADFS) is Azure AD Connect Health for ADDS.

Download Azure AD Connect Health Agent for ADDS from *https://go.microsoft.com/fwlink/?LinkID=820540*.

The installation procedure is like the one for Azure AD Connect Health Agent for ADFS.

To use Azure AD Connect Health for ADDS, open **Azure portal** > **Azure AD Connect Health** > **AD DS services** and select the forest name. See Figure 1-91.

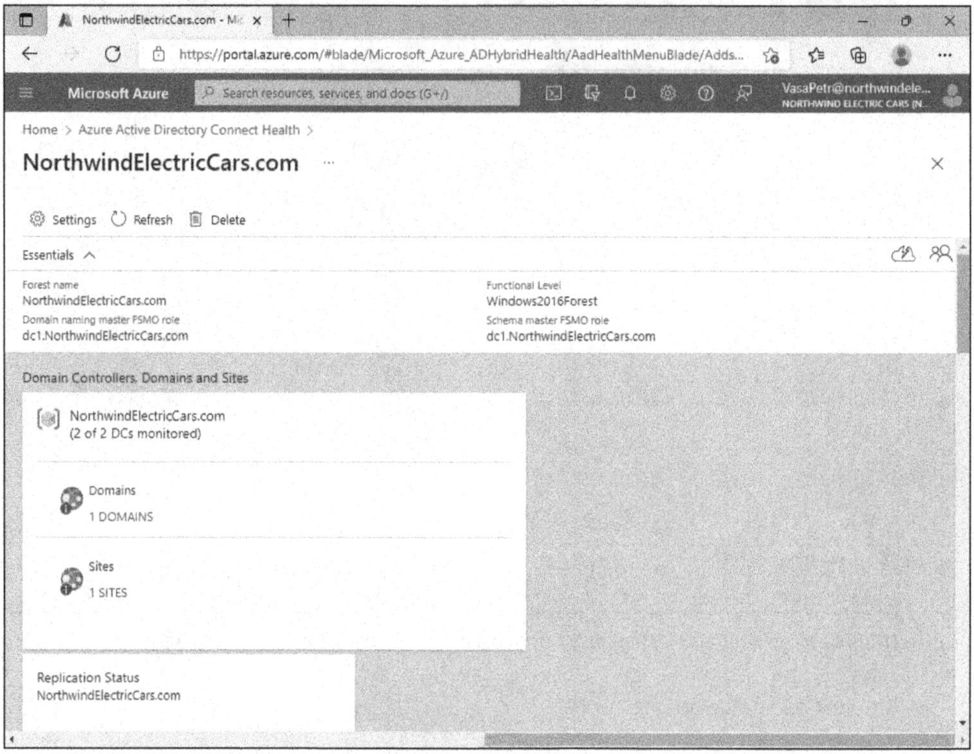

FIGURE 1-91 Azure Active Directory Connect health for ADDS

Use Azure AD Connect Health for ADDS to:

- View domain controllers, domains, and sites.
- View replication status.
- View alerts.
- Configure notification settings.
- Monitor LDAP Successful Binds/sec for each domain controller.
- Monitor NTLS Authentications/sec for each domain controller.
- Monitor Kerberos Authentications/sec for each domain controller.

Troubleshoot synchronization errors

As with many other solutions, troubleshooting of Azure AD Connect can be done on many levels—depending on the complexity of the problem, level of configuration customization, and skills of a troubleshooting person. For the purposes of this book, we will focus on troubleshooting using the Azure AD Connect wizard.

To troubleshoot synchronization using the Azure AD Connect wizard:

1. Ensure that the PowerShell execution policy is set to **RemoteSigned** or **Unrestricted**.
2. Open the Azure AD Connect wizard.
3. On the **Welcome to Azure AD Connect** page, select **Configure**.
4. On the **Additional tasks** page, select **Troubleshoot** and then select **Next**. See Figure 1-92.

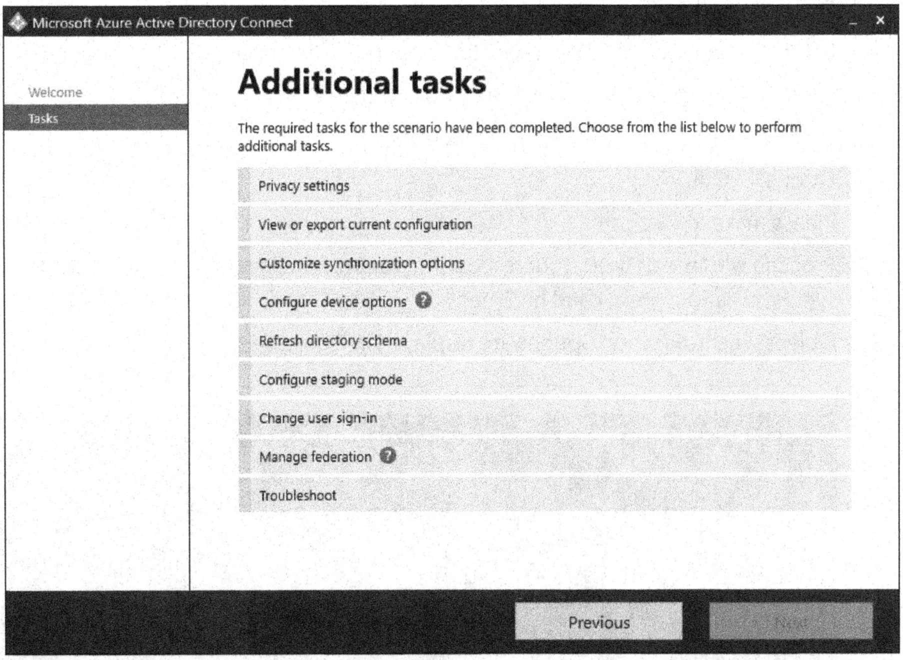

FIGURE 1-92 Azure AD Connect, Additional tasks page.

5. On the **Welcome to AADConnect Troubleshooting** page, select **Launch**.
6. The PowerShell-based troubleshooting tool will be displayed with a list of options. See Figure 1-93.

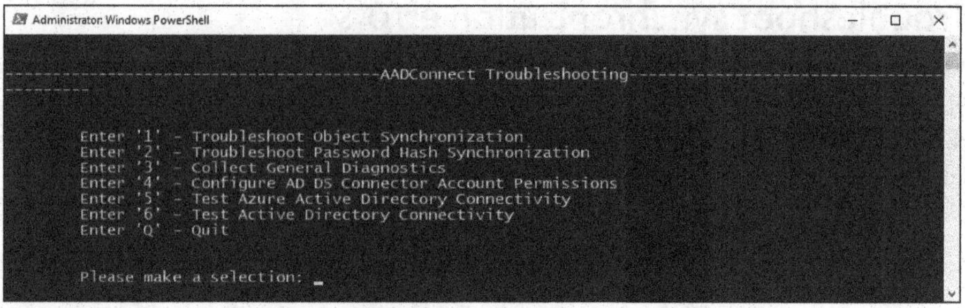

FIGURE 1-93 AAD Connect Troubleshooting.

Enter '1' - Troubleshoot Object Synchronization

Enter '2' - Troubleshoot Password Hash Synchronization

Enter '3' - Collect General Diagnostics

Enter '4' - Configure AD DS Connector Account Permissions

Enter '5' - Test Azure Active Directory Connectivity

Enter '6' - Test Active Directory Connectivity

Enter 'Q' - Quit

Please make a selection:

7. Proceed with the desired troubleshooting option. For example, to continue with object synchronization, press 1 and hit Enter.

8. Object synchronization options are displayed in Figure 1-94.

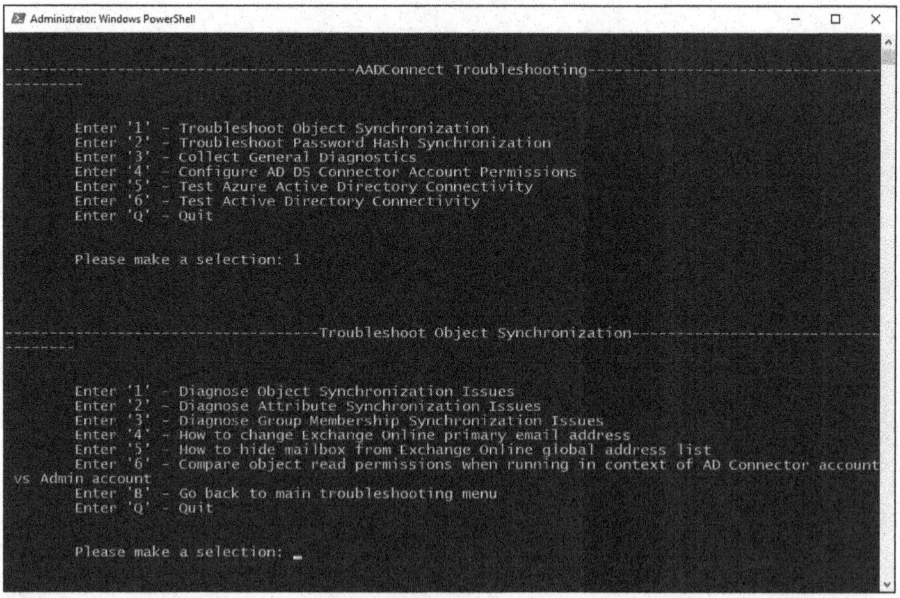

FIGURE 1-94 AAD Connect Troubleshooting, Troubleshoot Object Synchronization step.

Enter '2' - Diagnose Attribute Synchronization Issues

Enter '3' - Diagnose Group Membership Synchronization Issues

Enter '4' - How to change Exchange Online primary email address

Enter '5' - How to hide mailbox from Exchange Online global address list

Enter '6' - Compare object read permissions when running in context of AD Connector account vs Admin account

Enter 'B' - Go back to main troubleshooting menu

Enter 'Q' - Quit

Please make a selection:

9. Select the desired option. For example, if option 1 (**Diagnose Object Synchronization Issues**) is selected, you will be asked to provide the AD object Distinguished Name. Then, you will be asked to provide the Azure AD tenant Global Administrator or Hybrid Identity Administrator credentials.

10. Review the problems found, recommended actions, and the generated HTML report. See Figure 1-95.

FIGURE 1-95 AAD Connect Troubleshooting shows the result of object synchronization troubleshooting.

Chapter summary

- Azure AD roles can have permissions in Azure AD, permissions for Microsoft 365 products, or permissions across a Microsoft 365 stack.

- Azure AD roles can be built-in or custom.

- Role assignment includes the security principal, role information, scope, and type of assignment.

- The scope of assignment can be Directory, Administrative unit, or an Azure AD resource.

- The type of assignment can be permanent eligible, permanent active, time-bound eligible, or time-bound active.

- The UserPrincipalName (UPN) consists of a UPN prefix (user account name) and UPN suffix (domain name) divided by the @ symbol.

- After adding a new custom domain name to the tenant, you need to verify it—i.e., prove that you own the domain name by configuring DNS records.

- Registering a device in Azure AD is beneficial for single sign-on, signing in to the device with Azure AD credentials, device-based conditional access, and mobile device management enrollment scenarios.

- Three device join types are available in Azure AD: Azure AD Registration, Azure AD Join, and Hybrid Azure AD Join.

- Azure AD Registration is for Bring Your Own Device (BYOD) scenarios.

- Azure AD Join and Hybrid Azure AD Join are for corporate Windows 10/11 devices.

- A Hybrid Azure AD Joined device is a member of an on-premises AD domain, registered in Azure AD on top of that.

- All three options (Azure AD Registration, Azure AD Join, and Hybrid Azure AD Join) provide single sign-on (SSO) to Azure AD.

- Control the Hybrid Azure AD Join process for members of an on-premises domain by managing Service Connection Points (SCP).

- Use Seamless SSO in situations where a Primary Refresh Token (PRT) is not available.

- Place resources to administrative units for the purpose of delegating permissions.

- Use the Access management for Azure resources toggle to grant Global Administrator control over subscriptions associated with a tenant.

- Security groups are used for granting access to resources.

- Microsoft 365 groups are used for collaboration between users, as well as between users and guests.

- Group nesting is supported only between Security groups.

- Use dynamic groups to configure attribute-based rules to populate group memberships.

- Use Azure AD Self-Service Group Management to allow users to create and manage their groups.

- Use Group expiration policy to automatically remove Microsoft 365 groups that are no longer in use.

- Set the UsageLocation attribute for users before assigning Microsoft 365 licenses.

- Use Azure AD B2B to invite business partners to your tenant and provide them access to applications and resources.

- Limit guests' permissions with the Guest user access restrictions setting.

- Use Guest invite restrictions to limit who can invite guests. By default, any member or guest can invite new guests.

- Use Azure AD Connect to synchronize objects between an on-premises environment and Azure AD, configure hybrid authentication, and monitor the health of the hybrid environment.

- One Azure AD Connect server can synchronize with multiple on-premises AD forests but only one Azure AD tenant.

- Use staging Azure AD Connect servers to test configuration and as a standby.

- In a hybrid environment, authentication methods available include Password Hash Synchronization (PHS), Pass-Through Authentication (PTA), and Federation.

- Use Password Hash Synchronization as a recommended hybrid authentication method.

- Azure AD Connect cloud sync is a new synchronization service that utilizes lightweight agents on-premises and a synchronization engine in the cloud.

- Use Azure AD Connect Health to monitor the Azure AD Connect synchronization engine, on-premises ADDS environment, and ADFS environment.

Thought experiment

In this thought experiment, you demonstrate your skills and knowledge of the topics covered in this chapter. You can find the answers in the section that follows.

You are an enterprise administrator for a company that starts its Microsoft 365 journey. You have three on-premises AD forests that have forest trusts between them. You need to configure synchronization of users, groups, and devices identities between the on-premises environment and an Azure AD tenant that you are about to create.

Today, all corporate Windows 10 devices are joined to an on-premises AD domain and managed through Group Policy Objects. You need to provide single sign-on from these devices to Azure AD, keeping them joined to an on-premises domain for the time being.

1. What device registration model you will choose for corporate Windows 10 devices?

2. What synchronization mechanism will you use to synchronize identities between the on-premises environment and Azure AD?

3. What authentication method will you configure for the hybrid environment? Assume that there are no additional requirements beyond those explicitly stated above.

Thought experiment answers

This section contains the solutions to the thought experiment. Each answer explains why the choice is correct.

1. Hybrid Azure AD Join. Hybrid Azure AD Joined devices are members of the on-premises domain and registered to the Azure AD tenant at the same time.

2. Azure AD Connect. Azure AD Connect cloud sync doesn't support synchronization of device identities at the time of writing. On-premises forests having trusts between them is not a prerequisite for Azure AD Connect deployment, but it signals that there is network connectivity between forests, which is a prerequisite for Azure AD Connect deployment.

3. Password Hash Synchronization is the recommended authentication method because it doesn't have dependency on the on-premises environment for every sign-in.

CHAPTER 2

Implement an authentication and access management solution

Attacks on user accounts/passwords have increased significantly in recent years. Common brute force and password spray attacks are extremely effective against plain text passwords. Furthermore, leaked credentials are sold on the dark web, allowing anyone to instantly gain access to tens of thousands of user accounts and passwords. The root cause of these attacks is that passwords alone are ineffective in countering the level and sophistication of attacks against them. Azure AD offers robust multifactor authentication mechanisms that help safeguard access to critical organizational resources by adding another layer of security through the use of a secondary form of authentication. Azure AD also offers fine- and coarse-grain access management solutions, such as condition access, which enables organizations with varying security posture requirements to implement policies that meet their business requirements.

Skills covered in this chapter:

- Skill 2.1: Plan, implement, and manage Azure Multifactor Authentication (MFA) and self-service password reset
- Skill 2.2: Plan, implement, and manage Azure AD user authentication
- Skill 2.3: Plan, implement, and manage Azure AD conditional access
- Skill 2.4: Manage Azure AD Identity Protection
- Skill 2.5: Implement access management for Azure resources

Skill 2.1: Plan, implement, and manage Azure Multifactor Authentication (MFA) and self-service password reset

To improve the security posture of an organization and to mitigate threats associated with passwords, it is highly recommended to incorporate a multifactor option to authenticate the user. Adding an additional factor to user authentication immediately improves account security because a hacker must compromise additional factors to compromise the account.

Azure provides a range of options for configuring multifactor authentication (MFA) which requires careful planning and administration.

This skill covers how to:
- Plan Azure MFA deployment, excluding MFA Server
- Configure and deploy self-service password reset
- Implement and manage Azure MFA settings
- Manage MFA settings for users
- Extend Azure AD MFA to third-party and on-premises devices
- Monitor Azure AD MFA activity

Plan Azure MFA deployment, excluding MFA Server

Azure Multifactor Authentication (MFA) requires you to authenticate using two or more factors to establish identity successfully. These factors follow this pattern:

- Something you know: this could be a password, a passphrase, or a security question.
- Something you possess: this could be a token-generating device or a software-based application, such as a mobile app.
- Something you are: this could be a biometric property of a person, such as a face scan, fingerprint, or retina scan.

Azure MFA offers several options for user authentication to enable two-step verification. The underlying theme of two-step verification is to protect the sign-in process by making it incrementally more difficult for a malicious actor to compromise the account while also ensuring that the sign-in process is not cumbersome. For example, during a sign-in process, some users might prefer to enter their password followed by receiving a push notification on their device, whereas others might prefer to make a phone call because they do not have access to a smart device. As you will see in the following sections, carefully evaluating various authentication options is critical for Azure MFA end user adoption.

Determining a rollout strategy for Azure MFA

You need to think strategically about the rollout of Azure MFA within an organization. Striking a right balance between deployment velocity and its scope is the key to a successful rollout. Following are key points to keep in mind:

- Plan the deployment in small iterations by starting with a small subset of users who are receptive to change and whose daily tasks are least impacted by the rollout.

- Provide users with clear guidance regarding the registration process along with the MFA methods available to them for authentication.

- Continuously monitor for any issues reported by users, including steep learning curves, lack of preferred authentication methods, and technical challenges that may hamper the adoption.

- Ensure that support staff are trained well in advance before the rollout.

- Anticipate some resistance from a subset of users due to the change in their daily routine.

Licensing requirements for Azure MFA

Azure MFA licensing can be configured in a variety of ways. Understanding how licensing affects the availability of various MFA features to end users is an important part of planning. Table 2-1 provides a high-level breakdown of various Azure MFA features along with Azure AD and Microsoft 365 license requirements.

TABLE 2-1 Azure AD licenses and high-level MFA features

License Type	Description
Azure Active Directory Free	Includes security default features that prompt users for MFA as needed and provides baseline security to user accounts.
Azure Active Directory Premium P1	Same as Azure Active Directory Free. Includes the Azure AD Conditional Access feature, which allows implementation of fine-grain organization policies for MFA.
Azure Active Directory Premium P2	Same as Azure Active Directory Premium P1. Includes support for risk-based conditional access policies.
EMS E3, Microsoft 365 E3, and Microsoft 365 Premium	Includes Azure Active Directory Premium P1 features (as described above).
EMS E5 and Microsoft 365 E5	Includes Azure Active Directory Premium P2 features (as described above).

Table 2-2 lists the commonly used Azure AD MFA and access management features, as well as the Azure AD licenses that support them.

TABLE 2-2 Azure AD licenses and specific MFA features

Feature	Azure AD Free	Azure AD P1	Azure AD P2
Mobile app as a second factor	Yes	Yes	Yes
Phone call as a second factor	No	Yes	Yes
SMS as a second factor	No	Yes	Yes
Custom greetings for phone calls	No	No	Yes
Custom caller ID for phone calls	No	Yes	Yes
Conditional Access	No	No	Yes
Risk-based conditional access	No	No	Yes

Configure and deploy self-service password reset

Self-service password reset (SSPR) is a feature in Azure AD that allows users to change their password without seeking help from support or an IT administrator. With SSPR, users can follow a series of prompts to reset their password to unlock their account if they forget their password. It also helps the organization in saving costs because support staff can focus on other urgent matters.

To enable service-service password to reset:

1. Sign in as a Global Administrator to the Azure portal at *http://portal.azure.com*.

2. Navigate to **Azure Active Directory**.

3. Select **Password Reset** from the left-side pane, as shown in Figure 2-1.

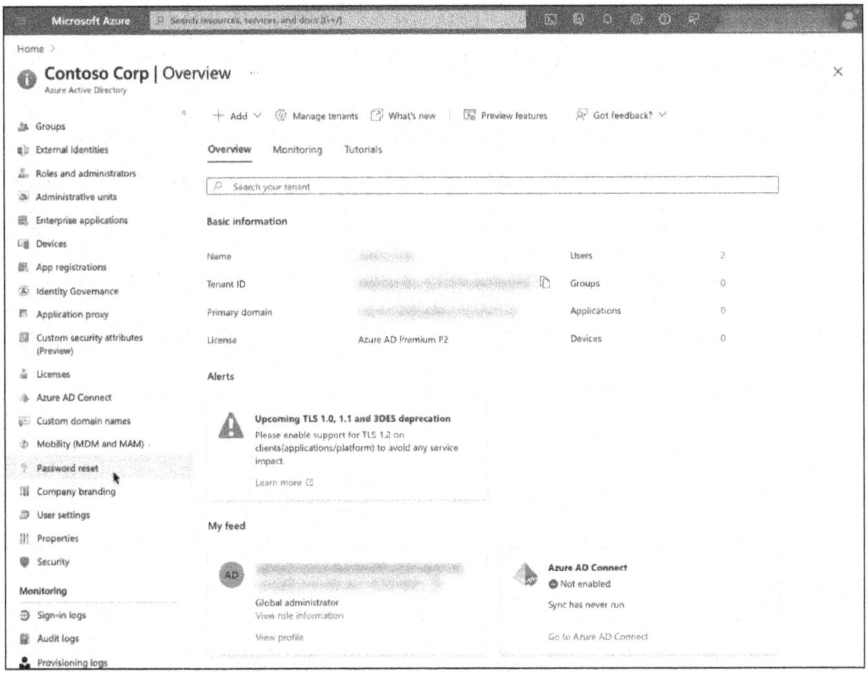

FIGURE 2-1 Password reset option in Azure AD.

4. On the **Properties** page, under the **Self service password reset enabled** option, select **All**, as shown in Figure 2-2. This will enable all users in the tenant to reset their password using SSPR. You can also choose a specific group by selecting the option **Selected**, which will only allow users in that group to reset their password.

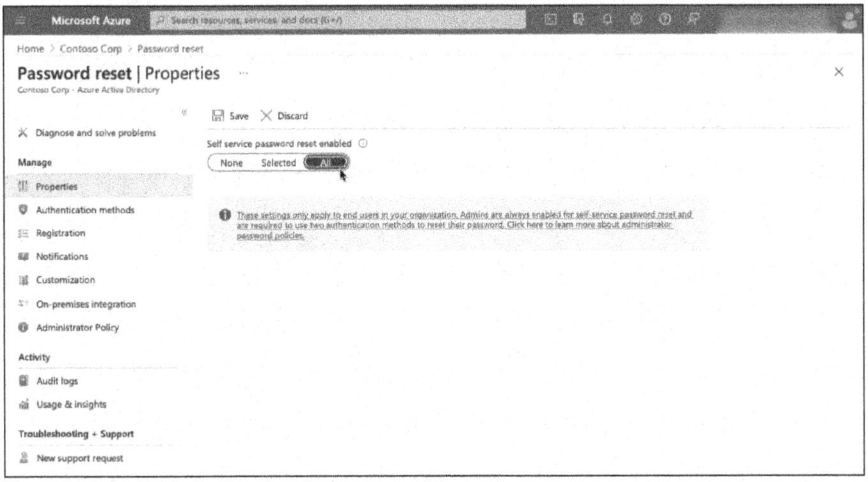

FIGURE 2-2 Password reset properties.

5. Click **Save**.

Register an authentication method for self-service password reset

Follow the steps below to sign in as a user and register a phone number that will be used during SSPR.

1. Sign in as a user to the My Sign-Ins portal at: *https://mysignins.microsoft.com.*

2. On the **Keep your account secure** page, enter the phone number and click **Next**, as shown in Figure 2-3. A text code will be sent to the phone number provided.

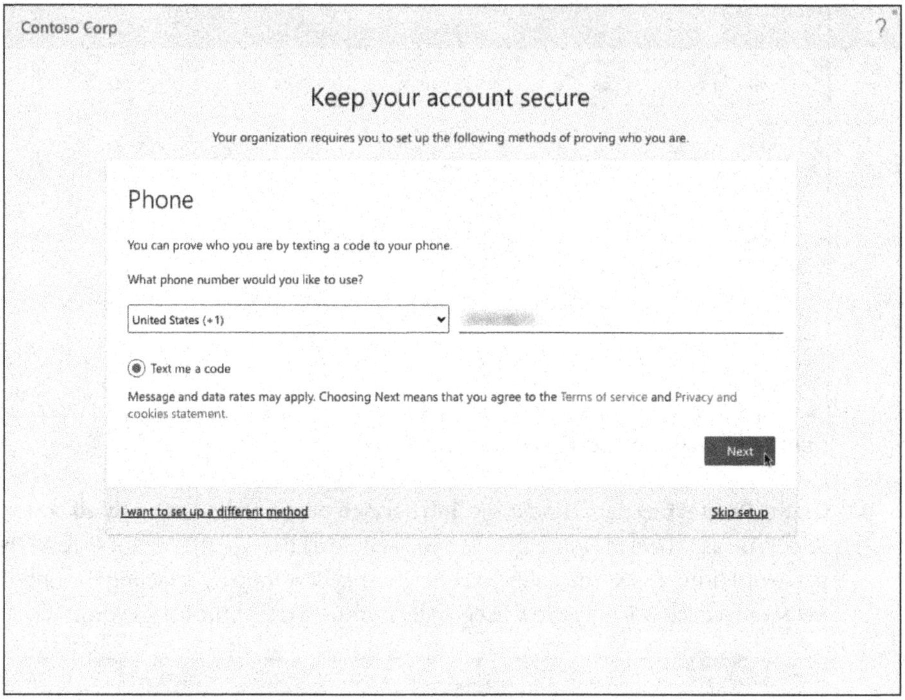

FIGURE 2-3 Phone number validation via SMS message.

3. Enter the text code received on the phone number and click **Next**. Figure 2-4 shows a sample text code sent to the phone number registered in the previous step.

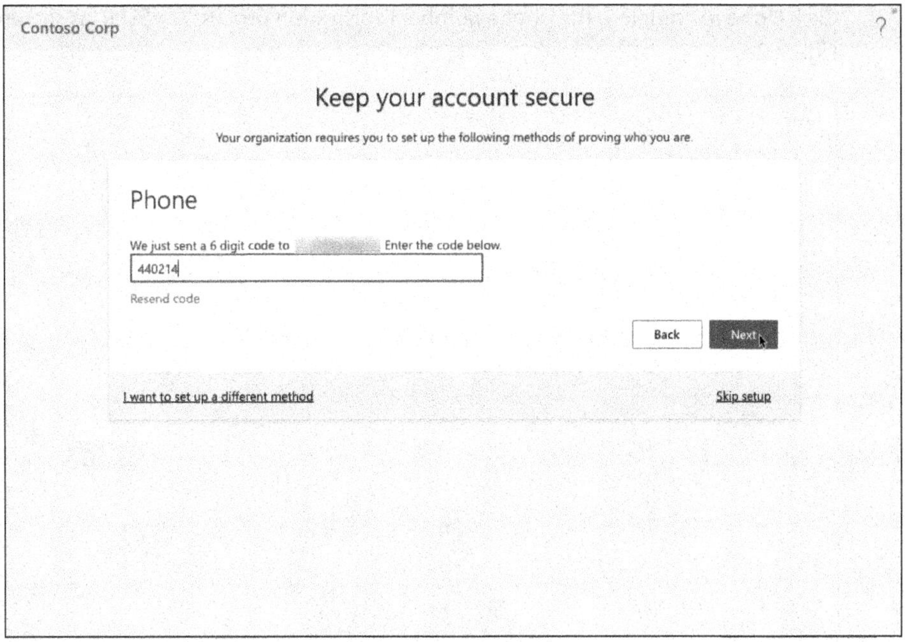

FIGURE 2-4 Phone number verification via 6-digit code.

4. You should see **SMS verified. Your phone was registered successfully** message, as shown in Figure 2-5. Click **Next**.

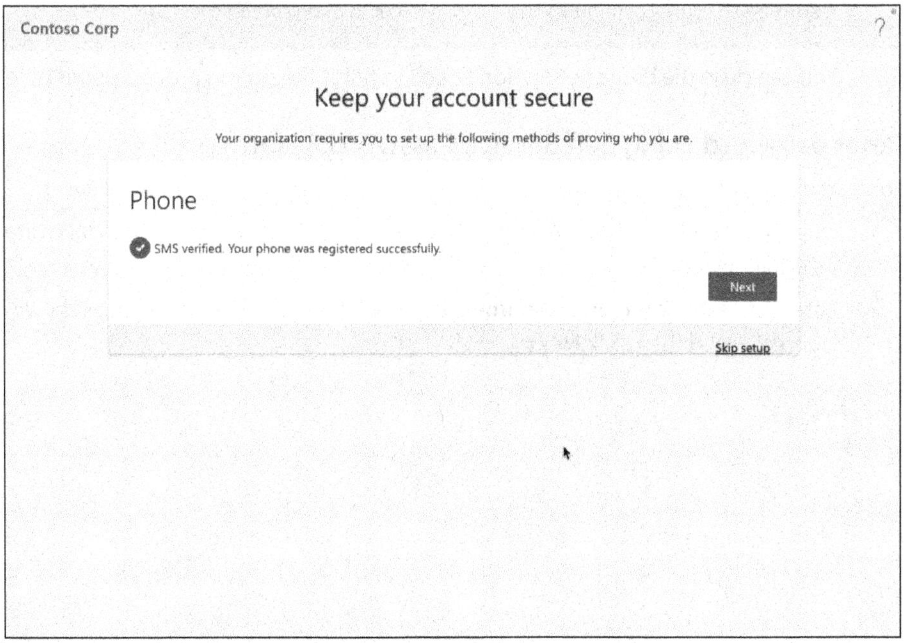

FIGURE 2-5 Phone number registration success.

5. Click **Done** to complete the phone number registration process for SSPR, as shown in Figure 2-6.

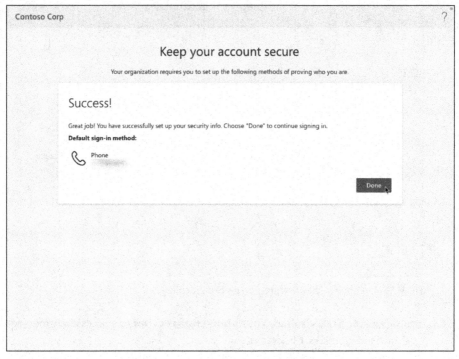

FIGURE 2-6 Security configuration information completion success message.

6. You can close the browser. You don't need to finish the sign-in process at this time.

Reset password using Self Service Password Reset

Follow the steps below to reset the user's password using Self Service Password Reset:

1. Navigate to the URL *https://passwordreset.microsoftonline.com/* using an InPrivate or Incognito browser session.

2. Enter the user's **Email** or **Username** and complete the CAPTCHA check, as shown in Figure 2-7, and then click **Next**.

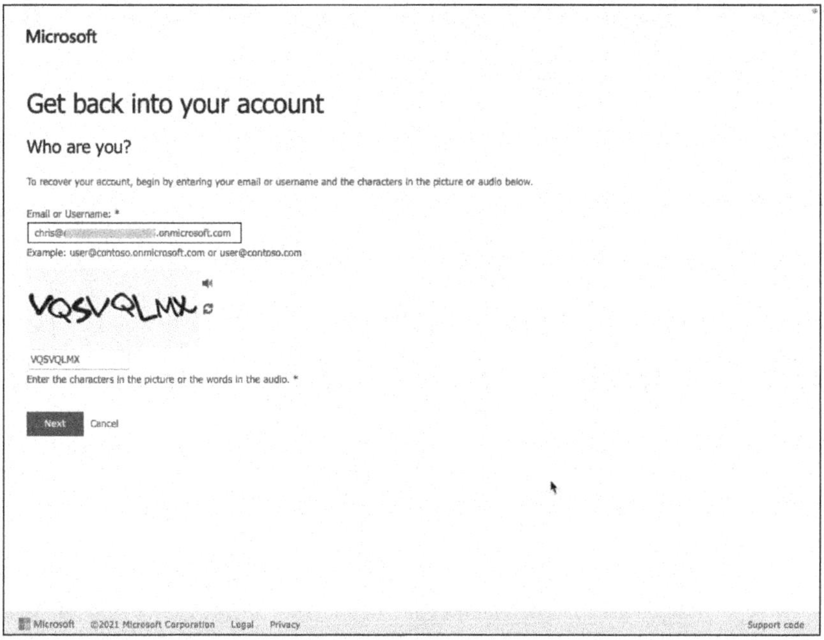

FIGURE 2-7 Get back into your account using email or username.

3. Enter the phone number associated with the account, as shown in in Figure 2-8, and then press **Text**. A text message with a verification code will be sent to this phone number.

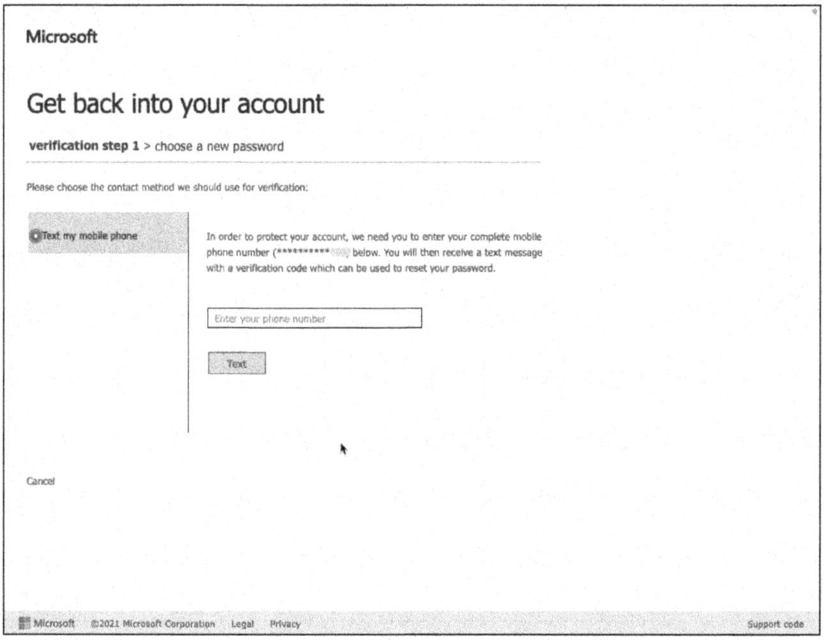

FIGURE 2-8 Enter a phone number.

4. Enter the verification code, as shown in in Figure 2-9, and then then press **Next**.

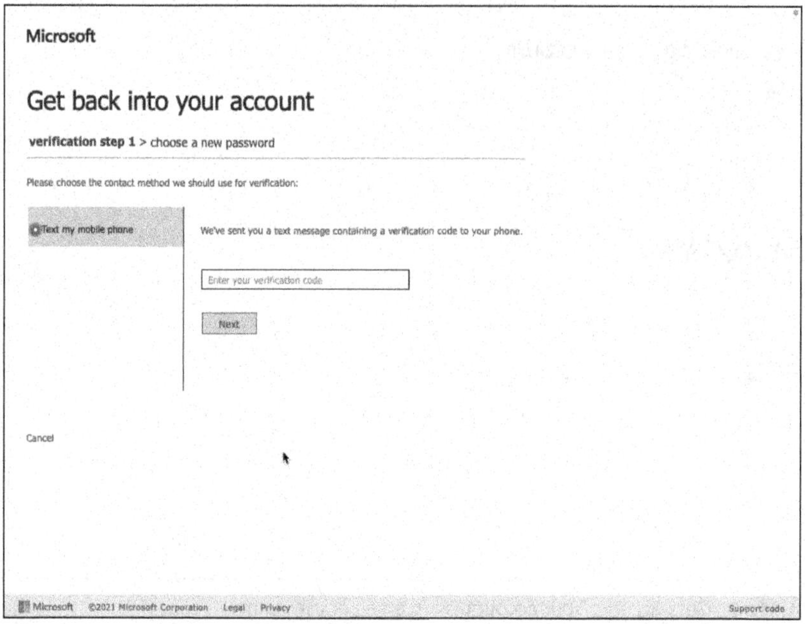

Microsoft

Get back into your account

verification step 1 > choose a new password

Please choose the contact method we should use for verification:

○ Text my mobile phone   We've sent you a text message containing a verification code to your phone.

    [Enter your verification code]

    [Next]

Cancel

Microsoft   ©2021 Microsoft Corporation   Legal   Privacy   Support code

FIGURE 2-9   Phone number verification.

5. Enter the new password, as shown in in Figure 2-10, and then click **Finish**.

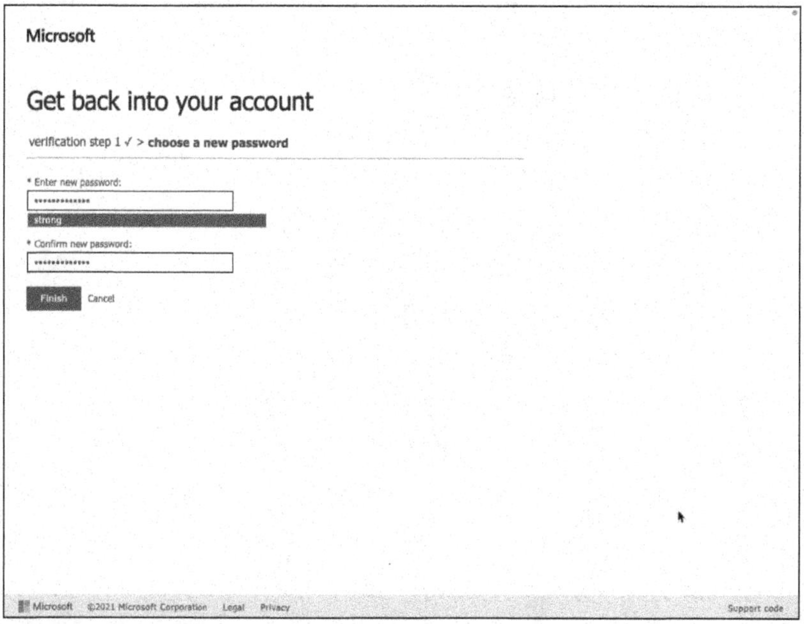

Microsoft

Get back into your account

verification step 1 ✓ > **choose a new password**

* Enter new password:

[•••••••••••••]

strong

* Confirm new password:

[•••••••••••••]

[Finish]   Cancel

Microsoft   ©2021 Microsoft Corporation   Legal   Privacy   Support code

FIGURE 2-10   Enter new password.

6. The success message "**Your password has been reset**" will appear on the page, as shown in Figure 2-11. This confirms that the user account password has been reset successfully. You can now close the browser.

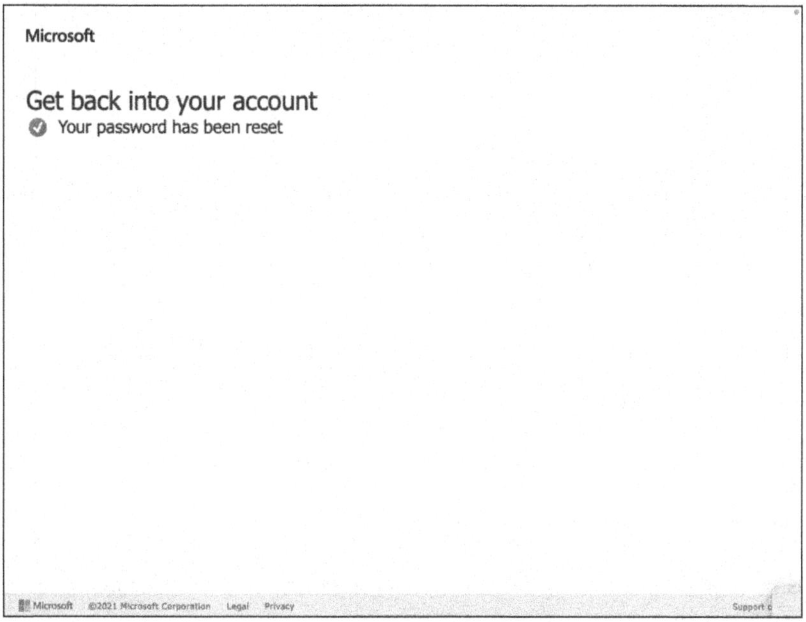

FIGURE 2-11 Password reset success.

Implement and manage Azure MFA settings

The steps below demonstrate how to set up and manage Azure MFA settings. Please note that you must have an active Azure subscription in order to complete the tasks in this skill and the others in this chapter. To sign up for a free trial subscription, visit *https://azure.microsoft.com/en-us/offers/ms-azr-0044p/*.

1. Sign in to the Azure portal, *https://portal.azure.com*, using a Global Administrator account.
2. Navigate to the Azure Active Directory dashboard by using the Azure Active Directory option available in the sidebar of the Azure portal.
3. Select the **Security** option located under the **Manage** section on the left side, as shown in Figure 2-12.

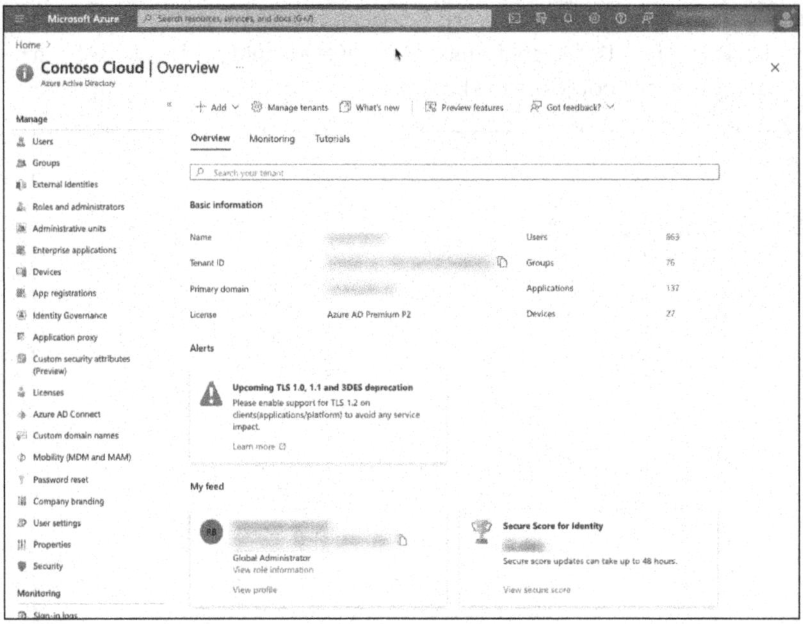

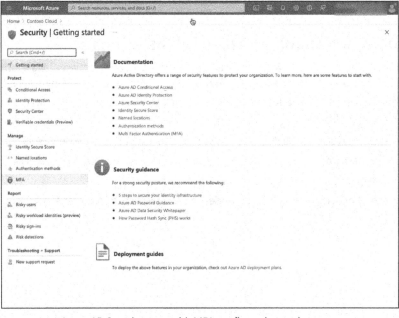

FIGURE 2-12 Azure AD home page with Security option.

4. Select the **MFA** option located under the **Manage** section on the Security page, as shown in Figure 2-13.

FIGURE 2-13 Azure AD Security page with MFA configuration options.

5. Select the **Additional cloud-based MFA settings** link located under Configure, as shown in Figure 2-14. This will open a new page with all available options for MFA.

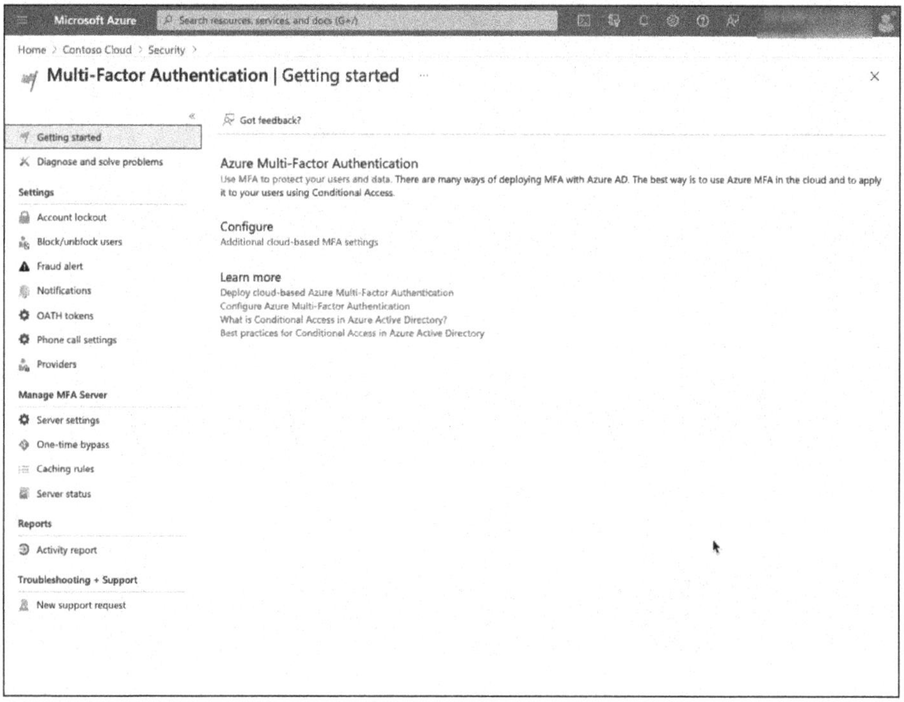

FIGURE 2-14 Azure AD Multi-Factor Authentication (MFA).

6. By default, all available MFA verification options are selected, as shown in Figure 2-15. You can deselect one or more of these verification options as needed based on your MFA planning. It is recommended that users have at least more than one MFA method available to them in case the primary method is unavailable. Please review Table 2-3 for more details about each MFA setting available on this page.

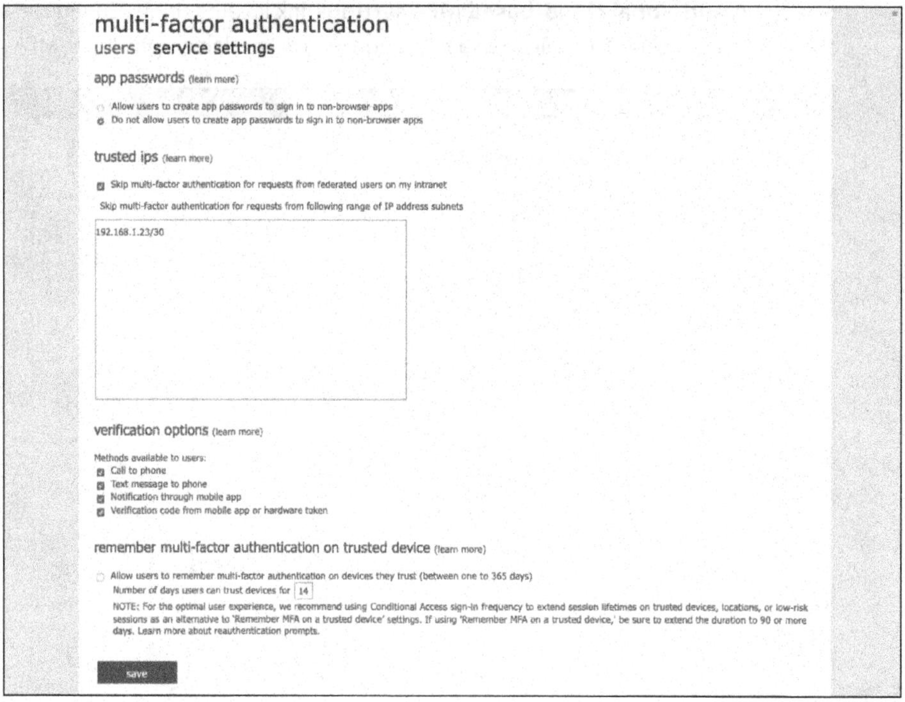

FIGURE 2-15 Azure AD MFA service settings.

TABLE 2-3 Azure AD MFA service settings

Setting	Description
App passwords	■ Allow users to create app passwords to sign in to non-browser apps ■ Do not allow users to create app passwords to sign in to non-browser apps
Trusted IPs	Allow bypass of multifactor authentication prompts for users who sign in from a defined IP address range
Verification Options	These are all the available verification options available for MFA: ■ Call to phone ■ Text message to phone ■ Notification through mobile app ■ Verification code from mobile app or hardware token
Remember MFA on trusted device	When enabled, this option allows users to skip subsequent MFA verifications for a set number of days (up to 365 days) after successfully signing in using MFA on a trusted device.

In addition to MFA service settings, Azure AD also provides miscellaneous configuration options for MFA, as summarized in Table 2-4.

TABLE 2-4 Azure AD MFA settings

Setting	Description
Account lockout	Temporarily lock accounts using MFA service when there are many denied authentication attempts in a row. This applies only to users who enter a PIN to authenticate. The following settings are available: ■ Number of MFA denials that trigger account lockout ■ Minutes until account lockout counter is reset ■ Minutes until account is automatically unlocked
Block/unblock users	Blocked users will not receive MFA requests. Users will remain blocked for 90 days from the time they are blocked. Blocked users can be manually unblocked by the administrator using the "Unblock" action.
Fraud alert	The fraud alert allows users to report fraudulent MFA attempts because of a suspicious MFA prompt—for example, when an MFA prompt is from an unknown source. Users can use their phone or the Microsoft authenticator app to report the fraudulent MFA attempt. There are two configuration options available: ■ Automatically block users who report fraud: This option blocks user accounts reporting the fraud for 90 days or until an administrator unblocks the account. ■ Code to report fraud during initial greeting: This option allows customizing the code (the default is 0) that the user enters to report a fraud before pressing #.
Notifications	Email notifications are sent to identity administrators when users report a fraud alert.
OATH tokens	OATH time-based one-time password (TOTP) SHA-1 tokens that refresh codes every 30 or 60 seconds are supported. OATH tokens are uploaded in a comma-separated values (CSV) file format. See *https://docs.microsoft.com/en-us/azure/active-directory/authentication/howto-mfa-mfasettings#oath-tokens*.
Phone call settings	Enables customization of the caller ID and voice greeting message that the user receives during an MFA attempt. When the caller ID is not customized, by default voice calls come from the phone number "+1 (855) 330-8653" within the United States. Make sure the user is aware of this number and that it is excluded from any spam filters.

Manage MFA settings for users

Administrators can manage the following MFA settings for a specific user:

- Phone number: Configure phone number used by the user to perform MFA via either SMS or a voice call.

- Email address: Configure the email address of the user. The email can be used for self-service password reset (SSPR) but not for an MFA option.

- Revoke existing MFA session: Remove any existing MFA sessions for the user and force MFA the next time the policy on the device requires it.

- Force re-registration of MFA: Clears the user's remembered MFA sessions and requires them to perform MFA the next time it's required by the policy on the device.

- Reset Password: Assigns a temporary password to a user account, which must be changed by the user during their next sign-in.

To configure phone authentication methods and the email address of a user:

1. Sign in as an administrator to the Azure portal at *http://portal.azure.com*.

2. Navigate to **Azure Active Directory**.

3. Select **Users** from the left pane, as shown in Figure 2-16.

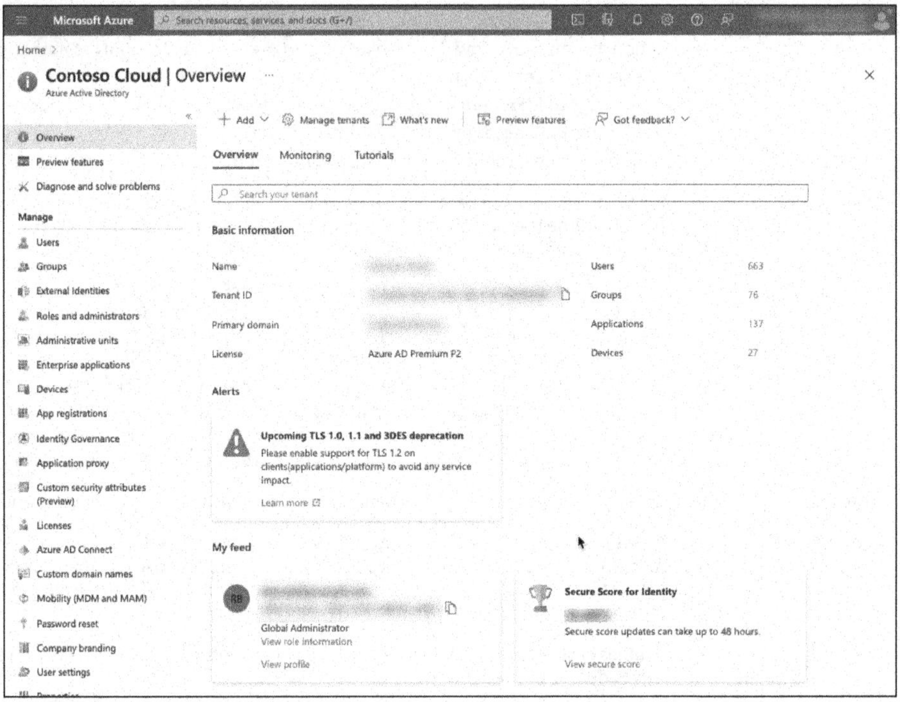

FIGURE 2-16 Azure AD Users option.

4. On the **Users** page, select the user you'd like to configure the authentication method for MFA. You can use the search bar, as shown in Figure 2-17.

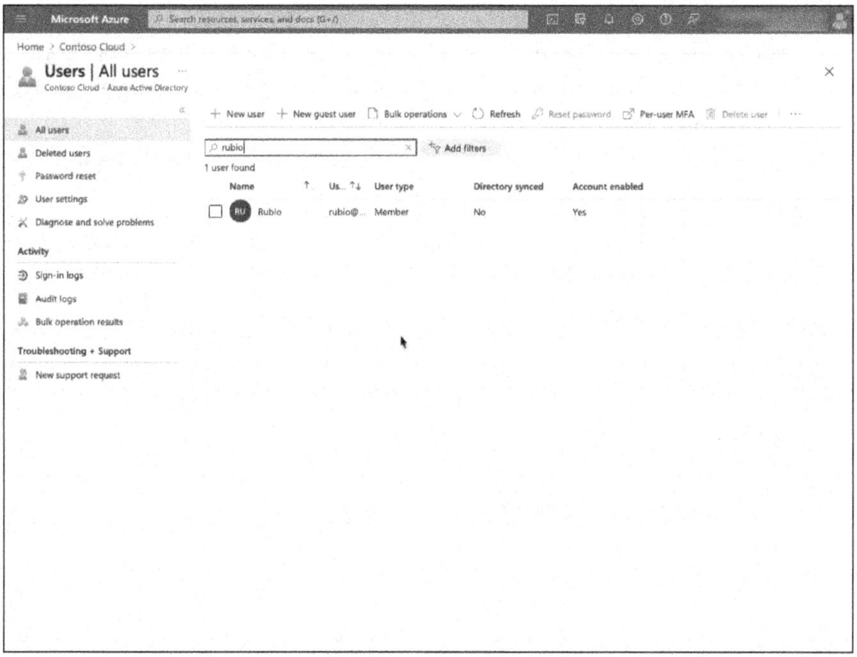

FIGURE 2-17 Azure AD All users.

5. Select **Authentication methods** from the left side, as shown in Figure 2-18.

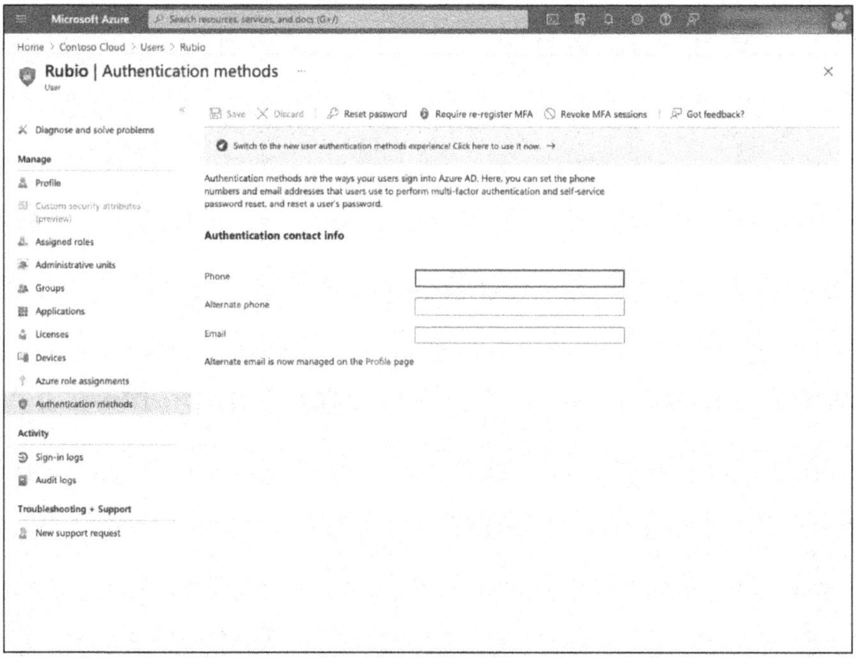

FIGURE 2-18 Azure AD Authentication methods.

6. Fill in the following information:

- Phone: This is the phone number used during the MFA authentication. Make sure there is a space between the region/country code and the phone number. For example, +1 1224567890.

- Phone: This is the alternate phone number used during the MFA authentication in case the primary phone number is not available.

- Email: The email address used during MFA authentication. An email address alone cannot be used for MFA.

7. Click the **Save** button located on the top row, as shown in Figure 2-19.

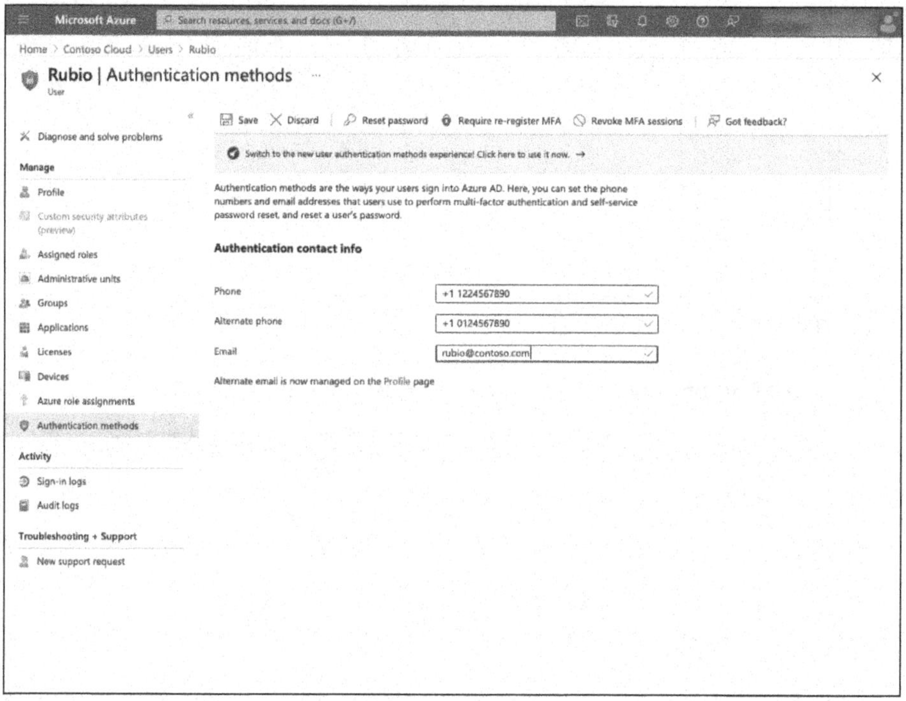

FIGURE 2-19 Azure AD Authentication contact info.

Extend Azure AD MFA to third-party and on-premises devices

To help you safeguard third-party and on-premises devices, Microsoft Intune can be used with Azure Active Directory (Azure AD) Conditional Access to mandate multifactor authentication (MFA) for device activation. MFA functions by requiring any two or more of the verification techniques listed below:

- Something you are aware of (typically a password or PIN)

- Something you possess (a reliable item that is difficult to copy, such as a phone)

- Something that identifies you physically (biometrics, such as a fingerprint)

MFA is supported for iOS/iPadOS, macOS, Android, and Windows 8.1 or later devices. Please note that when end users enroll their device, they now must authenticate with a second form of identification, such as a PIN, a phone, or biometrics. More information about extending MFA on devices can be found at *https://learn.microsoft.com/en-us/mem/intune/enrollment/multi-factor-authentication#configure-intune-to-require-multifactor-authentication-at-device-enrollment*.

Monitor Azure AD MFA activity

The Azure Active Directory (Azure AD) sign-ins report can be used to review and understand Azure AD Multi-Factor Authentication events. This report provides the following insights:

- Was the sign-in hampered by MFA?
- How did the user finish MFA?
- Which methods of authentication were used during a sign-in?
- Why couldn't the user complete MFA?
- How many users were asked to provide MFA?
- How many users failed the MFA challenge?
- What are the most common MFA issues that end users face?

Step-by-step instructions on how to access the sign-ins report can be found at *https://learn.microsoft.com/en-us/azure/active-directory/authentication/howto-mfa-reporting#view-the-azure-ad-sign-ins-report*.

Skill 2.2: Plan, implement, and manage Azure AD user authentication

When a user signs in to a device, application, or service, one of the primary functions of an Azure AD is to authenticate credentials. However, in Azure AD, there are multiple options for user authentication that go beyond simply verifying a username and password and provide a range of security protections such as phishing resistance, biometrics, and so on.

This skill covers how to:

- Plan for authentication
- Implement and manage authentication methods
- Implement and manage Windows Hello for Business
- Implement and manage password protection and smart lockout
- Implement certificate-based authentication in Azure AD
- Configure Azure AD user authentication for Windows and Linux virtual machines on Azure

---

Plan for authentication

Planning for authentication is an important part of determining which method provides the best combination of usability and security. Traditionally, username and password is the most popular authentication method used to verify user credentials. However, it is also the least secure method because it is easy to launch a brute force attack against the passwords. To improve security, it is highly recommended to replace the password or at least use an additional authentication method for sign-ins. Azure AD provides a range of passwordless MFA methods to the users.

Users can use Azure AD passwordless authentication methods such as FIDO2 security keys, Windows Hello for Business, and the Microsoft Authenticator app during sign-ins.

Table 2-5 provides a summary of various authentication methods that can be used for sign-ins. Please note that some of these methods can be used for both MFA and self-service password reset (SSPR). (SSPR is covered in a later section.)

TABLE 2-5 Azure AD authentication methods and usage.

Authentication method	Usage
Password	Azure AD MFA and SSPR
Microsoft Authenticator app	Azure AD MFA and SSPR Available to users using iOS and Android operating system. Users may register their mobile app at *https://aka.ms/mfasetup*. By using the Microsoft Authenticator app, users receive push notifications on their smartphone or tablet and then reject or approve the request. Users can also use the Microsoft Authentication app to generate an OATH verification code. During the sign-in process, this verification code can be used as a second form of authentication.
Voice call	Azure AD MFA and SSPR Voice call is placed by the Azure automated voice system to the user's phone number. The user receives the call and then must use a keypad to confirm or deny the authentication.
Text messages	Azure AD MFA and SSPR A text message containing a time-bound verification code is sent by Azure MFA via SMS to the user's mobile phone. The user must enter this verification code during the sign-in process within the specific time period to complete the verification process.
FIDO2 Security Key	Azure AD MFA and SSPR Fast Identity Online (FIDO) is an open standard for passwordless authentication. The user first needs to register a FIDO2 security key and then select it at the time of sign-in for authentication purposes. FIDO2 security keys are available in the form of USB devices, Bluetooth, and NFC.
Windows Hello for Business	Azure AD MFA and SSPR Windows Hello for Business (WHfB)is a fully integrated biometric authentication method based on facial recognition or fingerprint matching. Users need Windows 10 or a later version of the Windows operating system to use WHfB to sign in to Azure Active Directory.

OATH software token	Azure AD MFA and SSPR
	Users can use the Microsoft Authenticator app or other similar authenticator apps that can generate software-based OATH tokens to sign in to Azure Active Directory.
OATH hardware token	Azure AD MFA and SSPR
	OATH is an open standard to generate one-time password (OTP) verification codes. Azure Active Directory natively supports hardware-based OATH time-based one-time password SHA-1 tokens with 30 seconds or 60 seconds validity. Users can use hardware devices from their preferred vendors, which are compatible with OATH standards to generate OTPs and use them to sign in to Azure Active Directory.

EXAM TIP

When evaluating various authentication methods for MFA, keep in mind the overall context of the scenario provided in the question. For example, using the Microsoft Authenticator app might be a convenient option for certain demographics that may have access to a smartphone with a reasonable internet connection. However, a phone call may be a better option if the targeted demographic lacks access to smartphones or has intermittent internet connectively. Usually, the best choice of an MFA method is a combination of various factors, such as cost, adoption, and security.

Implement and manage authentication methods

As part of the Azure AD sign-in experience, basic password-based authentication should be supplemented or replaced with a more secure authentication method such as FIDO.

Working with FIDO2

The Fast IDentity Online (FIDO) Alliance's goal is to replace passwords with strong passwordless authentication that is both secure and usable. The latest version of the open specification for passwordless authentication, FIDO2, incorporates the W3C Web Authentication (WebAuthn) standard as well as the FIDO Client to Authenticator Protocol 2 (CTAP2). Users can sign in using an unphishable FIDO2 security key stored in a hardware device that can be accessed via commonly used protocols such as NFC (near-field communication), Bluetooth, and USB.

FIDO2 security keys can be used to sign in to Azure AD or hybrid Azure AD-joined devices to achieve single-sign-on to cloud and on-premises resources.

> **NEED MORE REVIEW?** **PASSWORDLESS AUTHENTICATIONS AND COMBINED REGISTRATION FEATURES**
>
> Read more about passwordless authentications' reliance on the combined registration feature at: *https://docs.microsoft.com/en-us/azure/active-directory/authentication/howto-authentication-passwordless-security-key#enable-the-combined-registration-experience.*

Enabling the FIDO2 security key method

To enable the FIDO2 security key method for Azure AD:

1. Sign in as an administrator to the Azure portal at *http://portal.azure.com*.

2. Navigate to **Azure Active Directory**.

3. Select **Security** from the left pane, as shown in Figure 2-20.

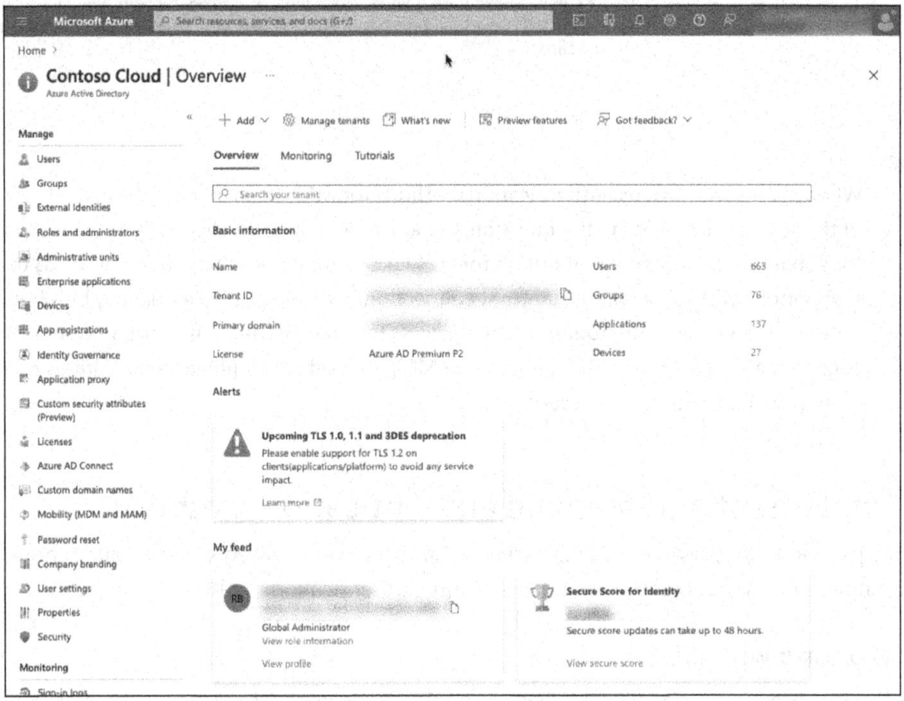

FIGURE 2-20 Azure AD home page with Security option.

4. Select **Authentication methods** from the left pane, as shown in Figure 2-21.

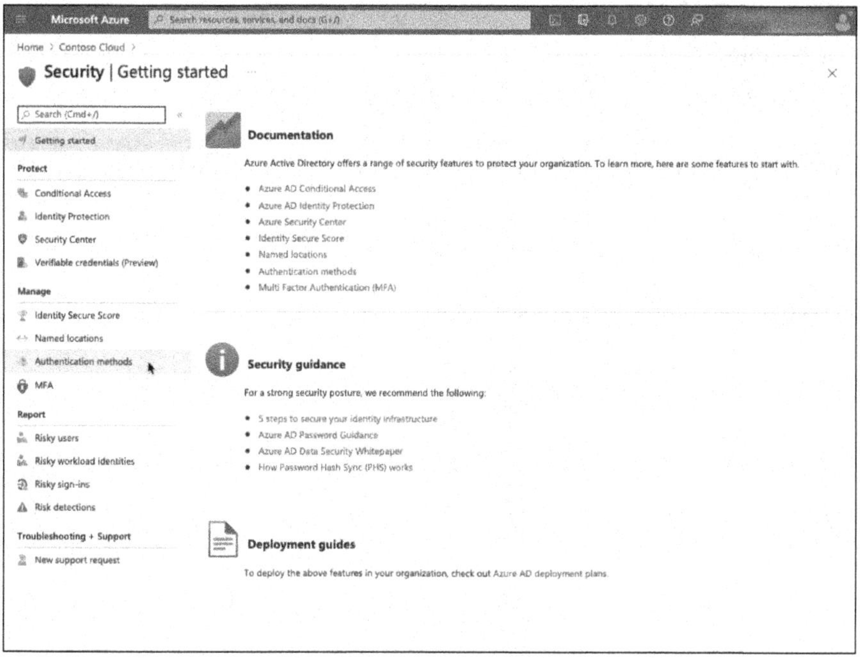

FIGURE 2-21 Azure AD Security settings with the Authentication methods option.

5. Select **FIDO2 Security Key** from the list of available methods, as shown in Figure 2-22.

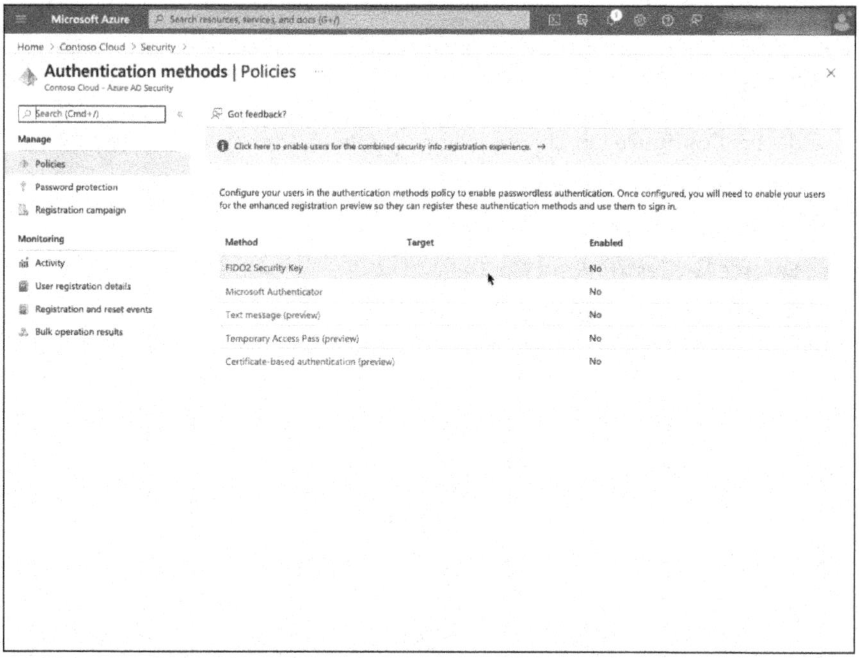

FIGURE 2-22 Azure AD Authentication methods.

6. Under the **Basics** tab, choose the following options, as shown in Figure 2-23.
   - **Enable:** Yes
   - **Target:** All users

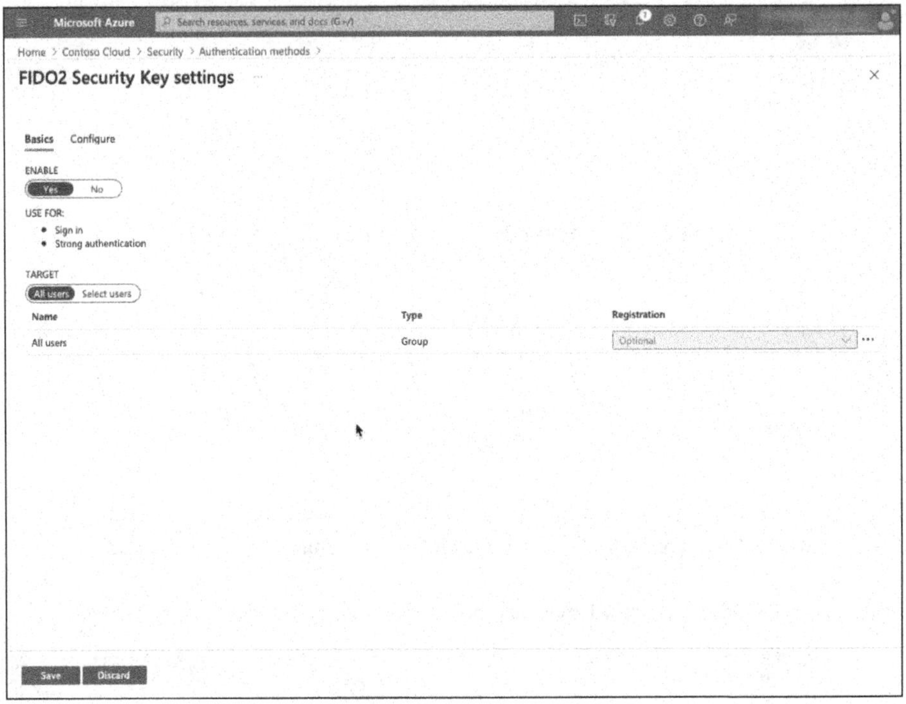

FIGURE 2-23   Azure AD FIDO2 Security Key settings.

7. Under the **Configure** tab, choose following options, as shown in Figure 2-24.
   - **Allow self-service set up:** Yes
   - **Enforce attestation:** No (Default)
   - **Enforce key restrictions:** No (Default)
   - **Restrict specific keys:** Block (Default)

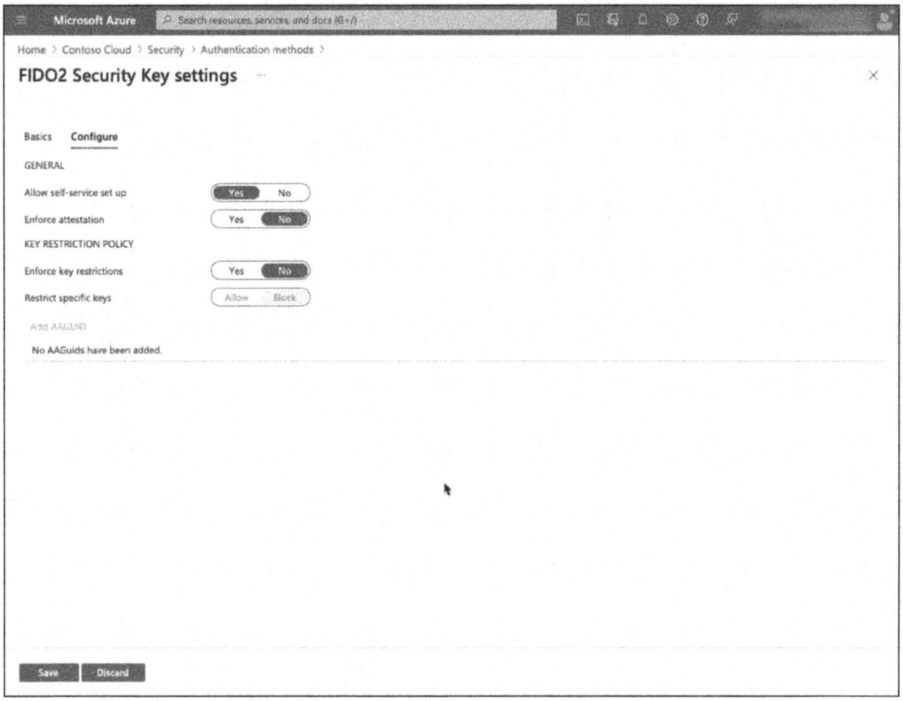

FIGURE 2-24 Azure AD FIDO2 Security Key configuration options.

8. Click **Save**.

Register a FIDO2 security key

The user must configure a FIDO2 security key using the steps below before it can be used for sign-in:

1. Navigate to the URL *https://myprofile.microsoft.com/*.

2. Sign in with the user account for which FIDO2 security key needs to be configured.

3. Select **Security info**, as shown in Figure 2-25. Make sure there is at least one Azure AD MFA method already registered; otherwise, you must first register for an MFA method before you can register a FIDO2 security key.

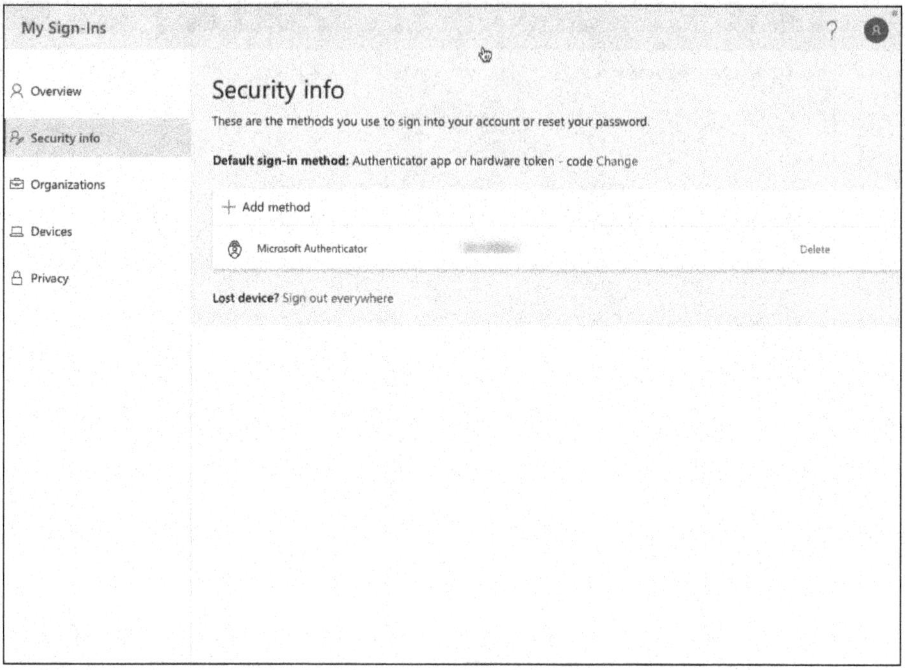

FIGURE 2-25 My Sign-Ins Security info.

4. Select **Security key** from the dropdown and click **Add**, as shown in Figure 2-26.

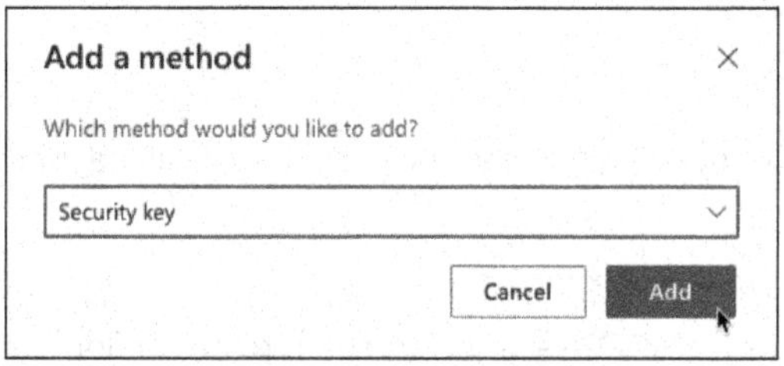

Add a method ✕

Which method would you like to add?

| Security key ⌄ |

Cancel   Add

FIGURE 2-26 Adding a security key as an authentication method.

5. Choose the type of security key, **USB device** or **NFC device**, that you would like to use, as shown in Figure 2-27.

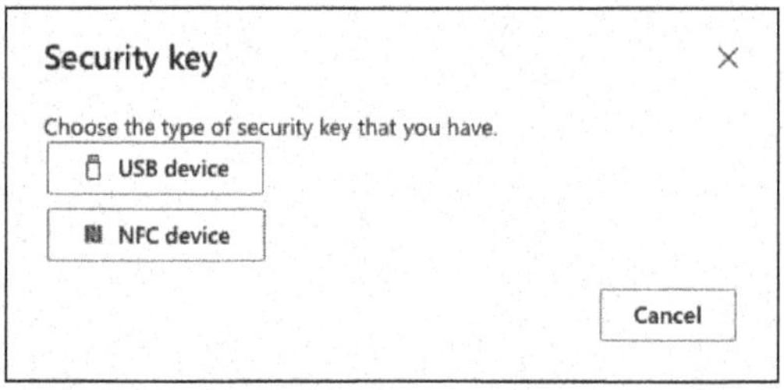

Security key ✕

Choose the type of security key that you have.

⌷ USB device

⧉ NFC device

Cancel

FIGURE 2-27 Security key type selection screen.

6. Complete the registration process by creating or using a PIN for the security key and then perform a biometric or touch for the gesture.

7. Provide a meaningful name for the key and select **Next**.

8. Finally, select **Done** to finish the process.

Sign in with passwordless credentials using a FIDO2 security key

The steps below demonstrate how to sign in with passwordless credentials using a FIDO2 security key.

1. Sign in to the Azure portal at *https://portal.azure.com/* using the account for which a FIDO2 security key is already registered.

2. Complete the sign-in process by providing the security key. For example, Figure 2-28 shows the pop-up message presented by the browser asking a user who has previously registered the security key using a USB device to use it to finish the authentication process.

FIGURE 2-28 Sign-in process with security key.

3. After the successful passwordless authentication using the security key, the user will be taken to the Azure portal (*https://portal.azure.com*), as shown in Figure 2-29.

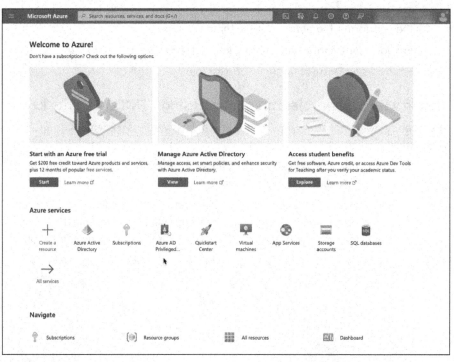

FIGURE 2-29 The Azure portal.

Implement and manage Windows Hello for Business

Windows Hello for Business allows users to use strong two-factor authentication to replace passwords on their Windows 10 or Windows 11 devices. Users are given a credential that is linked to their device and uses a biometric or PIN for authentication. Users can also use Windows Hello for Business to authenticate and sign in to Azure Active Directory, Active Directory, Microsoft Account, or any FIDO2-enabled service.

Keep the following key characteristics in mind when implementing Windows Hello for Business:

- The credentials for Windows Hello are based on a certificate or an asymmetrical key pair. Windows Hello credentials can be bound to a device, and the token obtained with the credential can also be bound to the device.

- During the registration process, the identity provider (such as Active Directory, Azure AD, or a Microsoft account) validates user identity and maps the Windows Hello public key to a user account.

- Depending on the policy, keys can be generated in the hardware Trusted Platform Module (TPM), v1.2 or v2.0 for enterprises and v2.0 for consumers or through software. When using TPM, the private key never leaves the device. During the registration process, the authenticating server assigns a public key to the user account.

- Two-factor authentication is used, which combines a key or certificate tied to a device with something the person knows (a PIN) or something physically associated with the person (biometrics).
- For keys, both personal (Microsoft account) and corporate (Active Directory or Azure AD) accounts use the single container.
- To help ensure user privacy, all keys are separated by identity providers' domains.
- The Windows Hello gesture is not shared with the server and does not roam between devices.
- Templates for biometrics are kept locally on a device.
- PINs are never saved or shared.

Table 2-6 lists various Windows Hello for Business features that help improve the overall security posture.

TABLE 2-6 Windows Hello for Business features

FEature	Description
Dual Enrollment	This feature enables administrators to enroll both non-privileged and privileged credentials to perform elevated administrative functions on their device. *https://docs.microsoft.com/en-us/windows/security/identity-protection/hello-for-business/hello-feature-dual-enrollment* Requirements: ■ Hybrid and On-premises Windows Hello for Business deployments ■ Enterprise joined or Hybrid Azure joined devices ■ Windows 10, version 1709 or later ■ Certificate trust
Dynamic Lock	This feature allows users to enhance security of their Windows device by configuring it to lock automatically when a Bluetooth- paired device signal falls below the maximum Received Signal Strength Indicator (RSSI) value. Requirements: ■ Windows 10, version 1703 or later
Multifactor Unlock	These features allow Windows 10 and Windows 11 devices to be configured such that users require a combination of authentication factors and trusted signals to unlock their devices. *https://docs.microsoft.com/en-us/windows/security/identity-protection/hello-for-business/feature-multifactor-unlock* Requirements: ■ Windows Hello for Business deployment (Hybrid or On-premises) ■ Azure AD, Hybrid Azure AD, or Domain Joined (Cloud, Hybrid, or On-Premises deployments) ■ Windows 10, version 1709 or newer, or Windows 11 ■ Bluetooth, Bluetooth-capable phone (optional)
Remote Desktop	This feature allows a remote desktop connection to a server or another device using a certificate deployed to a Windows Hello for Business container. Requirements: ■ Windows 10 ■ Windows 11 ■ Cloud only, Hybrid, and On-premises only Windows Hello for Business deployments ■ Azure AD joined, Hybrid Azure AD joined, and Enterprise joined devices

PIN Reset	This feature enables users to reset a forgotten PIN using the lock screen or from the sign-in options available in the Settings console. *https://docs.microsoft.com/en-us/windows/security/identity-protection/hello-for-business/hello-feature-pin-reset* Requirements: ■ Windows 10, version 1709 or later ■ Windows 11
Conditional Access	Azure Active Directory conditional access policies can be applied on devices using Windows Hello for Business. This enables organizations to apply an advanced set of conditions when a user tries to access a resource. *https://docs.microsoft.com/en-us/windows/security/identity-protection/hello-for-business/hello-feature-conditional-access* Requirements: ■ Azure Active Directory ■ Hybrid Windows Hello for Business deployment

EXAM TIP

Authentication with Windows Hello for Business is always key-based or certificate-based. That makes it more secure than Windows Hello, which relies on a connivence PIN technique that isn't backed up by certificate-based authentication or asymmetric encryption (public/private key): *https://docs.microsoft.com/en-us/windows/security/identity-protection/hello-for-business/hello-overview#the-difference-between-windows-hello-and-windows-hello-for-business*

When implementing Windows Hello for Business, you have many options to choose from. By providing multiple options, nearly every organization will be able to deploy Windows Hello for Business. The availability of numerous options makes the deployment appear complex; however, most organizations will realize they've already implemented most of the infrastructure required for the Windows Hello for Business deployment. It is critical to recognize that Windows Hello for Business is a distributed system that requires careful planning across multiple teams within an organization. Table 2-7 lists the most common Windows Hello for Business deployment types.

TABLE 2-7 Windows Hello for Business deployment types

Deployment type	Description
Cloud only	The cloud-only deployment model is appropriate for organizations that only have cloud identities and do not need access to on-premises resources. These organizations typically connect their devices to the cloud and rely solely on cloud resources such as Exchange Online, SharePoint Online, Microsoft Teams, etc. Furthermore, because these users do not use on-premises resources, they do not require certificates for services such as VPN, as everything they require is hosted in Azure.
Hybrid	The hybrid deployment model is intended for businesses that are using federation with Azure Active Directory or using Azure Active Directory connect using Azure Active Directory-hosted applications and want a single sign-in user experience for both on-premises and Azure Active Directory resources.
On-premises	The on-premises deployment model is intended for organizations that do not have cloud identities or use Azure Active Directory-hosted applications.

Implement and manage password protection and smart lockout

Azure AD Password Protection enables organizations to detect known weak passwords and block them from usage by the users. It also has capability to detect any variation of these weak passwords and block those from being used by the users. Azure AD Password Protection maintains a global banned passwords list, which is applied automatically to all users in the directory. In addition to the default global list of banned passwords, an organization can create their own custom list of banned passwords to meet their specific security requirements. Whenever a password is created or reset, it is checked against the banned password list, and only after it passes the check is the user allowed to use that password.

Azure AD Password Protection is available both for cloud-only users and for users who are synchronized from on-premises AD DS. The next section covers Azure AD Password Protection for cloud-only users, while a later section will cover deployment requirements and the configuration steps needed to enable Azure AD Password Protection for users synchronized from on-premises AD DS.

EXAM TIP

While the global banned passwords list is available with an Azure AD Free license, the ability to create and use custom banned passwords requires an Azure AD Premium P1 or P2 license.

Licensing requirements

The licensing requirements for global and custom banned password lists are as follows:

- **Azure AD Password Protection with global banned password list:** Cloud-only users require Azure AD Free, and users synchronized from on-premises AD DS require an Azure AD Premium P1 or P2 license to use this feature.

- **Azure AD Password Protection with custom banned password list:** Both cloud-only users and users synchronized from on-premises AD DS require an Azure AD Premium P1 or P2 license to use this feature.

Configure custom banned password list

The steps below show how to configure a custom banned password list:

1. Sign in to the Azure portal, *https://portal.azure.com*, using a Global Administrator account.

2. Navigate to the Azure Active Directory dashboard by using the Azure Active Directory option available in the sidebar of the Azure portal.

3. Select the **Security** option located under the Manage section on the left side, as shown in Figure 2-30.

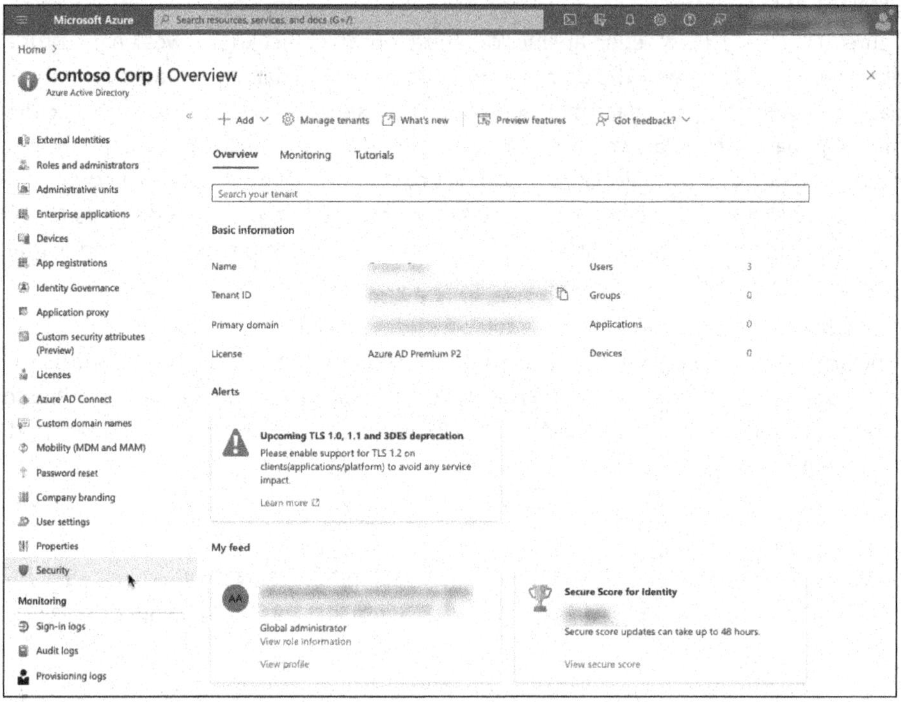

FIGURE 2-30 Azure AD home page with the Security option.

4. Select **Authentication methods**.

5. Select **Password protection**, as shown in Figure 2-31.

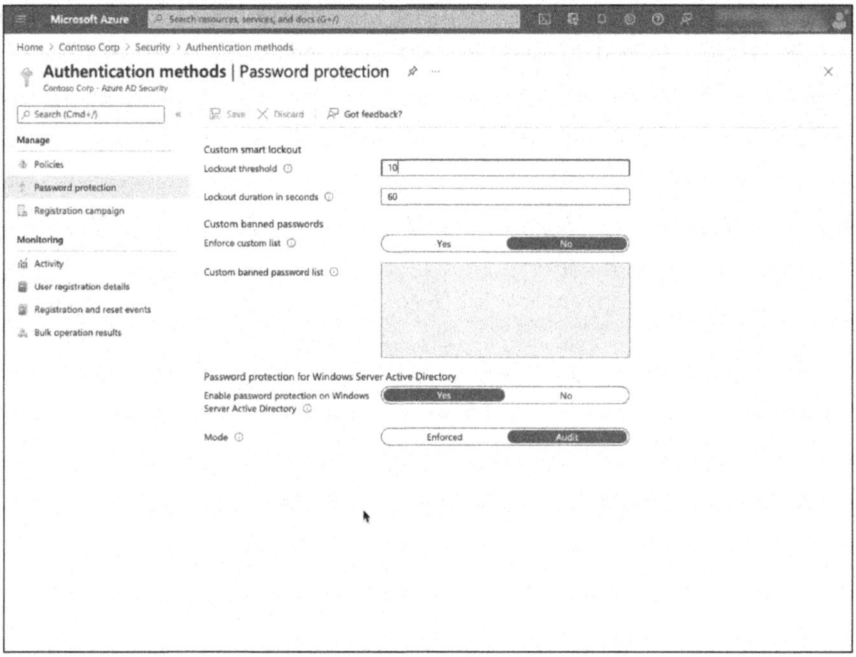

FIGURE 2-31 Password protection.

6. Set the **Enforce custom list** option to **Yes**, as shown in Figure 2-32.

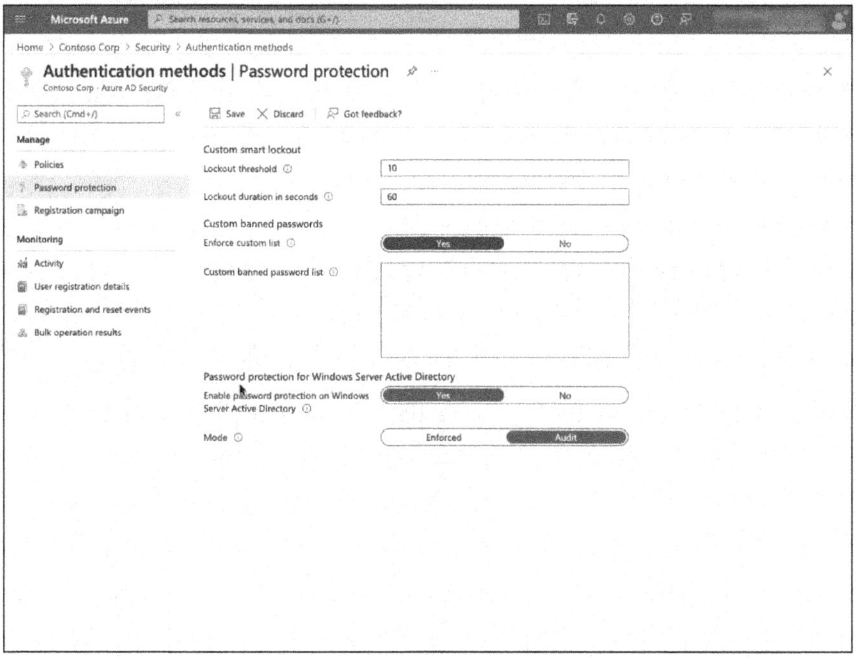

FIGURE 2-32 Enforce custom list.

7. Specify custom passwords to ban using the multi-line text box available for the **Custom banned password list**. Make sure to enter one term per line, as shown in Figure 2-33.

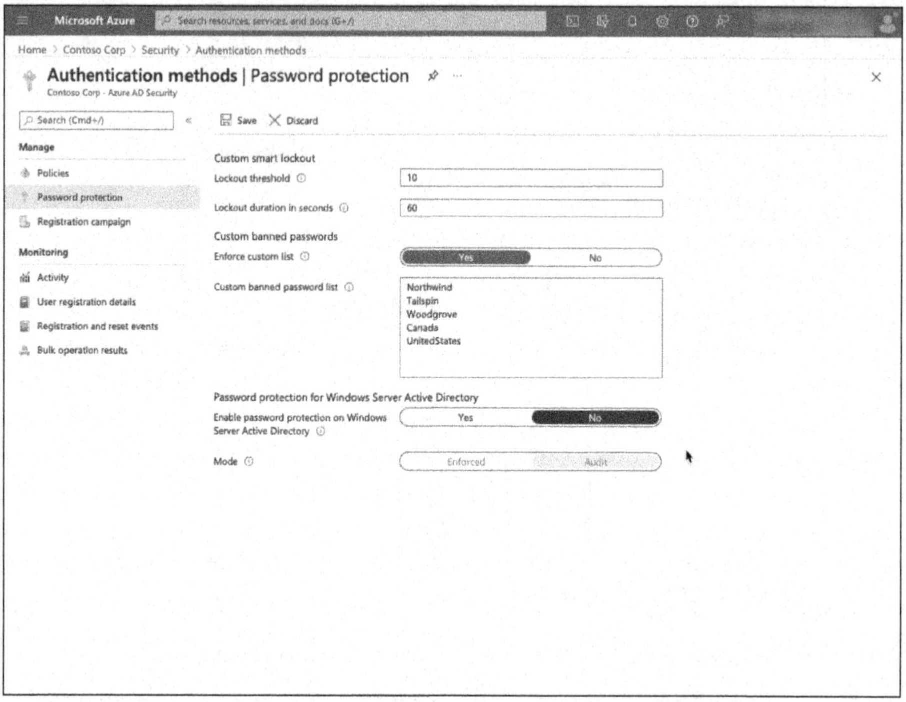

FIGURE 2-33 Custom banned password list.

Consider the following restrictions while creating a custom banned password list:

- A maximum of 1000 terms are allowed per list.
- The minimum term length is 4 characters.
- The maximum term length is 16 characters.
- Terms are case-insensitive. For example, Northwind, NorthWind, northwind, north-WIND, and norTHwinD are all considered identical terms.
- The list considers common character substitutions, such as "o" and "0" or "a" and "@."

8. Click **Save**. Keep all other settings at their default values. It may take up to several hours before the custom banned password list is fully applied.

Testing a custom banned password list

The steps below show how to test a custom banned password list:

1. Sign in to *https://mysignins.microsoft.com/* using the user account. You will change the password for this account in the next step.

2. Select **CHANGE PASSWORD**, as shown in Figure 2-34.

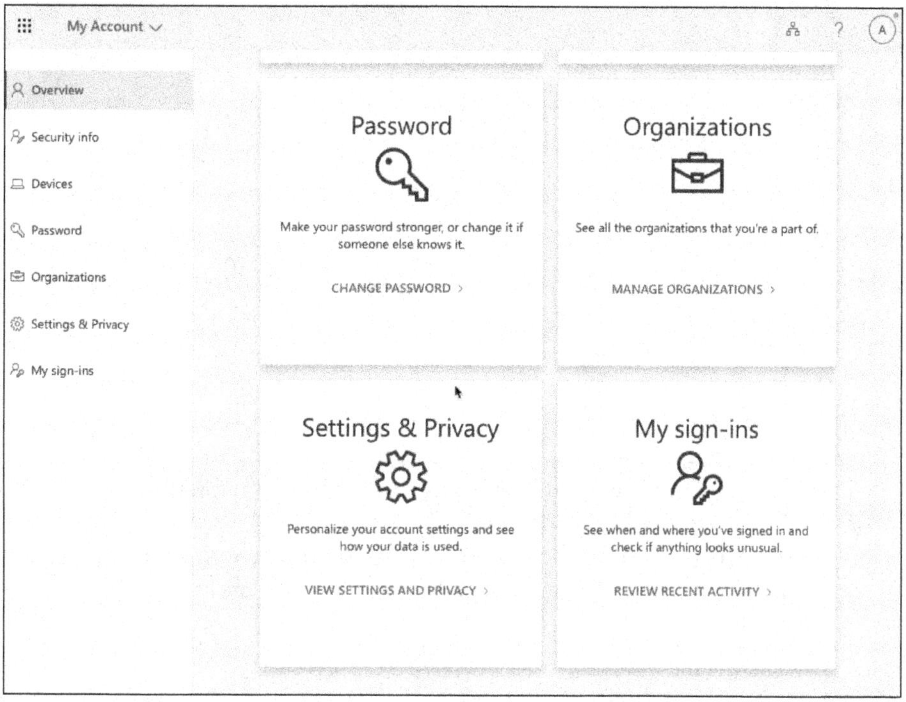

FIGURE 2-34   My Account.

3. On the **Change Password** page, enter the current password in the **Old password** textbox and then enter a new password containing a term that's on the custom banned password list that you defined earlier—for example, "Northwind100%."

4. Click **Submit**. You will get an error message, as shown in Figure 2-35. This message indicates that the password you entered contains words or characters that are banned by the administrator.

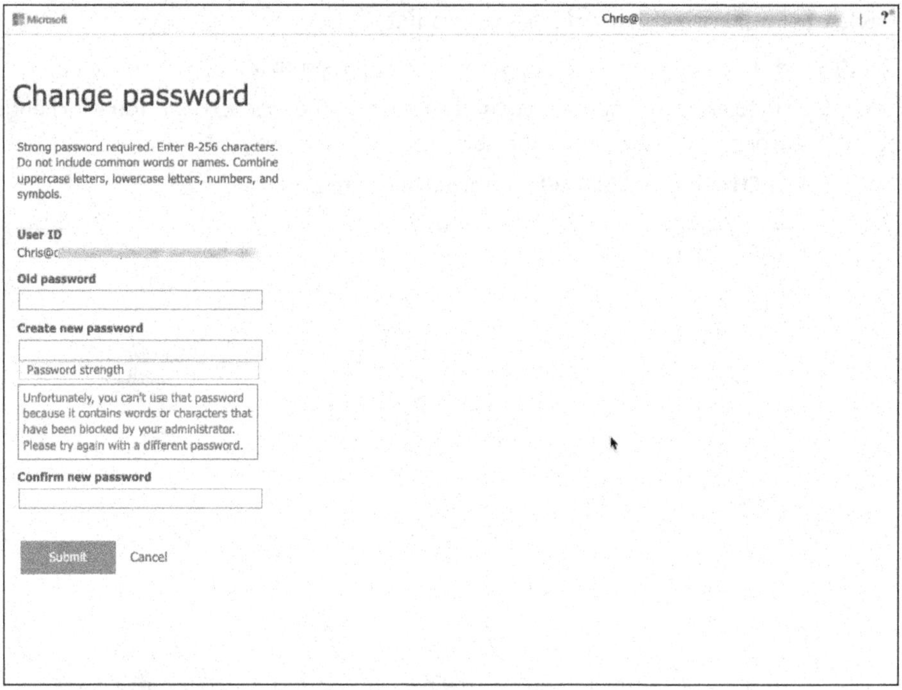

FIGURE 2-35 Change password failure due to a custom banned password list.

5. Click **Cancel** to leave the page without changing the password. Alternatively, you can choose a new password that does not contain terms that are listed within the banned password list.

6. Finally, close the browser.

Planning for on-premises Azure AD Password Protection deployment

The Azure AD Password Protection feature allows using the same global and custom banned password lists that are stored in Azure AD for on-premises passwords. Technically, these checks are performed whenever a password is reset or changed using on-premises AD DS domain controllers.

Plan for deployment of Azure AD Password Protection on-premises by verifying the following core requirements:

- Account with Active Directory domain administrator privileges in the forest root.
- Universal C Runtime installation on all machines where Azure AD Password Protection components are installed. This also includes a domain controller.
- Key Distribution Service (KDC) should be enabled on all domain controllers running Windows Server 2012 or later.

- Network access to the following two endpoints from machines where the Azure AD Password Protected service is installed:
    - Azure AD Password Protection functionality: *https://login.microsoftonline.com*
    - Authentication Requests: *https://enterpriseregistration.windows.net*
- At least one domain controller must be able to connect with one server running proxy service for Azure AD Password Protection. Specifically, the domain controller must be able to access RPC endpoint mapper port 135 and the RPC server port on the host running the proxy service.
- Download Azure AD Password Protection for Windows Server Active Directory software installation files from the Microsoft Download Center: *https://www.microsoft.com/en-us/download/details.aspx?id=57071*.
    - AzureADPasswordProtectionProxySetup.exe
    - AzureADPasswordProtectionDCAgentSetup.msi

Install and configure Azure AD Password Protection on-premises

Table 2-8 summarizes the tasks that must be completed for successful installation and configuration of the Azure AD Protection proxy service in your environment. Please use the links provided for each task in Table 2-8 to follow detailed step-by-step instructions provided by Microsoft. These instructions are kept up to date by Microsoft, and it is highly recommended that you follow them as-is without customizations.

TABLE 2-8   Azure AD Password Protection installation and configuration task list

Task	Description
Azure AD Password Protection proxy service installation	The Azure AD Password Protection proxy service is installed on a member server located within an on-premises AD DS environment. Its role is to communicate with Azure AD and maintain a copy of global and custom banned password lists. For step-by-step installation instructions, please read *https://docs.microsoft.com/en-us/azure/active-directory/authentication/ howto-password-ban-bad-on-premises-deploy#install-and-configure-the-proxy-service.*
Configure the proxy service to communicate through an HTTP proxy	Configure the HTTP proxy that the Azure AD Password Protection service will use to communicate with Azure AD. This step is optional. For step-by-step configuration instructions, please read *https://docs.microsoft.com/en-us/ azure/active-directory/authentication/howto-password-ban-bad-on-premises-deploy#configure-the-proxy-service-to-communicate-through-an-http-proxy.*
Configure the proxy service to listen on a specific port	<ul><li>The Azure AD Password Protection proxy service and DC agent communicates via RPC over TCP. The default configuration for the proxy service allows it to listen to any available RPC port, but this behavior can be changed by configuring it to use a specific port. This step is optional.</li><li>For step-by-step configuration instructions, please read *https://docs. microsoft.com/en-us/azure/active-directory/authentication/howto-password-ban-bad-on-premises-deploy#configure-the-proxy-service-to-listen-on-a-specific-port.*</li></ul>

Table 2-9 summarizes the task that must be completed for successful installation and configuration of the Azure AD Protection DC service. Please use the link provided for the task in Table 2-9 to follow detailed step-by-step instructions provided by Microsoft. These instructions are kept up to date by Microsoft, and it is highly recommended that you follow them as-is without customizations.

TABLE 2-9 Azure AD Password Protection DC agent service installation and configuration tasks list

Task	Description
Azure AD Password Protection DC agent service installation	The Azure AD Password Protection DC agent service installation can be automated using standard MSI procedures. For step-by-step configuration instructions, please read *https://docs.microsoft.com/en-us/azure/active-directory/authentication/howto-password-ban-bad-on-premises-deploy#install-the-dc-agent-service*.

After the successful installation and configuration of the Azure AD Password Protection proxy and DC agent service, follow the steps below to enable Azure AD Password Protection for on-premises environments:

1. Sign in to the Azure portal, *https://portal.azure.com*, using a Global Administrator account.

2. Navigate to the Azure Active Directory dashboard by using the Azure Active Directory option available in the sidebar of the Azure portal.

3. Select the **Security** option located under the Manage section on the left side.

4. Select **Authentication methods**.

5. Select **Password protection**.

6. Set **Enable password protection on Windows Server Active Directory** to **Yes**, as shown in Figure 2-36. Leave the **Mode** set to **Audit**.

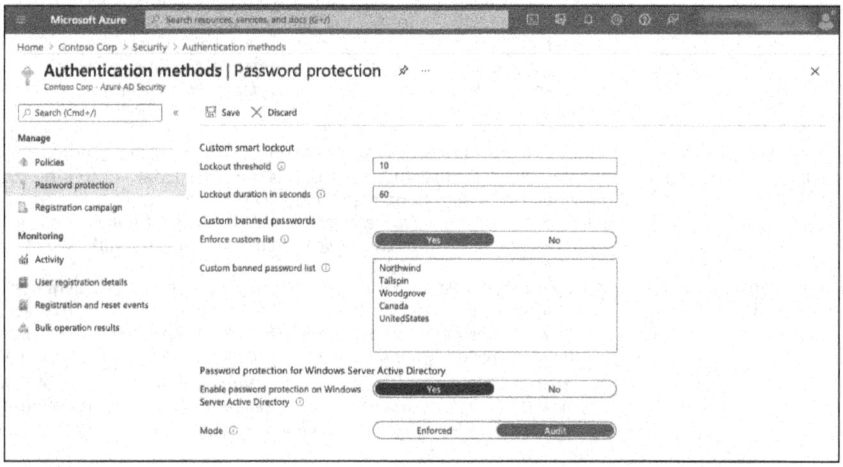

FIGURE 2-36 Password protection for Windows Server Active Directory.

7. Click **Save**.

Configure smart lockout thresholds

Azure AD smart lockout helps safeguard user accounts by locking out potential malicious actors who use brute force, password spray, or similar attack techniques to guess the passwords. Azure AD smart lockout works by locking the user account from sign-in attempts for one minute after several consecutive failed attempts. The lockout acts as a shield to protect the user account from being attacked from bots in an automated fashion. The exact number of failed attempts threshold resulting in the user account being locked depends on the type of Azure Cloud where the Azure AD tenant is located. For Azure Public Cloud and Azure China, the failed attempts lockout threshold is 10; for Azure US Government, the failed attempts lockout threshold is 3.

The default lockout values can be customized to match organizational needs. Please note that customizations to smart lockout values require an Azure AD Premium P1 or higher user license. The following steps show how to change the lockout threshold and duration:

1. Sign in to the Azure portal, *https://portal.azure.com*, using a Global Administrator account.

2. Navigate to the Azure Active Directory dashboard by using the Azure Active Directory option available in the sidebar of the Azure portal.

3. Select the **Security** option located under the Manage section on the left side.

4. Select **Authentication methods**.

5. Select **Password protection**.

6. Set the **Lockout threshold** and **Lockout duration in seconds** to values that match your needs.

   For example, Figure 2-37 shows the **Lockout threshold** set to 5, which means the account will be locked after 5 failed sign-in attempts by the user, and **Lockout duration in seconds** is set to 90. Keep in mind that if the first sign-in attempt after the lockout also fails, then the account locks out again. If a user account keeps getting lockouts repeatedly, the lockout duration increases over time. The exact duration by which the lockout increases is not released publicly as a safety measure to avoid malicious actors from exploiting it.

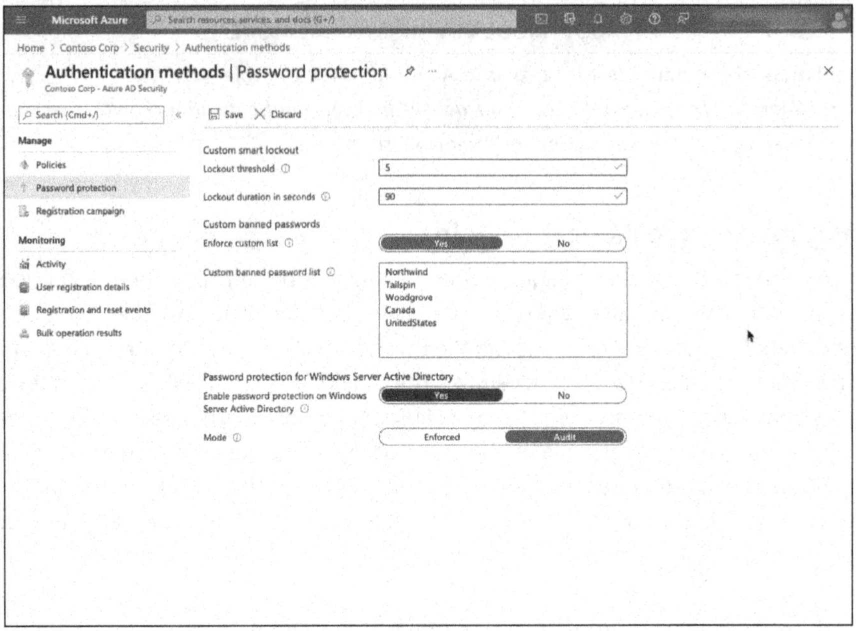

FIGURE 2-37 Lockout threshold and Lockout duration in seconds.

7. Click **Save**.

EXAM TIP

When a user account is locked by the smart lockout feature, it cannot be unlocked by the administrator, who must wait for the lockout period to expire. In this case, the user can use the self-service password reset feature (SSPR) to unlock the account by resetting their password.

Implement certificate-based authentication in Azure AD

For applications and browser sign-in, Azure Active Directory (Azure AD) certificate-based authentication (CBA) enables users to authenticate directly with X.509 certificates against their Azure AD account.

Following are some key advantages of using Azure AD CBA:

- **Improved user experience:** Users who require certificate-based authentication can now directly authenticate against Azure AD without the need for federated AD FS.
- **Ease of deployment:** Azure AD CBA is a free feature that does not require any paid editions of Azure AD to use, nor does it require complex on-premises deployments or network configuration, because users authenticate directly against Azure AD.
- **Security:** On-premises passwords do not need to be stored in any form in the cloud, and CBA works in tandem with conditional access features and authentication strength capability to enforce MFA.

In CBA, the username binding policy aids in the validation of the user's certificate. To determine the user, the Subject Alternate Name (SAN) PrincipalName in the certificate is mapped to the UserPrincipalName attribute of the user object by default. Table 2-10 shows the four supported binding methods. In general, mapping types are high-affinity if they are based on identifiers that cannot be reused (such as Subject Key Identifiers or SHA1 Public Key). These identifiers provide greater assurance that only one certificate can be used to authenticate the user.

TABLE 2-10 Azure AD CBA certificate bindings

Certificate mapping Field	Example values in certificateUserIds	User object attributes	Type
PrincipalName	■ "X509:<PN>adam@contoso.com"	■ userPrincipalName ■ onPremisesUser PrincipalName ■ certificateUserIds	■ low-affinity
RFC822Name	■ "X509:<RFC822>user@woodgrove.com"	■ userPrincipalName onPremisesUser PrincipalName certificateUserIds	■ low-affinity
X509SKI	■ "X509:<SKI>123456789abcdef"	■ certificateUserIds	■ high-affinity
X509SHA1PublicKey	■ "X509:<SHA1-PUKEY>123456789abcdef"	■ certificateUserIds	■ high-affinity

When a user uses CBA to authenticate to Azure AD, the user's sign-ins log will show the X.509 Certificate as the authentication method, as shown in Figure 2-38.

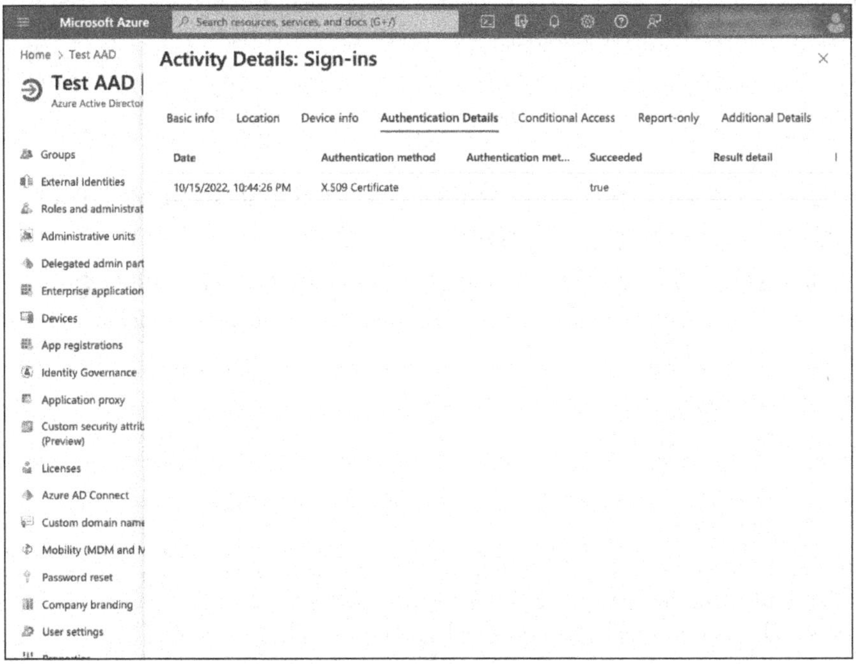

FIGURE 2-38 Azure AD user sign-in using X.509 certificate.

The following scenarios are supported by Azure AD CBA:

- User sign-ins to web browser-based applications on all platforms.
- User sign-ins to Office mobile apps, including Outlook, OneDrive, and so on.
- User sign-ins on mobile native browsers.
- Support for granular authentication rules for multifactor authentication by using the certificate issuer Subject and policy OIDs.
- Configuring certificate-to-user account bindings by using any of the certificate fields:
  - Subject Alternate Name (SAN) PrincipalName and SAN RFC822Name
  - Subject Key Identifier (SKI) and SHA1PublicKey
- Configuring certificate-to-user account bindings by using any of the user object attributes:
  - User Principal Name
  - onPremisesUserPrincipalName
  - CertificateUserIds

The following scenarios are not supported by Azure AD CBA:

- Certificate Authority hints aren't supported, so the list of certificates that appears for users in the certificate picket UI isn't scoped.
- Only one CRL Distribution Point (DP) for a trusted CA is supported.
- The CDP can be only HTTP URLs. Azure AD CDA does not support Online Certificate Status Protocol (OCSP) or Lightweight Directory Access Protocol (LDAP) URLs.
- Configuring other certificate-to-user account bindings, such as using the Subject, Subject + Issuer, or Issuer + Serial Number, are not available in this release.

More information on configuring Azure CBA can be found at *https://learn.microsoft.com/en-us/azure/active-directory/authentication/how-to-certificate-based-authentication.*

Configure Azure AD user authentication for Windows and Linux virtual machines on Azure

By integrating with Azure AD authentication, organizations can improve the security of Windows and Linux virtual machines (VMs) in Azure. Azure AD can be used as a primary authentication platform for:

- Windows Server 2019 Datacenter edition and later
- Windows 10 1809 and later
- Windows 11
- Linux virtual machines

More details on configuring Azure AD login for a Windows VM is available at *https://learn.microsoft.com/en-us/azure/active-directory/devices/howto-vm-sign-in-azure-ad-windows#enable-azure-ad-login-for-a-windows-vm-in-azure.*

More details on configuring Azure AD login for a Linux VM is available at *https://learn.microsoft.com/en-us/azure/active-directory/devices/howto-vm-sign-in-azure-ad-linux#enable-azure-ad-login-for-a-linux-vm-in-azure*.

Skill 2.3: Plan, implement, and manage Azure AD conditional access

Conditional access, at its core, offers organizations the ability to enable users to be productive anywhere and whenever they want while also protecting the organization's resources. Organizations use Azure AD conditional access to apply the fine-grain access control policies required to secure resource access. Conditional Access collects signals from a variety of sources to make decisions and enforce organizational policies.

This skill covers how to:

- Plan conditional access policies
- Implement conditional access policy assignments
- Implement conditional access policy controls
- Test and troubleshoot conditional access policies
- Implement session management
- Implement device-enforced restrictions
- Implement continuous access evaluation
- Create a conditional access policy from a template

Plan conditional access policies

Azure AD conditional access policy in a nutshell is an "if-then" statement. It is a powerful tool for organizations to implement rich access control policies, since it allows implementing both fine-grain and coarse-grain access control. Following are a few examples of conditional access policies:

- **If** the user belongs to HR Azure AD group and is requesting access to the HR application, **then** only grant access if the request is made from a device that is marked as compliant.
- **If** the user belongs to the Global Administrator role, has a high sign-in risk, and is requesting access to the Azure portal, **then** only grant access after the user successfully completes both the MFA challenge and a password reset.
- **If** the user belongs to a United States Sales Azure AD group, is making a request from a location outside of the United States (location based on IP Address), and is requesting access to a Microsoft 365 cloud application, **then** block the request.

- **If** a request is made by any user in the Azure AD directory to access LegacyHRApp application, **then** block the request.
- **If** a request is made by any user in the Azure AD directory to access cloud application using legacy authentication, **then** block the request.
- **If** a request is made by any user in the Azure AD directory to access any cloud application, **then** only grant access if they have signed Terms of Use (ToU) successfully.

Azure AD includes a handy What If tool that allows you to simulate the behavior of conditional access policies without running them. This aids in the planning of conditional access policies by providing visibility into potential user impact. Figure 2-39 shows the What If tool with input parameters, and Figure 2-40 shows the result of the What If tool.

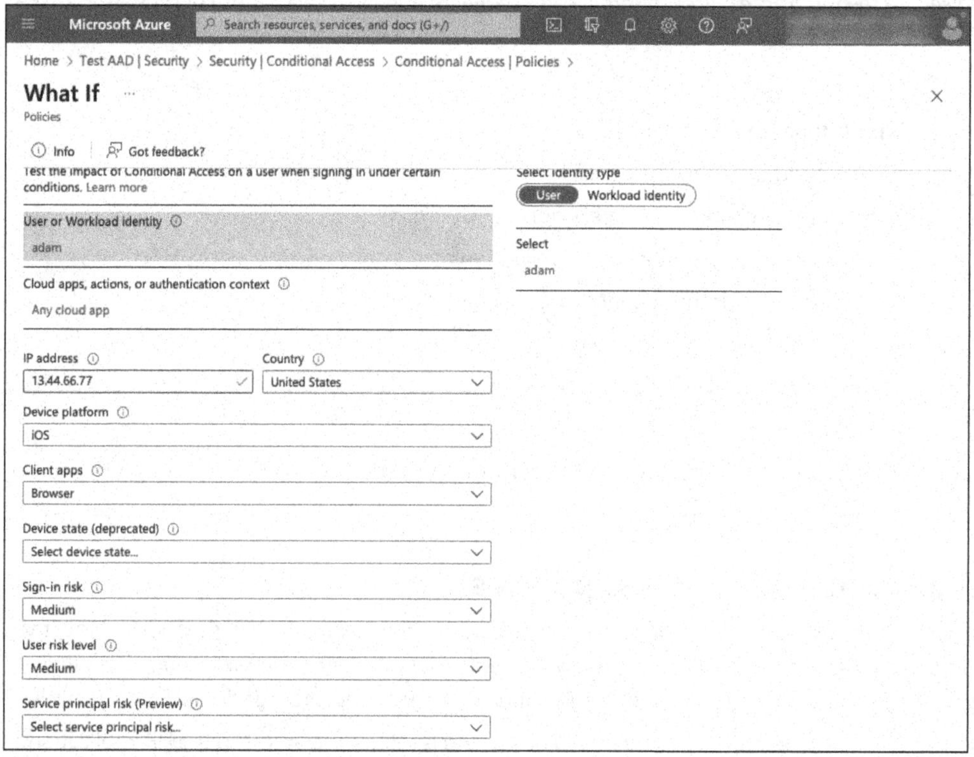

FIGURE 2-39 Azure AD What If tool parameters.

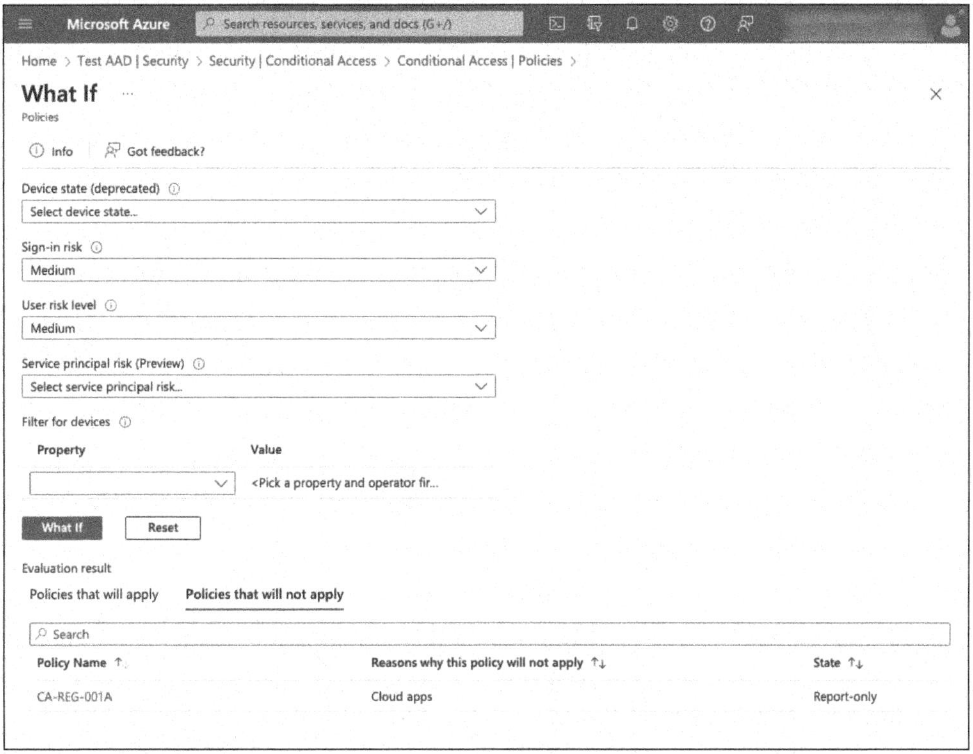

FIGURE 2-40 Azure AD What If tool results.

Licensing requirements

The Azure AD conditional access feature requires an Azure AD Premium P1 license or Microsoft 365 Business Premium license. Also, using risk-based signals like sign-in and user-risk requires the Identity Protection feature, which is available as part of the Azure AD Premium P2 license.

If the Azure AD premium licensing required for working with conditional access is not available, the message/banner shown in Figure 2-41 will be displayed. If a required license was held in the past but is no longer valid, the existing policies will be listed but cannot be modified.

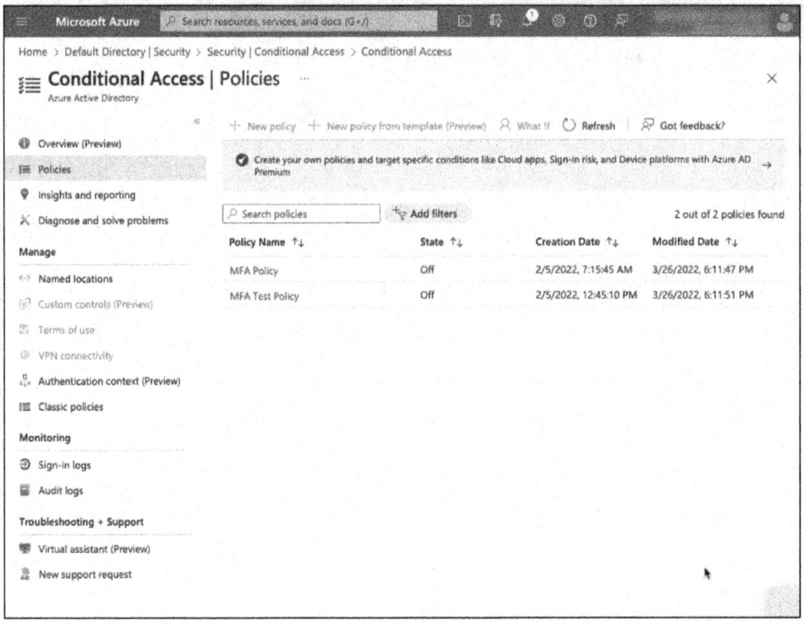

FIGURE 2-41 Azure AD Conditional Access licensing message.

Furthermore, certain conditional access policy features, such as the risk-based conditions like user risk level and sign-in risk level, as shown in Figure 2-42, are only available when an Azure AD Premium 2 (P2) license is used because they require the Identity Protection feature.

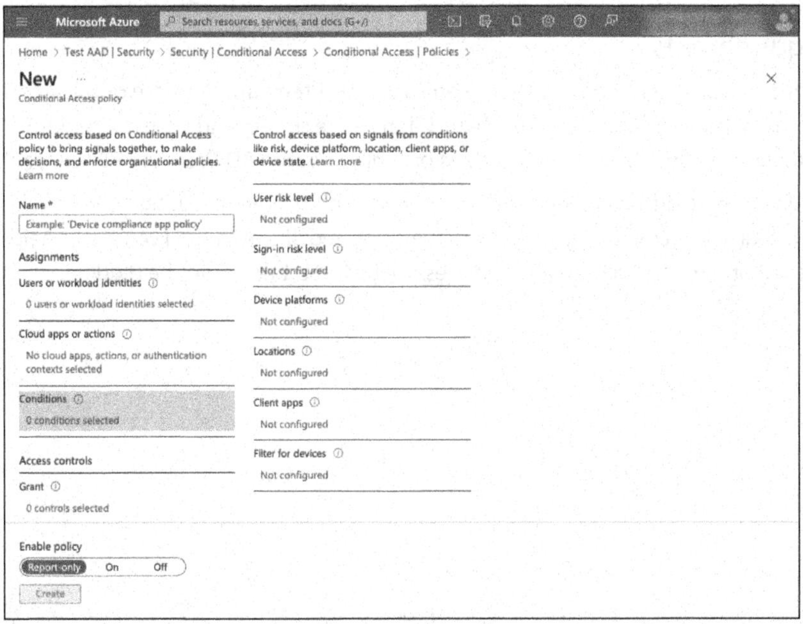

FIGURE 2-42 Azure AD P2 license is required for risk-based conditions.

Deployment planning for conditional access policies

Planning for Azure AD conditional access polices deployment is a critical step toward ensuring that users' productivity is not negatively impacted while security posture is improved by the conditional access policies enforced. Table 2-11 shows various proven practices that should be taken into consideration while planning the conditional access deployment.

TABLE 2-11 Azure AD conditional access deployment considerations

Consideration	Description
Use report-only mode	The report-only mode for conditional access policies enables you to view the results of real-time policy execution without enforcing the policy. This can be a very effective tool to evaluate the policies by reviewing the sign-in logs and gaining a better understanding of the impact of policies before enabling them in the production environment.
Configure break-glass accounts	Misconfigured conditional access policies may result in administrator accounts getting locked out from accessing critical applications, causing negative impacts on business continuity. To mitigate this issue, always configure multiple break-glass accounts. These accounts are then excluded from conditional access policies, hence enabling them to continue accessing the critical applications.
Avoid broad scope block-all policies	Conditional access policies can be implemented in both fine-grain and coarse-gain fashion. It is recommended to be as precise as possible when defining the conditional access policy to avoid accidentally impacting a broader range of users than expected.
Simulate policy execution using What If tool	The What If tool helps you test the conditional access policies by simulating user sign-in under various scenarios based on a combination of attributes such as user, application, location, and device platform. The result shows which conditional access policies would apply based on sign-in characteristics. Run the What-If tool before the actual deployment to understand the impact of the conditional access policies. Read more about the What If tool at *https://docs.microsoft.com/en-us/azure/active-directory/conditional-access/what-if-tool*.
Rollback policy	Azure AD allows three ways to roll back the conditional access policy: ■ Exclude the selected users and groups from policy ■ Disable the policy ■ Delete the policy.

Implement conditional access policy assignments

The assignments section of conditional access policy determines who, what, and where the conditional access policy applies to. Following are key components of conditional access policy assignments:

- **Users and Group:** Allows for the targeting of specific groups of users. For more information about users and group-based assignments in conditional access, please refer to *https://learn.microsoft.com/en-us/azure/active-directory/conditional-access/concept-conditional-access-users-groups*.

- **Directory Roles:** Allows administrators to specify which Azure AD directory roles should be used to determine assignment. Organizations, for example, may impose stricter policies on users with the Global Administrator role.

- **Guests or external users:** This option provides a variety of choices for targeting conditional access policies to specific guests or external user types, as well as specific tenants containing those types of users.

- **Cloud apps, actions, and authentication context:** Administrators can assign controls to particular applications, actions, or authentication contexts using conditional access policies. Administrators can select from a list of applications that includes built-in Microsoft applications as well as any Azure AD integrated applications, including gallery, non-gallery, and Application Proxy applications. Administrators can also define policy based on a user action rather than a cloud application, such as register security information or register or join devices, allowing conditional access to enforce controls around those actions. Finally, authentication context can be used by administrators to add an extra layer of security to applications. For more information about cloud apps, actions, and authentication context, please refer to *https://learn.microsoft.com/en-us/azure/active-directory/conditional-access/concept-conditional-access-cloud-apps*.

- **Conditions:** An administrator can use signals from conditions such as risk, device platform, or location to improve policy decisions within a conditional access policy. More information about conditions are available at *https://learn.microsoft.com/en-us/azure/active-directory/conditional-access/concept-conditional-access-conditions*.

This section will show you how to use various conditional access policy assignments to enforce Terms of Service (ToU). Please note that you will need an Azure AD P2 license to complete the tasks in this section.

Enforce Terms of Use (ToU) using conditional access policy

Organizations can use Azure AD Terms of Use (ToU) policies to convey information to end users in a simple way. This allows users to read essential disclaimers for legal or compliance needs.

Follow the steps below to add a new Terms of Use, which you will use later in the conditional access policy:

1. Sign in to the Azure portal, *https://portal.azure.com*, using a Global Administrator account.

2. Navigate to the Azure Active Directory dashboard by using the Azure Active Directory option available in the sidebar of the Azure portal.

3. Select **Identity Governance** located under the **Manage** section, as shown in Figure 2-43.

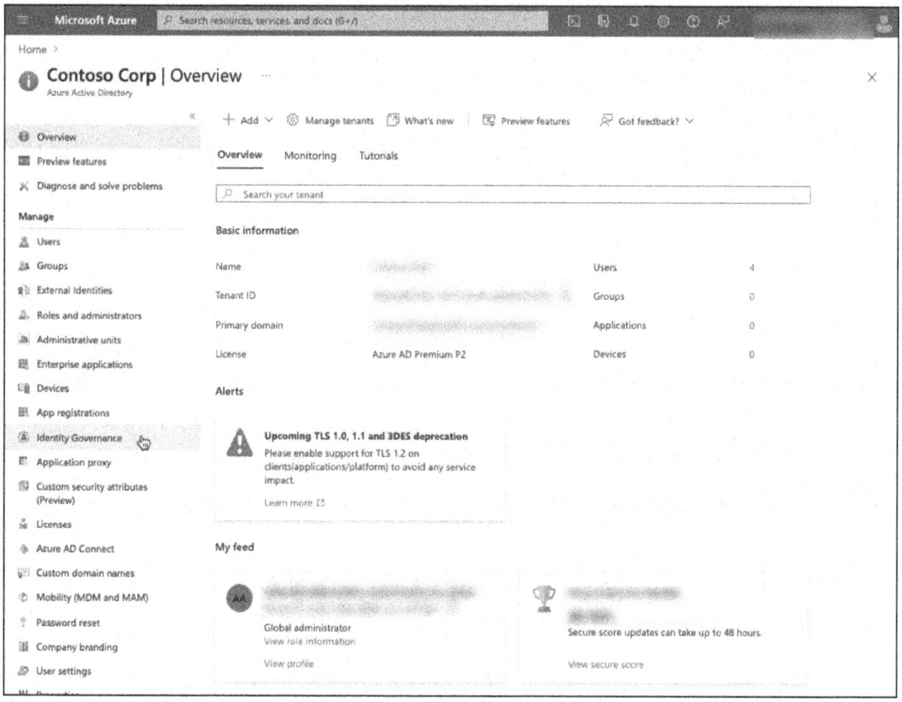

FIGURE 2-43 Azure AD Identity Governance.

4. Select **Terms of use** from the left side pane, as shown in Figure 2-44.

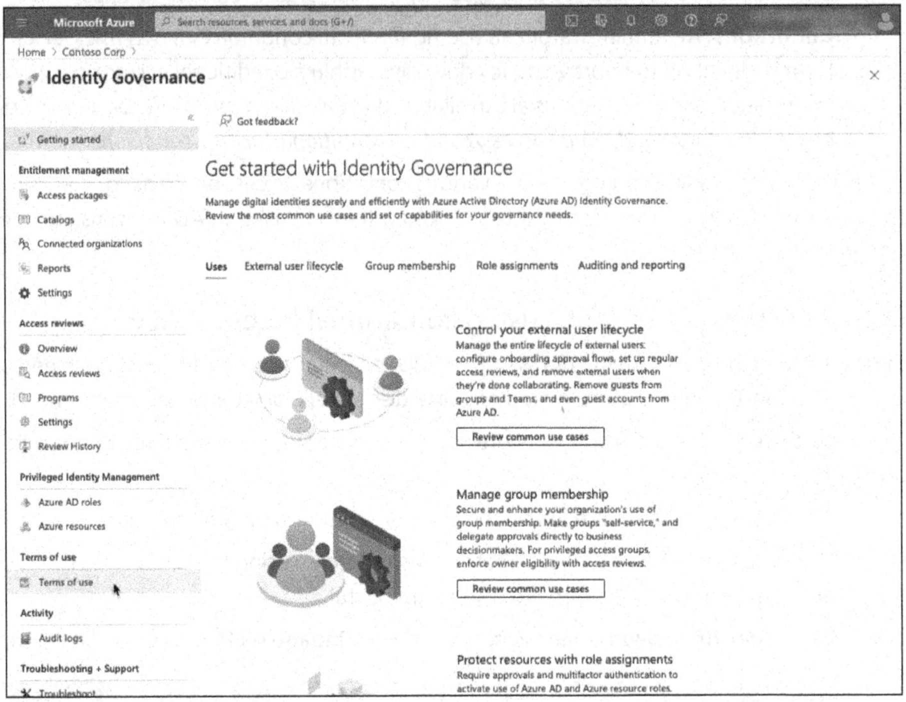

FIGURE 2-44 Terms of Use (ToU).

5. Click **New terms** from the top pane.

6. On the **New terms of use page**, fill in the following information. It should look like Figure 2-45.

- **Name:** Employee Terms of Use Agreement

- **Terms of use document:** Select any PDF document and upload, it since it is only going to be used for testing purposes. You can use the Microsoft SLA for testing purposes, which is available for download at *https://download.microsoft.com/download/2/C/8/2C8CAC17-FCE7-4F51-9556-4D77C7022DF5/MCA2017Agr_EMEA_EU-EFTA_ENG_Sep20172_CR.pdf*.

  - **Language:** Select English (or the language of your choice) from the dropdown menu.

  - **Display Name:** ToU.

- **Require users to expand the terms of use:** On (This will force users to read the entire document).
- **Require users to consent on every device:** Off.
- **Expire consents:** Off.
- **Duration before re-acceptance required (days):** 60.
- **Enforce with conditional policy template:** Create conditional access policy later.

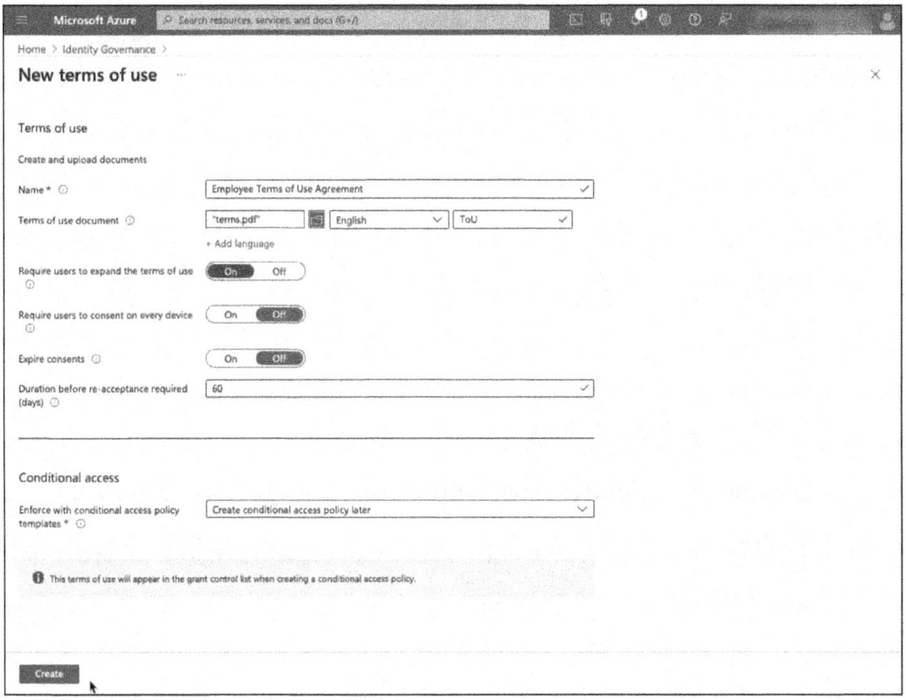

FIGURE 2-45 New Terms of Use.

Follow the steps below to create a new conditional access policy and enforce the Terms of Use (ToU) before users can sign in to the Azure portal.

1. Sign in to the Azure portal, *https://portal.azure.com*, using a Global Administrator account.
2. Navigate to the Azure Active Directory dashboard by using the Azure Active Directory option available in the sidebar of the Azure portal.
3. Select **Security** from the left side pane.
4. Select Conditional Access from the left side pane, as shown in Figure 2-46.

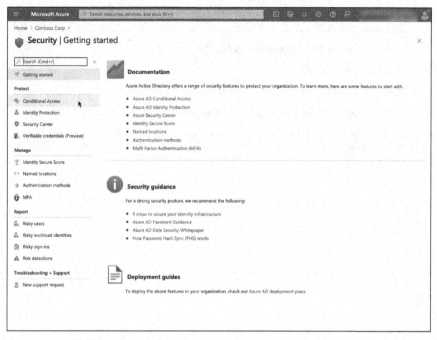

FIGURE 2-46   Conditional Access.

5.   Click + **New policy** and then select **Create new policy** as shown Figure 2-47.

FIGURE 2-47   Create new policy.

6. On the **New Conditional Access policy page**, enter **Enforce-ToU** for the **Name**, as shown in Figure 2-48.

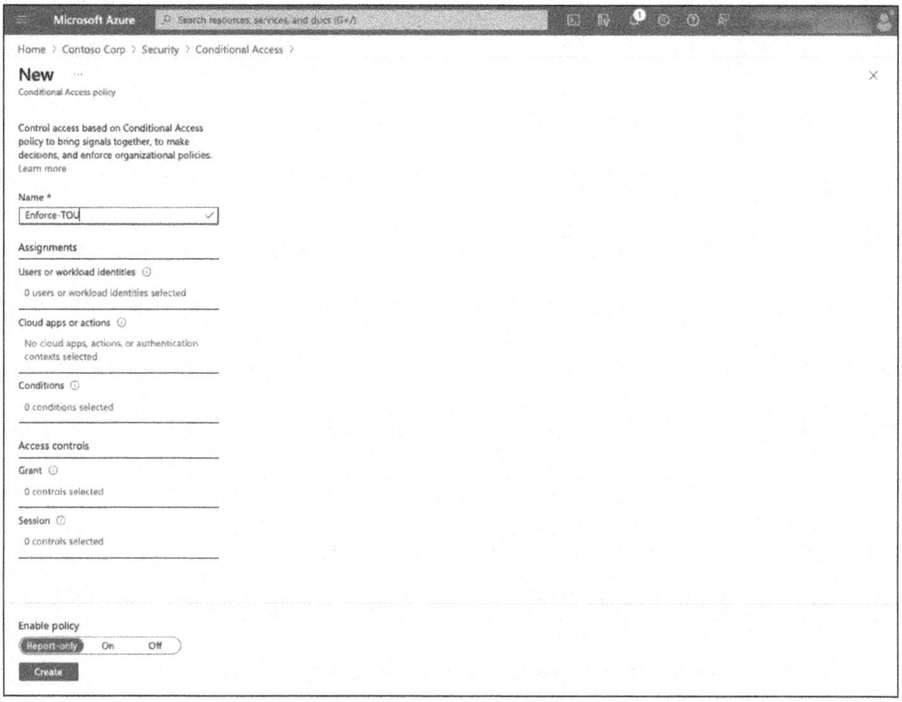

FIGURE 2-48 New Conditional Access policy.

7. Expand **Users or workload identities** and then set following information options. The result should look like Figure 2-49.

- **What does this policy apply to:** Users and groups.

- **Include:** All users.

- **Exclude:** Select the Global administrator role from the Directory roles drop-down menu.

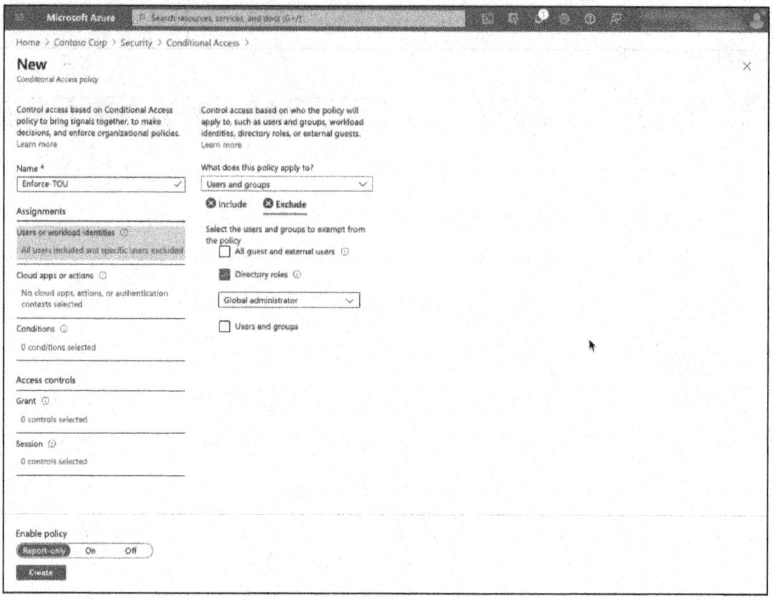

FIGURE 2-49 Users or workload identities.

8. Expand **Cloud apps or actions** and then set the following information options. The result should look like Figure 2-50.

    ■ **Select what this policy applies to:** Cloud apps.

    ■ **Include:** Click **Select apps** and then search for and choose **My Apps**.

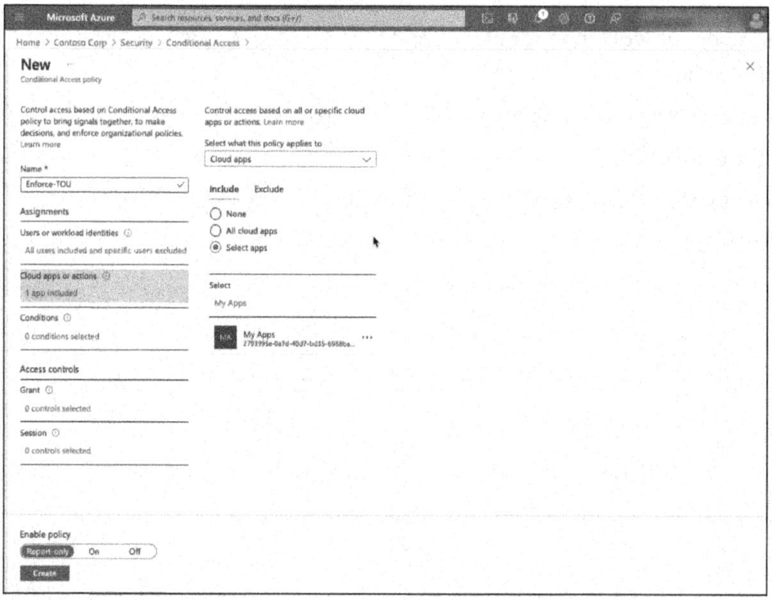

FIGURE 2-50 Cloud apps or actions.

9. Expand **Grant**, set the following information options, and then click **Select**. The result should look like Figure 2-51.

   ■ **Grant access:** Employee Terms of Use Agreement.

   ■ **For multiple controls:** Require all the selected controls.

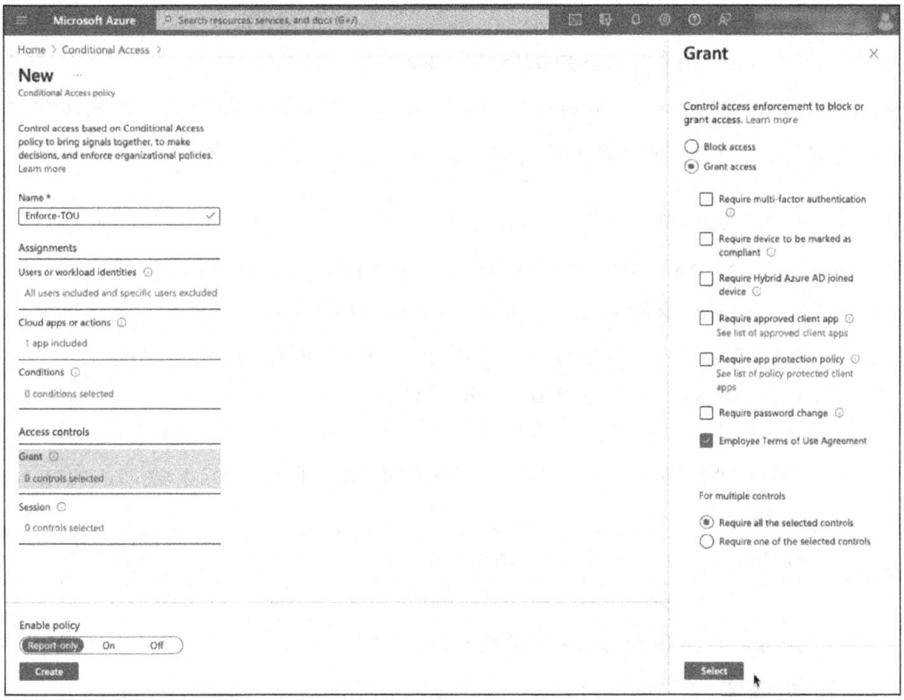

FIGURE 2-51 Grant options.

10. Set **Enable policy** to **On**.

11. Click **Create**.

Implement conditional access policy controls

The access control section of the conditional access policy determines how the conditional access policy is enforced. Following are key components of the conditional access policy access control:

■ **Grant:** The access control option can be used to allow or deny access to the resource. Learn more about Grant control at *https://learn.microsoft.com/en-us/azure/active-direc-tory/conditional-access/concept-conditional-access-grant*.

■ **Session:** Administrators can use session controls to provide limited experiences within specific cloud applications. Learn more about session control at *https://learn.microsoft.com/en-us/azure/active-directory/conditional-access/concept-conditional-access-session*.

This section will show you how to implement conditional access policy access control to deny access to a resource based on the sign-in risk. Please note that you will need an Azure AD P2 license to complete the tasks in this section.

Enforce MFA using the sign-in risk signal with conditional access policy

Follow the steps below to create a conditional access policy that uses the sign-in risk signal to enforce MFA for granting access to a cloud application.

1. Sign in to the Azure portal, *https://portal.azure.com*, using a Global Administrator account.

2. Navigate to the Azure Active Directory dashboard by using the Azure Active Directory option available in the sidebar of the Azure portal.

3. Select **Security** from the left side pane.

4. Select **Conditional Access** from left side pane, as shown in Figure 2-46.

5. Click **+ New policy** and then select **Create new policy**.

6. On the **New conditional access page**, enter **CA-SignIn** for the **Name**.

7. Expand **Users or workload identities** and then set the following information options. The result should look like Figure 2-49.

   - **What does this policy apply to:** Users and groups.

   - **Include:** All users.

   - **Exclude:** Select the Global administrator role from the Directory roles dropdown menu.

8. Expand **Cloud apps or actions** and then set the following information options.

   - **Select what this policy applies to:** Cloud apps.

   - **Include:** All Cloud Apps.

9. Expand **Conditions**, select **Sign-In risk**, and set the following information options:

   - Set **Configure** to **Yes**.

   - Select the sign-in risk level this policy will apply to:

     - **High**

     - **Medium**

     - **Low**

   - Press **Done** to save your choices.

10. Expand **Grant**, set the following information options, and then click **Select**.

    - **Block access**

    - **For multiple controls:** Keep the default option.

11. Set **Enable policy** to **On**.

12. Click **Create**.

Test and troubleshoot conditional access policies

In this section, you will learn how to test the previously created conditional access policies, as well as how to troubleshoot them.

Test conditional access policy to enforce Terms of Use (ToU)

The steps below show how to test a conditional access policy to enforce the Terms of Use (ToU) that you created earlier:

1. Sign in to the My Apps portal, *https://myapps.microsoft.com/*, with a user account that does not have a Global Administrator role assigned and has not read and accepted the Terms of Service (ToU).

2. Expand the **Terms of Use (ToU)**, and then select **Accept**, as shown in Figure 2-52. You must review the entire terms of use document by scrolling through it before you can accept it.

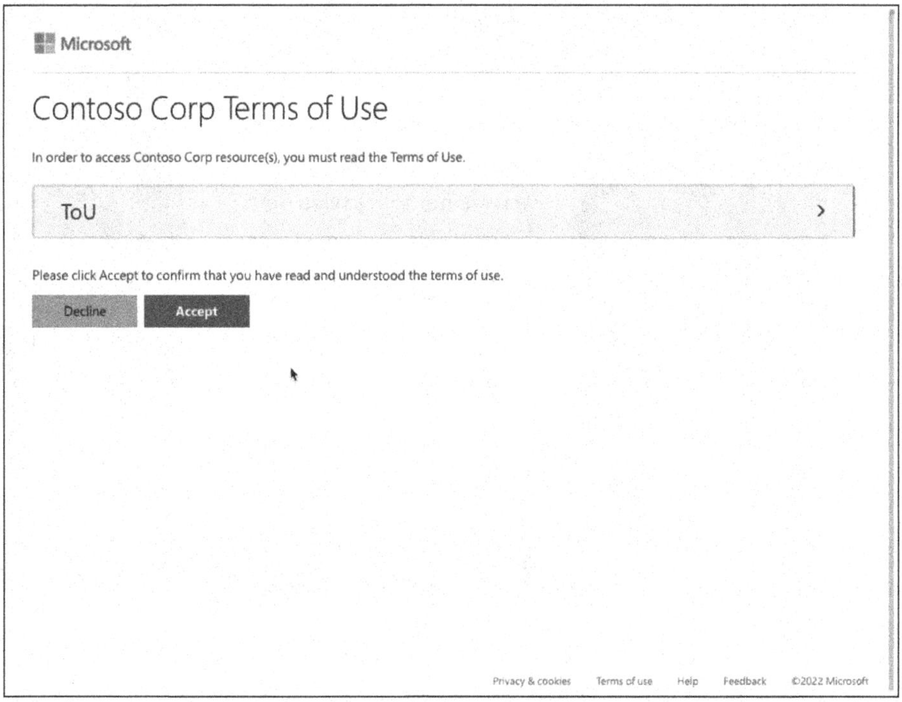

FIGURE 2-52 Terms of Use (ToU).

The sign-in process will complete, and the browser will redirect to My Apps Portal.

You have successfully tested the conditional access policy that enforces the Terms of Use (ToU) before the user can access the resource.

Test Enforce MFA using the sign-in risk signal with the conditional access policy

The Tor Browser (*https://www.torproject.org/*) is required to complete the steps below in order to simulate sign-in risk and test the conditional policy. If your organization prohibits the use of the Tor browser, you may need to install it on a virtual machine.

1. Launch the Tor browser.
2. Sign in to the Azure portal, *https://portal.azure.com*, with a user account that does not have a Global Administrator role assigned.

   Due to the high sign-in risk posed by the use of the anonymizer proxy Tor, user access will be blocked, and a message will display, as shown in Figure 2-53.

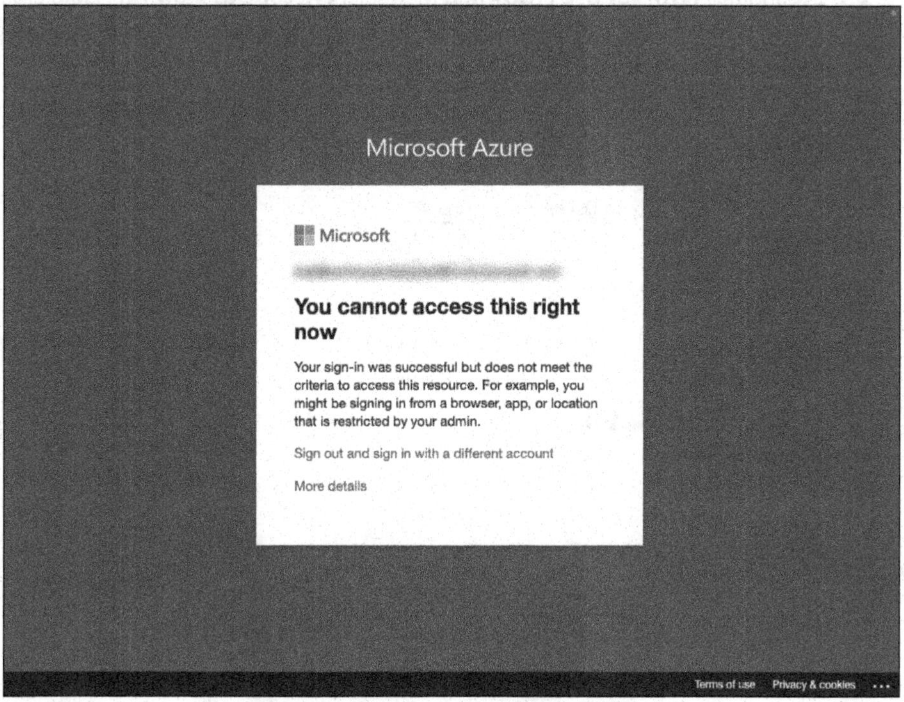

FIGURE 2-53 Sign-In blocked due to high risk.

Troubleshooting conditional access policy

When a conditional access policy is imposed, the user is given an explanation, as shown in Figure 2-53. This provides users with just enough information to understand why the policy is behaving as it does, but IT administrators may need more information to troubleshoot.

More information can be gathered to begin troubleshooting by expanding the More details option, as shown in Figure 2-54, which provides critical information useful for troubleshooting.

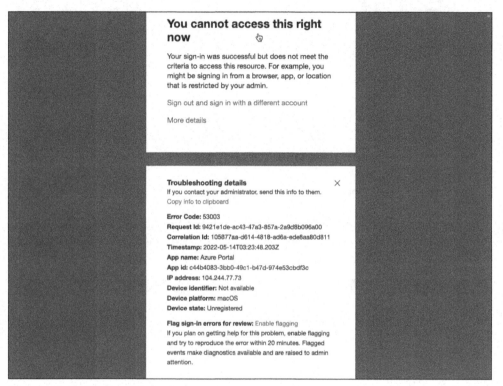

FIGURE 2-54 Troubleshooting details.

Administrators can further troubleshoot the issue by searching the Sign-In logs for Correlation ID, Timestamp, and other attributes available to them, as shown in Figure 2-54. To access the Sign-In logs and troubleshoot, follow these steps:

1. Sign in to the Azure portal, *https://portal.azure.com*, with a user account that has the Global Administrator role assigned to it or has the necessary permissions to view the Sign-In logs.

2. Navigate to the **Azure Active Directory** dashboard by using the Azure Active Directory option available in the sidebar of the Azure portal.

3. Select **Sign-In logs** located under the **Monitoring** section.

4. The Sign-In logs are displayed in chronological order, as shown in Figure 2-55. You can filter based on Correlation Id or other information.

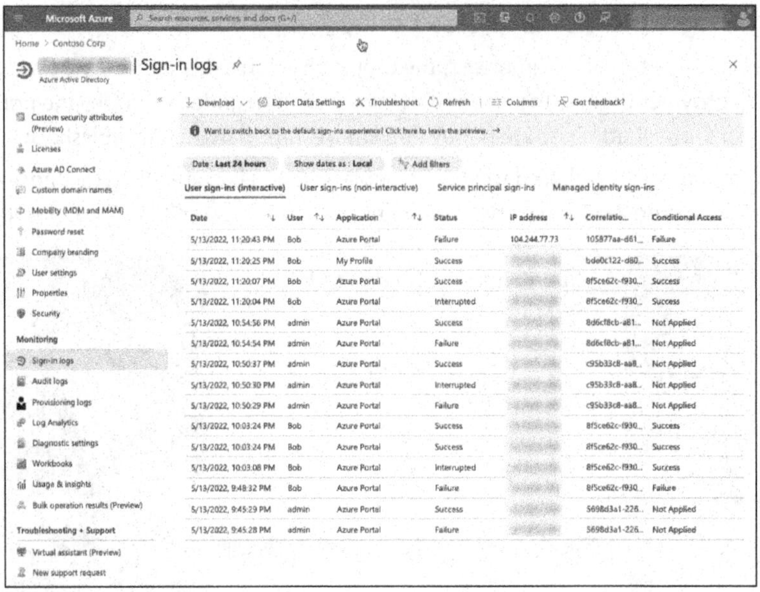

FIGURE 2-55 Sign-In logs.

5. Select the Sign-In log entry with Failure and matching Correlation ID from the information collected earlier. As shown in Figure 2-56, the Failure reason, Additional details, and Sign-In error code provide useful information for troubleshooting.

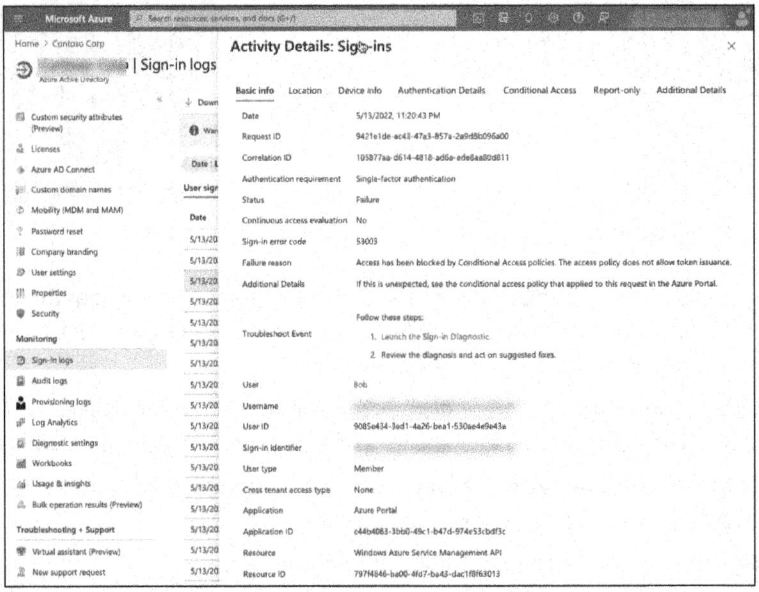

FIGURE 2-56 Activity Details for Sign-ins.

6. You may now close the browser.

Implement session management

Organizations frequently need to restrict sessions when dealing with scenarios involving corporate resources accessed from unmanaged or shared devices, as well as access to sensitive business data from external networks. To constrain the authentication session, administrators can use conditional access to create policies that target session management scenarios within organizations. Table 2–12 lists session management controls that an administrator can use to implement through conditional access policy to constrain the experiences within specified cloud applications.

TABLE 2-12   Azure AD session controls options for conditional access

Option	Description
Conditional access application control	The conditional access policy can be configured to use Conditional Access App Control to monitor and control user application access and sessions in real time based on access and session policies defined in Microsoft Defender for Cloud. More information on Conditional Access application control can be found at: *https://docs. microsoft.com/en-us/defender-cloud-apps/proxy-deployment-aad.*
Sign-in frequency	Sign-in frequency specifies how long a user must wait before being asked to sign in again when attempting to access a resource. Administrators can set a time limit (hours or days) or require reauthentication every time. Please note that the sign-in frequency setting is only applicable to apps that have implemented the OAUTH2 or OIDC protocols. More information on sign-in frequency can be found at *https://docs.microsoft.com/en-us/azure/active-directory/conditional-access/howto-conditional-access-session-lifetime#user-sign-in-frequency.*
Persistent browser session	Persistent browser session allows user to stay signed in after closing and reopening their browser. More information on Persistent browser session can be found at *https://docs.microsoft.com/en-us/ azure/active-directory/conditional-access/howto-conditional-access-session-lifetime#persistence-of-browsing-sessions.*
Customize continuous access evaluation	The customized continuous access evaluation configuration in the conditional access policy enables organizations to disable continuous access evaluation, which is enabled by default. More information on customizing continuous access evaluation can be found at *https://docs.microsoft.com/en-us/azure/active-directory/ conditional-access/concept-continuous-access-evaluation.*
Disable resilience defaults (Preview)	When the disable resilience defaults option is enabled, access to resources is disabled when existing sessions expire. More information on disable resilience defaults can be found at *https:// docs.microsoft.com/en-us/azure/active-directory/conditional-access/resilience-defaults.*

Implement device-enforcement restrictions

Conditional access policies can use the information returned from devices with Microsoft Intune installed to assess organization compliance requirements and grant or deny access to an organizational resource. For example, if access control is set to "Require device to be marked as compliant," the conditional access policy will use that compliance status to determine whether to grant or deny access to email and other organizational resources.

The steps below demonstrate how to create a conditional access policy that requires users to use an approved client app or an app protection policy when accessing corporate cloud apps from a personal device running iOS or Android.

1. Sign in to the Azure portal, *https://portal.azure.com*, using a Global Administrator account.

2. Navigate to the **Azure Active Directory** dashboard by using the Azure Active Directory option available in the sidebar of the Azure portal.

3. Select **Security** from the left side pane.

4. Select **Conditional Access** from the left side pane, as shown in Figure 2-46.

5. Click **+ New policy** and then select **Create new policy**.

6. On the **New conditional access** page, enter **CA-DeviceCompliancePolicy** for the Name.

7. Expand Users or workload identities and then set the following information options.

   - **What does this policy apply to:** Users and groups.
   - **Include:** All users.
   - **Exclude:** Select the Global administrator role from the Directory roles dropdown menu.

8. Expand **Cloud apps or actions** and then set the following information options.

   - **Select what this policy applies to:** Cloud apps
   - **Include:** All Cloud Apps

9. Expand **Conditions**, select **Device platforms**, and set the following information options:

   - Set **Configure** to **Yes**.
   - **Select the device platforms:**
     - **iOS**
     - **Android**
   - Press **Done** to save your choices.

10. Expand **Grant**, set the following information options, and then click **Select**.

    - **Grant access** and then select the checkboxes for **Require approved client app** and **Require app protection policy**.
    - **For multiple controls:** Require all the selected controls.

11. Set **Enable policy** to **On**.

12. Click Create.

Read more about device enforcement using conditional access at *https://learn.microsoft. com/en-us/mem/intune/protect/conditional-access-intune-common-ways-use#device-based- conditional-access*.

Implement continuous access evaluation

Continuous Access Evaluation (CAE) is an Azure AD feature that allows organizations to respond to policy violations or security issues in near real time. It allows the communication between the token issuer, which is Azure AD, and the relying party, which is the client application making the request for token issuance. This two-way conversation enables the relying party to detect changes in properties, such as network location, and notify the token issuer. It also allows the token issuer to notify the relying party to stop respecting tokens for a specific user due to account compromise, disablement, or other issues.

Continuous access evaluation automatically creates a conditional access policy when it is enabled. However, a conditional access policy can be customized to disable continuous access evaluation as needed. Read more about continuous access evaluation and conditional access at *https://learn.microsoft.com/en-us/azure/active-directory/conditional-access/concept-conditional-access-session#customize-continuous-access-evaluation.*

Create a conditional access policy from a template

Conditional access policy templates are intended to make it easier for administrators to implement new policies that adhere to Microsoft security recommendations. These templates are intended to provide maximum protection while adhering to commonly used policies across a wide range of customer types and locations.

Follow the steps below to create a conditional access policy from a template that will enforce multifactor authentication for admins.

1. Sign in to the Azure portal, *https://portal.azure.com*, using a Global Administrator account.
2. Navigate to the Azure Active Directory dashboard by using the Azure Active Directory option available in the sidebar of the Azure portal.
3. Select **Security** from the left side pane.
4. Select **Conditional Access** from the left side pane, as shown in Figure 2-46.
5. Click + **New policy from template (preview)**.
6. Select **Identities** from template category and press the **Next** button.
7. Select **Require multifactor authentication for admins** and press the **Next** button.
8. Press the **Create Policy** button.

Skill 2.4: Manage Azure AD Identity Protection

Azure AD Identity Protection (AADIP) is the crown jewel in Microsoft's Identity Security offering and can be fully leveraged with an Azure AD P2 license (or equivalent). Microsoft analyzes 6.5 trillion signals per day from internal and partner sources to identify and protect customers from threats. Identity Protection signals can be fed into tools like Conditional Access to make access decisions, or they can be fed back to a security information and event management (SIEM) tool for further investigation based on organization's needs.

> **This skill covers how to:**
> - Implement and manage a user risk policy
> - Implement and manage sign-in risk policy
> - Implement and manage MFA registration policy
> - Monitor, investigate, and remediate elevated risky users
> - Implement security for workload identities

Implement and manage a user risk policy

Identity Protection can evaluate what it recognizes to be usual behavior for a user and use that knowledge to form risk calculations. Calculation of the likelihood that an identity has been compromised is known as user risk. Users can self-remediate if a risk is discovered by executing a self-service password reset and dismissing the user risk event to avoid causing unnecessary noise for administrators.

EXAM TIP

Azure AD Identity Protection as a feature and service is already deployed in your tenant, irrespective of your licensing status, and has been detecting risk since the inception of the tenant. Risk remediation involves configuration of risk policies (user/sign-in/workload) or performing manual remediation (UX/API).

Licensing requirements

Microsoft offers two flavors of premium licensing: P1 and P2. Aside from any additional licensing for workload identities, the Identity Protection feature set is divided up across these license options, as shown in Figure 2-57.

CAPABILITY	DETAILS	AZURE AD FREE/ MICROSOFT 365 APPS	AZURE AD PREMIUM P1	AZURE AD PREMIUM P2
Risk policies	User risk policy (via Identity Protection)	No	No	Yes
Risk policies	Sign-in risk policy (via Identity Protection or Conditional Access)	No	No	Yes
Security reports	Overview	No	No	Yes
Security reports	Risky users	Limited Information. Only users with medium and high risk are shown. No details drawer or risk history.	Limited Information. Only users with medium and high risk are shown. No details drawer or risk history.	Full access
Security reports	Risky sign-ins	Limited Information. No risk detail or risk level is shown.	Limited Information. No risk detail or risk level is shown.	Full access
Security reports	Risk detections	No	Limited Information. No details drawer.	Full access
Notifications	Users at risk detected alerts	No	No	Yes
Notifications	Weekly digest	No	No	Yes
	MFA registration policy	No	No	Yes

FIGURE 2-57 AADIP Licensing details.

As shown in Figure 2-57, P2 licensing contains all the bells and whistles, including:

- The ability to remediate risk by end-users through risk remediation policies.
- The ability to monitor risk and view details of the risk detected and remediated.
- Stream into your existing framework, Security Information and Event Management (SIEM), for threat and incident response by using Microsoft's extensible Graph APIs.

Throughout this skill, we will assume P2 licensing on the tenant to understand the full depth of concepts and capabilities.

Prerequisites

Configuring Identity Protection requires the administrator to assume one of the following roles depending on the action needed to be taken within the Identity Protection blade:

- Global Administrator—giving them complete access to AADIP
- Security Administrator—allowing them everything a global administrator (GA) can do except reset a user's password
- Security Operator—allowing access to Identity Protection reports and alerts
- Security Reader—allowing access to Identity Protection reports and read-only access to alerts configuration

Configure user risk security policy

Azure AD Identity Protection offers native options to remediate risk within the Identity Protection blade. These are called Security Policies (also called IPC policies, where IPC stands for Identity Protection Center), and these are great for enabling end user risk remediation quickly and easily in your tenant.

To configure a user risk security policy:

1. Browse to **portal.azure.com** > **sign-in** > **Azure Active Directory** > **Security** > **Conditional Access** > **New policy**.

2. Choose a **user/group** to be included in the policy, as shown in Figure 2-58.

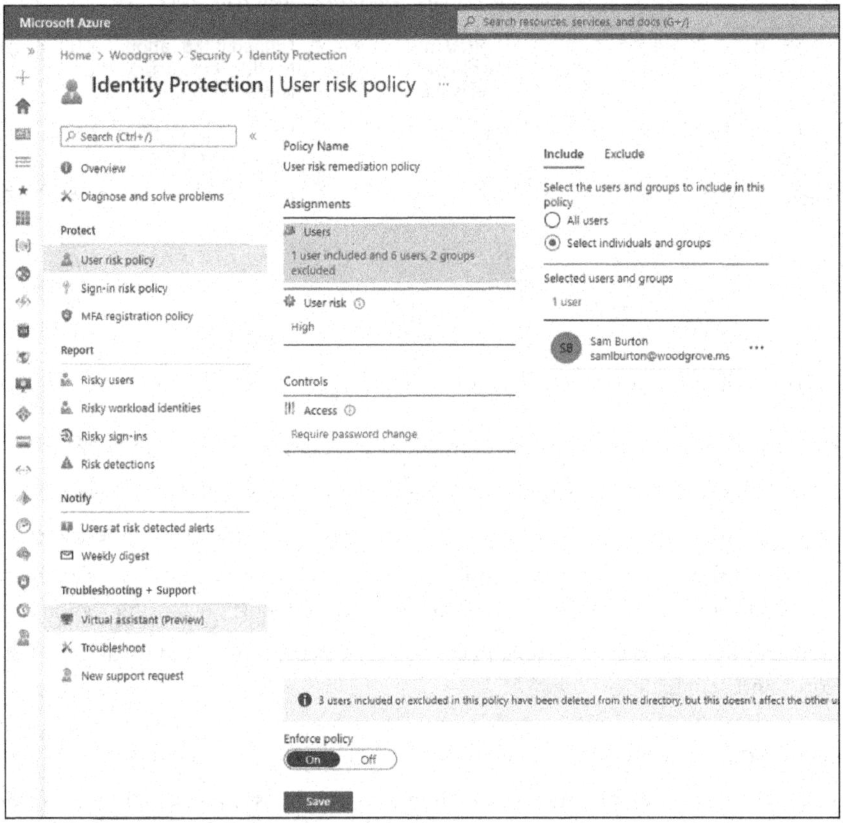

FIGURE 2-58 User risk security policy.

3. Select the **risk levels** that you'd like to trigger end-user risk remediation for. Microsoft recommends setting up the policy for **High** user risk to have a good balance between security and productivity. Setting up a policy for all levels of risk might trigger too many requests to change the password, leading to more predictable and less random passwords.

4. You can set the Grant Control to either **Block** or **Allow access requiring MFA**.

5. Remember to select **Enforce policy** before selecting **Save**.

   As you can see, security policies don't give us options to apply remediation with any sort of useful granular control. Therefore, risk remediation via Conditional Access was developed.

Configure risk-based conditional access user risk policy

The advantage of configuring risk-based conditional access policies is the granular control it offers in both Condition Control as well as Grant Control. You can also combine Session Controls with the Grant Controls. You may create multiple policies for each sign-in risk and/or user risk, for different risk levels and scoping different users, applications, locations, etc. If multiple sign-in risk policies conflict with each other, the most stringent action will be taken from among the two Condition Controls.

To configure a user risk remediation conditional access policy:

1. Browse to **portal.azure.com** > **sign-in** > **Azure Active Directory** > **Security** > **Conditional Access** > **New policy**.
2. Choose a **user/group** to be included in the policy.
3. For user risk remediation CA policies, it is recommended to choose **All cloud apps** as the applications you want access to be monitored for risk remediation.
4. Under **Conditions**, shift the **Configure** slider to **Yes** and choose **User risk**. Then choose the levels of risk to be targeted for end-user remediation. Microsoft recommends setting the policy for **High** user risk.
5. You can combine multiple condition controls (except sign-in risk) with the user risk condition control to lend granularity to your risk remediation scope.
6. You can get creative with your **Grant Controls** by combining them. For example, as shown in Figure 2-59, you can see how user risk can be remediated in combination with forcing another action on the user: The default grant control that must be chosen is **Require Password Change**. This is the *only* grant control that remediates risk on a user. Here, you will see a note that says that this grant action is allowed when policy is assigned to **All cloud apps**, which is why user risk policies are recommended to be applied to all cloud apps, above.

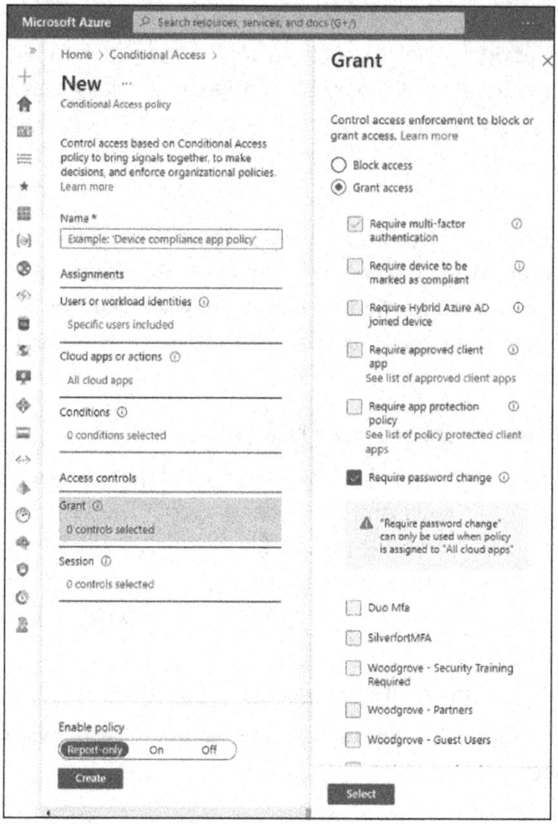

FIGURE 2-59 CA user risk policy.

7. Press **Select**.
8. Finally, Press **Create**.

EXAM TIP

It is not recommended to have both security policies as well as conditional access risk policies enabled simultaneously for risk remediation. This causes conflicts, results in unpredictable outcomes, and is generally a recipe for troubleshooting nightmares for your ID-SOC team.

Implement and manage sign-in risk policy

Sign-in risk is remediable provided it is real-time sign-in risk with MFA. All other sign-in risk detections are offline, accrued after the sign-in takes place and therefore contribute to user risk. A sign-in risk remediation policy therefore cannot, post-hoc, remediate risk accrued after the sign-in takes place. User risk CA policies therefore help with the mitigation of accrued offline sign-in risk.

Configure sign-in risk security policy

To create a sign-in risk security policy:

1. Browse to **portal.azure.com** > **sign-in** > **Azure Active Directory** > **Security** > **Identity Protection**.

2. Select **Sign-in risk policy**, as shown in Figure 2-60.

3. Choose a **user/group** to be included in the policy.

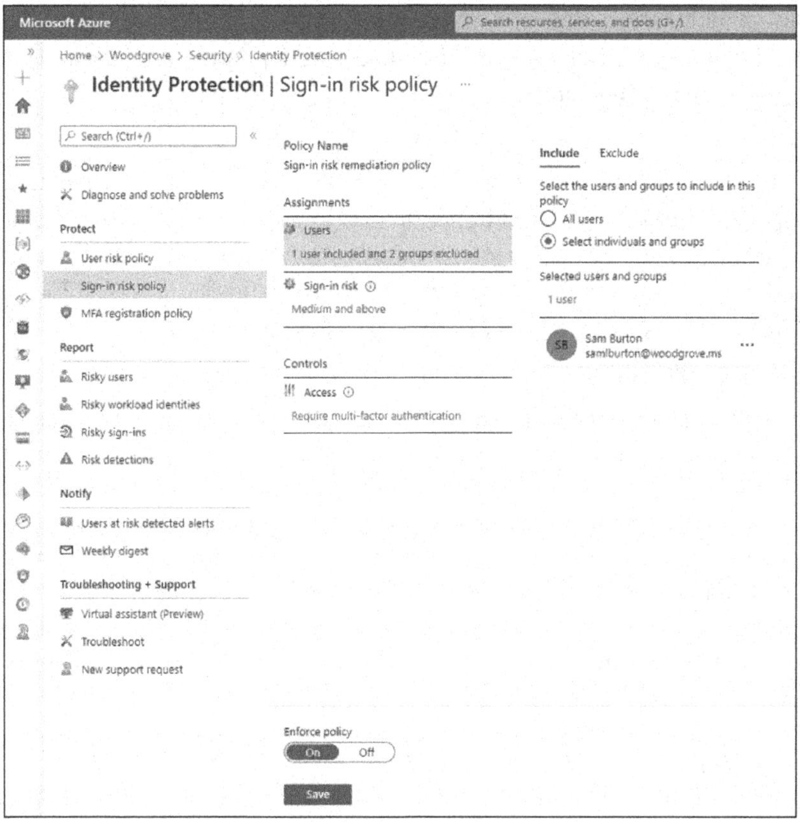

FIGURE 2-60 Sign-in risk security policy.

4. Select the risk levels that you'd like to trigger end-user risk remediation for. Microsoft recommends setting the policy for **Medium** and **High** sign-in risk to have a good balance between security and productivity. Setting up a policy for all levels of risk might trigger MFA fatigue or accidental approvals.

5. You can set the Grant Control to either **Block** or **Allow access requiring MFA**.

6. Remember to select **Enforce policy** before selecting **Save**.

EXAM TIP

It is good practice to exclude your break-glass accounts/groups from risk-based policy. Ideally, your break-glass accounts should have Grant Control set to Block access to all resources except management portals such as the Azure portal.

Sign-in risk CA policy

To configure a sign-in risk conditional access policy:

1. Browse to **portal.azure.com** > **sign-in** > **Azure Active Directory** > **Security** > **Conditional Access** > **New policy**.
2. Choose a **user/group** to be included in the policy.
3. Choose the applications you want access to be monitored for risk remediation.
4. Under **Conditions**, shift the **Configure** slider to **Yes** and choose **Sign-in risk**. Then choose the levels of risk to be targeted for end-user remediation. Microsoft recommends setting up the policy for **Medium** and **High** sign-in risk.
5. Set the **Grant access** to **Require multi-factor authentication**.
6. Finally, select **Create**.

Note the following regarding choosing custom controls as a grant control with risk-based conditional access. Although this can be chosen as a grant control action, this does not remediate risk on the sign-in. If a sign-in risk based conditional access policy is configured with custom controls as a grant option, the end-user will be prompted for the relevant custom control when attempting a risky sign-in, and if the control challenge, multifactor authentication (MFA), is satisfied, the end user will be granted access but the risk on the sign-in will not have been mitigated. The reason is because custom controls as designed today don't apply an MFA claim on the issued refresh token. All it does is provide a binary signal of Satisfied/Not Satisfied to the conditional access engine. Since there is no MFA claim issued on the refresh token, Identity Protection does *not* recognize it as a valid remediation action. Also, a third-party IdP (Identity Provider) federated with Azure AD will issue an MFA claim (if the third-party IdP is configured to do MFA) on the token it issues to Azure AD. Therefore, in such a case, Identity Protection respects the completed MFA and remediates risk provided that conditional access policy is set with grant control and requires MFA where MFA is completed through the federated IdP.

AADIP and B2B

The Azure AD ecosystem classifies B2B users into many types:

- An Azure AD B2B user is defined as an identity using their organizational credentials in one Azure AD tenant to access resources in another Azure AD tenant.
- There are B2B users using Microsoft (MSA) personal accounts like Hotmail, Outlook, etc.
- There may also be B2B users hosted in non-Azure AD/vendor tenants.

- There is the scenario where B2B users are homed in non-Microsoft personal accounts from popular vendors like Gmail, Yahoo!, etc.
- And finally, there are accounts hosted on third-party on-premises identity systems.

There are a couple of principles to note when considering protection of B2B users using risk remediation policies:

- Identity Protection is officially supported for Azure AD B2B users only.
- Sign-in risk for an Azure AD B2B user is considered a property native to the resource tenant that the B2B user is attempting to access.
- User risk for an Azure AD B2B user is considered a property of the user, and hence native to the home tenant that the B2B user belongs to.

This brings about curious behaviors that one must keep in mind when deploying risk remediation policies for Azure AD B2B guest users:

- If an Azure AD B2B guest user develops sign-in risk while accessing a resource not in the home tenant, they will be prompted for MFA in the resource tenant and will be able to remediate risk through authentication methods registered either in the home tenant or in the resource tenant.
- The risky sign-in is visible in the home tenant as well as the guest tenant.

Implement and manage MFA registration policy

Using MFA reduces the adversarial attack surface on identities. Microsoft's MFA registration policy makes it simple for you to enroll your users in MFA. You can also gradually introduce it to your users by grouping them and configuring the group in the MFA registration policy. Scoped users will have a 14-day registration period that begins when they sign in interactively the next time. Users can continue to postpone registration for 14 days. The user must complete MFA registration at the end of the 14-day period before they can complete their sign-in process.

Configuration steps

Configuration can be a bit confusing, since Azure Active Directory has a separate MFA blade under Security. But the MFA registration policy is actually available for configuration in the Identity Protection blade.

1. Browse to **portal.azure.com** > **sign-in** > **Azure Active Directory** > **Security** > **Identity Protection** > **MFA registration policy**.

2. Choose the **users and groups** to be scoped for MFA registration. You can also set exclusions by user or group.

3. You have one compulsory control checkbox: **Require Azure AD MFA registration**.

    - Slide the **Enforce policy** slider to **On**.
    - Select **Save**.

Deployment considerations

Some deployment considerations to note:

- The MFA registration policy is a P2 offering.
- This feature is different from what is offered under **portal.azure.com** > **sign-in** > **Azure Active Directory** > **Authentication Methods** > **Registration Campaign**, popularly known as the "Nudge" feature. The registration campaign "nudges" a user without a deadline to onboard to a stronger authentication method, like the Authenticator app. This is therefore a feature complementary to the MFA registration policy.
- The registration campaign offering is a P1 offering.

Monitor, investigate, and remediate elevated risky users

The true value of Identity Protection is gleaned from the thorough understanding of how risk is presented against users, sign-ins, and workload identities in a tenant. These are available through UX tools like the Risk Reports, via API, and also through streaming data options to your SIEM (Security Information and Event Management) tool of choice.

Understanding risk reports

Identity Protection offers three reports for three entity-level triage views of risk seen on the tenant:

- Risky Users report
- Risky Sign-ins report
- Risky Detections report

Each of these reports can be viewed in the **Azure** portal by browsing to **Azure Active Directory** > **Security** > **Identity Protection**. The report allows for data export via CSV/JSON format. General functions like searching/sorting by any column is available as standard. By default, the risk reports are filtered (to optimize page load times). Be sure to remove all filters depending on the needs of your investigation.

EXAM TIP

The risk reports have different log-rotation periods. The Risky Users report tracks risky users since the beginning of time (from the perspective of tenant inception). The Risky Sign-in report tracks with the log rotation period of the sign-in logs (30 days). The Risk Detections report has a log-rotation period of 90 days.

Risky Users report

The Risky Users report is a table of all the risky users in your tenant. By default, it is filtered for all active users that are risky. Look at the various options the report offers for triaging risky users, as shown in Figure 2-61.

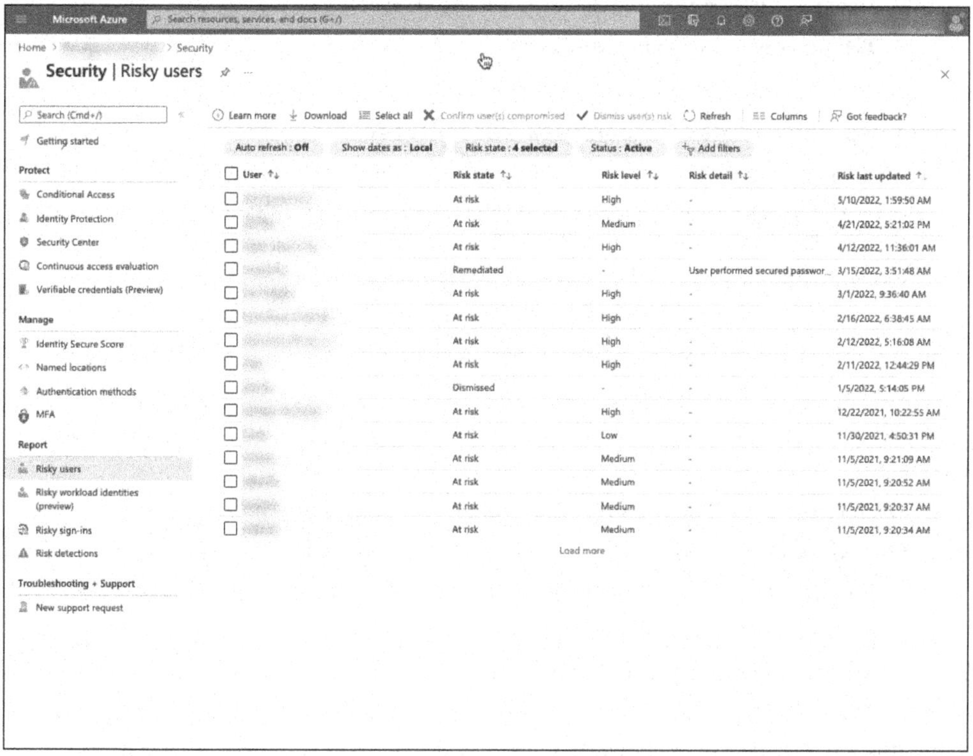

FIGURE 2-61 The Risky Users report.

- **Risk State:** This depicts the current risk state of the user. It can take the following values:
  - **At Risk** (determined to be still risky)
  - **Confirm Compromised** (a special type of "at risk" state to denote that the administrator determined the user risky)
  - **Remediated** (determined to be no longer at risk, remedied by end user secure password change)
  - **Dismissed** (a special type of "no longer at risk" state, where the user is determined by the admin to be not risky)

- **Risk Level:** This depicts the risk level calculation by AADIP at the time when the risk was last updated. This can take the values High, Medium, Low, or None.

- **Risk Detail:** This offers more information about the transition of Risk States from the first Risk Level determined. It can take the following values:
  - **User performed secure password change/reset**
  - **Admin confirmed compromised**
  - **Admin dismissed all risk for user**
  - **Admin generated temporary password for user**

- **Risk last updated:** This is a key value to check when trying to understand why a user is risky. You might look into a user's associated sign-ins or risk detections to understand the contributions of risk to that user. In case you find nothing in either, then this field becomes useful, for if the date/timestamp is greater than 90 days from its log-rotation, that is the reason for not seeing any risk detections associated with the risky user.

- **Risk processing state:** This is useful when admin actions (such as Confirm Compromised/Dismissal) are taken.

In the User Details pane, as shown in Figure 2-62, additional triage and investigation options are offered:

- **User's risky sign-ins:** Takes you to a filtered view of the Risky Sign-ins report.

- **User's risk detections:** Takes you to a filtered view of the Risk Detection report.

- **Reset password:** Allows the admin to reset the user's password to a temporary string (a useful option for help desk staff, especially when a Block risky user policy is configured).

- **Confirm user compromised/Dismiss user risk:** Options to manually control the risk state of a user.

- **Block user:** Disables access for the user.

- **Investigate with Azure ATP:** This is a useful option for users that have accrued risk from detections that are non-native detections. Today, it takes you to the Microsoft Defender for Cloud portal, but as new detections from other products in the Microsoft Suite are surfaced/integrated, that link will change to a redirection to the Microsoft 365 Defender portal, where you can investigate the scenario in depth.

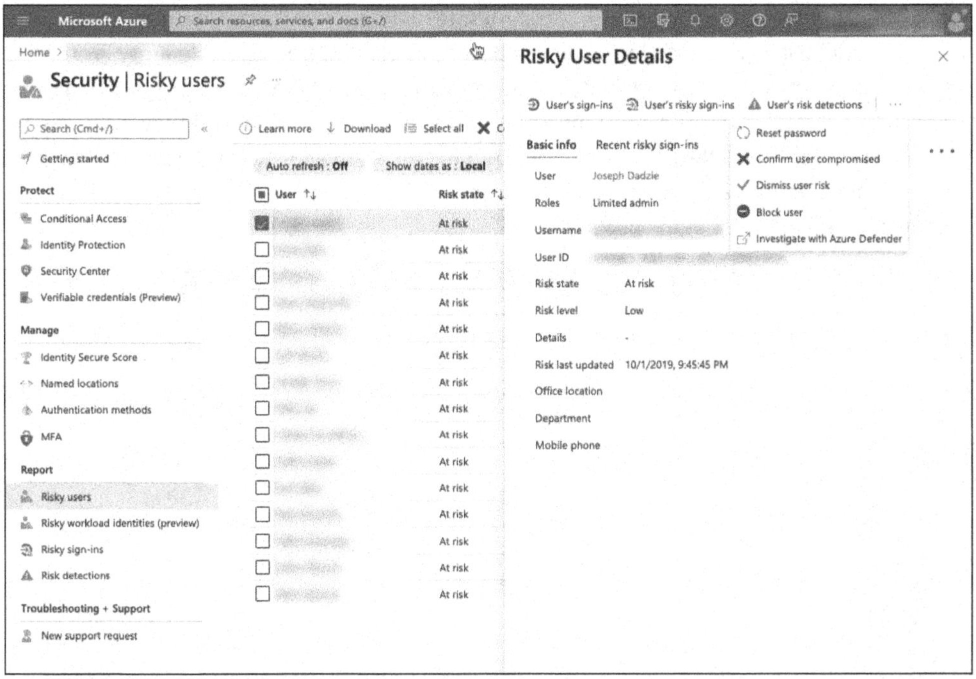

FIGURE 2-62 Risky Users Details.

> ***EXAM TIP***
>
> **The Block User option works reliably for cloud identities only! For federated or synchronized identities, this action will be overridden by Azure AD Connect, which enforces the on-premises directory as the source of authority.**

Risky Sign-ins report

The Risky Sign-ins report, as shown in Figure 2-63, is a table of all the risky sign-ins occurring in your tenant. By default, it is filtered for all unremedied sign-ins.

Pay attention to the following:

- **Configure Trusted IPs:** In triaging risky sign-ins, one may often find risk attributed to legitimate sign-ins from known IP addresses. In such a case, this option can be used to configure all the trusted IPs for the environment. Identity Protection ignores risk calculations for sign-ins sourced from trusted IPs.
- **Risk level (real-time):** Reports the real-time risk calculated against the sign-in.
- **Risk level (aggregate):** Reports the cumulative risk (real-time and offline) incurred against the sign-in.
- **Confirm sign-in compromised/Confirm sign-in safe:** Like the options for risky users, these admin actions also elevate/nullify the risk score associated to the sign-in.

Neither "Confirm compromise" nor "Confirm safe" actions "familiarize" features for a sign-in or user today. So if you have a block policy and a user is blocked because of Identity Protection calling out risk due to unfamiliarity in the conditions around the sign-in, simply confirming the sign-in to be safe will not resolve the issue for the user. In all likelihood, if they log in from the same location again, they might be called out for risky behavior again. Microsoft always recommends setting grant controls such as "Require MFA" or "secure password change" for sign-in and user risk policies, respectively.

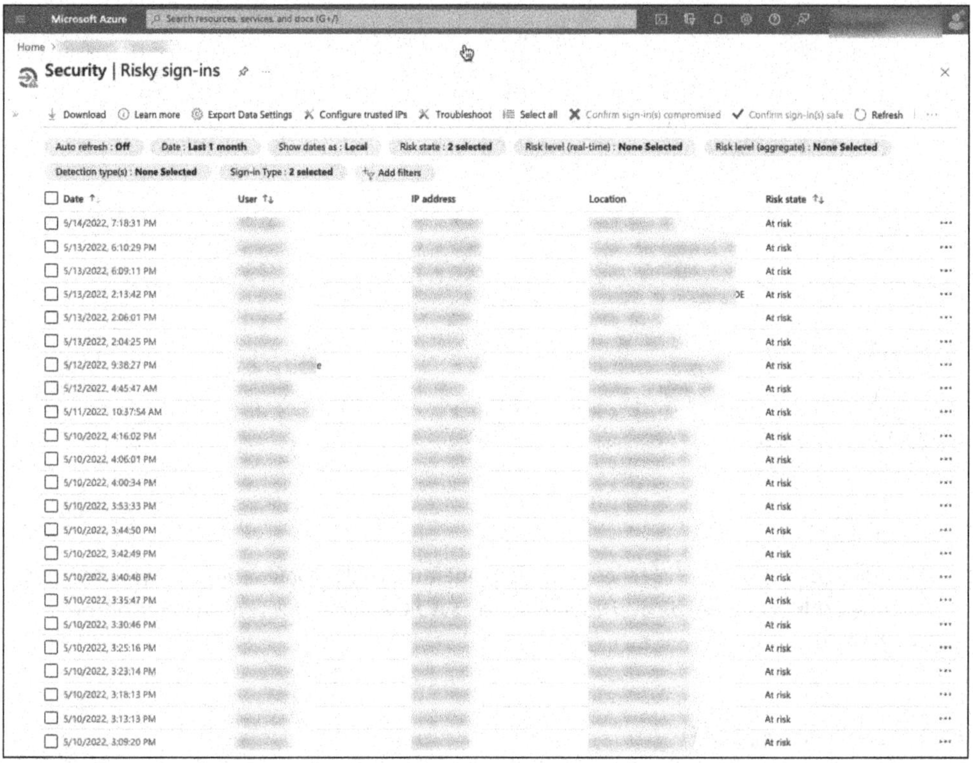

FIGURE 2-63 Risky sign-ins.

You can select an entry from the report to bring up the Risky Sign-in Details pane, as shown in Figure 2-64, which contains more information, including:

- **Sign-in time:** Records the timestamp of the sign-in.
- **Time detected:** Records the timestamp when Identity Protection first deemed the sign-in risky.
- **Detection last updated:** Records the timestamp when the last end-user, AI, or admin action was taken on the sign-in.

When looking at the activity of a user at risk—be it their account risk or session (sign-in) risk—it is important to look at the entirety of their activity. Identity Protection does not just protect user activity during *interactive* sign-ins but also monitors and evaluates risk for *non-interactive* sign-ins as well. These sign-in types can be sorted through a filter available in the Risky Sign-ins report. Thus, while you might find a user to be risky with no associated sign-ins, it is possible that their silent non-interactive sign-ins are contributing to aggregate/account risk. Non-interactive user sign-ins are those performed on a user's behalf by a client application or a background service. These sign-ins, unlike interactive user sign-ins, do not require the user to provide an authentication factor. Instead, a token or code is used by the device or client app to authenticate or access a resource on behalf of the user.

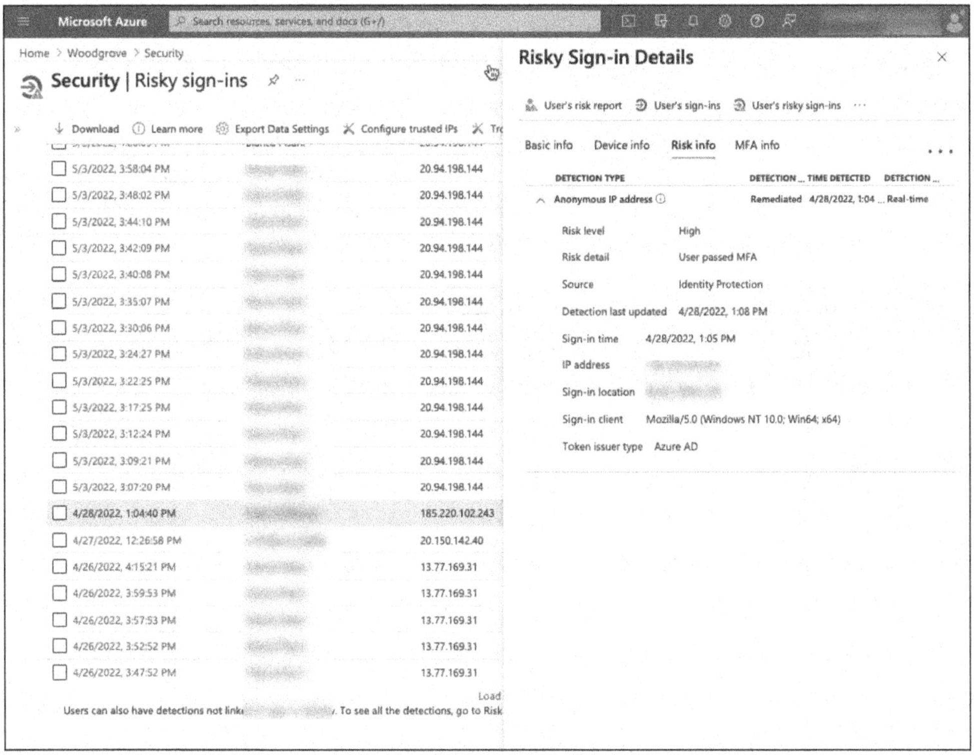

FIGURE 2-64 Risky Sign-ins Details.

EXAM TIP

The sign-in risk's time detected and detection last updated times are very useful in troubleshooting what occurred on a sign-in. Microsoft publishes offline detections within 48 hours of a sign-in. These times can be used to validate that you indeed see this in your tenant. In other instances, these times can help you draw a timeline between sign-in, in-app activity, remediation attempts, any AI (offline risk engine)-based activity and admin actions on a sign-in and its associated detection(s).

Risk Detections report

The Risk Detections report, as shown in Figure 2-65, is a table of all the risky detections in your tenant. Risk detections form the basis of all risk incurred on users and sign-ins in the tenant. One or more risk detections may be associated to a particular sign-in or user. By default, it is filtered for all active detections.

When thinking about risk reporting for B2B users, there are a couple of things to note:

- If an Azure AD B2B guest user develops or possesses risk and attempts to access a resource in the non-home tenant, and if the user is covered by a user risk policy and is subsequently blocked (per the above!), this phenomenon is not visible in the resource tenant risky user reports.

- Administrators cannot dismiss risk for Azure AD B2B guest users in the resource tenant.

Identity Protection has recently improved the signal-to-noise ratio (SNR) for low-risk risky sign-ins. The detection systems now run both in real-time and offline (post authentication) to understand whether sign-ins and users are compromised. The offline machine learning model scores sign-ins with different features and algorithms to determine whether a sign-in was compromised. The output of this offline model is the aggregate sign-in risk level, which represents the most recent evaluation of whether that sign-in was compromised.

> **NEED MORE REVIEW? HOW RISK DETECTIONS WORKS**
>
> Read more about Azure AD Risk Detections at: *https://docs.microsoft.com/en-us/azure/active-directory/identity-protection/concept-identity-protection-risks.*

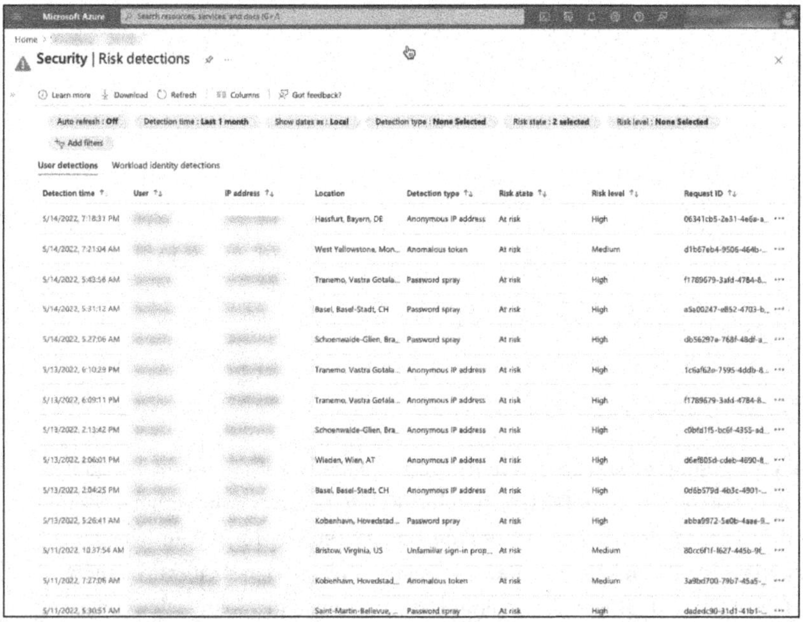

FIGURE 2-65 Risky detections.

Risk remediation considerations

Remediation involves reversing the contribution of risk to the entity's risk score. Remediation can be performed on a sign-in or a user. When a risky sign-in is remediated, all contribution to the sign-in risk score, by the associated risk detections to that sign-in, is reversed. When a risky user is remediated, all contribution to the user risk score, by the associated risk detections to that user, contributing either directly or indirectly (via aggregate risk), is reversed.

When a user, workload, or a user's sign-in is deemed to be at risk, it needs to be alleviated to ensure that a certain level of security is maintained in your tenant. Risk indicates the possibility of compromise. To mitigate that risk, an administrator may either manually remediate user/sign-in risk or choose to utilize end-user remediation options by configuring a risk remediation conditional access policy. Risks on workload identities don't support remediation methods today, and the only action allowed upon detecting risk is "Block."

The advantage of using end-user remediation via policies is that the remediation signal is fed back into Identity Protection to improve the precision of the risk determination in your tenant. This results in:

- Helping achieve balance between security and productivity
- Reduced time-to-response (TTR) toward risk detected, since this responsibility is passed on to the end-user
- Reduces help desk/Identity admin overhead by reducing the volume of risk data to be triaged manually

There are two types of risk remediation methods supported today:

- Sign-in risk remediation via MFA
- User risk remediation via a secure password change

Identity Protection offers two independent methods to remediate risk via policy:

- Identity Protection Security Policies
- Risk-based Conditional Access Policies

If conditional access allows the triggering of MFA for each interactive logon, and intelligently too with Session Management, Reauthentication, and Continuous Access Evaluation (CAE) controls, what is the use of MFA triggered through risk detection?

First, always-on MFA can introduce MFA fatigue. It increases the likelihood of a user inadvertently approving an MFA request. This can offer the attacker an opportunity to obtain a token with an MFA claim, who might, if smart enough, register their own MFA credential against the compromised identity to gain persistence.

Second, there are many detections in the detection suite that don't just protect sign-in at authentication but also learn from behavior throughout a user's journey accessing resources and utilizing endpoints. Detections can determine abnormal behavior through this information, like suspicious email behavior can trigger risk within Identity Protection.

Third, Identity Protection offers its various risk detection protections not just for interactive sign-in scenarios but for non-interactive sign-ins as well. This means that risk is determined each time a new Access Token/Refresh Token pair is issued. Therefore, a user's SSO experience is protected by Identity Protection silently. Thus, Identity Protection offers an important layer of protection in an MFA-protected environment where it intelligently monitors login and resource access activity to trigger in-line asynchronous authentication verification from the end-user to protect access to resources.

Identity Protection notifications

AADIP sends two types of automated notification emails to help you manage user risk and risk detections:

- **Users at risk detected email**—To enable immediate investigation of users at risk
- **Weekly digest email**—Offering a summary of new risky users and real-time risky sign-ins detected over the last calendar week

To configure the Users at Risk email in the **Azure portal**, browse to **Azure Active Directory** > **Security** > **Identity Protection** > **Users at risk detected alerts**.

To configure the weekly digest email for recipients in your tenant, in the **Azure portal**, browse to **Azure Active Directory** > **Security** > **Identity Protection** > **Weekly digest**.

There are two corner case scenarios related to notifications:

- The corner case scenarios with User at Risk email notifications: To prevent a barrage of emails, only one email is sent over risk detected in a 5-second period. Also, if risk is detected for an older sign-in (offline risk) and an email has already been sent for a more recent sign-in, then email notifications are throttled for the older sign-in. Finally, if end-user remediation via policies is deployed, it is quite possible that a user remediates their risk state before you address the email notification sent to alert their risk state.

- The corner case scenarios with Weekly Digest email notifications: Users in the Global Administrator, Security Administrator, or Security Reader roles are automatically en-rolled to receive the weekly digest emails. An attempt is made to send it to the first 20 members in each role. Only users who hold one of the above roles at the time the email is sent can receive the email. Those eligible for the role but who are not elevated into it at the time the email is sent won't receive the email.

EXAMP TIP

AADIP currently doesn't support sending emails to group-assigned roles.

SIEM Integrations

An essential part to managing identity security at scale is the ability to spool authentication and threat events to a SIEM to aid incident response, threat hunting, and troubleshooting. AADIP generates the following kinds of logs:

- User Risk Events (User risk detections)
- Risk information in sign-ins
- Risky users
- Audit data
- Risky Service Principals
- Service Principal Risk Events

Exporting risk data

Using this method, organizations can choose to store Identity Protection-related risk data for longer periods than the default retention period in Azure AD. To do so, on the **Azure portal**, simply browse to **Azure Active Directory** > **Diagnostic settings** > **Edit setting**, as shown in Figure 2-66, and select between archiving data to a storage account, streaming it to an event hub, or making it available to Log Analytics or a partner solution.

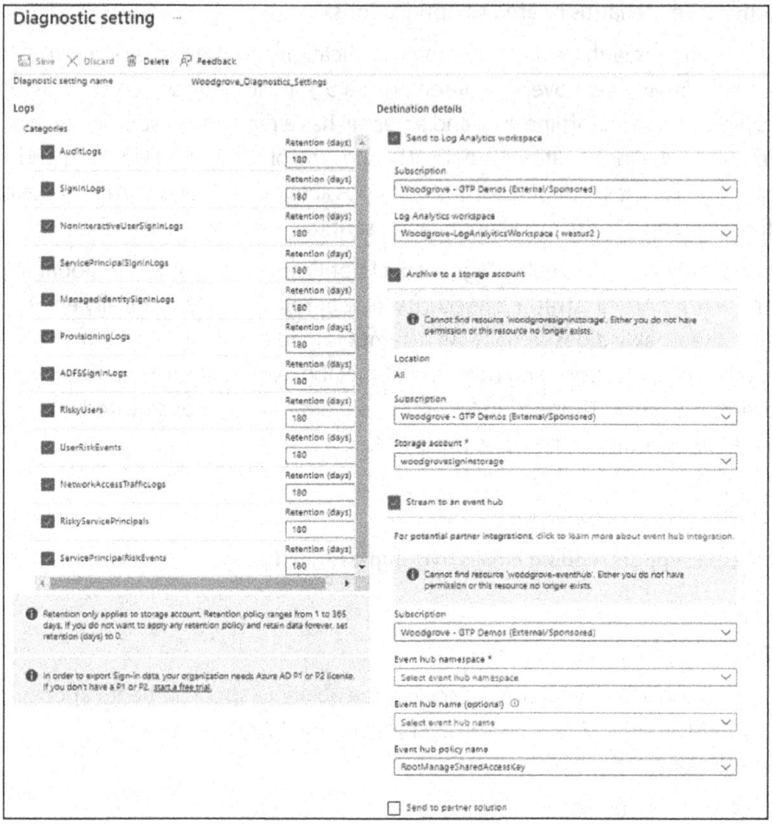

FIGURE 2-66 Diagnostic settings.

Microsoft's own version of cold storage would be to stream data into a storage account. However, if you want to make the data available for use within the Microsoft ecosystem, you could choose to stream it to Event Hub. Event Hub supports first- and third-party (non-Microsoft) connectors that allow integration of third-party SIEMs to pull the data off Event Hub. You could also make the data available in Log Analytics to write threat-hunting queries on a sample set of data on-the-fly. Finally, Microsoft supports direct integration with some partner vendor solutions such as Apache Kafka, Datadog, ElasticDB, and Logz.io.

> **NEED MORE REVIEW?   INTEGRATE AZURE AD LOGS WITH AZURE MONITOR LOGS**
>
> Read more about integrating Azure AD logs with Azure Monitor at:
> *https://docs.microsoft.com/en-us/azure/active-directory/reports-monitoring/*
> *howto-integrate-activity-logs-with-log-analytics*

Implement security for workload identities

Just as with risk-based policies for user principals, Microsoft now offers risk detections and remediation options for workload identities as well! For licensing considerations for workload identities, always refer to the licensing requirements detailed at *https://docs.microsoft.com/en-us/azure/active-directory/identity-protection/overview-identity-protection#license-requirements*. Currently, an active P2 license in the tenant can help secure workload identities with Identity Protection. However, when this feature is more generally available, additional licensing may be required.

A workload identity can be any application, service principal, or managed identity that attempts access to resources without human intervention. Workload identities need to be separated from user identities because their native characteristics differ from user identities. For example, a workload identity cannot perform multifactor authentication based on biometric proofs. Their credentials require security provisions whose requirements are very different from the security provisions of user credential methods. Something you know—a password or the storage of a memorized secret—is typically not the responsibility of an identity provider, but this is not so for workload identities. They are typically also privileged with permissions that are not normally or liberally assigned to user identities requiring greater monitoring and review.

Configure risk-based Conditional Access policy for workload identities

Today, Conditional Access for workload identities offers only "Block" as a grant control. Therefore, Conditional Access offers mitigation of risk rather than remediation (at the time of writing this book), but it is expected that there will be automatic remediation options in the future. To create a Workload Identity risk policy in Conditional Access:

1. Browse to **portal.azure.com** > **sign-in** > **Azure Active Directory** > **Security** > **Conditional Access** > **New policy**.

2. Choose a workload identity to be included in the policy. Here, although Microsoft regresses to an older term (viz., service principal), this is only because, as part of public preview, only single-tenant service principals are in scope—i.e., third-party SaaS applications and multi-tenanted applications that you may have published, as well as Managed Identities, are out of scope for now!

3. Under **Cloud apps or actions**, choose **All cloud apps**.

4. Under **Conditions**, for **Service principal risk (preview)**, shift the **Configure** slider to **Yes** and choose **Service principal risk**. Then choose the levels of risk to be targeted for end-user remediation. Here, you can also combine this with a location condition limiting access for the scoped service principals. Service principals usually have fixed/finite IPs; therefore, the Location condition is a convenient option to narrow down access.

   As mentioned above, only the **Block** grant condition is supported today. But watch for remediation options in the future! See Figure 2-67.

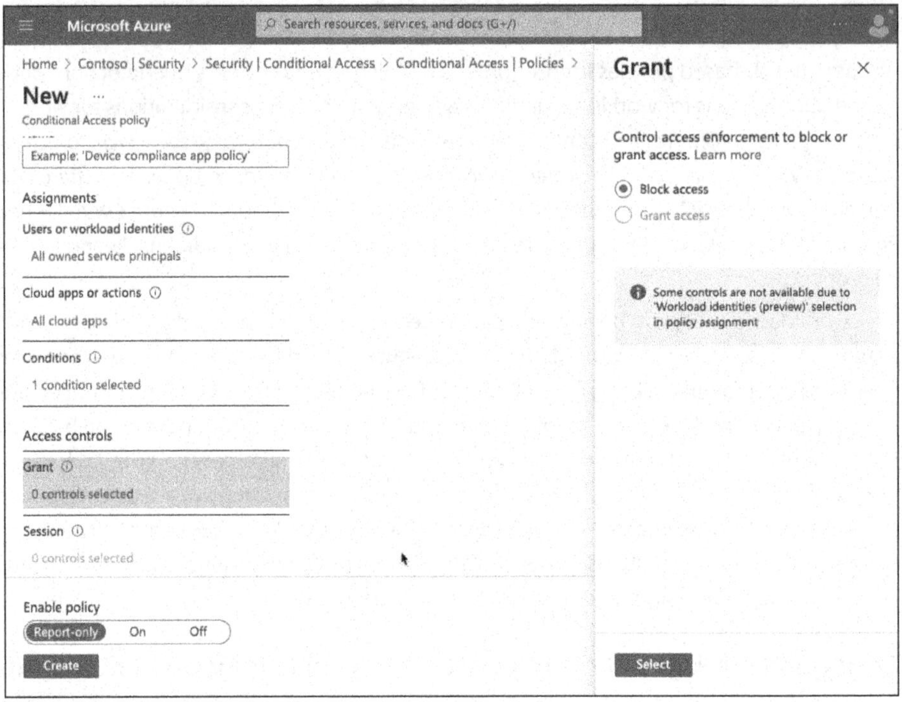

FIGURE 2-67 CA workload identity risk policy.

Monitor, investigate, and remediate workload identity risk

The options available for security administrators to monitor, investigate, and remediate risk on user identities is now also extended to workload identities. Risk data is available via:

- The Risky Workload Identities blade
- Graph APIs
- Azure Monitor

There are some important differences to these options from those offered for User Identities.

As mentioned earlier, Workload Identity risk policies in Conditional Access today offer only mitigation of risk. However, Microsoft strongly recommends that further action be taken upon detecting risk on Workload Identities, including:

- Inventory credentials on the identities called out at risk.
- Delete credentials when the identity is suspected to be compromised.
- Add new credentials, preferably X.509 certificates.
- When using workload identities with Azure KeyVault (AKV), remediate any AKV secrets that the workload identity has access to, by rotating them.

Microsoft has published a detailed guide for Security Operations teams to help them in their monitoring and incident response effort around securing Applications: *https://docs.microsoft.com/en-us/azure/active-directory/fundamentals/security-operations-applications*. There is also an Azure AD Toolkit, a PowerShell module, that offers easy CLI options for performing some of the above recommended operations: *https://github.com/microsoft/AzureADToolkit*.

Another major difference to note is that, for user identities, there are two types of risk reported:

- User Account Risk
- Sign-in Session Risk

All risk detections for user identities fall under the above two risk classifications. For Workload Identities today, all risk detections offered contribute to workload identity account risk only—i.e., there are no risk detections for workload identities contributing to risk determined at the workload identity sign-in or session level (as of this book's writing, which is not to say this will remain so in the future!). For details on the different types of workload identity risk detections, refer to *https://docs.microsoft.com/en-us/azure/active-directory/identity-protection/concept-workload-identity-risk#workload-identity-risk-detections*. Therefore, it follows that while there are two risk reports, as shown in Figure 2-68 and Figure 2-69, respectively, offered for User Identities, for Workload Identities today, administrators can monitor, investigate, and remediate risk via the Risky Workload Identities report.

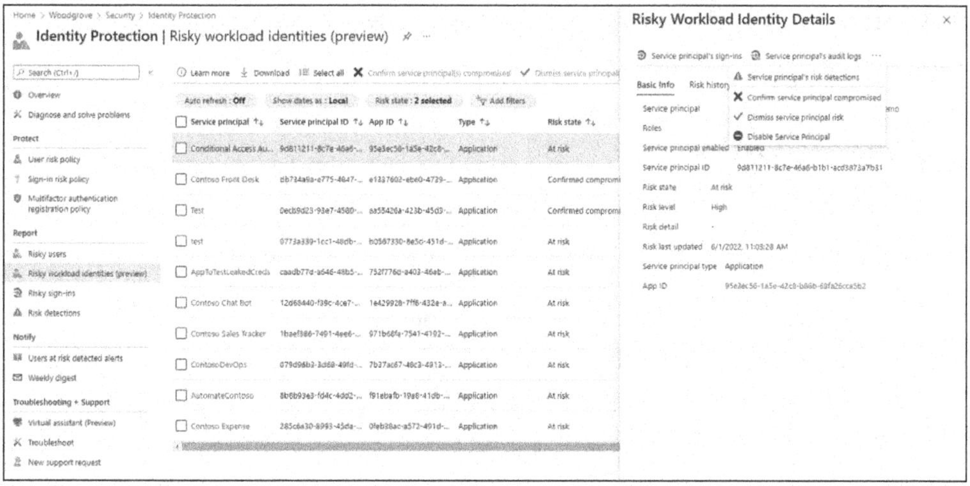

FIGURE 2-68 Workload Identity Risk report.

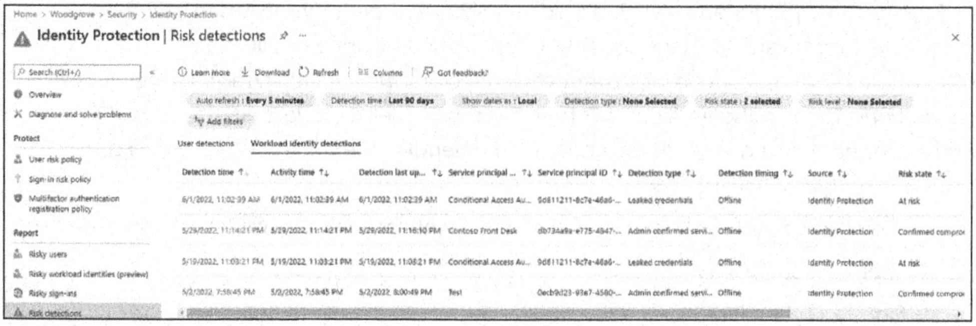

FIGURE 2-69 Workload Identity Risk detections report tab.

Skill 2.5: Implement access management for Azure resources

Using Azure roles to assign and manage access to resources is an important part of the Administrator's job. It is always recommended to follow the principle of least privilege, which states that only the absolute minimum permissions should be granted to users and groups. Azure provides both built-in roles and the ability to create custom roles as needed to ensure that organizations can create roles that meet their needs. Also, management of secrets, credentials, certificates, and keys is a challenge in any cloud-based system. This is where managed identities come in and relieve developers of the burden of managing credentials.

> **This skill covers how to:**
> - Assign Azure roles
> - Configure custom Azure roles
> - Create and configure managed identities
> - Use managed identities to access Azure resources
> - Analyze Azure role permissions
> - Configure Azure Key Vault RBAC and policies

Assign Azure roles

The primary mechanism you use to control access to Azure resources is Azure role-based access control (Azure RBAC). Role assignment can be done at the following levels:

- Users
- Groups
- Service Principal
- Managed Identity

The Azure portal, Azure PowerShell, Azure CLI, Azure SDKs, or REST APIs can all be used to assign roles. The Access control (IAM) page in Azure, as shown in Figure 2-70, can be used to assign Azure roles. In each subscription, you can have up to 2000 role assignments. Role assignments at the subscription level, resource groups, and resource scopes are all subject to this restriction. Each management group can have up to 500 role assignments. Read more about role-based access assignment at *https://learn.microsoft.com/en-us/azure/role-based-access-control/overview*.

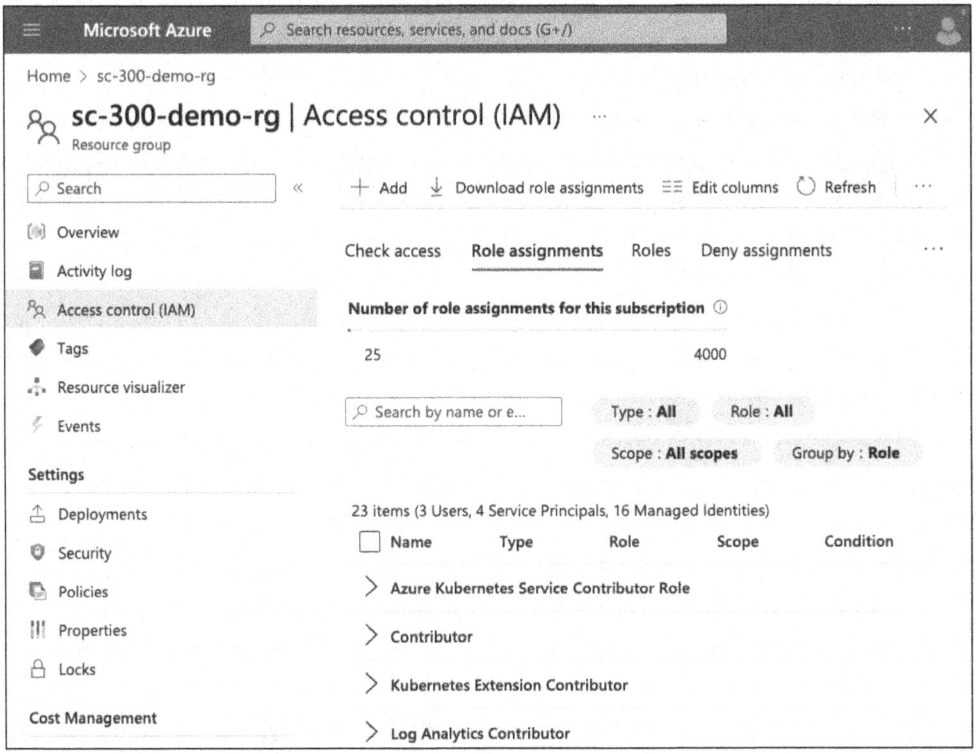

FIGURE 2-70   Azure role assignments.

Configure custom Azure roles

Similarly to built-in roles, custom roles can be assigned to users, groups, or other resources in Azure. When building a custom role, administrators can adhere to the concept of least privilege so that it includes only the permissions necessary for the new role and nothing else. Custom roles can be shared between subscriptions and are kept in the directory. The Azure AD directory may contain as many as 5000 custom roles. The Azure portal, Azure PowerShell, Azure CLI, or REST API can all be used to create custom roles.

To create a new custom role using the Azure portal, follow these steps:

1. Sign in to the Azure portal, *https://portal.azure.com*, a using Global Administrator account.

2. Navigate to the Azure Active Directory dashboard by using the Azure Active Directory option available in the sidebar of the Azure portal.

3. Select **Roles and administration** from the left side pane.

4. Fill in the **Basics** as needed and then press **Next**.

5. Select the permissions that match your requirements and press **Next**. Figure 2-71 shows the permissions assignment page along with a search bar to find the permission by name or description.

6. Finally, review the details and press **Review + create** to finish creating the new custom role.

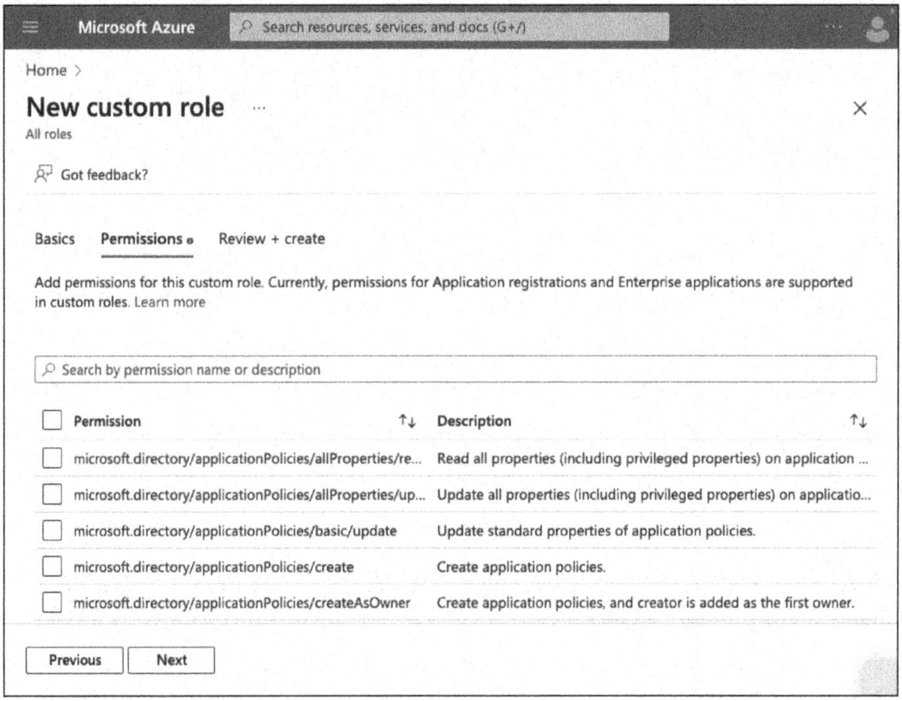

FIGURE 2-71 Create a custom role.

Read more about configuring custom roles at *https://learn.microsoft.com/en-us/azure/ role-based-access-control/custom-roles#steps-to-create-a-custom-role*.

Create and configure managed identities

The management of secrets, credentials, certificates, and keys is a common challenge when developing a cloud solution. These secure elements are used to ensure that communication between services is secure. Developers no longer need to manage these credentials thanks to managed identities.

While developers can safely store secrets in Azure Key Vault, services require access to Azure Key Vault. Managed identities provide applications with an automatically managed identity in Azure Active Directory to use when connecting to resources. The managed identity supports Azure AD authentication. Applications can obtain Azure AD tokens using managed identities without having to manage any credentials.

There are two types of managed identities:

- **System assigned:** The system-assigned managed identity is created in Azure AD and is linked to the service instance's lifecycle. When you delete the resource, Azure automatically deletes the identity. Only that Azure resource can use this identity to request tokens from Azure AD by design. Figure 2-72 shows an example of system-assigned managed identity role assignment for the Azure virtual machine instance.

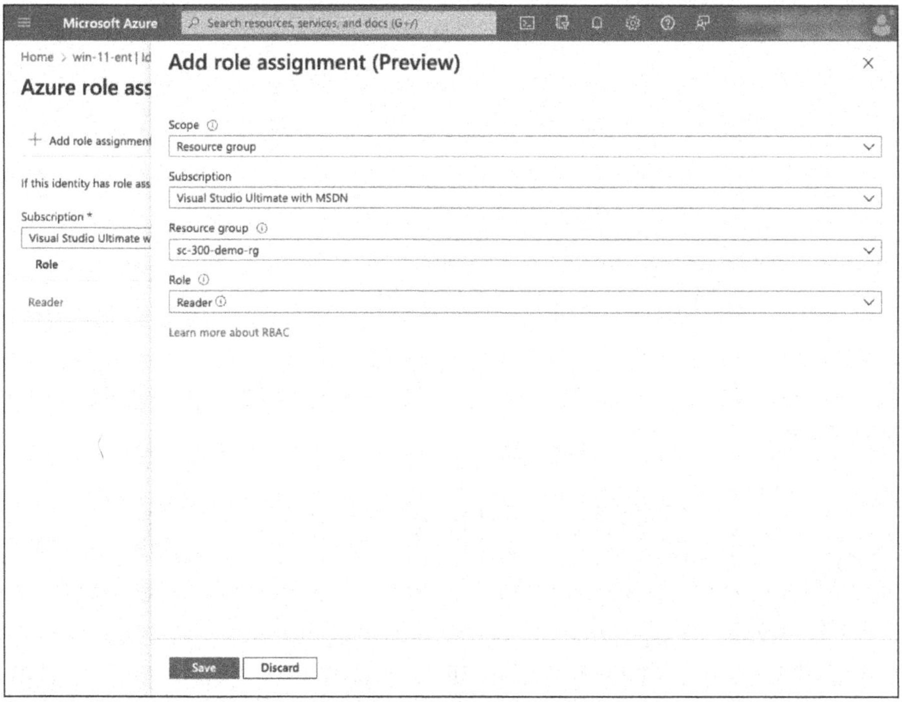

FIGURE 2-72   System-assigned managed identity assignment to an Azure resource (VM).

- **User assigned:** This type of managed identity is managed independently of the resources that make use of it. It can be assigned to one or more Azure service instances. Figure 2-73 shows an example of user-assigned managed identity assignment to an Azure virtual machine instance.

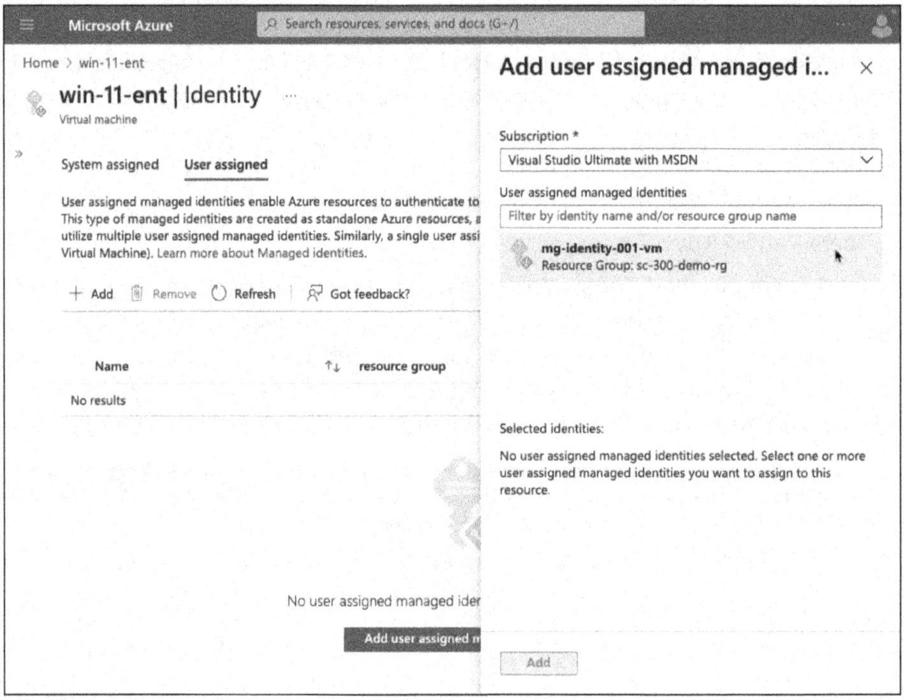

FIGURE 2-73 User-assigned managed identity assignment to an Azure resource (VM).

Please keep in mind that each Azure service that supports managed identities has its own timeline. More information about Azure services and support for managed identities can be found at *https://learn.microsoft.com/en-us/azure/active-directory/managed-identities-azure-resources/managed-identities-status*.

Use managed identities to access Azure resources

After you've assigned a managed identity to an Azure resource, you can grant the managed identity access to other resources. When working with managed identities, keep the following points in mind:

- In Azure, you create a managed identity by selecting either system-assigned managed identity or user-assigned managed identity. The complete list of Azure services that support managed identities can be found at *https://learn.microsoft.com/en-us/azure/active-directory/managed-identities-azure-resources/services-support-managed-identities*.

- Assign the managed identity to the source Azure resource, such as an Azure Virtual Machine, when dealing with a user-assigned managed identity.

- Ensure that the managed identity is authorized to access the target service. For example, Figure 2-74 shows how an Azure virtual machine's system-assigned managed identity can be granted access to the Azure Monitor logs analytics workspace. In this case, the source resource is an Azure virtual machine, and the target resource is a logs analytics workspace.

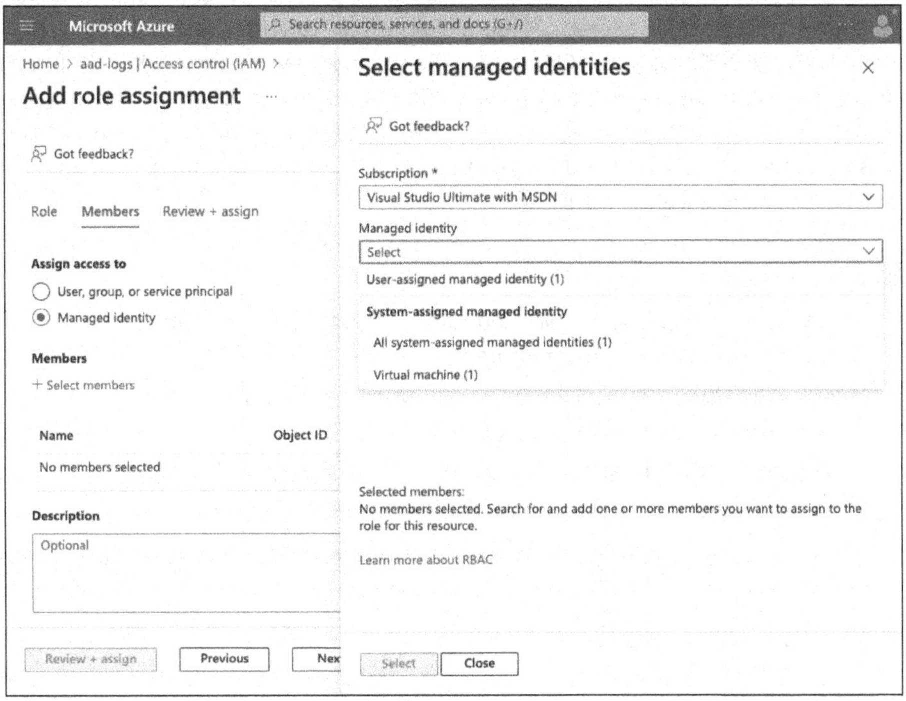

FIGURE 2-74 Managed identities assignment.

Analyze Azure role permissions

All users in Azure AD are given a set of default permissions. The type of user, their role assignments, and their ownership of individual objects all contribute to defining user access.

The set of default user permissions differs depending on whether the user is a native user of the tenant or was brought over as a guest user from another directory as part of a business-to-business (B2B) collaboration.

The following are the default permissions assigned to member and guest users.

- Member users can register applications, manage their own profile photo and mobile phone number, change their password, and invite B2B visitors.
- Guest users have limited directory access. They can edit their own profile, change their password, and view information about other users, groups, and apps. They cannot, however, read all directory information.

Configure Azure Key Vault RBAC and policies

Access to Azure Key Vault can be granted using either role-based access control (RBAC) or Key Vault access policies. Access policies provide more granular control but can be more challenging to manage.

A Key Vault access policy specifies whether a user, application, or group can access Key Vault secrets, keys, and certificates. Access policies can be assigned via the Azure portal (as shown in Figure 2-75), the Azure CLI, or Azure PowerShell. Please note that Key Vault can store up to 1024 access policy entries, each of which grants a unique set of permissions to a specific security principal. Due to this limitation, it is recommended to assign access policies to groups of users rather than individual users whenever possible. Using groups makes managing permissions within an organization much easier.

Please see the links below for step-by-step instructions on configuring Azure Key Vault RBAC and access policies.

- Azure portal: *https://learn.microsoft.com/en-us/azure/key-vault/general/assign-access-policy?tabs=azure-portal*

- Azure CLI: *https://learn.microsoft.com/en-us/azure/key-vault/general/assign-access-policy?tabs=azure-cli*

- Azure PowerShell: *https://learn.microsoft.com/en-us/azure/key-vault/general/assign-access-policy?tabs=azure-powershell*

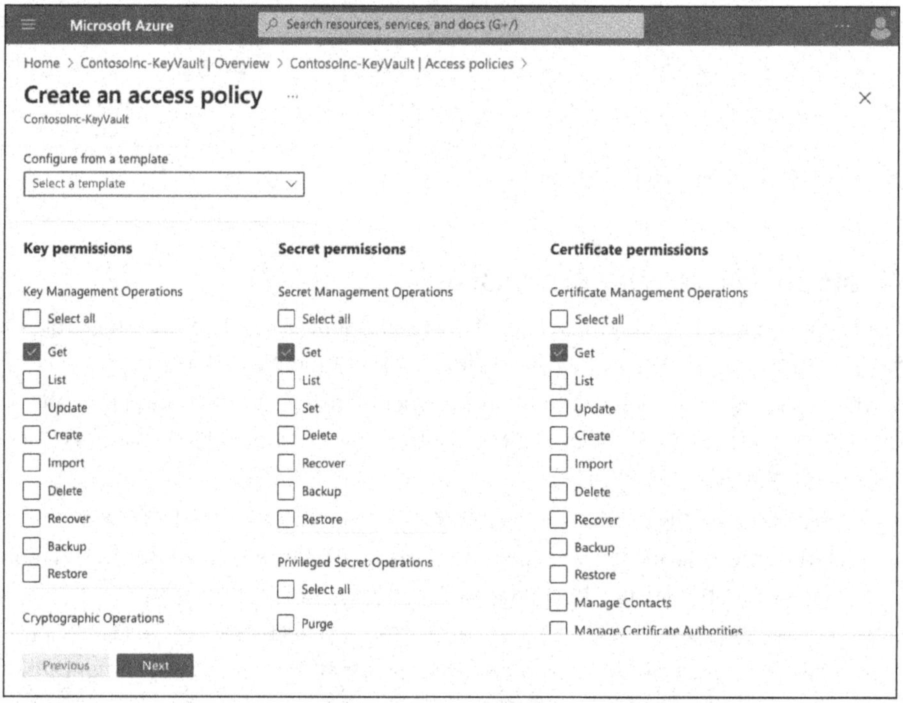

FIGURE 2-75 Create a Key Vault access policy.

Azure Key Vault also supports Azure RBAC for managing key, secret, and certificate permissions. RBAC enables you to manage all permissions across all Key Vaults from a single location. Permissions can be assigned to management groups, subscriptions, resource groups, or individual resources using the RBAC model. RBAC must be enabled for the Key Vault, as shown in Figure 2-76, and then the Access control (IAM) option can be used to view and assign roles as needed, as shown in Figure 2-77.

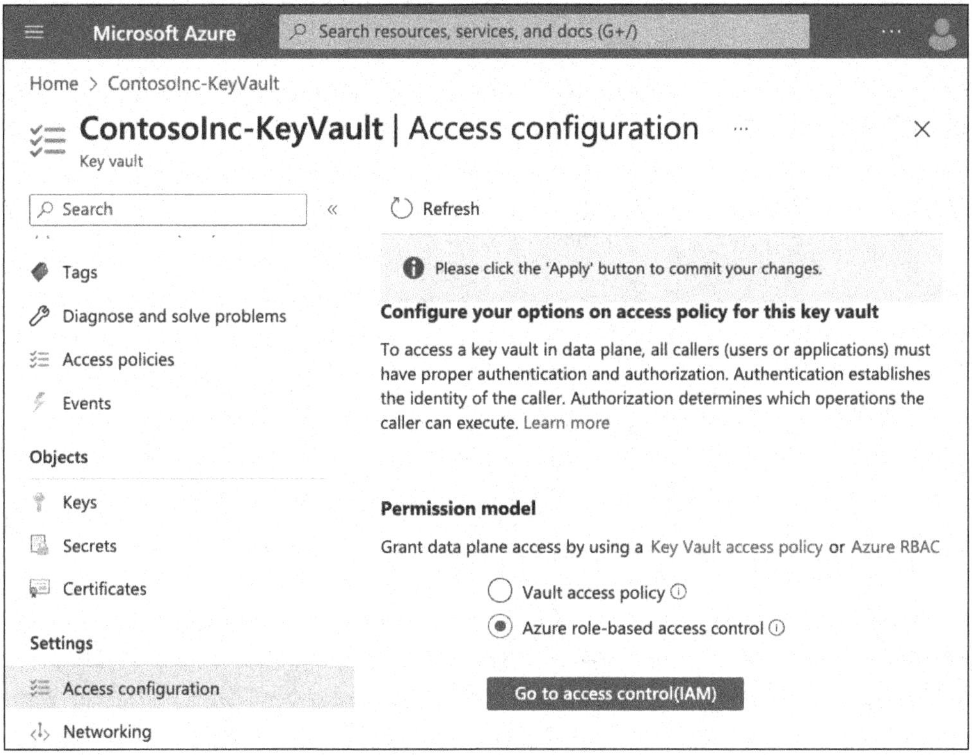

FIGURE 2-76 Enable Azure role-based access control in Key Vault.

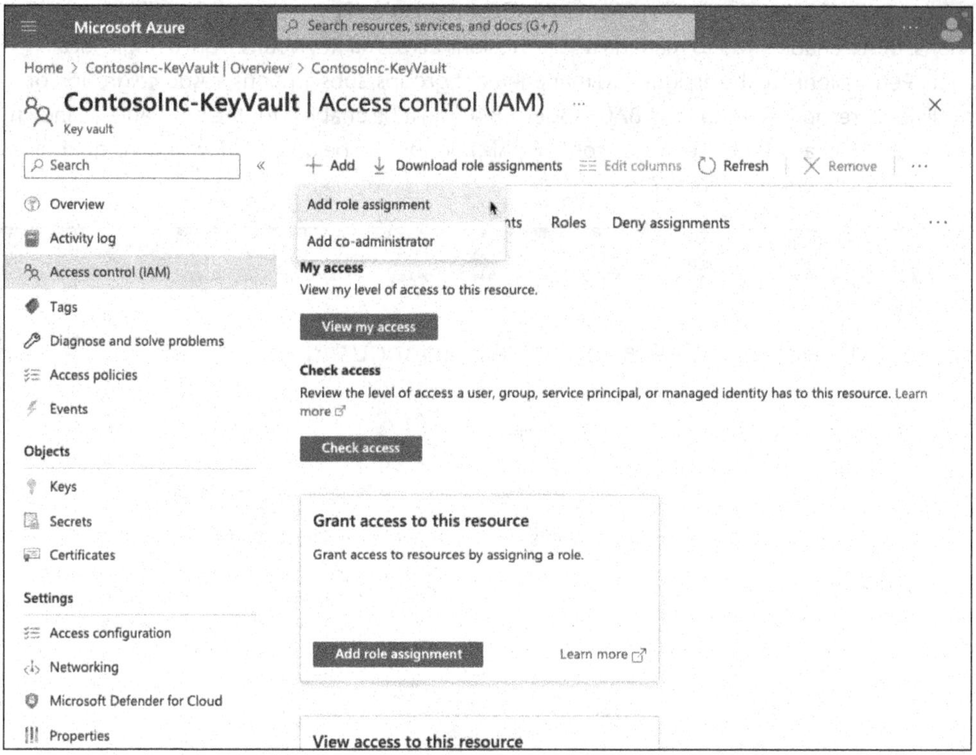

FIGURE 2-77 Access control (IAM) in Key Vault for viewing and assigning roles.

Keep in mind that configuring Azure RBAC permissions for Key Vault nullifies all existing access policy permissions. This may cause outages if equivalent Azure roles are not assigned.

For more information on configuring access to Key Vault keys, certificates, and secrets with an Azure role-based access control, visit *https://learn.microsoft.com/en-us/azure/key-vault/general/rbac-guide*.

Chapter summary

- Azure AD Multifactor Authentication (MFA) allows organizations to add an additional factor to user authentication, which increases account security readily because a hacker must compromise additional factors to get access to the account.
- Azure AD provides a range of passwordless MFA authentication methods to users.
- Users can use Azure AD passwordless authentication methods such as FIDO2 security keys, Windows Hello for Business, and the Microsoft Authenticator app during sign-ins.

- Self-service password reset (SSPR) is a feature in Azure AD that allows users to change their password without seeking help from support or an IT administrator.

- Azure AD smart lockout helps safeguard user accounts by locking out potential malicious actors who use brute-force, password spray, or similar attack techniques to guess the password.

- Azure AD tenant restrictions enable organizations with strict information access and compliance requirements to control the access to any SaaS application that uses modern authentication protocol and relies on Azure AD tenant for single-sign-on (SSO).

- Azure AD Conditional Access enables organizations to apply the fine-grain access control policies required to secure resource access.

- Azure AD Conditional Access collects signals from a variety of sources to make decisions and enforce organizational policies.

- Azure AD Terms of Use (ToU) policies make it easy for end users to see important legal or compliance disclaimers.

- Azure AD Identity Protection (AADIP) can evaluate what it recognizes to be usual behavior for a user and use that knowledge to form risk calculations.

- Calculation of the likelihood that an identity has been compromised is known as user risk.

- Azure AD Identity Protection (AADIP) provides three risk related reports: the Risky Users report, Risky Sign-ins report, and Risky Detections report.

- Azure role-based access control (RBAC) is the primary mechanism to control access to Azure resources.

- Managed identities provide an automatically managed identity in Azure AD for applications to use when connecting to other Azure resources.

Thought experiment

In this thought experiment, demonstrate your skills and knowledge of the topics covered in this chapter. You can find answers to this thought experiment in the next section.

You work for Contoso, Inc., a large industrial company, as an Azure AD administrator.

Staff of Contoso, Inc. utilize passwords as their primary authentication mechanism, with no additional factor, and their credentials were recently exposed, raising serious security concerns. Staff also have a habit of selecting poor passwords with no verification for password quality. Also, Contoso, Inc. currently lacks capabilities to detect leaked credentials or anomalous user behavior.

The IT department recently upgraded all staff machines to the Windows 11 operating system, which was a costly process, and the company wanted to ensure that users received the best possible combination of security and usability.

Finally, Contoso, Inc.'s Compliance department requires that Azure AD logs be retained in Azure storage for retention purposes.

With this information in mind, answer the following questions:

1. How can Contoso, Inc.'s security posture be improved to ensure that even if user credentials are leaked, their security prevents hackers from accessing the user account?

2. What measures need to be taken to ensure that staff passwords do not contain words considered unsuitable for passwords?

3. What feature will allow Contoso, Inc. users to use biometrics for authentication on Windows 11?

4. Which Azure AD setting allows configuring of Azure AD logs to be sent to Azure Storage service?

Thought experiment answers

This section contains solutions to the thought experiment. Each answer explains why the answer choice is correct.

1. Azure Multifactor Authentication (Azure MFA). Azure MFA should be used to improve the security posture of an organization and to mitigate threats associated with passwords. Adding an additional factor to user authentication immediately improves account security because a hacker must compromise additional factors to compromise the account.

2. Azure AD Password Protection. Azure AD Password Protection maintains a global banned passwords list, which is applied automatically to all users in the directory. In addition to the default global list of banned passwords, organizations can create their own custom list of banned passwords to meet their specific security requirements.

3. Windows Hello for Business (WHfB). It allows users to use strong two-factor authentication to replace passwords on their Windows 11 devices. Users are given a credential that is linked to their device and that uses biometrics for authentication.

4. Azure AD Diagnostic settings. It enables the sending of Azure AD logs to the Azure Storage service.

CHAPTER 3

Implement Access Management for Apps

Azure Active Directory (Azure AD) enables enterprises to support a simple, secure, and easy application access model. This chapter covers how enterprise admins can discover applications, enable single sign-on (SSO) experiences for applications, enable application management, and provide insights based on integrated reporting. We also focus on the deployment of various types of applications, including cloud apps and on-premises web applications, and provide an understanding of how the security model works and how applications and application access can be secured.

Skills covered in this chapter:

- Skill 3.1: Plan, implement, and monitor the integration of Enterprise apps for SSO
- Skill 3.2: Implement app registrations
- Skill 3.3 Manage and monitor application access by using Microsoft Defender for Cloud Apps

Skill 3.1: Plan, implement, and monitor the integration of Enterprise apps for SSO

Enterprise applications govern the majority of the end user application experience. This skill focuses on how the applications are discovered, how different types of applications can be integrated with Azure AD, and key access management fundamentals in real-world scenarios.

> **This skill covers how to:**
> - Discover apps by using Microsoft Defender for Cloud Apps or an ADFS application activity report
> - Design and implement app management roles
> - Understand and plan various built-in roles for application management
> - Configure pre-integrated gallery SaaS apps for SSO and implement access management
> - Integrate custom SaaS apps for SSO
> - Implement application user provisioning
> - Integrate on-premises apps by using the Azure AD Application Proxy
> - Monitor and audit access/sign-ons to Azure AD integrated Enterprise applications
> - Implement and configure consent settings

Discover apps by using Microsoft Defender for Cloud Apps or an ADFS application activity report

Increasingly, more enterprises are adopting the SaaS (Software as a Service) model for the majority of commercial off-the-shelf applications and increasingly adopting modern applications that leverage SAML/OIDC/OAuth Standards, making it easy to subscribe to services. In the modern world, you will hear the mention of new tools such as a CASB (Cloud Access Security Broker), which is responsible for enforcing security within cloud service providers and users. Microsoft Cloud App Security (MCAS), now called Microsoft Defender for Cloud Apps, is CASB software that provides visibility and enforces organizational policies for such applications.

Microsoft Cloud App Security

MCAS, now also known as Microsoft Defender for Cloud Apps, offers multiple options to discover applications being used by the enterprises, and it can receive signals from various channels including outbound internet proxy logs, reverse proxy, and API integration. Cloud Discovery is most used to discover applications that are being used in the organization. Sometimes also referred to as Shadow IT, it can provide comprehensive visibility into non-approved applications being used by business units or individuals. The administrator can further choose to enforce controls per the enterprise policies.

Architecture

Microsoft Defender for Cloud Apps or Cloud App Security can improve the visibility into cloud apps and provide additional security controls. The following describes some of the most used features. Figure 3-1 also describes how they are architecturally enforced.

- Identify cloud applications used in the organization using discovery functionality
- Implement API-based app connectors that provide deeper management and visibility into the applications
- Extend conditional access controls and apply sessions controls and understand deeper application usage patterns
- Allow/disallow or enable sanctioned or unsanctioned applications

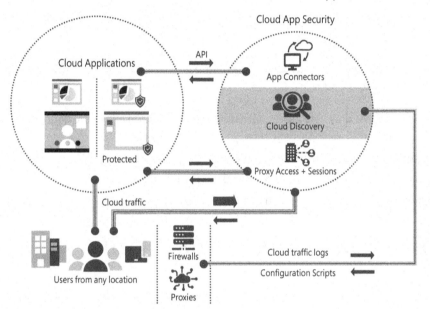

FIGURE 3-1 Cloud App Discovery architecture.

> **NEED MORE REVIEW?**   **Cloud app Discovery**
>
> For more information about the different editions of Cloud App Security, visit:
> *https://docs.microsoft.com/en-us/defender-cloud-apps/editions-cloud-app-security-o365*

Cloud Discovery

One of the key functions of Cloud App Security is the Cloud Discovery feature. You can configure use logs from your firewalls or proxies to generate insights. The process of log collection can also be automated for periodic retrieval and continuous report updates. The cloud discovery is an intelligent report with enriched metadata to help admins get insights into usage patterns and risks. Figure 3.2 shows the various cloud apps discovered by the cloud discovery engine.

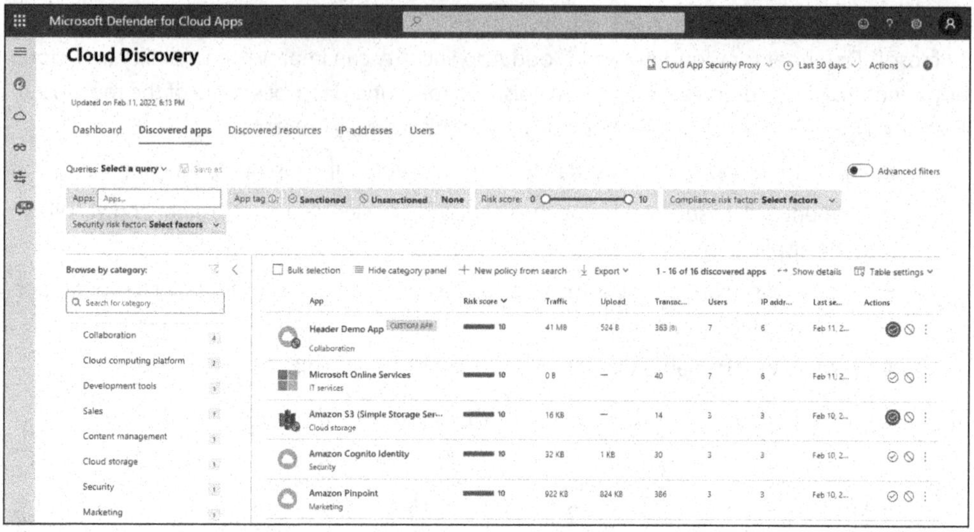

FIGURE 3-2 Cloud App Discovery portal.

Cloud discovery can not only detect the application usage, but it can enrich the data with a lot of metadata about the application. In general, you might have a view into:

- Generic application usage across the organization
- Automatic categorization into sanctioned and unsanctioned applications
- Automatic metadata enrichment such as risk score, compliance information, etc.
- Usage insights based on traffic, users, IP addresses, etc.
- Rich filtering capabilities based on usage and enriched metadata include
  - App tag
  - Apps and domains
  - Categories
  - Compliance risk factors (PCI-DSS, HIPAA, and more)
  - Legal risk factors
  - General risk factors
  - Risk scores
  - Security risk factors
  - Usage

Sanctioned apps

While Microsoft Cloud App Security can provide great insights with cloud discovery, this capability cannot enable or disable access. It does provide intelligent insights to the admins who can recommend using similar reputable SaaS applications rather than something that might put the entire organization at risk. Additionally, if you use some specific solutions like Microsoft Defender for Endpoint or some other supported proxy solutions, you can generate scripts and block access to identified unsanctioned applications. In Figure 3-3, you can see the Unsanctioned apps tab highlighted and the details of the applications in this category.

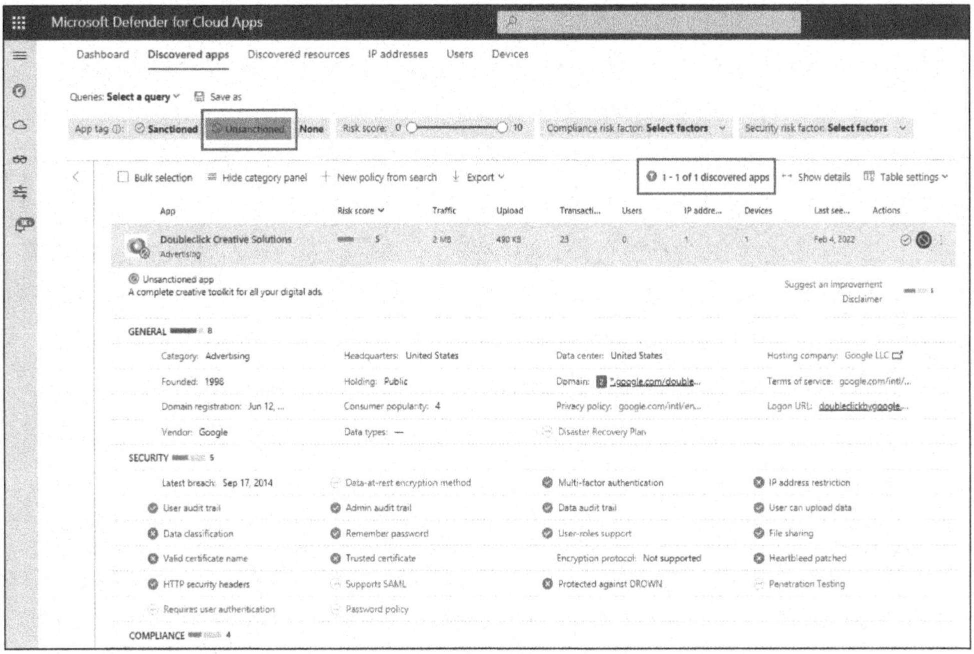

FIGURE 3-3 Application details discovered by cloud discovery.

***NEED MORE REVIEW?* SANCTIONING DISCOVERED APPS**

For more information on sanctioning/un-sanctioning discovered apps, visit:

https://docs.microsoft.com/en-us/defender-cloud-apps/governance-discovery

Active Directory Federation Service

ADFS, or Active Directory Federation Service, servers provide an organization to set up federations with business partners and provide single sign-on (SSO) capabilities to trusted parties. One of the key tenants of the more modern applications has been the ability to separate users' authentication from applications—protocols such as SAML, OIDC, and OAuth allow you to enable this feature. Although these protocols have existed for quite some time, they are sometimes also referred to as modern protocols, since you can leverage them to apply modern controls like Multifactor Authentication (MFA), device-based compliance, etc. Many enterprises today still have federation servers to allow their users to connect to SaaS apps. In-house line-of-business (LOB)/custom applications sometimes call private applications and leverage the same infrastructure to federate with Microsoft 365/Azure AD Services. Figure 3-4 shows the ADFS Server in federation mode and how different applications can be federated with ADFS.

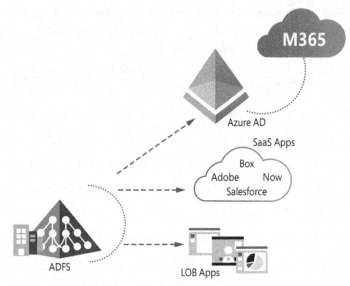

FIGURE 3-4 ADFS Servers with federated apps inclunding o365/Azure AD.

However, increasingly more companies are taking advantage of advanced cloud Native Azure AD features like Conditional Access, Azure AD Multifactor Authentication, and device-based policy. Enterprises extend the similar controls/policies for their SaaS applications and line-of-business (LOB) applications to achieve a more modern security plane with consistent controls and policies for both cloud and on-premises applications. One of the first steps they take is to integrate applications with Azure AD directly, as shown in Figure 3-5.

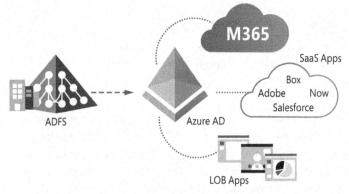

FIGURE 3-5 Applications directly connected to Azure AD.

ADFS usage and insights

ADFS Usage and insights can help generate reports to assist in the migration of applications from ADFS to Azure AD. The ADFS application activity report provides key decision points to help with prioritization of the apps for migration, including app usage and potential issues that might affect migration. Figure 3-6 shows an example of the ADFS application activity report with detected insights highlighting the date range filter and the key fields reported.

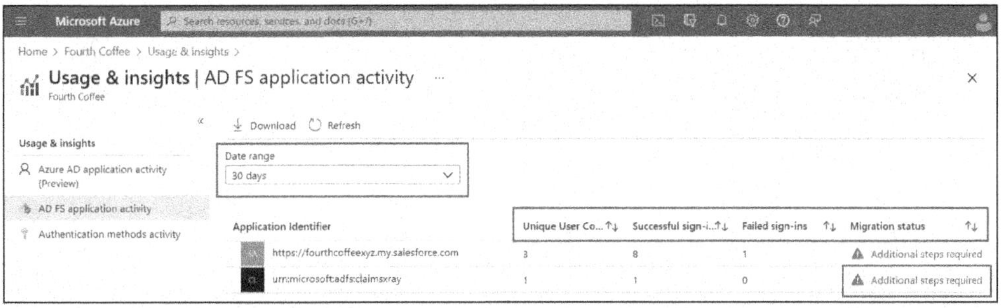

FIGURE 3-6 ADFS application activity.

Prerequisites for the ADFS Usage and insights include the following: the AD Connect health service must be enabled, ensure that you have the ADFS Connect health on ADFS Server(s), and a few auditing permissions that must be enabled along with certain Local security policy settings depending on the ADFS Server version. For the applications to show up on the console, there should be success/failure events in the event logs related to the applications. Information regarding the application and related information is controlled via role-based access control (RBAC).

The following roles can view the reports:

- Global administrators
- Global readers
- Application administrator
- Cloud application administrator
- Security readers
- Report readers

The ADFS Application Activity report can help with the following areas:

- **Discover ADFS Application**: The report will include applications that users have signed in to during the last 30 days. The report skips Microsoft-related relying parties like Microsoft Office 365.
- **Planning:** The tool shows you the number of unique users and sign-in information, which can be used to plan for application migration and for planning risk associated with the criticality of applications based on usage.

- **Identify issues and recommendations**: The Azure AD service automatically runs several tests to identify potential migration issues and provide recommendations on how those can be fixed. Figure 3-7 shows how potential issues are reported and details on possible resolutions in the highlighted sections.

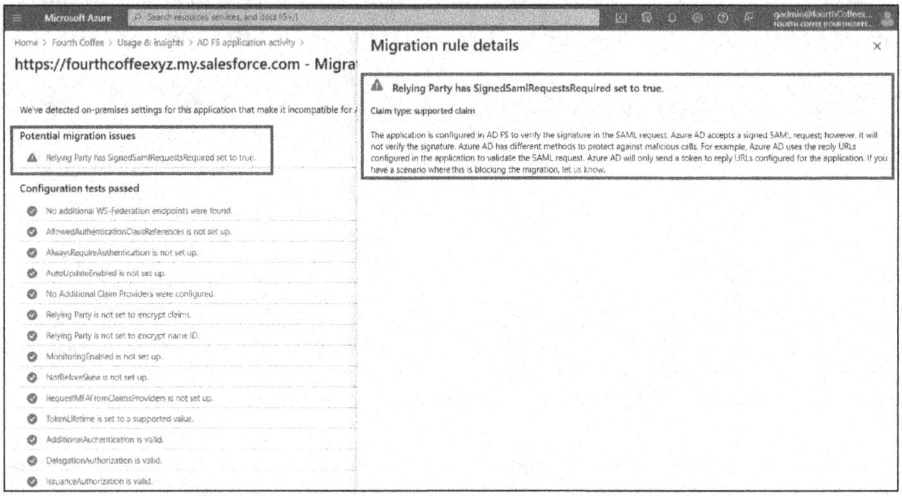

FIGURE 3-7 ADFS application migration details.

Once the insights are generated, you might see the below results in the migration status. Administrators can further click on details to find a more detailed analysis of the status.

- **Ready to migrate:** No modification is required for the application and ADFS.

- **Needs review:** You will need to review certain settings; some application configuration elements can't be migrated to Azure.

- **Additional steps required:** This will require some changes to the application's settings before the application can be migrated. In general, the most effort is required for an application reported in this state.

> **NEED MORE REVIEW?** **ADFS APPLICATION ACTIVITY REPORT**
>
> For more information about this, visit: *https://docs.microsoft.com/en-us/azure/active-directory/manage-apps/migrate-adfs-application-activity*

Design and implement app management roles

This objective focuses on understanding the various design aspects of the roles available for managing applications in Azure AD. In general, before applications are secured using Azure AD, planning is required to understand the delegation model, types of applications, and what activities these roles allow them to perform.

Restricting apps creation

Before we start planning the application management roles, one of the key things Azure AD does is to allow all users to perform application registrations and manage their settings. However, in most enterprises these are governed and assigned to appropriate roles. This can be achieved in the user settings by setting the **Users can register applications** under **App registrations** to **No** (as highlighted in Figure 3-8).

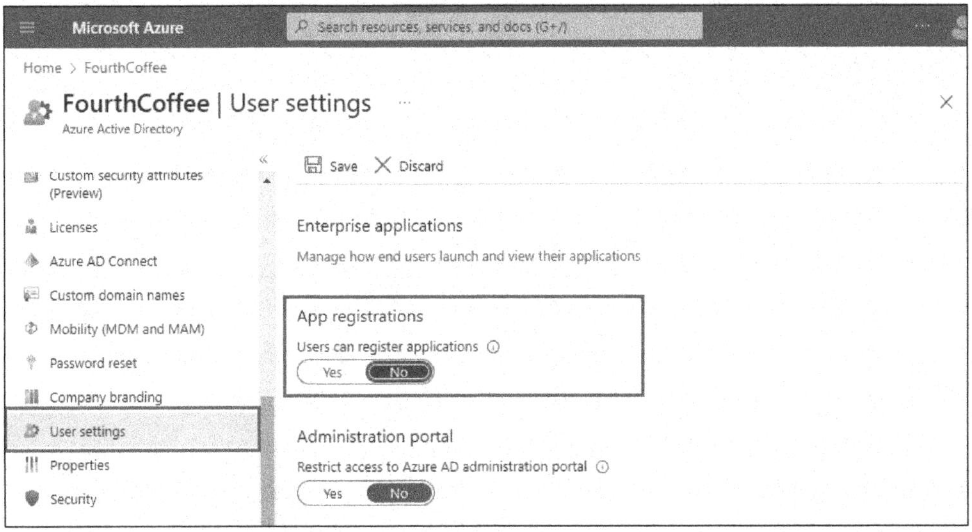

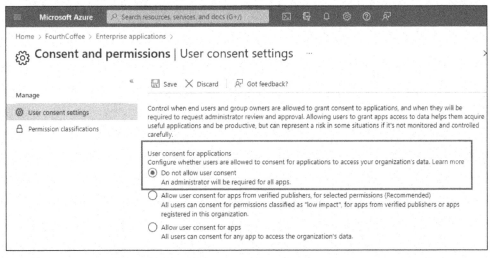

FIGURE 3-8 App registration control on Azure AD.

On the **Enterprise applications** blade, under **Consent and Permissions**, in the **User consent for applications** option, choose **Do not allow user consent** (highlighted in Figure 3-9).

FIGURE 3-9 Consent setting to block users for app consent.

You also need to configure the consent settings for **group owners** as part of the overall consent management (as highlighted in Figure 3-10).

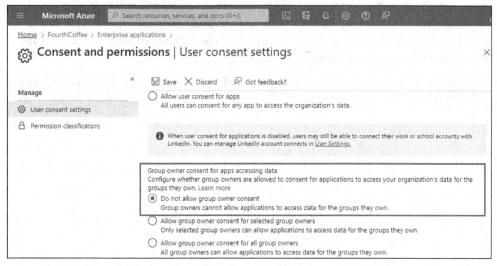

FIGURE 3-10 Additional Consent setting to block users for app consent.

When the above settings are configured, end users are unable to consent to any application, which might be an issue in the real world as users need access to the applications. Azure AD provides administrators with options to allow users to safely request consent for new applications where the user consent is reviewed by an approving request. These requests must also be delegated to the users/groups/roles in the enterprise. Figure 3-11 highlights the **admin consent requests** control.

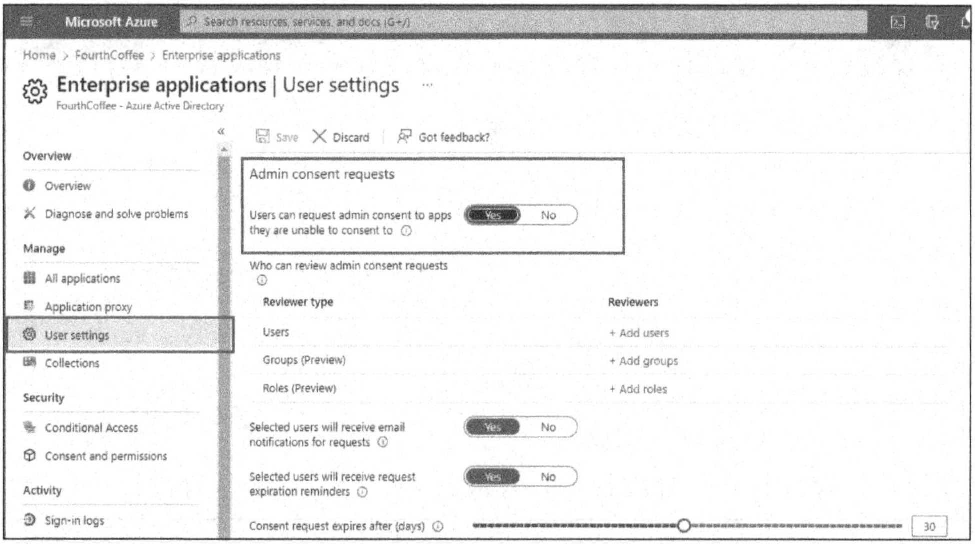

FIGURE 3-11 Enterprise app setting to request admin for app consent.

Even with the **Users can request admin consent** settings, admins might still be over-whelmed with the number of requests. Additionally, you can choose to safely consent to applications that are from publishers verified with Microsoft as part of the Application Integration certification. This provides a higher attestation that the application is verified and can be traced to the app owners with a reduced risk of consent abuse and hence safer to consent automatically as highlighted in Figure 3-12.

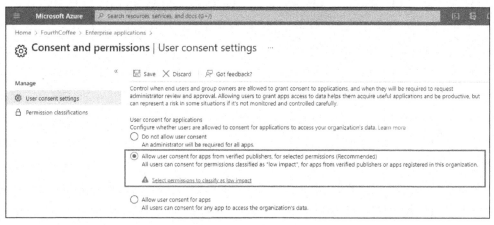

FIGURE 3-12 App registration setting to allow consent for verified publishers.

Application ownership

You can assign users to specific built-in roles such as application developers to create application registrations. The users are granted ownership for any applications they create, thereby giving them ownership permissions that allow them to manage all settings of that specific application. Figure 3-13 shows the owners of the application; the creator of the application is added as the default owner.

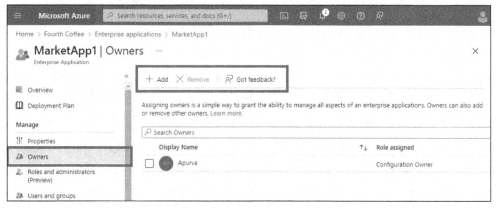

FIGURE 3-13 Adding application owners for the Enterprise applications.

Similar settings exist for the App Principals or App Registrations. You can see the owner details and how they can be added highlighted in Figure 3-14.

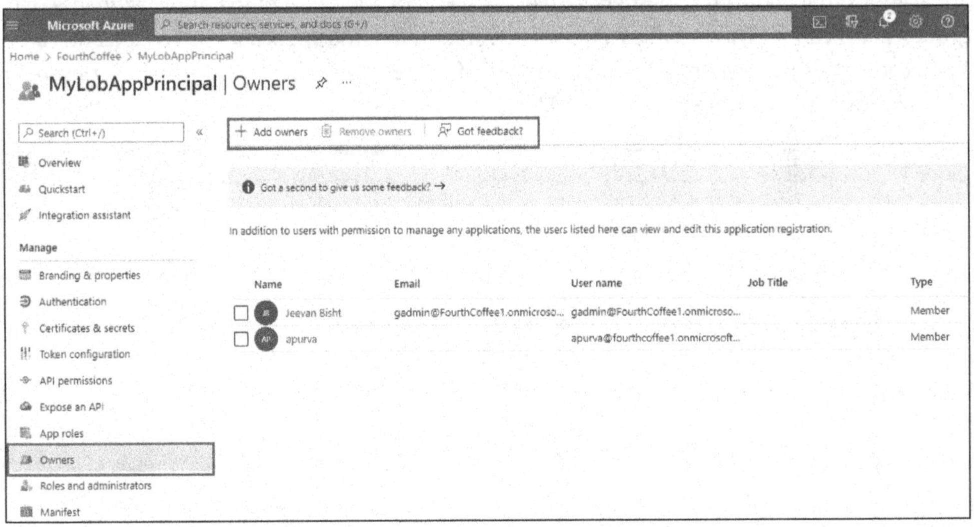

FIGURE 3-14   Adding owners for the app registration for a LOB app.

NOTE   **THE FOLLOWING RESTRICTIONS APPLY TO THE APP PRINCIPAL OWNER CONFIGURATION:**

- Groups cannot be assigned as owners of an Enterprise application or app registration.
- A service principal can be the owner of the application registration.
- New app registrations are hidden from users by default. To enable the app, in the Azure portal navigate to **Azure Active Directory > Enterprise applications** and select the app. Then on the Properties page, toggle **Visible to users?** to **Yes**.
- The app can have more permissions than app owners. An application owner can perform tasks impersonating the applications.

Understand and plan various built-in roles for application management

Azure AD offers multiple roles to allow delegation and management of applications. Three built-in roles are available related to application management, as described in Table 3-1, along with their capabilities.

TABLE 3-1 Azure AD roles for the application management

Role	Description
Application Administrator	Can create and manage all aspects of app registrations and Enterprise apps
Application Developer	Can create application registrations independent of the **Users can register applications** setting
Cloud Application Administrator	Can create and manage all aspects of app registrations and Enterprise apps except App Proxy

EXAM TIP

It is important to understand each of the built-in application admin roles and have a clear distinction of what types of applications every role can manage.

Custom roles

While the built-in roles allow delegation in certain scenarios, they might be too broad, or you might need to tailor the roles for application developers for specific applications. Custom roles allow admins to create a role definition that can be assigned to different users. For example, you create a custom role for developers and assign them to specific developers to manage their own application as a scope.

The process of creating custom roles is a two-stage process:

- **Define the custom role**

  The role definition is generally a subset of permissions assigned to the built-in-roles; you can choose what permissions to grant from the list.

- **Assign the role**

  By default, custom roles are assigned at the default organization-wide scope to grant access permissions for all app registrations within the organization. For more information, please read *https://learn.microsoft.com/en-us/azure/active-directory/roles/custom-create#assign-a-custom-role-scoped-to-a-resource*.

NOTE CUSTOM ROLE RESTRICTIONS

If you have the setting **Restrict access to the Azure AD Administration** configured to yes, custom roles do not grant access to the Azure AD portal.

To create a custom role, complete the following steps:

1. Sign in to the Azure AD portal with **Global Administrator** credentials.
2. On the Azure Active Directory blade, under **Manage**, select **Roles and administrators**.

3. On the **Roles and administrators** blade, select **New custom role** (as highlighted in Figure 3-15).

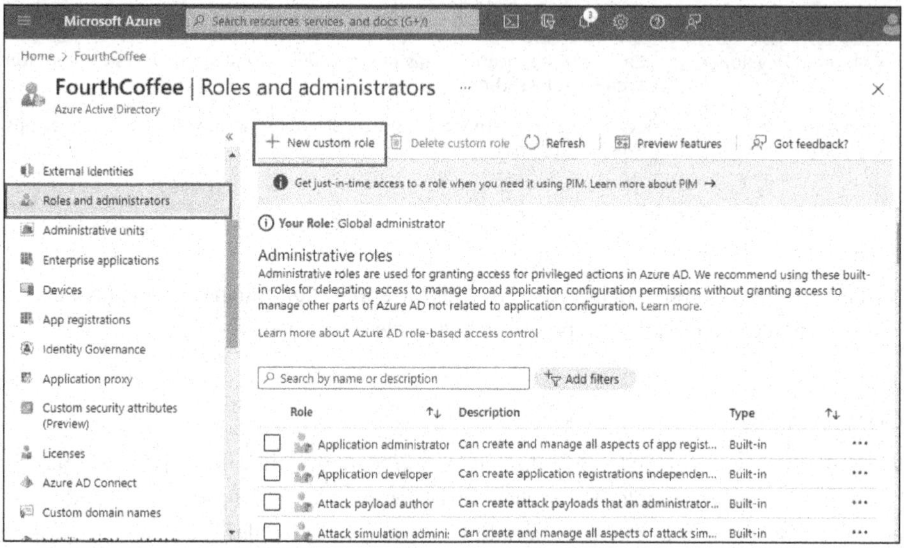

FIGURE 3-15 The Azure AD console for adding new custom roles.

4. In the **New custom role** blade, on the **Basics** tab, in the **name** box, enter the **AppManagers** role, provide a role description, and click Next (as highlighted in Figure 3-16).

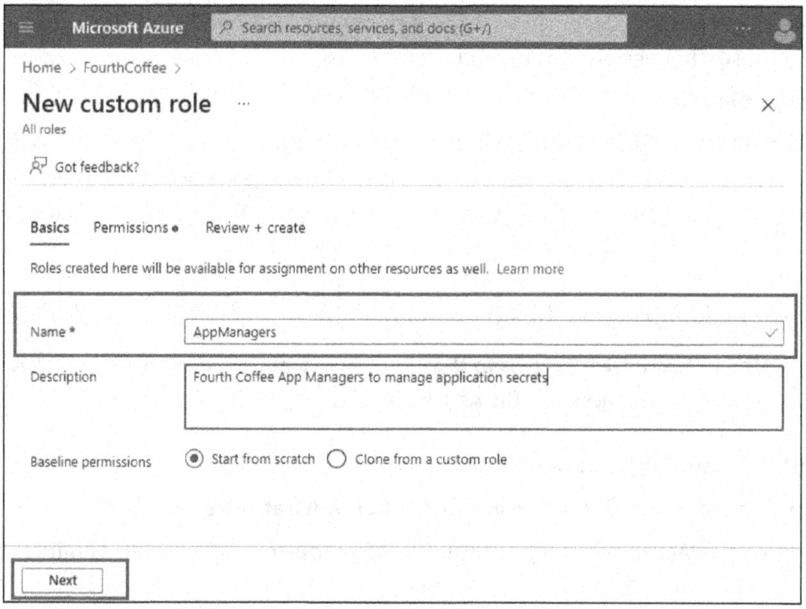

FIGURE 3-16 Basic Information for custom roles creation.

5. Go to the Permissions tab and review the available permissions.

6. In the Search by permission name or description box, enter **Manage,** specify the required permissions, and click **Next** (as highlighted in Figure 3-17).

7. Click **Next**.

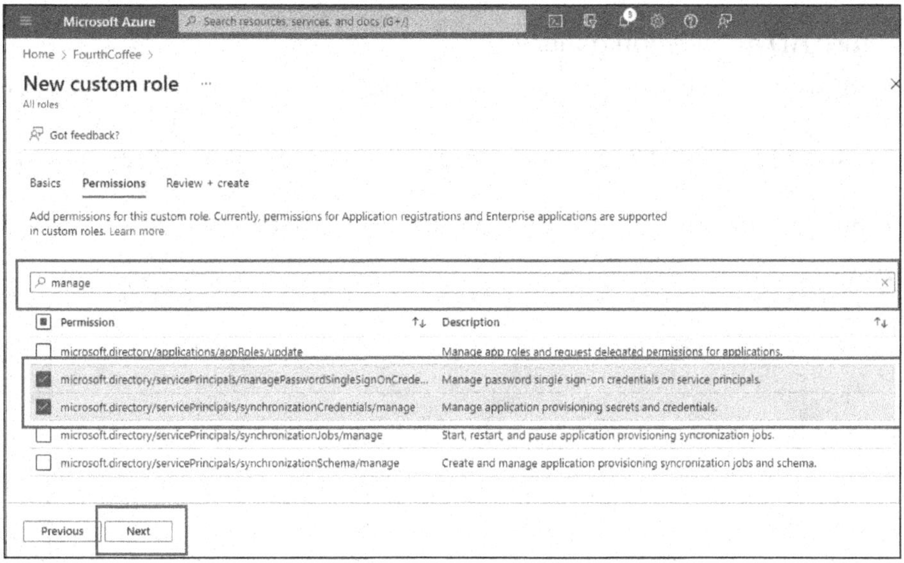

FIGURE 3-17 Custom role wizard to select permissions from built-in permissions.

8. In the results, select the desired permissions and then select Next.

9. Review the changes and then select Create.

10. The role you just created should be available for assignment under **Roles and administrators**. In this example, we sort by Type as Custom and specify **AppManagers**, as highlighted in Figure 3-18.

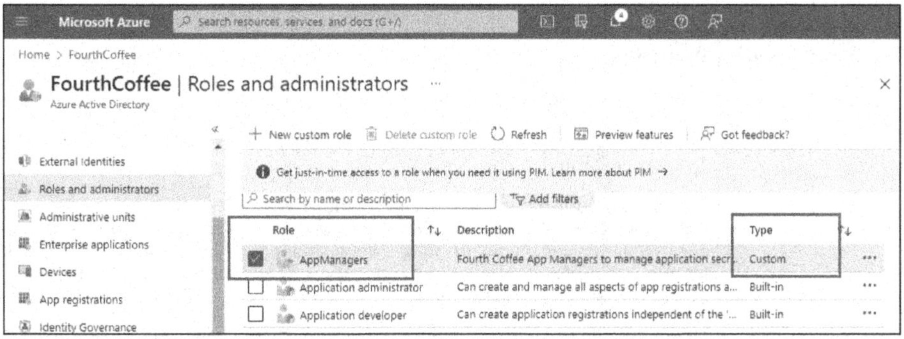

FIGURE 3-18 Custom role available in the console.

Configure pre-integrated gallery SaaS apps for SSO and implement access management

In this section, we cover what Azure AD gallery applications are, the key configuration attributes, and how to implement access control for the applications.

Azure AD application gallery

Azure AD offers thousands of pre-integrated applications as part of the Azure AD gallery. See Figure 3-19. These help reduce the admin's efforts and provide a pre-verified applications integration experience. Multiple types of applications are available for integration, and we will learn to search, add an application, and learn the key steps involved in gallery app integrations. There are four primary types of applications in the Azure AD Gallery, as described in Table 3-2.

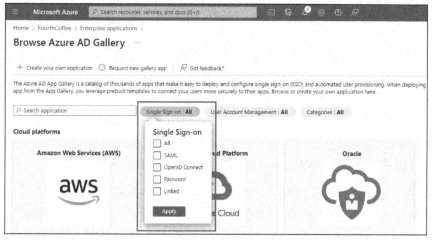

FIGURE 3-19   Azure AD Gallery.

TABLE 3-2   Azure AD Gallery application

Application type	Description
OpenID Connect	Choose OpenID Connect and OAuth 2.0 if the application you're connecting to supports it.
SAML	Choose SAML whenever possible for existing applications that do not use OpenID Connect or OAuth.
Password	Choose password-based when the application has an HTML sign-in page. Password-based SSO is also known as *password vaulting*. Password-based SSO enables you to manage user access and passwords to web applications that don't support identity federation. It's also useful when several users need to share a single account, such as to your organization's social media app accounts.
Linked	Linked sign-on allows you to add a link to an application in My Apps and/or the Office 365 application launcher for selected users.
	You can add a link to a custom web application that currently uses federation, such as Active Directory Federation Services (ADFS). The Linked option doesn't provide sign-on functionality through Azure AD credentials.

Azure AD Gallery offers a search experience to quickly identify the application among the thousands in the offering. This allows admins to efficiently navigate to the required application. It offers multiple filters to choose applications from various business categories, support for user account provisioning, and single sign-on methods.

To search for the applications in the Azure AD console, follow these steps:

1. In the Azure portal, select Enterprise Applications, and then select new Application.

2. In the search window, type the application name—in this example, we type **salesforce**.

3. Select the Salesforce application to view the properties, as shown in Figure 3-20.

   The search wizard will also indicate if the application supports **Federated SSO** or **Provisioning** (User/Group/Both).

4. Click the **Create** button to add an instance of the application.

FIGURE 3-20 Adding an application from the Azure AD Gallery.

Once the application is created, one of the first things you do is configure the various application attributes or properties; the application properties are listed below. Administrators can control user experience for an application by controlling the key application properties. The properties described below are common to Enterprise applications as well app registrations, as shown in Figure 3-21.

- **Application Name**

  Specify the application name so it can be easily discovered by end users.

- **Logo**

  Azure AD allows administrators to define custom logos. The logo art specifications are 215 x 215 in the PNG format.

- **Notes**

  This field is useful for the management of the application, in case there might be more than one instance of the same application that is configured differently and used by different business departments. This field is plain text and can be used for administrator notes.

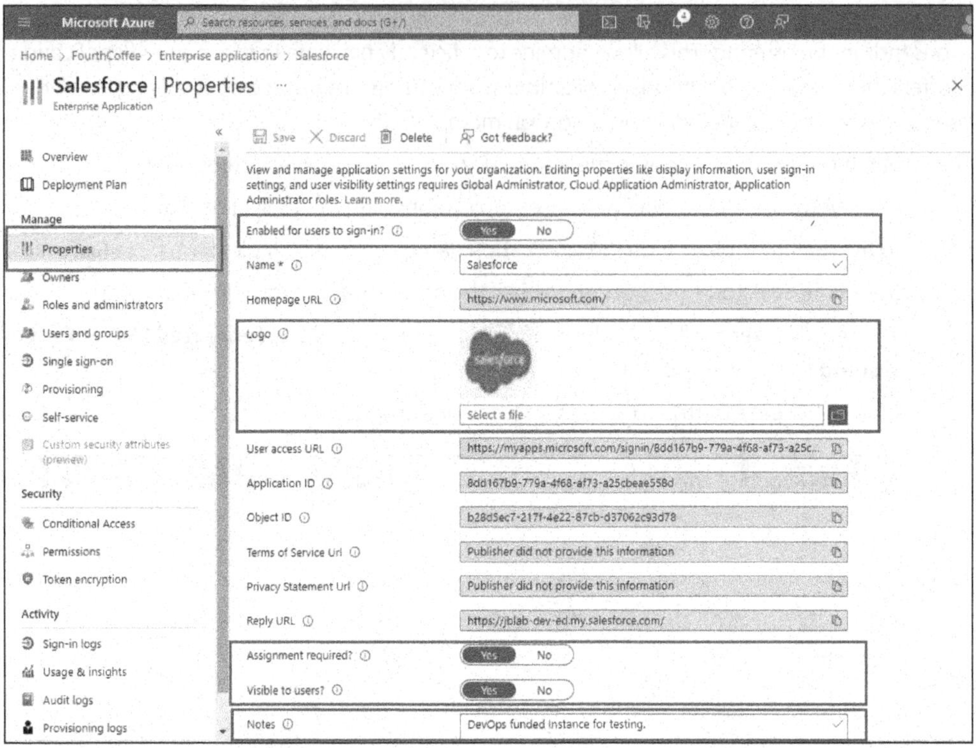

FIGURE 3-21 Enterprise Application Properties

■ **Application Behavior Controls**

Three main settings can be adjusted to meet both user and business requirements: **Enabled for users to sign in, User assignment required**, and **Visible to users.**

Table 3-3 contains a quick summary of the various settings that can impact the end user experience and application discovery/visibility by the end users. These options exist to accommodate different types of applications like Web apps, APIs, etc. In certain cases, you want users to be able to launch the app, while in other instances of APIs you want to hide the apps from end users.

TABLE 3-3 Application behavior controls

Setting	Yes	No
Enabled for users to sign-in	Assigned users will be able to sign in to this application, either from My Apps, from the User access URL, or by navigating to the application URL directly.	No users will be able to sign in to this app, even if they are assigned to it.
Assignment Required	Users and other apps or services must first be assigned this application before being able to access it.	All users will be able to sign in, and other apps and services will be able to obtain an access token to this service.
Visible to Users	Assigned users will see the application on My Apps and the Office 365 app launcher.	No users will see this application on their My Apps and the Office 365 app launcher.

Implement access management

Access management is a key aspect of any Identity and Access Management (IAM) solution. Azure AD provides a powerful yet simple interface to manage applications access for users.

Applications can be assigned to appropriate users and groups. One of the key planning items related to application access is the group for application access. While you can assign users to the application, it's recommended to use a group for each application or application role if the application supports multiple roles. In Figure 3-22, as an example, a group of users called **Salesforce-ChatterUsers** is assigned to the App Role **Chatter Free User**.

To assign users to an app, complete the following steps:

1. On the **Salesforce** app in the **Enterprise Applications** blade, on the **Overview** page, under Manage, you can select **Users and groups**.

2. On the **Users and groups** page, on the menu, select **+Add user/group**.

3. On the **Add Assignment** blade, select **Users and groups**.

4. In the **Users and groups** pane, select your application group account and then press the **Select** button.

5. (Optional) You might have an option to select Role if applicable to your app.

6. Select **Assign**.

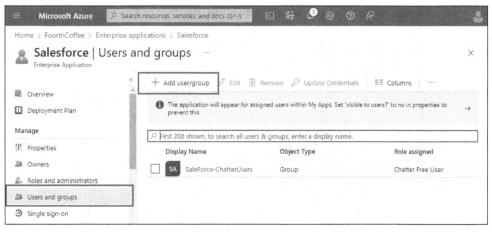

FIGURE 3-22 Assigning users and groups to an application.

In this section, we learned about what the Azure AD Application Gallery is, how we can search for an application, create an application from the gallery, view and set key properties associated with an application, and implement access control. Each SaaS application or gallery app might have a different single sign-on (SSO) configuration, which was not covered here. Detailed configuration around single sign-on is covered in the next section, "Integrate custom SaaS apps for SSO."

> **NEED MORE REVIEW?**   **INTEGRATE SAAS APPLICATIONS WITH AZURE ACTIVE DIRECTORY**
>
> For more information on Azure AD application integration, visit:
>
> - *https://docs.microsoft.com/en-us/azure/active-directory/saas-apps/tutorial-list*
> - *https://docs.microsoft.com/en-us/azure/active-directory/manage-apps/add-application-portal-setup-sso*

Integrate custom SaaS apps for SSO

Azure AD offers thousands of pre-integrated applications in the gallery but also allows for the flexibility to add any software-as-a-service (SaaS) application if it's missing from the gallery. In this section, we will learn how one can integrate custom SaaS application with Azure AD.

Custom app integration

Azure AD can be used as an identity provider for many types of applications. Apart from having native support for Office 365 applications, you can further integrate various other types of applications.

- The Azure AD Gallery offers application templates that can be easily set up.
- You can request missing applications from Azure AD for integration.
- Additionally, you can manually configure applications for single sign-on using either SAML (Security Assertion Markup Language) or OIDC (OpenID Connect). Figure 3-23 shows how Azure AD can support different types of application integration.

FIGURE 3-23   Azure AD and supported application integration.

The Microsoft Identity platform has support for multiple protocols, and generally developers have a choice to integrate using one over another. Table 3-4 describes the key differences between key protocols and how they are used.

TABLE 3-4 Comparison between different supported protocols

SAML	OPENID CONNECT
SAML authentication is commonly used with identity providers such as Active Directory Federation Services (ADFS) federated to Azure AD and is therefore frequently used in Enterprise applications and generally has a larger footprint	OpenID Connect is commonly used for apps that are purely in the cloud, such as mobile apps, websites, and web APIs. Generally, all new applications are created using OIDC.
SAML	**OAuth**
Security Assertion Markup Language (SAML) is used for authentication.	OAuth is used for authorization.
OpenID Connect	**OAuth**
OpenID Connect (OIDC) is used for authentication. OpenID Connect is built on top of OAuth 2.0, which means the terminology and flow are similar between the two. You can even authenticate a user using OpenID Connect and get authorization to access a protected resource that the user owns using OAuth 2.0 in one request.	OAuth is used for authorization.

EXAM TIP

It is important to understand key differences with each protocol and their use.

Custom SaaS app integration

While you can use any custom application, we will walk through a popular app called ClaimsXray, which is used to troubleshoot SAML SSO issues. The goal of this exercise is to:

- Understand custom SaaS app integration
- Customize default claims being sent and view them

NOTE **WHAT IS A SAML CLAIM?**

A claim is information that an identity provider states about a user inside the token they issue for that user. In the SAML token, this data is typically contained in the SAML Attribute Statement. The user's unique ID is typically represented in the SAML Subject, also called the Name Identifier.

Let's begin the custom SSO integration for the application ClaimsXray using the following steps:

1. Launch the Azure AD Admin console by navigating to **https://aad.portal.azure.com/** and then clicking **Enterprise Application**.

2. Click **Create your own application**.

3. Specify the name **ClaimsXray**.

4. Select **Integrate any other application you don't find in the gallery (non-Gallery)** (as shown in Figure 3-24).

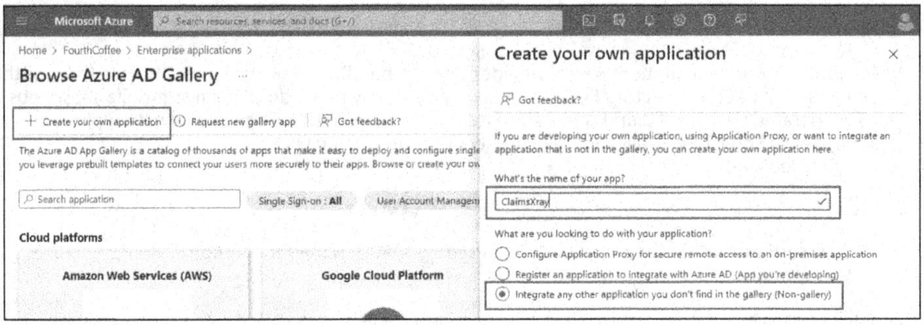

FIGURE 3-24 Assigning users and groups to an application.

5. Click **Single-Sign-On** and choose **SAML** (as shown in Figure 3-25).

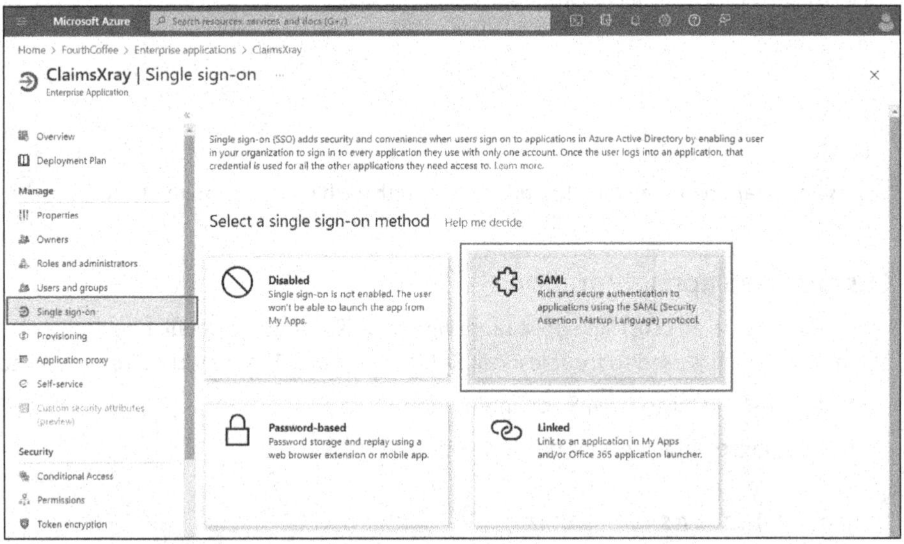

FIGURE 3-25 Specify the SSO using SAML.

6. Configure the single sign-on. Configure the SSO parameters as shown in Figure 3-26. Starting in the Basic SAML Configuration, specify:

A. Identifier: **urn:microsoft:adfs:claimsxray**

B. Reply URL: **https://adfshelp.microsoft.com/ClaimsXray/TokenResponse**

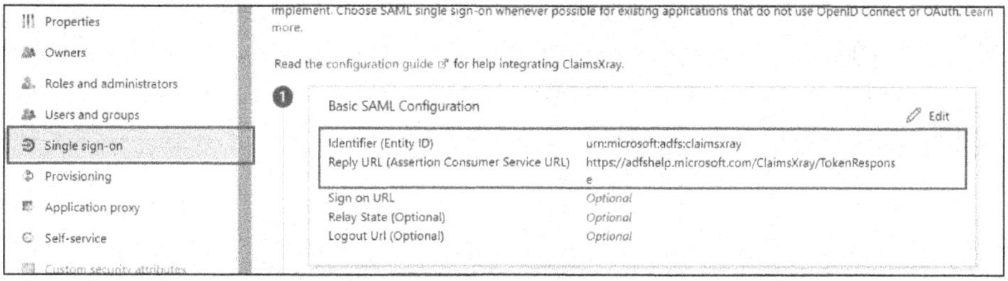

FIGURE 3-26 Definining Basic SAML Configuration.

7. Azure AD will supply some default claims, which are commonly used across applications. For the purpose of this exercise, we will add additional claims apart from the default set. Click **Edit,** as seen in Figure 3-27.

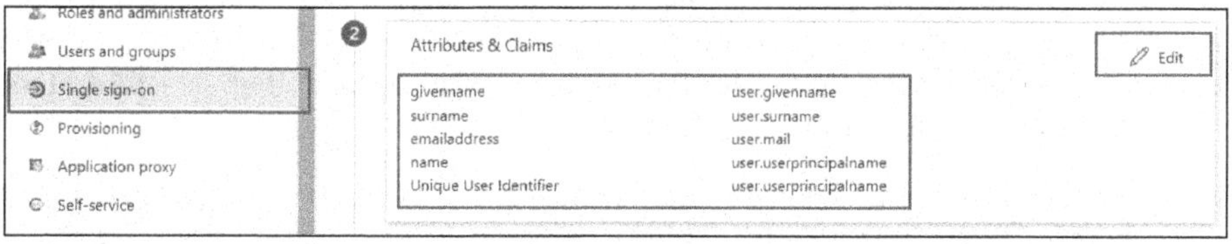

FIGURE 3-27 Modifying the custom claims.

8. In this setup, we will add a new claim called **Custom-EmployeeID** (but it can be anything that your application is expecting), and we will map it to the user property **user.employeeid** value, as seen in Figure 3-28.

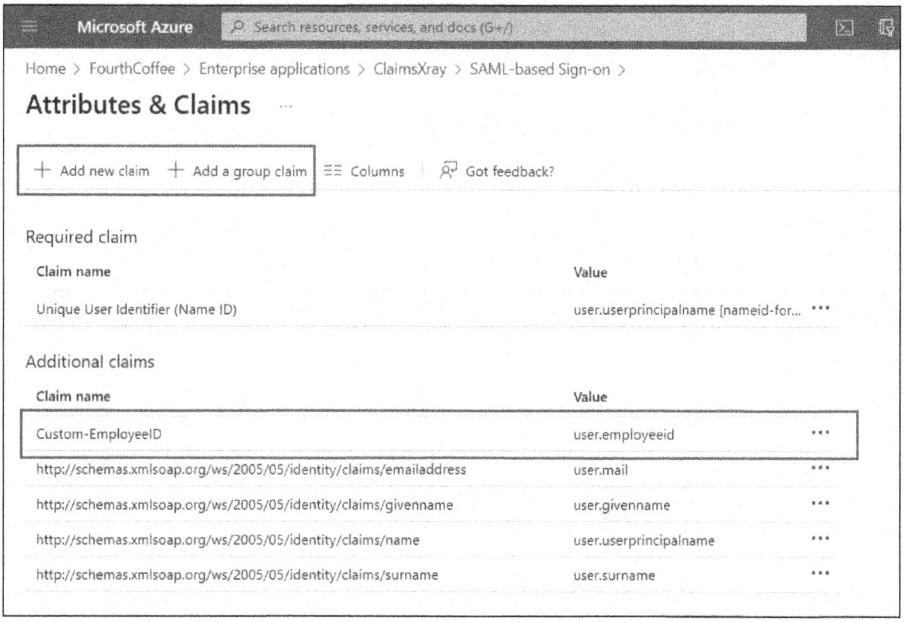

FIGURE 3-28 Adding a custom claim.

9. Once you have added the custom claims—in this case, **Custom-EmployeeID**—it should be available as part of your Attributes & Claims configuration. Verify that the custom claim was added, as shown in Figure 3-29.

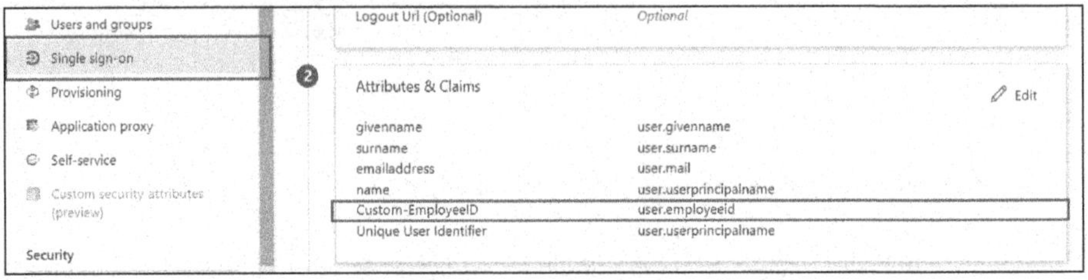

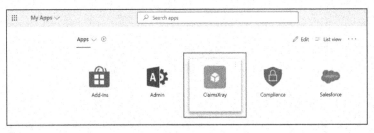

FIGURE 3-29   The custom claim is now part of the Attributes & Claims.

10. In this step, we will configure app authorization—i.e., who all can access this application. The recommended best practice is to assign via group membership, but for the test's purpose we can also add a user. Click **Users and groups** and then select **Add User/ Group** (as highlighted in Figure 3-30).

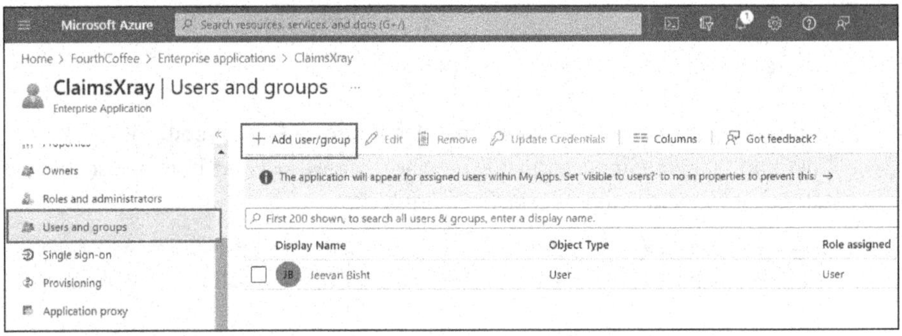

FIGURE 3-30   Assigning users and groups to an application.

11. Now we will verify that the application is available for the user and that the integration is working.

   A. Launch **My Apps** by browsing to *https://myapplications.microsoft.com/*.

   B. Launch the **ClaimsXrayApp** by clicking the **ClaimsXray** app icon (as shown in Figure 3-31).

FIGURE 3-31   Launch an application from My Apps.

12. Once the **ClaimsXray** icon is clicked, it launches a web application. As mentioned earlier, this web application is used to view all the SAML claims including the custom claim that was added. You can see that the **Custom-EmployeeID** claim is printed with the appropriate claim for the user who launched the application (as highlighted in Figure 3-32).

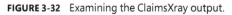

Claim ↑↓	Value
Custom-EmployeeID	SECRET123
http://schemas.microsoft.com/claims/authnmethodsreferences	http://schemas.microsoft.com/ws/2008/06/identity/authenticationmethod/password http://schemas.microsoft.com/claims/multipleauthn
http://schemas.microsoft.com/identity/claims/displayname	Jeevan Bisht
http://schemas.microsoft.com/identity/claims/identityprovider	https://sts.windows.net/bf040b23-572f-4894-a8c1-eb4cc8c443f7/

FIGURE 3-32 Examining the ClaimsXray output.

This summarizes the custom application SSO integration with Azure AD; however, some SaaS providers would also like to get the SaaS applications listed as part of the Azure AD gallery to customers, so they can easily search the application and integration guide. Finally, we also can request Azure Active Directory application integration if we plan to provide our services across multiple tenants or offer software-as-a-service (SaaS) service.

> **NEED MORE REVIEW?** **HOW TO PUBLISH YOUR APPS IN THE GALLERY**
>
> For more information on requesting to publish your application in the Azure Active Directory application gallery, visit: *https://docs.microsoft.com/en-us/azure/active-directory/manage-apps/v2-howto-app-gallery-listing*

Implement application user provisioning

In this section, we will talk about the need for application provisioning and how Azure AD can help with automating both provisioning and deprovisioning of the user.

Application user provisioning

In the modern world, most applications are moving to the SaaS (software-as-a-service) model. We have protocols like OpenID Connect (OIDC) and Security Assertions Markup Language (SAML) that can help set up single sign-on (SSO), but users also need to be provisioned into the applications. The term *provisioning* refers to the ability of automatically creating user identity and certain app roles for the given applications.

Application administrators have historically relied on either manual or Excel/CSV files imported into flow-based tools, sometimes referred to as *manual provisioning,* or have used approaches like SAML just-in-time (JIT) provisioning. These methods allow provisioning users, but as people leave or change roles it is equally important to deprovision, or remove, access. Otherwise, it might present security risks due to excessive data access or unnecessary application license cost overruns. Figure 3-33 shows how Azure AD can help achieve this goal with automation and standards-based integrations called SCIM (System for Cross-Domain Identity Management).

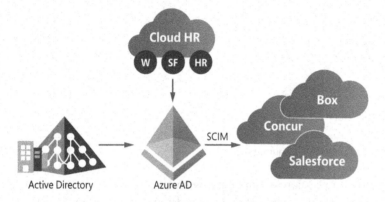

FIGURE 3-33 Azure AD support for provisioning.

Azure AD includes applications integration with support for automatic provisioning and deprovisioning of user's identities to adapt to changing business needs and user roles.

In general, some of the functions of the app provisioning include features mentioned in Table 3-5.

TABLE 3-5 App provisioning capabilities

Function	Description
User Provisioning	Automatically create new accounts in the right systems for new people when they join your team or organization.
User Deprovisioning	Automatically deactivate accounts in the right systems when people leave the team or organization.
Group Provisioning	Ability to provision groups to applications that support them.
Customization	Attributes can be customized to map either to existing attributes or apply transformations.
Governance	Monitor and auditing capabilities for users getting provisioned in the application.

NEED MORE REVIEW?   **WHAT IS APP PROVISIONING?**

For more information on app provisioning in Azure Active Directory, visit:

https://docs.microsoft.com/en-us/azure/active-directory/app-provisioning/user-provisioning

Automated vs Manual provisioning

Azure AD supports a range of applications supporting both modes:

- **Automated Provisioning** refers to the fact that Azure AD has a provisioning connector for the application.

- **Manual Provisioning** implies that the accounts must be created manually. This can be done via dumping identities into text/csv files and running import operations in the applications. Sometimes enterprises also run some scheduled tasks to have custom logic for the export/import of users.

Azure Active Directory Gallery applications supporting user provisioning can be clearly identified or filtered in the Azure AD Enterprise application by applying a filter on the **User Account Management** field, as highlighted in Figure 3-34. The Gallery application also has a small **Provisioning** icon if it supports automated provisioning.

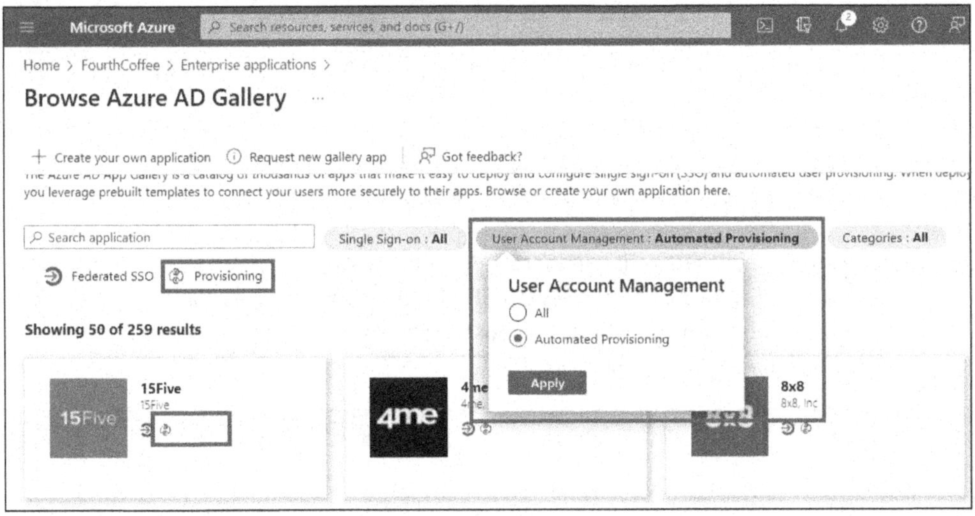

FIGURE 3-34 Application filter to identify applications that support provisioning.

Figure 3-35 shows the Salesforce application enabled for automated provisioning. The configuration steps on how to configure provisioning will vary from application to application.

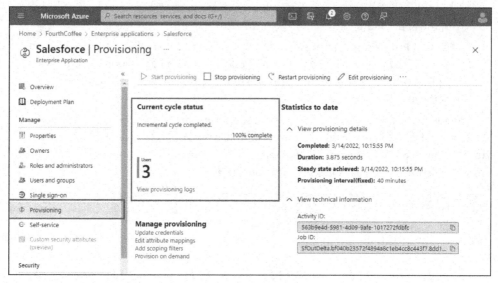

FIGURE 3-35   The Salesforce application enabled for provisioning.

Once the provisioning setting is configured, the automation is achieved by simply assigning the Specific groups. Figure 3-36 shows **MyOrgSFAdmins** as they are automatically provisioned in the Salesforce application as **System Administrators**. As the users are removed from the group, they would be automatically deprovisioned.

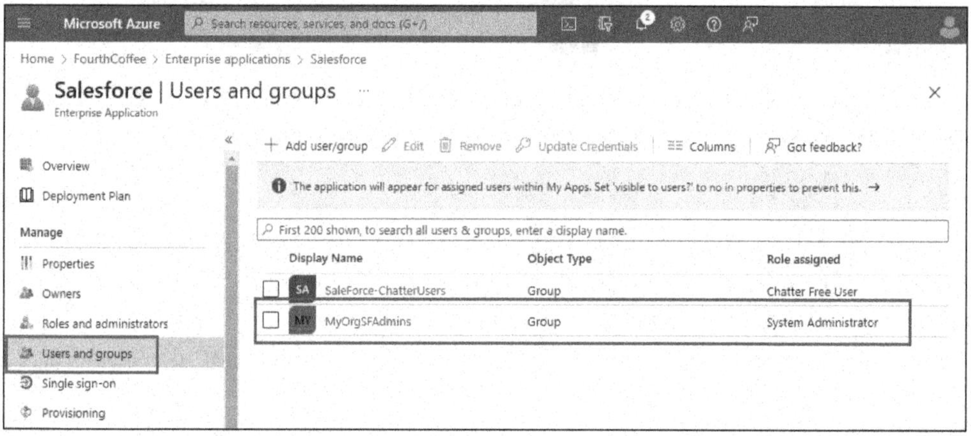

FIGURE 3-36   Salesforce automated roles provisioning based on group membership.

System for Cross-domain Identity Management (SCIM)

While API-based or proprietary automated provisioning exists, these are generally different from application to application and require extensive knowledge of the schemas and APIs before a connector can be created. These challenges were addressed using a new standard called SCIM, which is the de facto standard for provisioning when used with application support OIDC or SAML for industry standards-based integration.

SCIM standards define REST APIs to create, update, and delete objects with a predetermined schedule for common attributes like username, email, etc. across two endpoints: /Users and /Groups. This means that now developers can simply make standards-based REST calls to the defined endpoints to complete operations like creating users and groups. Figure 3-37 shows how SCIM endpoints can be used to provision required attributes for the application.

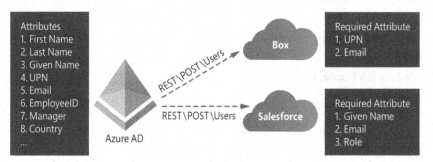

FIGURE 3-37 SCIM endpoints for attributes provisioning.

In summary, SCIM adds support for standards-based integration for SaaS applications or LOB applications without worrying about how objects are represented inside the applications, providing a more consistent and faster way to create apps with provisioning support.

Integrate on-premises apps by using the Azure AD Application Proxy

The Azure AD Application Proxy service is a part of Azure AD. It enables secure remote access to applications on-premises or hosted on public clouds to remote users, generally considered a replacement to VPN for accessing private/internal applications. It requires a minimum Azure AD Premium P1 license. A typical use of App Proxy is to provide access to LOB web applications but is not limited to on-premises SharePoint sites, Remote Desktop, or web applications that might require head-based authentication—e.g., WebSocket applications like Qlik and Tableau.

Azure AD Application Proxy features

Here are some of the key features that enterprises can utilize the Azure AD Application Proxy service for:

- Provides a secure way to access web-applications remotely.
- You can enforce modern security controls like MFA device compliance when accessing the web applications remotely via the Application Proxy service without modifying the web application or rewriting any code.
- Support for a wide set of applications, such as LOB web applications, IWA (Integrated Windows Authentication), applications using head-based authentication, Remote Desktop Gateway Service, or any client apps integrated with ADAL/MSAL.
- Support for custom domain names externally. You can publish the application with familiar URLs—e.g., app1.contoso.com—making it simpler for end users to access applications.
- Integration with the MyApps portal—all the Application Proxy applications can be published to the MyApps portal for ease of discovery.

Azure AD Application Proxy roles

The Azure Application Proxy service supports Azure AD role-based access control (RBAC). The Azure AD Application Proxy management role can be delegated to an application administrator instead of relying on a global administrator. Two key operations that Azure AD Application Proxy admins generally perform are covered in Table 3-6.

TABLE 3-6 Azure AD App Proxy Operations and Roles

Roles	Description
Connector Installation	You must have local administrator rights on the Windows server machine to install the connector in addition to the admin being part of the Application Administrator role, which is required to register the connector instance with Azure AD during the installation process.
Application Management	This includes both application publishing and management. Application administrators can manage all applications in the directory, including registrations, SSO settings, user and group assignments and licensing, Application Proxy settings, and consent. It doesn't grant the ability to manage Conditional Access.

Application Proxy flow

Let's examine the architecture for the Application Proxy service. Figure 3-38 shows the architecture and the flow overview.

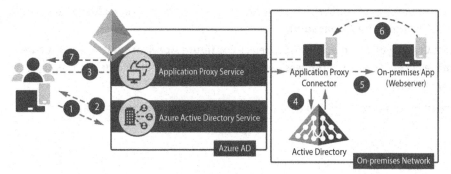

FIGURE 3-38 Azure AD Application Proxy architecture.

1. The user hits the application end point, and the user is directed to Azure to acquire a token and meet all requirements enforced by the administrators. Since App Proxy is integrated with Azure AD, advanced features like MFA, risk-based policy, device compliance, etc. are available as part of the Conditional access controls natively.

   Note: While the Azure AD Application Proxy requires a P1 license, to use advanced conditional policy elements like Sign in Risk or User Risk, you need at least a P2 license.

2. Once the authentication is successful, Azure AD issues a token to the client.

3. Then the client passes the token to the Application Proxy service, which retrieves basic information like UPN (User Principal Name) and SPN (Service Principal Name) from the token and sends the requests to one of the connectors in the connector group for the assigned application.

4. If the application is configured to KCD (Kerberos Constraint Delegation), it will reach out to local domain controllers for a Kerberos ticket on behalf of the user (optional).

   Note: Connectors do not have to be AD domain joined if your applications do not require KCD.

5. The connector sends the request to the on-premises application.

6. The response from the application is sent through the Application Proxy connector and the App Proxy service back to the user.

   Note: At no point does any port open from the public internet directly to the on-premises application, which has security benefits over traditional application publishing where incoming ports need to be opened, punching holes in the public facing firewall.

7. Users can successfully access the web applications.

Adding the Application Proxy application

In this exercise, we will cover the essential settings to publish an on-premises application using the Azure AD App Proxy. Follow these steps:

1. Launch the Azure AD Admin console by navigating to *https://aad.portal.azure.com/* and then click **Enterprise Application.**

2. Select **Create your own application**, select **Configure Application Proxy for secure remote access to an on-premises application**, and specify the **Name** of the app (as shown in Figure 3-39).

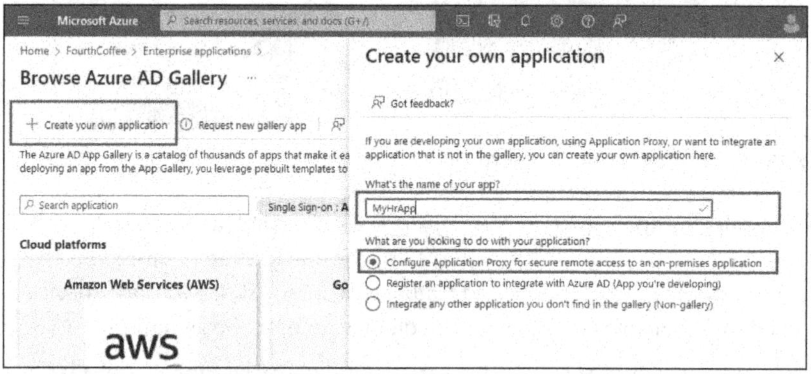

FIGURE 3-39 Adding the App Proxy application from the Azure AD console.

3. You will notice that the Application Proxy shares similar properties to the SaaS application, such as Owners, Roles, Administrators, Users and Groups, etc., which are therefore not discussed here. Our focus is the **Application Proxy** blade and Application Proxy specific configurations, such as the internal URL, etc., as shown in Figure 3-40. All the details are also shown in Table 3-7.

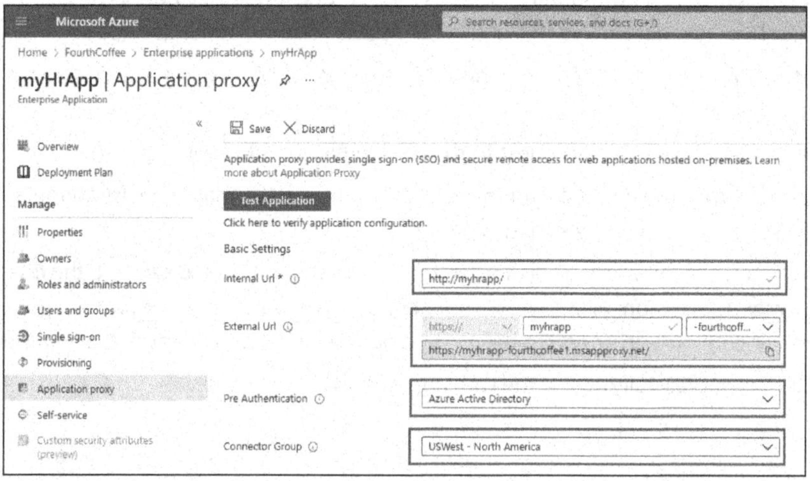

FIGURE 3-40 Application Proxy settings.

TABLE 3-7 App Proxy service configuration parameters

Field	Description
Name	The application name presented in Azure and the MyApps portal.
Internal URL	The URL is used to access the application internally on the private network. This should be reachable from the App Proxy Connector. The URL can be set to the root or can be branched to specific apps—for example, if you only wish to publish a certain part of the website, such as *http://hr.woodgrove.com/HrPolicy/*.
External URL	This address is used to access the application from outside of your private network. You can either use the default app proxy domain *.msapproxy.net or choose your own custom domain. **Note:** A custom domain will require External DNS updates and a public certificate for the domain name.
Pre-Authentication	You can choose: **Azure Active Directory** Users are redirected to Azure AD for the sign-in process and need to be authenticated before they can access the application. You can enforce security controls like MFA (Multifactor Authentication), Conditional Access, etc. **Passthrough** Users are not authenticated by Azure AD Application Proxy services; this is more suitable if your backend application can handle authentication requests.
Connector Group	Connector groups are sets of connectors that serve the requests for the Application Proxy service. You can assign a single connector group to multiple applications. You can have multiple connector groups based on application types or geographic location if desired. You have a minimum of two connectors in a production connector group. Do not use the default connector group for production applications.

4. There are additional sets of Configuration properties on the same page if you drill down the page. Figure 3-41 covers the Additional Settings details, while Table 3-8 covers the details of the most used options.

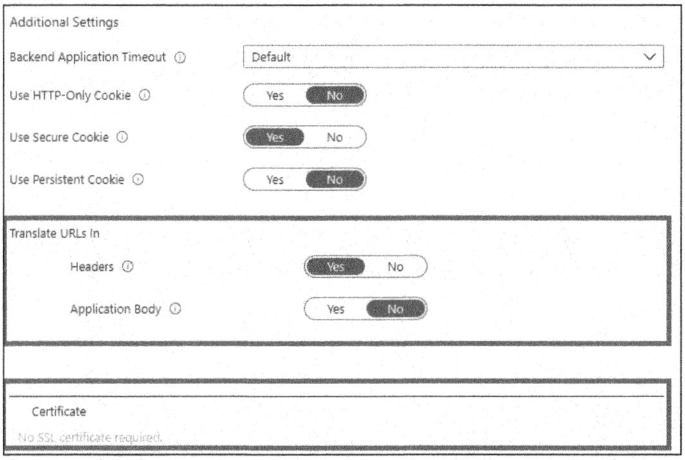

FIGURE 3-41 Additional Azure AD App Proxy Application configuration settings.

In the additional configuration parameters, there are two most widely used settings, as described in Table 3-8.

TABLE 3-8   Additional App Proxy configuration

Field	Description
Translate URLs In	You might use an external name that is different from the application internal names. The App Proxy service can automatically replace the HTML links on the pages to reflect the correct URL when they are exposed through App Proxy services.
Certificate	The certificate is required whenever you require a custom domain name for an application when published using an App Proxy—for example, *hrweb.contoso.com vs hrweb. contoso.msappproxy.net*.

> **NEED MORE REVIEW?   AZURE AD APPLICATION PROXY SETUP WALKTHROUGH**
>
> Use the reference links to walk through the overall process of setting up an Azure AD Application Proxy application with Kerberos constrained delegation (KCD):
>
> - *https://mslearn.cloudguides.com/guides/Provide%20secure%20remote%20 access%20to%20on-premises%20applications%20with%20Azure%20AD%20 Application%20Proxy*
> - *https://docs.microsoft.com/en-us/azure/active-directory/app-proxy/application-proxy-add-on-premises-application*

Monitor and audit access/sign-ons to an Azure AD integrated Enterprise application

Azure AD provides a rich set of capabilities to the admins to understand the status of the platform. These might include changes happening within the platform—for example, an application administrator added a new application, or a configuration update occurred to the conditional access service generally considered as auditing capabilities. There might be other transactional logging to monitor which users are logging in from what devices and IP addresses, etc., and whether or not the sign-in was successful, this information might be captured in other logs like sign-in logs.

Audit logs

Audit logs are key in tracking changes to services for both tracking and compliance purposes. The data is considered privileged information and can only be accessed by these roles:

- Security Administrators
- Security Reader
- Report Reader
- Global Reader
- Global Administrator

Both **Audit logs** and **Sign-in logs** are available in the **Monitoring** section of Azure Active Directory. If you launch the audit logs from the Monitoring blade, it will display information about all components. Figure 3-42 shows the Audit log and its details.

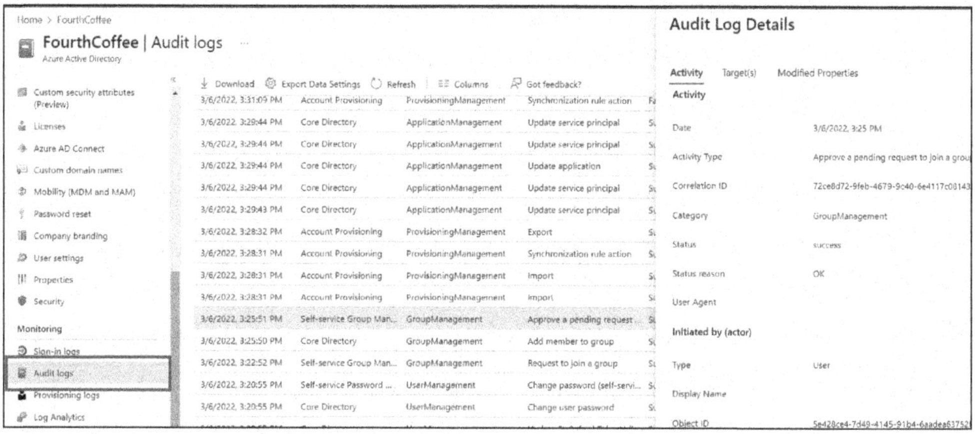

FIGURE 3-42 Azure Active Directory Audit logs.

The default view can be customized to add/remove additional information. In general, administrators can specify additional columns to view, have a 24-hour/7/30 days view of the audit log data, and the capability to Download/export the data as a CSV file (as shown in Figure 3-43).

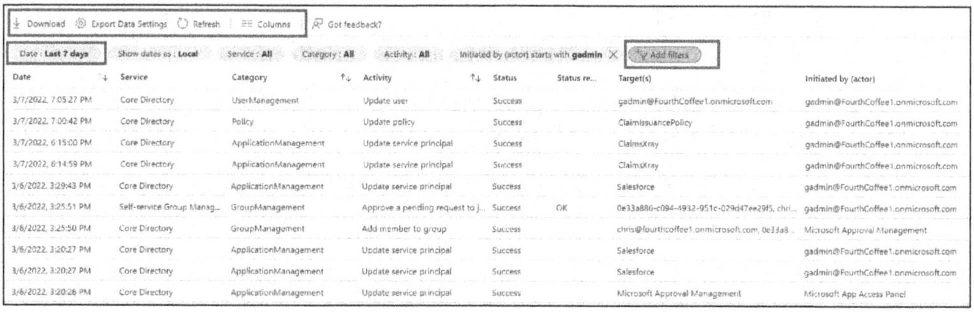

FIGURE 3-43 Azure Active Directory Audit logs filters and settings.

You can launch the audit logs from Enterprise applications, and the logs are filtered to the Enterprise application events. You can get insights like those shown in Figure 3-44.

- When was an application added?
- Who created the service principal?
- Who provided the consent for the app?
- Who added the application?
- Who modified the application?

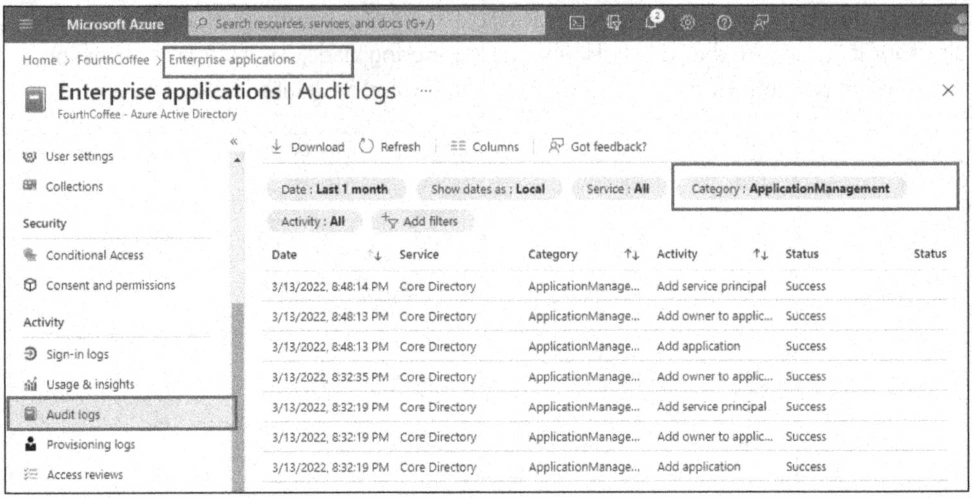

FIGURE 3-44 Azure Active Directory Audit Logs from Enterprise applications.

Usage insights

Azure AD can present a summarized view of application usage indicators like successful authentication, failed authentication, and how many users can access the application. These insights are a valuable set of information, as they can help the admins understand patterns that might otherwise be difficult to parse through logs, as shown in Figure 3-45.

To Access the insights reports:

1. Launch the Azure AD console and choose **Enterprise applications**.

2. From the **Activity section**, select **Usage & insights** to open the report.

3. Click the **Azure AD Application activity** report.

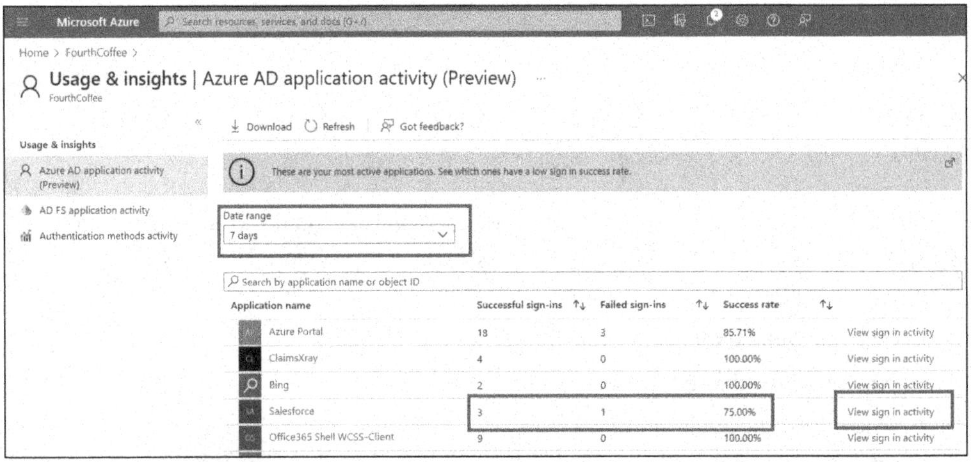

FIGURE 3-45 Azure AD application activity report showing app summary statistics.

This report can be used to determine multiple things, including but not limited to:

- What does the application usage look like?
- Are users in general able to successfully access the application?
- Trend Analysis for application access, such as what time is the app accessed, etc.

The **View sign-in activity** option can provide additional insights into the sign-in activity by day and details on what the common sign-in errors are, as shown in Figure 3-46.

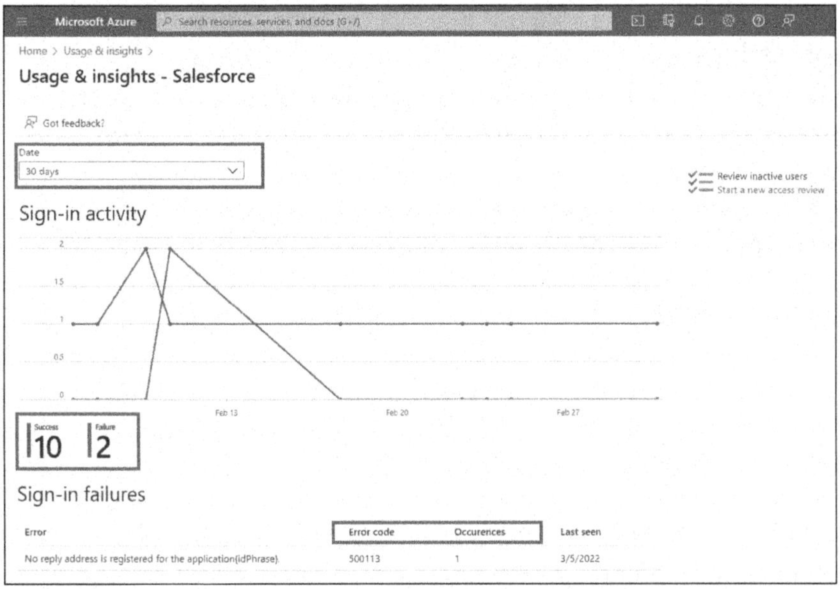

FIGURE 3-46 App activity showing usage including login success and failures for a given period.

Additionally, this information presented by Success and Failure in Figure 3-46 can be associated with the sign-in events where you can see detailed information for that specific sign-in event. Figure 3-47 shows the sign-in details for the specific application.

FIGURE 3-47 A sign-in event show details about the event.

Implement and configure consent settings

Azure AD allows applications to take advantage of scale and flexibility for application integration. This allows users to consent to applications across multiple service providers using their work accounts. However, Azure AD does provide organizations the ability to regulate what apps their users are consenting to avoid unwanted exposure to malicious applications that a normal user might not be aware of without sacrificing their experience on the platform. By default, all users can consent to any application that does not require admin consent.

User consent settings

In general, consent settings allow an admin to set limits on when end users are allowed to grant consent to apps and when they will be required to request administrator review and approval, as shown in Figure 3-48.

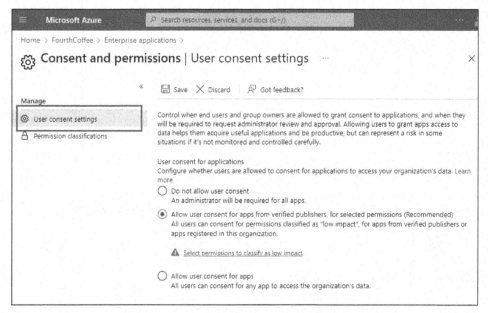

FIGURE 3-48 The User consent settings page.

Table 3-9 describes the impact of the various User consent settings options.

TABLE 3-9 User consent configuration options

Consent setting	Description
Disable user consent	Users cannot grant permissions to applications. Users can continue to sign in to apps they had previously consented to or that are consented to by administrators on their behalf, but they will not be allowed to consent to new permissions or to new apps on their own. Only users who have been granted a directory role that includes the permission to grant consent will be able to consent to new apps.
Users can consent to apps from verified publishers or your organization, but only for permissions you choose	All users can only consent to apps that were published by a verified publisher and apps that are registered in your tenant. Users can only consent to the permissions you have classified as "low impact." You must classify permissions to choose which permissions users are allowed to consent to.
Users can consent to all apps	This option allows all users to consent to any permission that does not require administrator consent for any application.
Custom app consent policy	This option provides the ability to specify more granular controls, which is done using the Azure AD PowerShell.

Administrators further have the capability to define what low-risks permissions consent looks like for their organizations. Consent settings provide them with the capability to classify the permissions as per their policies, making it efficient and safe for users to consent with limited exposure. For example, in Figure 3-49 the admin is specified.

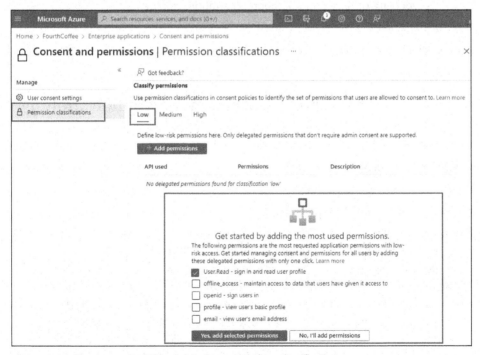

FIGURE 3-49 User consent settings related to permissions classification.

Skill 3.2: Implement app registrations

Azure AD organizations leverage Azure AD as the Identity platform for applications designed to represent line-of-business (LOB) applications and the ability to serve as SaaS applications to other Azure AD tenants. The application registration model and its security controls are critical to understand for a successful integration experience.

> **This skill covers how to:**
> - Plan your line-of-business application registration strategy
> - Implement application registrations
> - Configure application permissions and implement application authorization

Plan your line-of-business application registration strategy

Azure AD offers wide support for application integration. In general, enterprises can take advantage of the security and scale of the global service. We'll cover these topics:

■ Fundamentals of App Registration

■ What is an Application Object?

■ What is a Service Principal Object?

It is important to understand how the application is represented in Azure AD. There are two representational states: **Application Objects** and **Service Principal Objects**.

■ **Application Objects** are used to define and describe the application to Azure AD. This enables Azure AD to understand how to issue tokens to an application based on its configuration. Where the Application Object is created is called its home directory, especially in the case of multi-tenanted applications. The application object might contain information such as the Name, Redirect URIs, Certificate & Secrets, App Roles, SSO metadata, etc. Figure 3-50 shows the application object properties.

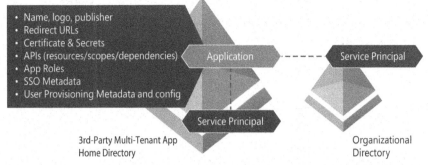

FIGURE 3-50 Azure AD Application Object key properties.

- **Service Principals** govern applications connected to Azure AD. While the Application Object can only exist in the home directory, the instances for the application can exist in tenants where it's being used called Service Principals. It can include the actual directory-specific configurations like logos, Name, users/group assignments, conditional access policies, Roles assignment, claims transformations, etc. Figure 3-51 shows the relationship between an Application and Service Principal.

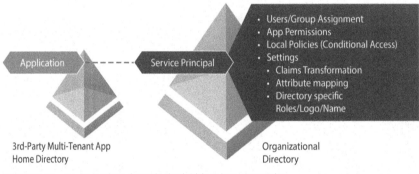

FIGURE 3-51 Azure AD Service Principal Object key properties.

The relationship between Application Object and Service Principal Objects

An application will have an Application Object in its home directory. It will have a Service Principal in any other directory that uses the application. If the application is being used in the home directory, it will have both a Service Principal and an Application Object in the same directory, as represented by **CustomApp** in the diagram shown in Figure 3-52. Figure 3-52 depicts the relationship between various types of Application Objects.

The **CustomApp** represents:

- Your custom developed application as integrated with Azure AD
- Any apps you connected for SSO
- Internal apps published using the Azure AD Application Proxy

It is also important to note that Microsoft has the following two directories:

- Microsoft Apps (**Microsoft service** directory like Office 365)
- Pre-integrated third-party applications (Azure AD **App Gallery**)

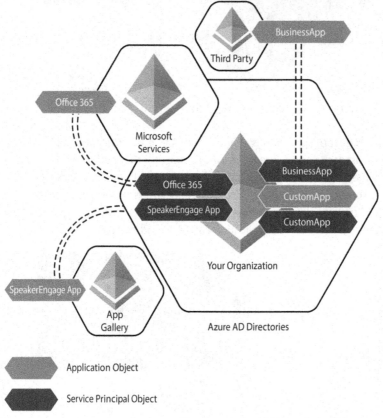

FIGURE 3-52 Azure AD application and Service Principal Object relationship.

Service Principals can be created using multiple entry points including the Azure AD console, Azure AD PowerShell, and Microsoft Graph API. When consenting for the application, users can also force the creation of the Service applications implicitly if the users' registrations are not blocked. Figure 3-53 depicts the implicit Service Principal registration flow when users try to access the application for the first time.

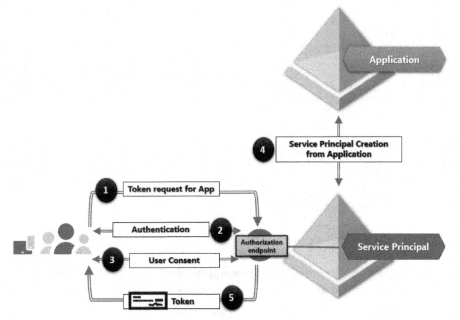

FIGURE 3-53 Service Principal creation flow from user consent.

The flow for implicit service principal creation is documented as follows:

1. A user attempts to sign in with the app. The **authorization endpoint** requests a token for the application.

2. The user credentials are acquired and verified for **authentication**.

3. The user is prompted to provide **user consent** for the app to gain access to the application tenant (as in Figure 3-54).

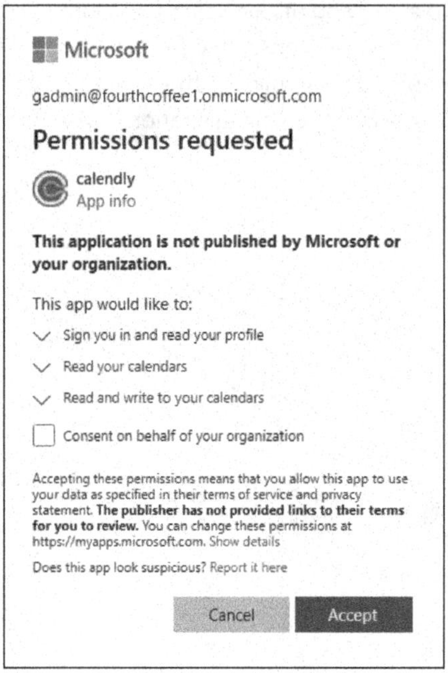

FIGURE 3-54 Application consent screen.

4. Azure AD uses the **Application Object** in the **Application** tenant as a blueprint for creating a **Service Principal** in the User tenant, and a Service Principal is created.

5. The user receives the requested **token** to access the application.

> **NOTE** **BLOCKING END USERS FROM CREATING SERVICE PRINCIPALS**
>
> To prevent users from registering their own applications:
>
> - In the Azure portal, go to the **User settings** section under **Azure Active Directory console**.
> - Change **Users can register applications** to **No**.

Implement application registrations

Application registration is the process of establishing a trust relationship between the identity platform and your application. The application could be a client app commonly including web, web API, or mobile apps.

One of the following Azure AD roles is required for app registrations:

- Application administrator
- Application developer
- Cloud application administrator

EXAM TIP

It is important to understand each of the built-in application admin roles and have a clear distinction of what types of applications every role can manage.

The next section covers the App registration process and various configuration parameters.

To register the application:

1. Log in to the Azure portal.
2. Under Manage, select **App registrations**, and then select **new registration**.
3. Enter a **Name** for your application.

   Specify the **Supported account types** or sign-in audience (who can use the application).
4. Specify **Redirect URI (optional)**. A redirect URI is where Azure AD will redirect a user's client and sends security tokens after authentication. In a production app, there is often a public endpoint where your app runs.
5. Select **Register** to complete the initial app registration, as shown in Figure 3-55.

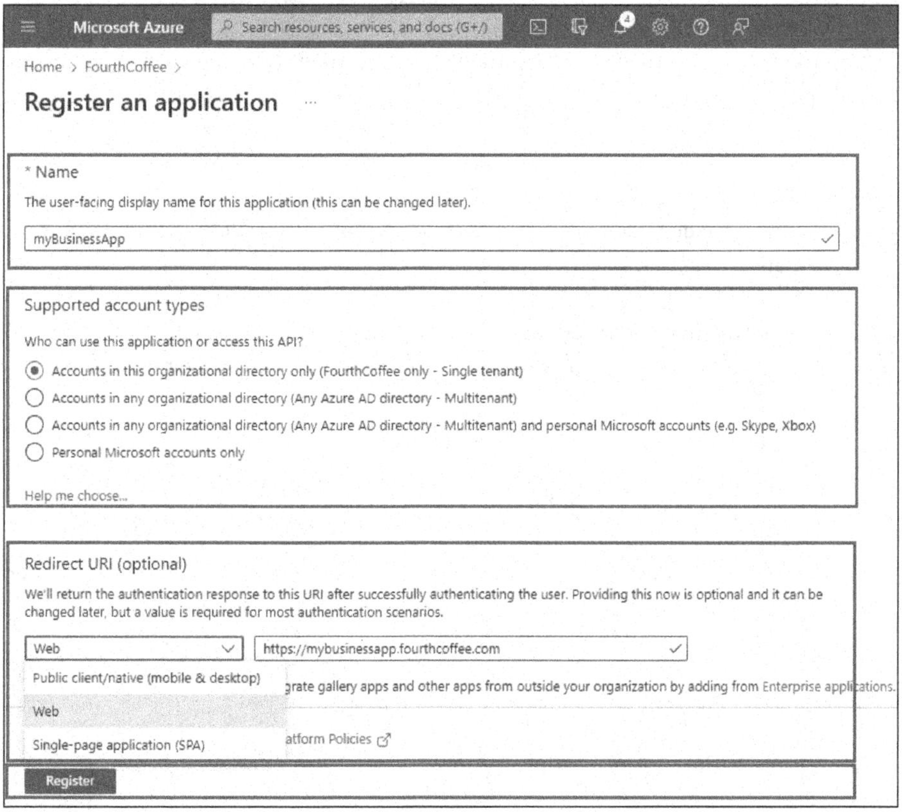

FIGURE 3-55 App registration configuration page.

Azure AD supports multiple types of accounts, as shown in Figure 3-55. Table 3-10 describes when to use specific account types. The most common option used for applications inside an enterprise is **Accounts in this organizational directory only**.

TABLE 3-10 Azure AD App Registration supported account types

Supported account types	Description
Accounts in this organizational directory only	Select this option if you're building an application for use only by users (or guests) in your tenant. Often called a line-of-business (LOB) application, this app is a single-tenant application in the Microsoft Identity platform.
Accounts in any organizational directory	Select this option if you want users in any Azure AD tenant to be able to use your application. This option is appropriate if, for example, you're building a software-as-a-service (SaaS) application that you intend to provide to multiple organizations. This type of app is known as a multi-tenant application in the Microsoft Identity platform.
Accounts in any organizational directory	Select this option to target the widest set of customers. By selecting this option, you're registering a multi-tenant application that can also support users who have personal Microsoft accounts.
Personal Microsoft accounts	Select this option if you're building an application only for users who have personal Microsoft accounts. Personal Microsoft accounts include Skype, Xbox, Live, and Hotmail accounts.

EXAM TIP

It is important to understand the details of the **supported account types** and **sign-in audience** related to each option.

6. **Authentication blade.** Azure AD supports applications for various platforms. In this blade, we configure the platform for which the application is being targeted, as shown in Figure 3-56.

   A. Under **Manage**, select **Authentication**.

   B. Under **Platform configurations**, select **Add a platform.**

   C. Select the appropriate applications type (not required for this exam).

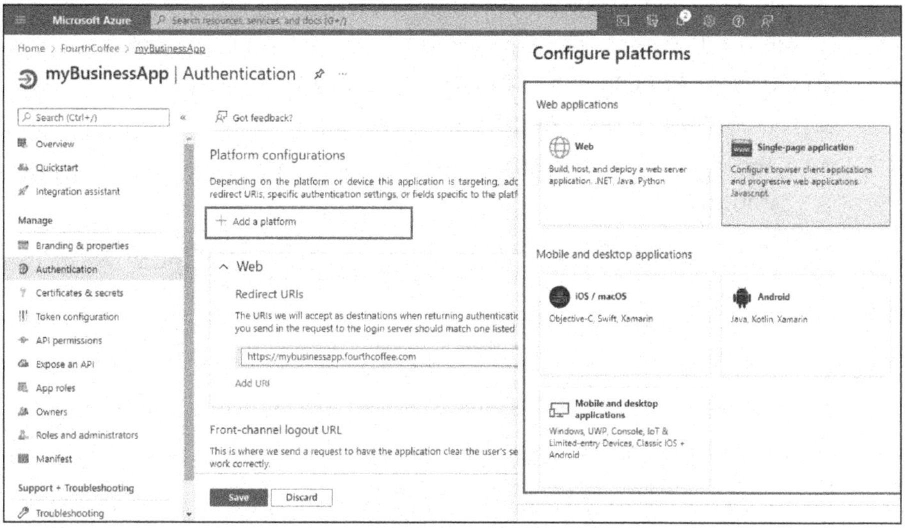

FIGURE 3-56 App registration platform configuration page.

Azure AD supports multiple platforms for application registration, and each application type has additional configuration parameters, as described in Table 3-11.

TABLE 3-11 App Registration Platform configuration settings

Platform	Configuration settings
Android	For apps written in Java, Kotlin, or Xamarin, configuring your Android app enables your users to get device-wide SSO through the Microsoft Authenticator and seamlessly access your application. You need to specify **Package Name** and **Signature Hash**.
iOS/macOS	For apps written using Objective-C, Swift, or Xamarin, configuring your iOS or macOS app enables your users to get SSO and seamlessly access your application. You need to specify the **Bundle ID**.
Mobile and desktop applications	For apps written for Windows, UWP, Console, IoT & limited-entry devices, classic iOS + Android, select one of the suggested **redirect URIs** or specify a **custom redirect URI**.
Single-page application	Configure browser client applications and progressive web applications. JavaScript. You need to specify a **redirect URI** that the URIs will accept as destinations when returning authentication responses (tokens) after successfully authenticating or signing out users. The redirect URI you send in the request to the login server should match the one listed here. Also referred to as reply URLs.
Web	Support for Web server applications like .Net, Java, Python, etc. You need to specify a **Redirect URI** that the URIs we will accept as destinations when returning authentication responses (tokens) after successfully authenticating or signing out users. The redirect URI you send in the request to the login server should match the one listed here. Also referred to as reply URLs.

7. **Certificates & Secrets blade.** App registration supports multiple options for the application authentications—typically client secret and secret in more secure workloads. To specify the authentication, configure the setting as follows:

   A. Under **Manage**, select **Certificates & Secrets.**

   B. Choose one of the credentials (Figure 3-57 shows the client-secret configuration being added).

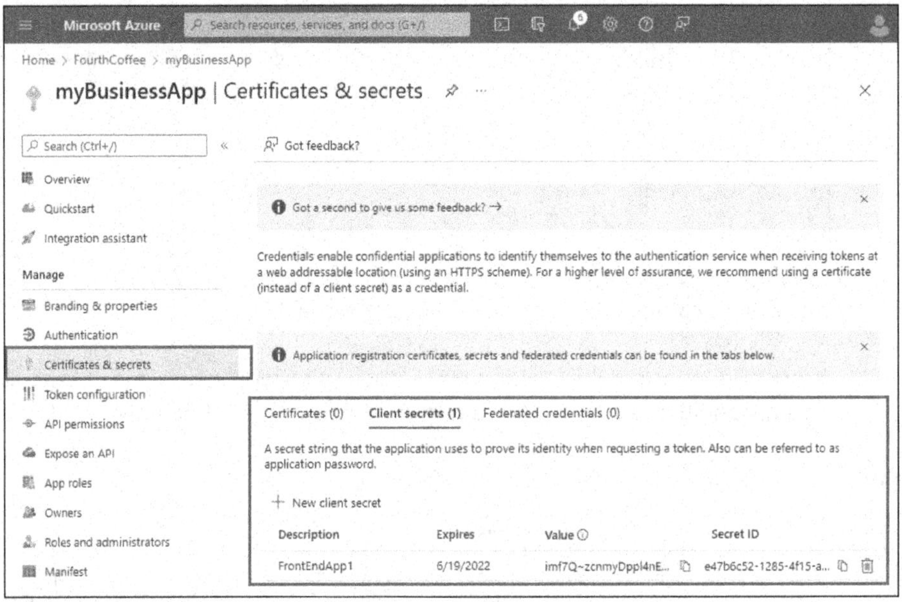

FIGURE 3-57 App Registration configuration for certificates and secrets.

Credentials enable confidential applications to identify themselves to the authentication service when receiving tokens at a web addressable location (using an HTTPS scheme). Table 3-12 covers various options and their scheme details.

TABLE 3-12 App Registration supported authentication methods

Option	Description
Certificate	Certificates can be used as secrets to prove the application's identity when requesting a token. Also, it can be referred to as public keys. Your certificate must be one of the following file types: .cer, .pem, .crt
Client Secret	A secret string that the application uses to prove its identity when requesting a token. Also, it can be referred to as an application password.
Federated Credentials	Allow other identities to impersonate this application by establishing a trust with an external OpenID Connect (OIDC) identity provider. This federation allows you to get tokens to access Azure AD protected resources that this application has access to, such as Azure and Microsoft graph.

EXAM TIP

For a higher level of assurance, use a certificate (instead of a client secret) as a credential. You will find that Client Secrets are most commonly used during development.

8. **Token configuration blade.** Azure AD provides flexibility to the developers to adapt to their standards. The configuration allows you to specify things like optional claims, token format, etc., to meet business requirements. To modify the default claim, follow these steps:
   A. Under **Manage**, select **Certificates & Secrets**.
   B. Specify **Optional Claims**, as seen in Figure 3-58.

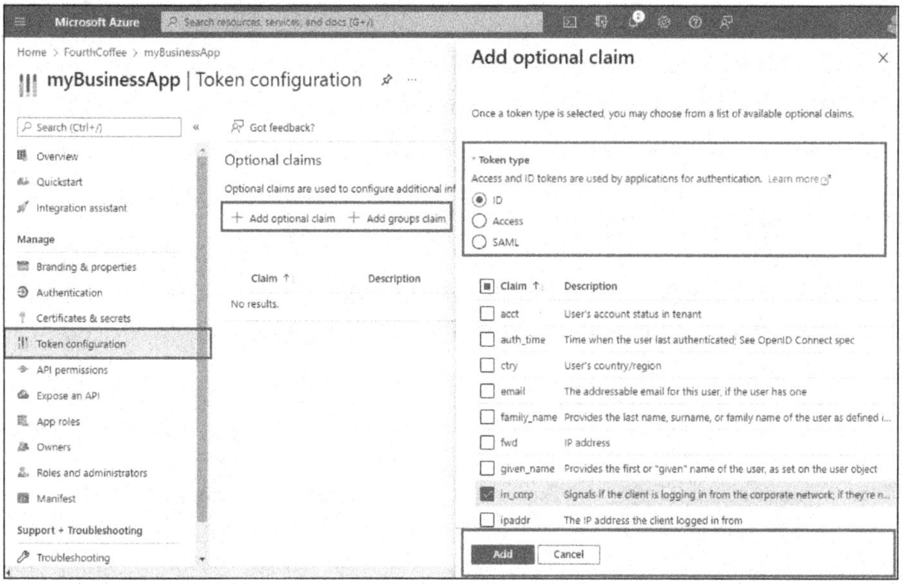

FIGURE 3-58 App registration Token configuration page.

Optional claims are used to configure additional information, which is returned in one or more tokens. You can **Add optional claim** and/or **Add groups claim.** You also configure various token types depending on the applications, as shown in Figure 3-58. Table 3-13 describes the various format details.

TABLE 3-13 Token types for optional claims

Token Type	Description
idToken	idToken for the OIDC ID token, the optional claims returned in the JWT ID token.
accessToken	accessToken for the OAuth access token, the optional claims returned in the JWT access token.
saml2Token	Saml2Token for SAML tokens, the optional claims returned in the SAML token. The Saml2Token type applies to both SAML1.1 and SAML2.0 format tokens.

Configure application permissions and implement application authorization

Let's start with the fundamentals of the authorization model and a basic understanding of scopes, permissions, and consent.

- **Understanding permissions and scopes**
- **Configure API permission**

Understanding permissions and scopes

Using the OAuth 2.0 protocol, Azure AD can support a third-party application access web-hosted resource on behalf of a user. Each application that integrates with Azure AD is identified using its **resource identifier** or **Application ID URI**. Let's look at some Microsoft Service Applications as an example:

- Microsoft 365 Mail API: https://outlook.office.com
- Microsoft Graph: https://graph.microsoft.com
- myBusinessApp: *https://myBusinessApp.fourthcoffee.com* (Custom example)

OAuth 2.0 is considered the authorization protocol. There are predefined permissions for the applications for some Microsoft examples. In OAuth 2.0, these *scopes* are often referred to as *permissions*. The permissions are strings:

- Mail.Read - Send mail as any user
- Calendar.Read – Read calendars in all mailboxes
- Mail.ReadWrite - Read and write mail in all mailboxes
- Expense.Report.ReadAll – Read all expense reports (Custom defined for example)

Developers can utilize these APIs to build a great user experience using the concept of least privilege where possible, asking only the permissions required for the app to be functional and effective. Some high-privilege permissions can only be granted by the administrator's consent. In the above list, Mail.ReadWrite might be one such example that could allow the app to read and write email on behalf of all users in the company. Figure 3-59 shows a custom scope configuration from the app.

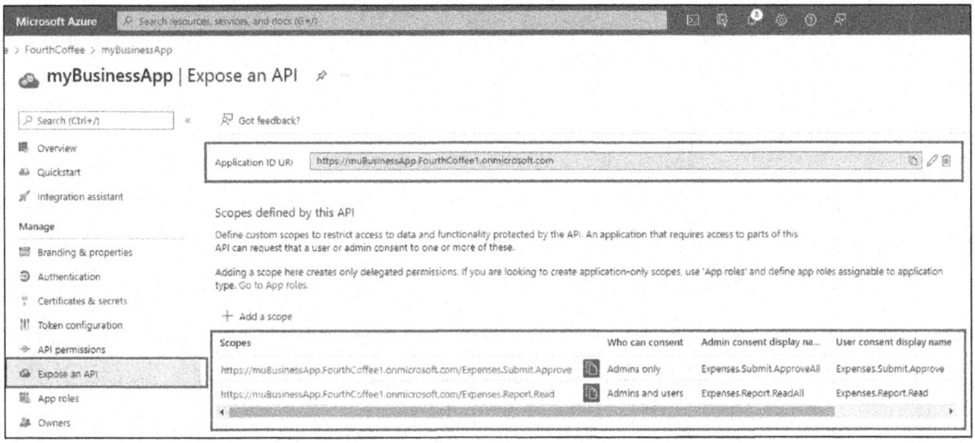

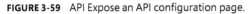

FIGURE 3-59 API Expose an API configuration page.

Azure AD supports two types of permissions:

- **Delegated permissions**

  These are assigned to the applications that require permission to act as the sign-in user when making calls to the target resources. In general, the user or administrator can provide consent.

- **Application permissions**

  These are assigned to applications that run without a signed-in user and are generally background services or processes/daemons. Only users in the administrator roles can consent to application permissions.

Delegated permissions have ***effective permissions***, which means that if an operation had a scope or permission similar to User.ReadWrite.All, this application would behave differently. Assume that an end user with no elevated permission consented to the application. The user would be scoped only to his profile because privileges are limited. On the other hand, if the Administrator launched the same application, she would be able to effectively update profiles for every user in the entire organization. Application permissions are not affected by this.

OpenID Connect (OIDC) is an authentication protocol based on the OAuth2 protocol (which is used for authorization). OpenID Connect has a few well-defined scopes that are also hosted on Microsoft Graph: openid, email, profile, and offline_access, as shown in Figure 3-60.

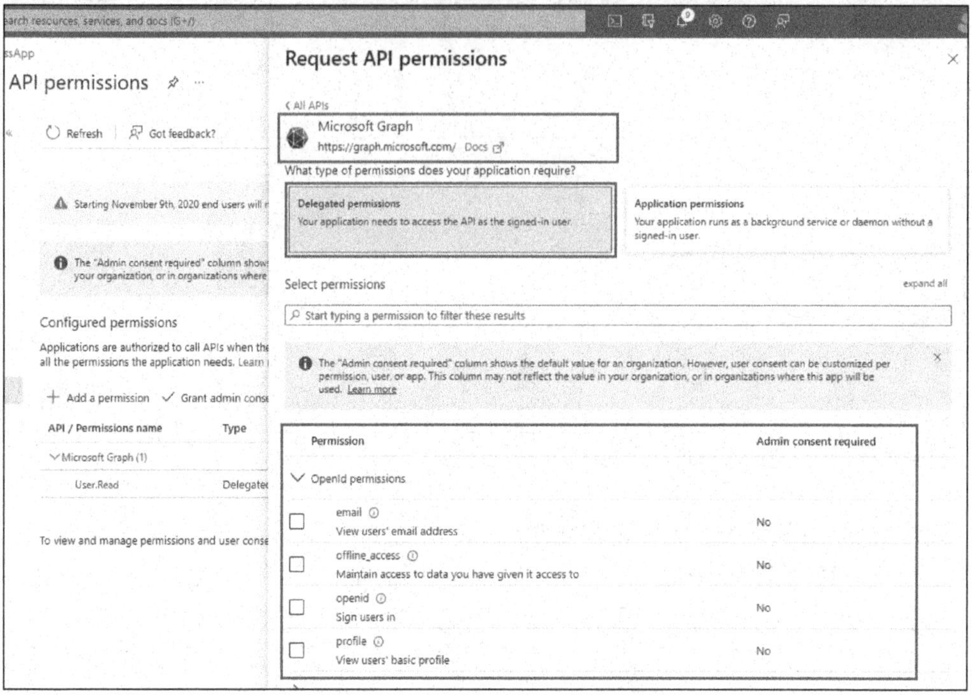

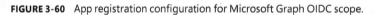

FIGURE 3-60 App registration configuration for Microsoft Graph OIDC scope.

Scopes are considered critical for application security and behavior. Table 3-14 captures the various options and their impact on user access.

TABLE 3-14 OIDC scope details

Scope	Description
Email	The email scope can be used with the openid scope and any others. It gives the app access to the user's primary email address in the form of the email claim.
Offline access	The offline_access scope gives your app access to resources on behalf of the user for an extended time. On the consent page, this scope appears as the ***Maintain access to data you have given it access to*** permission. When a user approves the offline_access scope, your app can receive refresh tokens from the Microsoft Identity platform token endpoint. Refresh tokens are long-lived, and your app can get new access tokens as older ones expire.
profile	The profile scope can be used with the openid scope and any others. It gives the app access to a substantial amount of information about the user. The information it can access includes, but isn't limited to, the user's given name, surname, preferred username, and object ID.
Openid	If using sign-in by using OpenID Connect, it must request the openid scope. The openid scope shows on the work account consent page as the ***Sign you in*** permission and on the personal Microsoft account consent page as the ***View your profile and connect to apps and services using your Microsoft account*** permission.

Tokens

There are primarily three types of tokens used in OAuth 2.0/OIDC:

- Access tokens - tokens that a resource server receives from a client, containing permissions the client has been granted.

- ID tokens - tokens that a client receives from the authorization server, used to sign in a user and get basic information about them.

- Refresh tokens - used by a client to get new access and ID tokens over time. These are opaque strings and are only understandable by the authorization server.

> **NEED MORE REVIEW?** **OAUTH 2.0 AND OIDC**
>
> For more information on OIDC protocols, roles, and scope, visit: *https://docs.microsoft.com/en-us/azure/active-directory/develop/active-directory-v2-protocols#protocols*

The OIDC scope would result in the consent request for the users. The app can request the permissions it needs by using the scope query parameter. When a user signs in to an app, the app sends a request for permission. Each permission is indicated by appending the permission value to the resource's identifier (the Application ID URI).

After the user enters their credentials, the Azure AD platform endpoint checks for a matching record of user consent. If the user has not consented to any of the requested permissions in the past, nor has an administrator consented to these permissions on behalf of the entire organization, the Azure AD endpoint asks the user to grant the requested permissions, as shown in Figure 3-61.

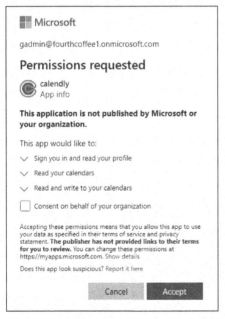

FIGURE 3-61 Application consent screen with required scopes.

However, the consent prompt experience can be configured in two ways:

- **User consent**

  When the user approves the permission request, consent is recorded, and the user doesn't have to consent again on subsequent sign-ins to the application. This must be done by every single user trying to access the application.

- **Tenant-level consent**

  The administrator can grant consent for the application to act on behalf of any user in the tenant. If the admin grants consent for the entire tenant, the organization's users won't see a consent page for the application.

Configure API permissions

As a part of the app configuration, one of the steps is configuring the API permissions. Both Enterprise applications and API Registration can be granted consent and must be done differently. The Global Administrator role is required to provide admin consent.

In the following section, we will review how we can grant consent for App Registrations.

To grant Admin consent for App Registrations:

1. Browse to **Azure Active Directory** > **App registrations** > **myBusinessApp app**.

2. In the left navigation, under Manage, select **API permissions**. (Figure 3-62 highlights the permissions menu and shows that Admin consent has not yet been granted.)

3. Under **Configured permissions**, select **Grant admin consent**.

4. Review the additional dialog presented, and then select **Yes**.

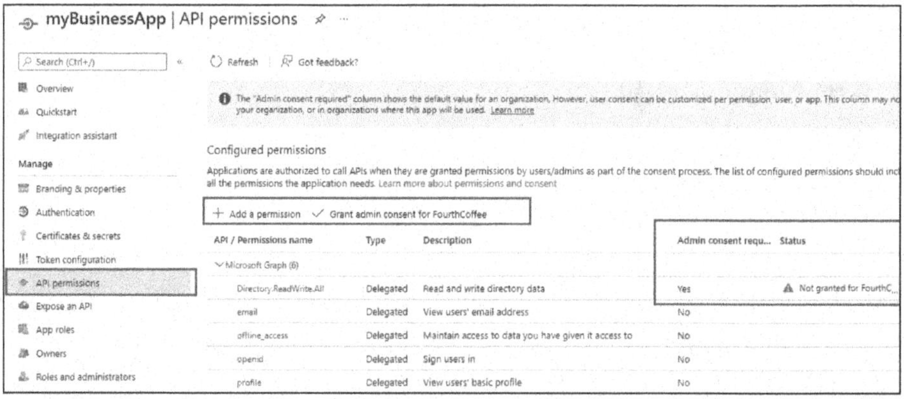

FIGURE 3-62 App registration configuration showing admin consent status and control.

In the below section, we will review how we can grant consent for the Enterprise applications.

To grant admin consent in Enterprise applications:

1. Browse **to Azure Active Directory** > **Enterprise applications** > app (myBusinessApp in this example).

2. On the **myBusinessApp** app blade, in the left navigation, under **Security**, select **Permissions**.

3. Under Permissions, select **Grant admin consent** and review the admin consent granted list (both are highlighted in Figure 3-63).

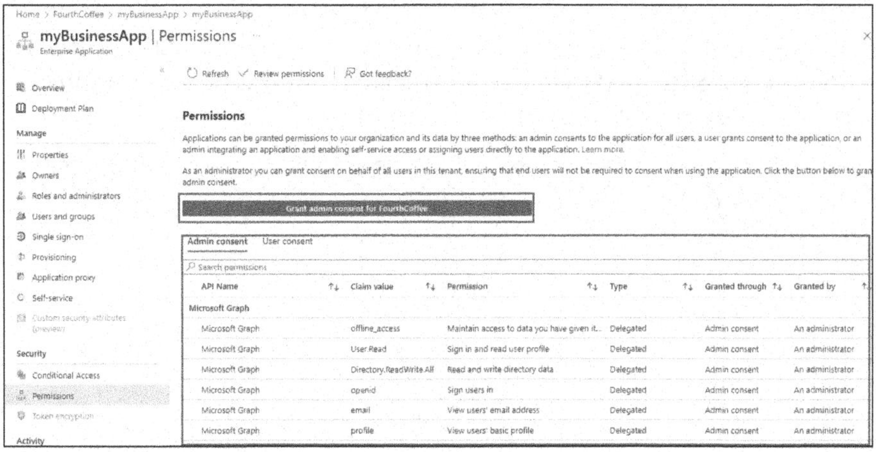

FIGURE 3-63   Granting Admin consent for the application.

NOTE GRANTING ADMIN CONSENT VIA A URL

Administrators can also provide tenant-wide admin consent by browsing to a specially crafted URL, *https://login.microsoftonline.com/{tenant-id}/adminconsent?client_id={clientId}*, where:

- {client-id} is the application's client ID.
- {tenant-id} is your organization's tenant ID or verified domain name.

Some of the high-privilege permissions can be admin restricted. If your app requires access to admin-restricted scopes for organizations, you should request them directly from a company administrator, also by using the admin consent endpoint.

Application consent permissions are granted via the admin consent endpoint. This grant isn't given on behalf of any specific user; instead, the client application is granted permissions directly. These are generally requested by non-interactive applications or services that run in the background.

EXAM TIP

If you think a malicious application was somehow permitted and you are compromised, you should:

- Remove all users assigned to the application.
- Revoke all permissions granted to the application.
- Revoke refresh tokens for all users.

Implement application authorization

App roles can be configured to emit role claims for each role the service principal or users were granted to the user. The applications can use these claims to implement claim-based authorization. These claims need to be configured per the requirement of the applications, and Azure AD provides many ways to achieve this for both Enterprise applications and App Registrations.

For example, in the following example, the application has two roles: **ClaimsViewer** and **User**. Chris is assigned to the **User** role and Jeevan Bisht is assigned to the **ClaimsViewer** role, as highlighted in Figure 3-64.

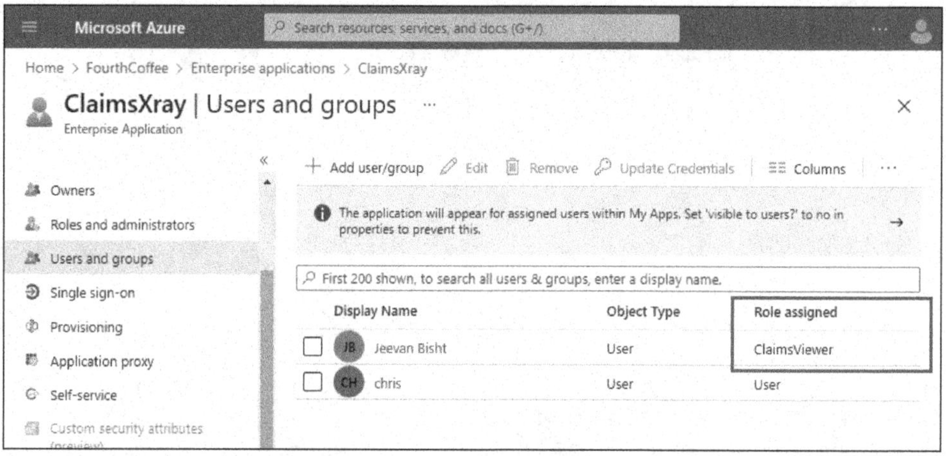

FIGURE 3-64   App roles assigned to users.

Once the user successfully authenticates, he would receive a token with claims including role claim. The application can implement different experiences for the **ClaimsViewers** and **User** roles. Figure 3-65 is just an example taken from the ClaimsXray app to print the claims from the token and highlight the value for the current user.

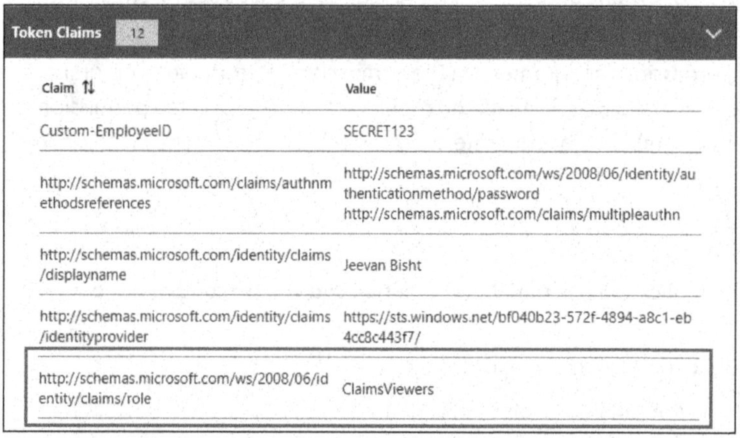

FIGURE 3-65   The role claim part of the issue token using the ClaimsXray app.

Creating app roles

Azure AD supports role-based access control to allow developers to apply authorization in their applications by using claims-based authorization for both users/groups and applications. This can be done by creating roles and assigning them to appropriate users/API. RBAC allows developers to easily enforce authorization using Azure AD capabilities.

In this section we will review how to create app roles. Do as follows:

1. Log in to the **Azure Active Directory Portal**.

2. Under **Manage**, select **App registrations**, and then select the application you want to define app roles in.

3. Select **App roles**, and then select **Create app role**, as highlighted in Figure 3-66.

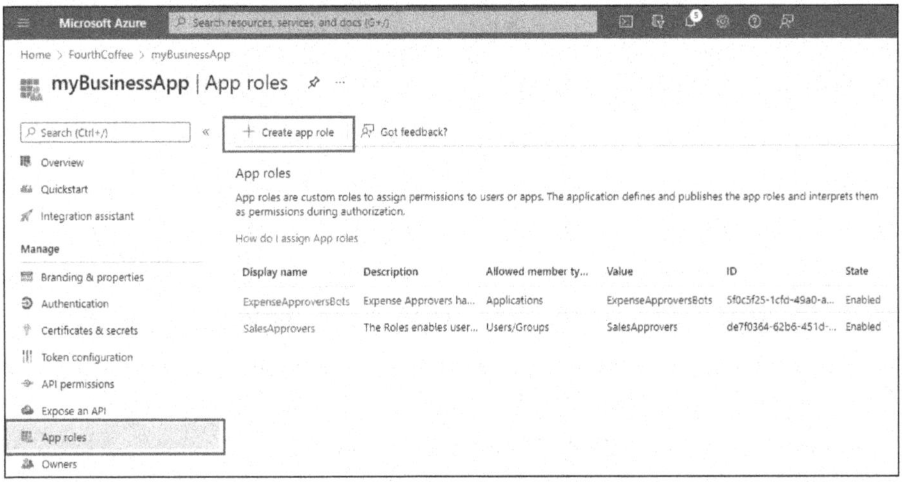

FIGURE 3-66 App registration configuration page for App roles.

4. Specify the details for app in the Create app role windows. Figure 3-67 highlights all the required fields. In this example, we are creating an AppRole called **ExpenseApprovers** whose value when passed to the application will be **ExpenseApprovers**. Also notice the Description field; this will used by App admins to understand the role context. App roles can be assigned to users, applications, or both.

5. Click **Apply.**

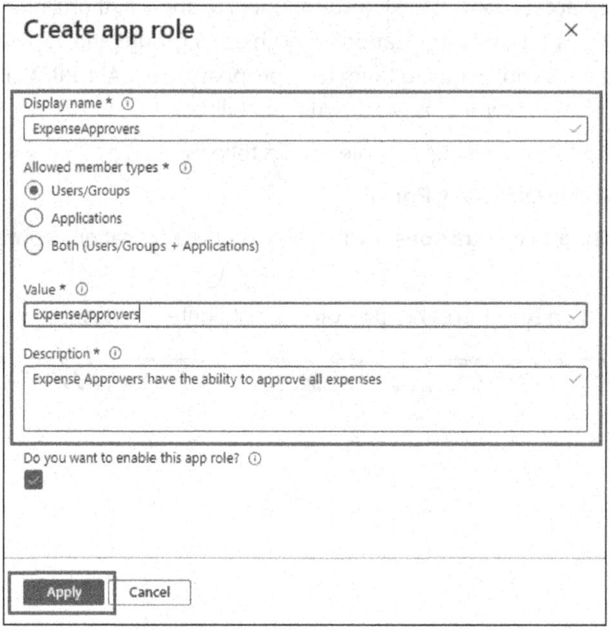

FIGURE 3-67 Custom roles definition.

In the previous section, we created a custom app role. These roles can be assigned to users/groups or applications, although both require configuration on different blades.

To assign app roles to applications, do the following:

1. Log in to the Azure portal.

2. In Azure Active Directory, select **App registrations**.

3. Find and select the application to which you want to assign an app role.

4. Select **API permissions** > **Add a permission**.

5. Select the **My APIs** tab (you should have a choice of **Microsoft APIs**, **APIs my organization uses**, and **My APIs**) and then select the app for which you defined app roles (**myBusinessApp** in this example, as highlighted in Figure 3-68).

6. Select **Application permissions**.

7. Select the role(s) you want to assign. (Figure 3-68 highlights the sequence and the API role that we created in the previous section.)

8. Select the **Add permissions** button to complete the addition of the role(s).

The new roles should appear in your app registration's API permissions pane.

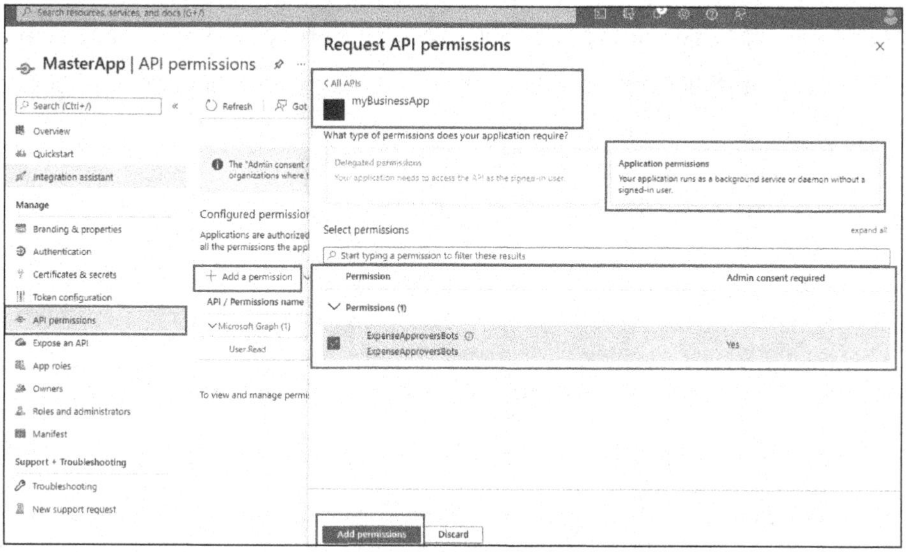

FIGURE 3-68 App registration configuration for adding API permissions.

> **NOTE ADMIN GRANTED CONSENT**
>
> These are application permissions, not delegated permissions. An admin must grant consent to use the app roles assigned to the application.

To assign users and groups to roles:

1. Log in to the Azure portal.

2. In **Azure Active Directory**, select **Enterprise applications** in the left navigation menu. Find and select the application to which you want to assign users or security groups to roles (**myBusinessApp** in our example).

3. Under **Manage**, select **Users and groups**.

4. Select **Add user/group**.

5. Select the **Users and groups** tab from the Add Assignment pane. A list of users and security groups is displayed. Choose a user and click the Select button.

6. Select a role in the **Add assignment** pane. All custom roles will be displayed.

7. Choose a role and click the Select button. (Figure 3-69 highlights the role assigned to both users.)

8. Select the Assign button to finish the assignment of users and groups to the app.

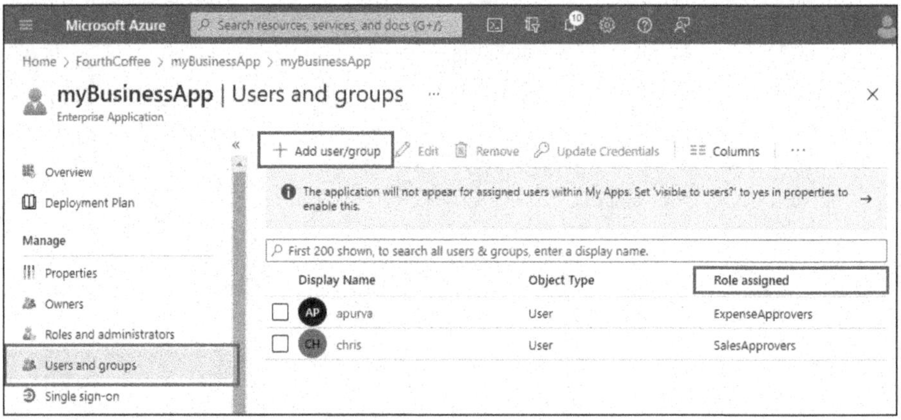

FIGURE 3-69 Assigning app roles to users and groups.

EXAM TIP

App roles are preferred in multi-tenant applications, since developers can easily map users to required functionality in their own code without having dependency on GroupName or GroupID, which might change with different tenants. Assigning groups to app roles is a general practice that SaaS app developers use when the application needs to be provisioned in multiple tenants.

Multi-tenant app considerations

Multi-tenant apps follow the same pattern for the app registrations; however, there are certain best practices that you should be aware of, which are highlighted in the following list:

- Use the principle of least user access to ensure that your app only requests permissions it requires.

- Test your apps against Conditional Access policies.

- Provide clear names and descriptions for any permissions you expose as part of your app.

NEED MORE REVIEW? **TENANCY IN AZURE ACTIVE DIRECTORY**

For more information on single/multi-tenant applications, visit: *https://docs.microsoft.com/ en-us/azure/active-directory/develop/single-and-multi-tenant-apps*

Skill 3.3: Manage and monitor application access by using Microsoft Defender for Cloud Apps

The threat landscape is constantly evolving, and modern applications need protection beyond authentication. There are threat scenarios such as high-privilege consent and insider risk that we can apply protection for using access or session policies to get a wider perspective and control of what users might be experiencing or what they can do. This skill focuses on how additional controls can be applied to the discovered applications using Microsoft Defender for Cloud Apps app connectors for greater visibility, and applying additional controls like sessions controls to web and OAuth apps using the Microsoft Defender for Cloud Apps policy engine.

This skill covers how to:

- Implement application-enforced restrictions
- Configure connectors to apps
- Deploy Conditional Access App Control for Apps using Azure Active Directory
- Create access and session policies in Microsoft Defender for Cloud Apps
- Implement and manage policies for OAuth apps

Implement application-enforced restrictions

Azure Active Directory offers a very powerful ability to control granular access with Conditional Access. However, in certain conditions you would want to allow applications to leverage the signals from Azure AD such as a device being complaint or not and offering a differentiated experience. This allows flexibility for the organizations to create different yet secure access when users are accessing the services from different devices. This control, however, is only available today for Office 365 SharePoint Online/OneDrive and Exchange online. Figure 3-70 shows how to enable app enforced restrictions in the conditional access policy.

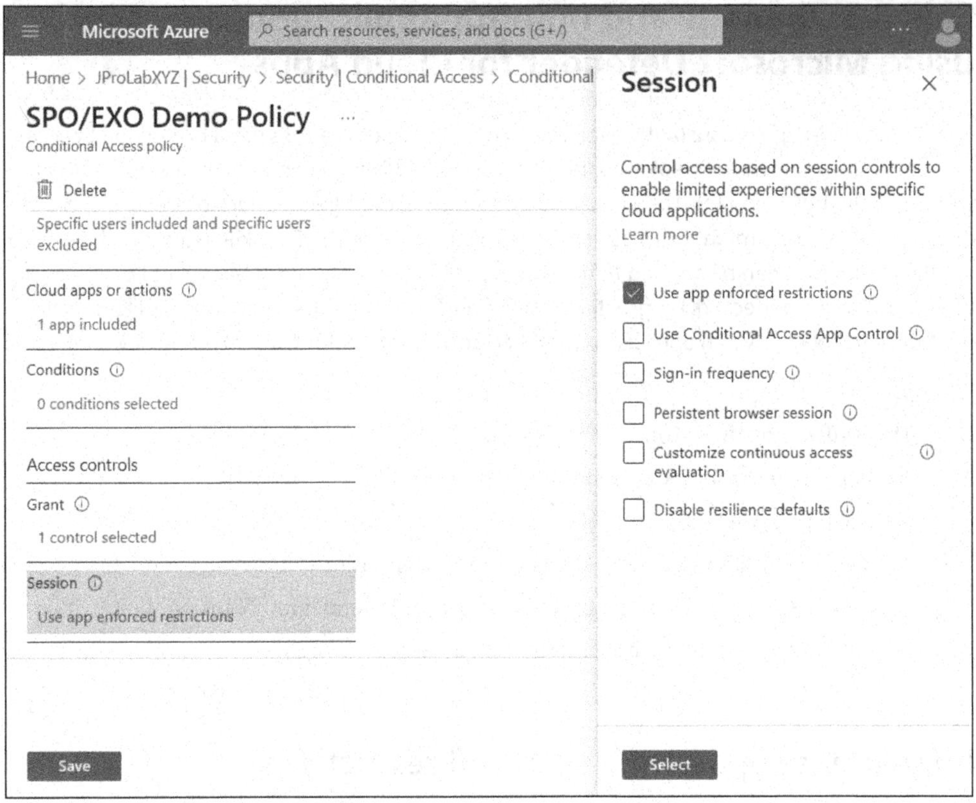

FIGURE 3-70 Conditional access policy with session control for app enforced restriction.

Once the conditional access policy is configured, you will also need to configure the applications to be able to utilize the app restrictions. The configuration details can be found at the below links:

- **SharePoint Online**: *https://docs.microsoft.com/en-us/sharepoint/control-access-from-unmanaged-devices*
- **Exchange Online**: *https://techcommunity.microsoft.com/t5/outlook-blog/conditional-access-in-outlook-on-the-web-for-exchange-online/ba-p/267069*

We will quickly review a few high-level options for the SharePoint admin center configuration. You can achieve the following using the app enabled restrictions, as shown in Figure 3-71:

- Block access from unmanaged devices (most restrictive)
- Allow limited, web-only access. This provides full access to complaint devices, but for non-compliant/unmanaged devices, this restricts their ability to download, print, or sync—ensuring the data is not unintentionally leaked on unmanaged devices.

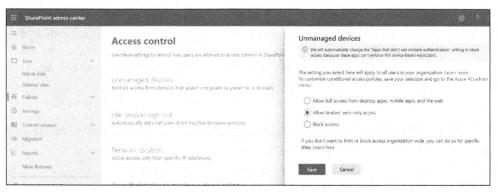

FIGURE 3-71 SharePoint admin center configuration for unmanaged devices.

Once the policy is configured, if a user tries to access the SharePoint from an unmanaged/non-compliant device, they will see the warning in the SharePoint app, as shown in Figure 3-72, which allows the user to access the application but does not allow downloading/printing or syncing.

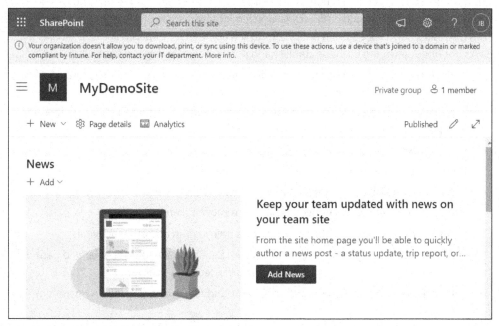

FIGURE 3-72 SharePoint limited web-only access end user experience.

Limiting a specific SharePoint site

SharePoint also supports the ability to block or limit access to a specific SharePoint site or OneDrive. However, this ability is only available from PowerShell. This experience might be required by enterprises that protect all SharePoint data using conditional access and consider their data sensitive; however, they might allow one or more specific sites to be accessed with fewer restrictions. For all sites where you enable conditional access policies, you should disable "Anyone" links; otherwise, the setting has no impact. Below is an example of restricting a specific SharePoint site using PowerShell with limited access and allowing only read-only access.

```
Set-SPOSite -Identity https://<SharePoint online URL>/sites/<name of site or OneDrive
account> -ConditionalAccessPolicy AllowLimitedAccess -ReadOnlyForUnmanagedDevices $true
```

For more information, visit *https://docs.microsoft.com/en-us/sharepoint/control-access-from-unmanaged-devices#advanced-configurations*.

Configure connectors to apps

Microsoft Defender for Cloud Apps supports the use of the API connectors to provide enhanced visibility and control over applications. It uses the APIs provided by the service providers. In some cases, these could be SaaS applications like Box, GitHub, etc. but also other cloud platforms like AWS, GCP, etc. Microsoft Defender for Cloud Apps works with these providers to optimize the API and the framework used and honors contracts such as API throttling and other platform-enforced restrictions. This avoids API hammering when requesting certain API intensive tasks like file search or file scans, which might be a series of API calls in short spans. This means it's normal for certain operations to run continuously, spread across in smaller tasks, for hours, ensuring both the stability and performance of target systems.

Connectors can bring additional information depending on what the service providers support. In general, you can find information across the following areas:

- **Account governance**—Provides ability for governance activities like suspending/revoking accounts, resetting passwords, etc.
- **Account Information**—Insights/visibility into users, privileges, account information, state of users (active/disabled), group memberships, etc.
- **App Permissions**—View and issue tokens and permissions.
- **App Permission Governance**—Ability to remove tokens.
- **Audit Trail**—Insights/visibility into users/admin sign-in and other activities.
- **Data Scan**—Ability to perform unstructured data scan with both regular and periodic scans (every 12 hours) or whenever a change is detected (real-time).
- **Data governance**—Abilities such as overwriting files, managing files in quarantine, or deleting files.

Tables 3-15 to 3-17 provide samples of the details of integration of Microsoft Defender for Cloud Apps integration to understand the integration capabilities with different service providers. For the complete list of supported applications, please visit the Microsoft Defender for Cloud Apps documentation.

TABLE 3-15 User and activities

Application	List Accounts	List Groups	List Privileges	Log On Activity	User Activity	Administrative Activity
AWS	Yes			Yes	NA	Yes
Azure	Yes	Yes		Yes		Yes
Box	Yes	Yes	Yes	Yes	Yes	Yes
Dropbox	Yes	Yes	Yes	Yes	Yes	Yes
Office 365	Yes	Yes	Yes	Yes	Yes	Yes
Salesforce	Yes	Yes	Yes	Yes	Yes (with SF Sheid)	Yes
ServiceNow	Yes	Yes	Yes	Yes	Partial	Partial

TABLE 3-16 User/app governance and security configuration visibility

Application	User Governance	View App Permisions	Revoke App permissions	Security configuration visibility
AWS		NA	NA	
Azure			Not supported by provider	
Box	Yes	Not supported by provider	Yes	Yes
Dropbox				
Office 365	Yes	Yes	Yes	
Salesforce	Yes	Yes	Yes	Preview
ServiceNow				Preview

TABLE 3-17 Information protection

Applicaiton	Dlp – Periodic Backlog Scan	Dlp – Near Real Time Scan	Sharing Control	File Governance	Apply Sensitivity Labels From Microsoft Purview Ip
AWS		Yes – S3 Bucket Discover only	Yes	Yes	NA
Azure					
Box	Yes	Yes	Yes	Yes	Yes
Dropbox	Yes	Yes	Yes	Yes	
Office 365	Yes	Yes	Yes	Yes	Yes
Salesforce	Yes	Yes		Yes	
ServiceNow	Yes	Yes	NA		

Deploy Conditional Access App Control for apps using Azure Active Directory

While Microsoft Defender for Cloud Apps offers integration with multiple IDPs and both catalog apps and custom apps, we will focus only on Azure AD integration as part of the scope for this exam. As part of the Conditional Access App Control, let's review the prerequisites.

Prerequisites:

- Azure Active Directory Premium P1 or higher
- Microsoft Defender for Cloud Apps
- Apps must use SAML 2.0 or OpenID Connect
- Apps must be configured for Single Sign-on (SSO) with Azure Active Directory

High-level steps for catalog app integration are as follows and detailed next:

- **Step 1:** Azure AD integration with Microsoft Defender for Cloud Apps.
- **Step 2:** Log in with the user assigned to the app for Defender to receive policy.
- **Step 3:** Verify the app connection in the Microsoft Defender for Cloud Apps console and enable access and session controls.
- **Step 4:** Enable the application available for Conditional Access App Control.
- **Step 5:** Perform the test deployment.

Step 1: Azure AD integration with Microsoft Defender for Cloud Apps

Identify the SAML 2.0 or OpenID Connect apps that are integrated with Azure and follow the steps below to configure conditional access to integrate with Microsoft Defender for Cloud Apps.

1. Open the Azure AD console and navigate to **Security** > **Conditional Access**.
2. On the **Conditional Access** pane, create a new policy by selecting **New policy** > **Create new policy.**
3. On the **New** pane, in the **Name** text box, enter the policy name.
4. Under **Assignments**, select **Users or workload identities** and specify users/groups that will be used for onboarding (initial sign-on and verification).
5. Under **Assignments**, select **Cloud apps or actions** and assign the apps and actions you want to control with Conditional Access App Control.
6. Under **Access controls**, select **Session**, select **Use Conditional Access App Control**, and choose the built-in policy **Monitor only (Preview)**. You can also choose Block downloads (Preview) or Use custom policy to set an advanced policy in Microsoft Defender for Cloud Apps, and then select **Select**, as shown in Figure 3-73.

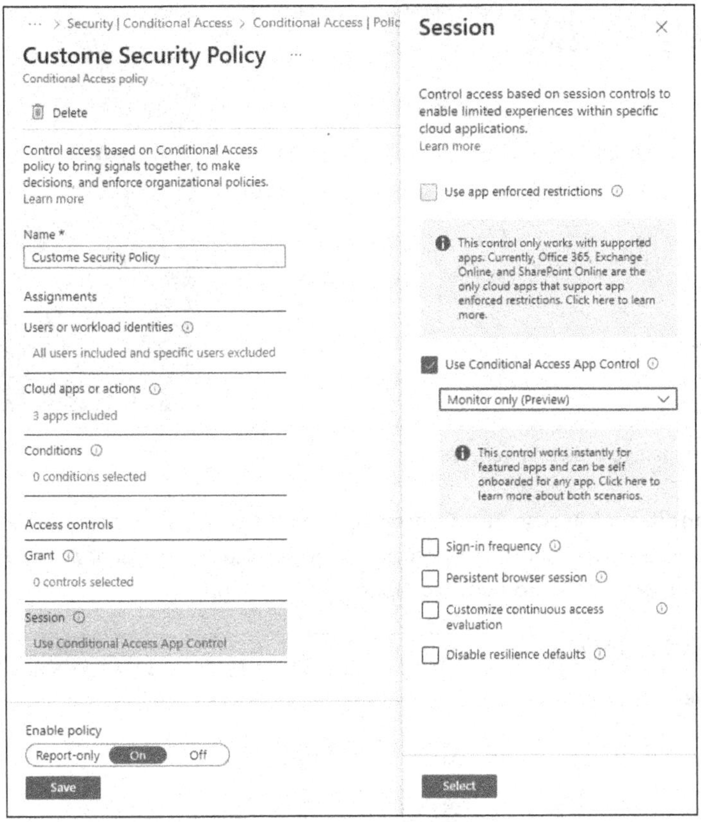

FIGURE 3-73 Enabling conditional access app control.

7. Under **Enable policy**, select **On** and then select **Create/Save**.

Step 2: Log in with the user assigned to the app for Defender to receive policy

After the creation of conditional access policies, you need to sign in to each application under the scope of the conditional access for Microsoft Defender for Cloud Apps to sync the policy details to its service. Without this step, the application might not appear in the Microsoft Defender for Cloud Apps console.

Step 3: Verify the app connection in the Microsoft Defender for Cloud Apps console and enable access and session controls

At this point, we will enable/verify that the access and session control are configured for the apps in scope. For this step, do as follows:

1. Go to the **Microsoft** Defender for Cloud **Apps** portal, select the **settings cog** on the top-left title bar of the portal, and then select **Conditional Access App Control**. See Figure 3-74.

FIGURE 3-74 Navigate to the Conditional Access App Control configuration.

2. Review the **Conditional Access App Control apps** table (shown in Figure 3-75), look at the **Available controls** column, and verify that both **Access control** or **Azure AD Conditional Access** and **Session control** appear for your apps.

Connected apps

App connectors   **Conditional Access App Control apps**   Security configuration apps

The Conditional Access App Control adds real-time monitoring and control capabilities for your apps.
To enable Conditional Access App Control capabilities on your apps, follow the deployment instructions.   ⚙ Device identification settings

ⓘ New Azure AD apps were discovered by Conditional Access App Control. View new apps.

Filters: ◉ Advanced filters

App: **Select apps** ⌄   App category: **Select category** ⌄   Last connected: Select a date

+ Add   ↓ Export   ⓘ ▽ Hide filters 🔲 Table settings ⌄

App ∧	Status	Available controls ⓘ	Was conne...	Last activity	
Calendly - General Online meetings	✅ Connected	Azure AD conditional access Session control	Jul 31, 202...	Jul 31, 202...	⋮
FindTime - General Productivity	✅ Connected	Azure AD conditional access ⊕ Onboard with session control	7/31/22, 9...	Jul 31, 202...	⋮
Microsoft 365 admin center - General Business management	⚠ No activities	Azure AD conditional access ⊕ Onboard with session control	Jan 12, 20...	—	⋮

FIGURE 3-75 Microsoft Defender for Cloud Apps connect apps console.

Step 4: Enable the application available for Conditional Access App Control

For this step, do as follows:

1. Review the list of apps, and on the row in which the app you're deploying appears, choose the three dots at the end of the row, and then choose **Edit app**.

2. Select **Use the app with session controls** and then select **Save**. See Figure 3-76.

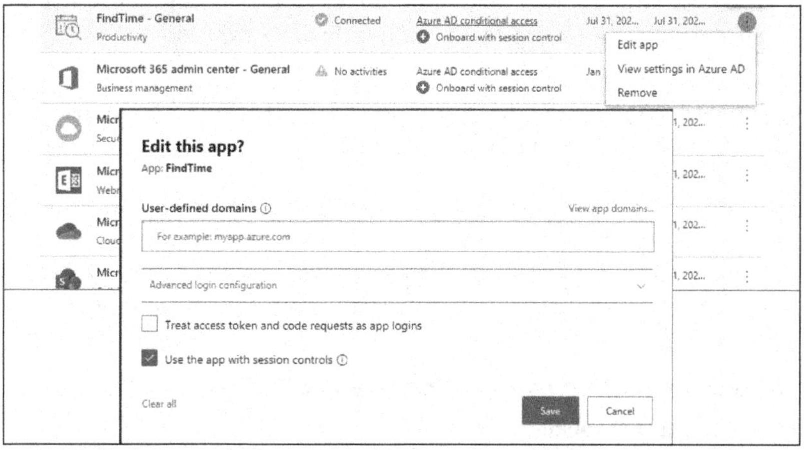

FIGURE 3-76 Enabling an app for session controls.

Step 5: Perform the test deployment

We need a fresh session for testing to make sure the test users log out from the existing session and then try to access the applications that are in scope for the policy. So do as follows:

1. Log in to the **Microsoft Defender for Cloud Apps** portal, and under **Investigate**, select **Activity** log, and make sure the login activities are captured for each app.

2. You can filter by clicking **Advanced** and then filtering using **Source** equals **Access control**. See Figure 3-77.

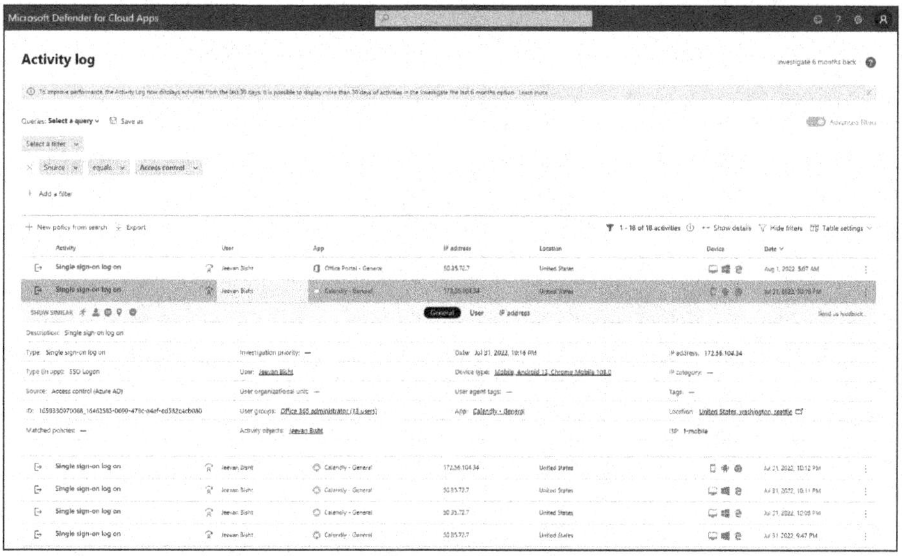

FIGURE 3-77 Activity log scope to access control.

3. You can see the device details such as desktop/mobile, etc., while testing. You should test the login from all the applications, including browsers or any mobile application. Ensure that the activities are correctly captured in the activity log.

Create access and session policies in Microsoft Defender for Cloud Apps

With access policies, you can enable real-time monitor and access control to cloud apps based on factors like app, device, location, and user. Microsoft Defender for Cloud Apps also offers certificate-based authentication to identify devices apart from the Hybrid Joined and Azure AD joined devices as conditions and checks. This can be useful in multiple scenarios to prove the relevance of devices.

To create a new access policy, follow this procedure:

1. Browse to **Control** > **Policies**.
2. Click **Create policy** and select **Access policy**. See Figure 3-78.

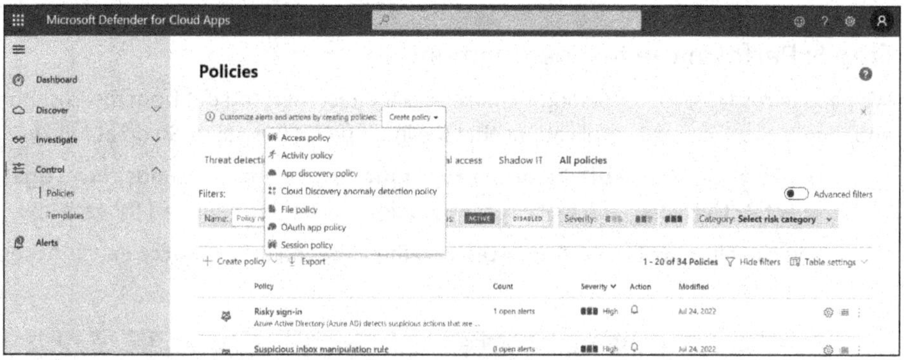

FIGURE 3-78 Microsoft Defender for Cloud Apps control policy menu.

3. In the **Access policy** wizard, assign a name for your policy, such as "Block access from non-corporate devices" (as shown in Figure 3-79) and provide a brief **Description**.
4. Define the **Policy Severity** and **Category** for access control.

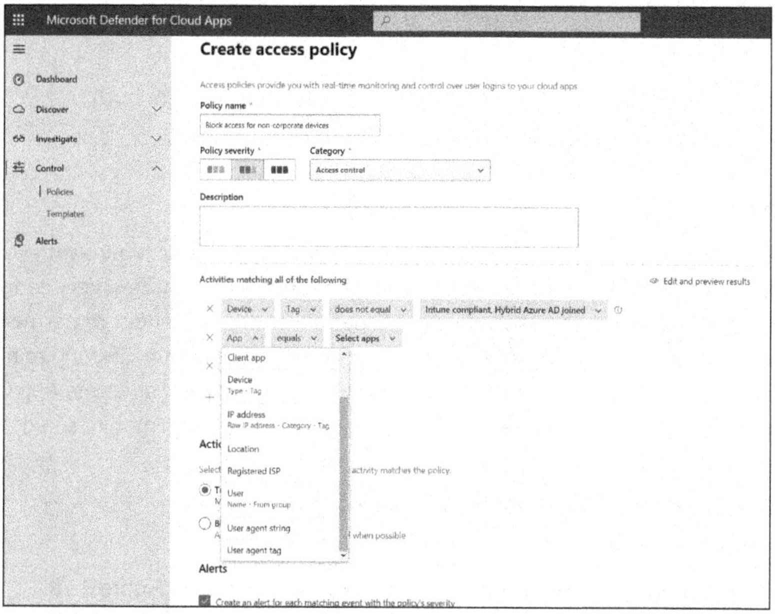

FIGURE 3-79 Access policy wizard.

5. In the **Activities matching all of the following** section (shown in Figure 3-79), under **Activity source**, select additional activity filters to apply to the policy. Filters include the following options:

- **App:** Use this filter to target specific apps.
- **Client app:** Use this filter to target a browser or client app if applicable.
- **Device tags**: Use this filter to identify unmanaged devices.
- **Device type**: Use this filter to identify PC/Mobile/Tablet/Other.
- **Location**: Use this filter to identify Countries/Unknown (Risky) Locations
- **IP address**: Use this filter to filter per IP addresses or use previously assigned IP address tags or categorized by classified services like VPN/Cloud Providers/Risky, etc. You can also define RAW IP addresses.
- **Registered ISP:** Use this filter to identify a specific ISP based off their IPs.
- **User:** Use this filter to target specific users/groups.
- **User agent string:** Use this filter to match exact user agent strings.
- **User agent tag**: Use this filter to enable the heuristic to identify mobile and desktop apps. This filter can be set to equals or does not equal. The values should be tested against your mobile and desktop apps for each cloud app.

6. Under **Actions**, select one of the following options:

- **Test**: Set this action to explicitly allow access according to the policy filters you set.
- **Block**: Set this action to explicitly block access according to the policy filters you set.

7. You can Create an **alert** for each matching event with the policy's severity.

   - Set an alert limit.
   - Select whether you want the alert as an email, a text message, or both.
   - Send alerts to Power Automate for automation.

Session Policies

Session policies can enable real-time session-level monitoring, providing admins with visibility into cloud apps and the ability to adapt to business requirements and policies. Very commonly, instead of allowing or blocking access completely, especially in case of vendor or partner access with session control, you can allow access while monitoring the session and/or limiting specific session activities using the reverse proxy capabilities of Conditional Access App Control. Session control applies to browser-based apps. To block access from mobile and desktop apps, create an Access policy.

To create a new session policy, follow this procedure:

1. Go to **Control** > **Policies**.
2. Select **Create policy** and then select **Session policy**, as shown in Figure 3-78.
3. Session Policy offers predefined catalog and suggested actions as templates. As shown in Figure 3-80, we will create a policy with no template option.

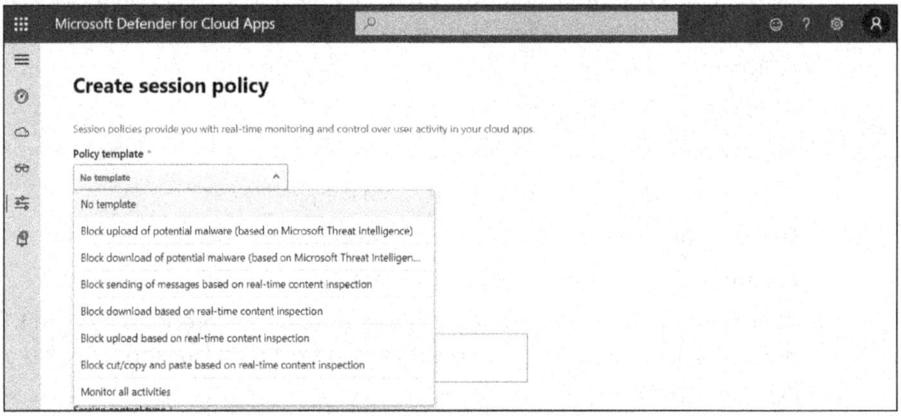

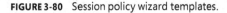

FIGURE 3-80 Session policy wizard templates.

4. In the **Session policy** window, assign a name for your policy, such as "Block printing SSN number for EXO/SPO/TEAMS for Associates," as shown in Figure 3-81.
5. In the **Session control type** field:
   - Select **Monitor only** if you only want to monitor activities by users. This selection will create a monitor-only policy for the apps you selected where all sign-ins, heuristic downloads, and activity types will be downloaded.

- Select **Block activities** to block specific activities, which you can select using the Activity type filter. All activities from selected apps will be monitored (and reported in the Activity log). The specific activities you select will be blocked if you select the Block action. The specific activities you selected will raise alerts if you select the Test action and have alerts turned on.

- Select **Control file download (with inspection)** if you want to monitor user activities. You can take additional actions like blocking or protect downloads for users.

- Select **Control file upload (with inspection)** if you want to monitor user activities. You can take additional actions such as blocking or protecting downloads for users.

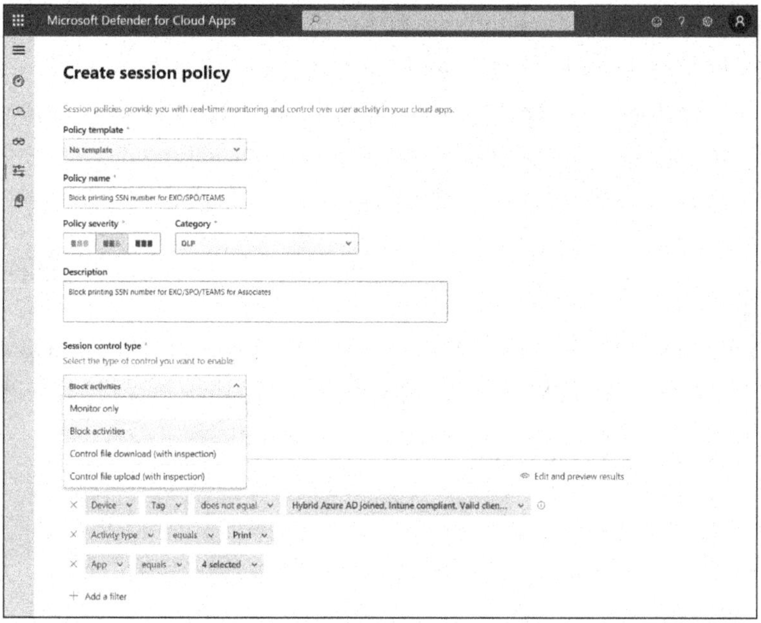

FIGURE 3-81 Session policy wizard.

6. In the **Activities matching all of the following** sections, Under Activity source, select additional activity filters to apply to the policy. Filters include the following options:

- **App:** Use this filter to target specific app(s).

- **Activity type:** Use this filter to select specific activities to be controlled, such as:

  - Print

  - Clipboard actions: Copy, Cut, and Paste

  - Send items in apps such as Teams

- **Client app:** Use this filter to target a browser or client app if applicable.

- **Device tags:** Use this filter to identify unmanaged devices.

- **Device type:** Use this filter to identify PC/Mobile/Tablet/Other.

- **Location:** Use this filter to identify Countries/Unknown (Risky) Locations
- **IP address:** Use this filter to filter per IP addresses or use previously assigned IP address tags or categorize by classified services like VPN/Cloud Providers/Risky, etc. You can also define RAW IP address.
- **Registered ISP:** Use this filter to identify a specific ISP based off their IPs.
- **User:** Use this filter to target specific users/groups.
- **User agent string:** Use this filter to match exact user agent strings.
- **User agent tag:** Use this filter to enable the heuristic to identify mobile and desktop apps. This filter can be set to equals or does not equal. The values should be tested against your mobile and desktop apps for each cloud app.

7. Under **Actions**, select one of the following options:
   - **Test:** Set this action to explicitly allow access according to the policy filters you set.
   - **Block:** Set this action to explicitly block access according to the policy filters you set.
   - **Require step-up authentication (Preview):** Re-evaluate Azure AD Conditional Access policies based on the authentication context.
   - **Protect:** This option is available only if you selected Control file download/upload (with inspection) under Session policy.
      - **Apply Label:** If your organization uses Microsoft Purview Information Protection, you can set an Action to apply a sensitivity label set in Microsoft Purview Information Protection to the file.
      - **Apply custom Permissions:**
         1. None
         2. Viewer – View Only
         3. Reviewer – View, Edit
         4. Co-Author – View, Edit, Copy, Print
         5. Co-Owner – All Permissions
      - **Block Download** any file that is unsupported by native protection where native protection is unsuccessful.

8. You can create an alert for each matching event with the policy's severity as follows:
   - Set an alert limit.
   - Select whether you want the alert as an email, a text message, or both.
   - Send alerts to Power Automate for automation.

> **NOTE SETTING SESSION/ACCESS POLICY**
>
> You can't remove an app from the Conditional Access App Control page once it's added. If you don't set a session or access policy on the app, the Conditional Access App Control won't change any behavior for the app.

Implement and manage policies for OAuth apps

While Microsoft Defender for Cloud Apps offers a default set of investigation (discussed briefly later in this chapter) just by the virtue of connecting with Azure AD, you can define granular policies around app permissions to get notifications automatically when the criteria are met. This could help admins secure control of the application permission being consented. Another example could be alerting of high permissions level when a certain threshold of uses is exceeded. You can also mark the permissions as approved or banned, which will disable the correlating enterprise application in Azure AD.

Let's review how this policy is created. Lauch the Microsoft Defender for Cloud Apps portal by visiting **portal.cloudappsecurity.com**. Then do as follows:

1. Go to **Control** > **Policies**.

2. Select **Create policy** and then select **OAuth App policy**.

3. In the **OAuth App policy** window, assign a name for your policy, such as Detect Apps requesting High Permissions Level (as shown in Figure 3-82).

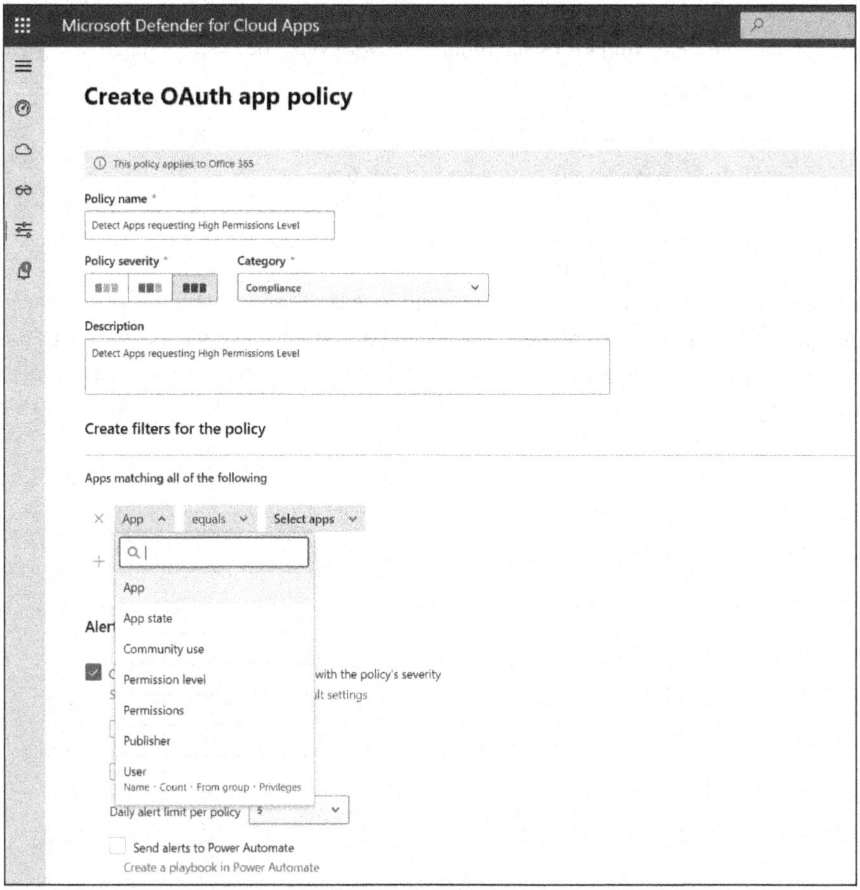

FIGURE 3-82 OAuth app policy creation wizard.

4. In the **Activities matching all of the following** sections, Under Activity source, select additional activity filters to apply to the policy. Filters include the following options:

- **App:** Use this filter to target specific app(s).
- **App State:** Use this filter to state Approved/Banned/Undetermined.
- **Community use:** Use this filter to use to Common/Rare/Uncommon.
- **Permissions Level:** Use this filter to use Low/Medium/High Level severity.
- **Permissions:** Use this filter to use specific permissions (e.g., Directory Read, etc.).
- **Publisher:** Use this to specify the exact publisher name text.
- **User**
    i. **Count:** The count of users impacted.
    ii. **From Group:** User this to specify target group(s).
    iii. **Name:** Use this to specify target users(s).
    iv. **Privileges:** Use this to specify exact roles like Administrator/Non-Administrators.

5. You can Create an **alert** for each matching event with the policy's severity.

- Set an alert limit.
- Select whether you want the alert as an email, a text message, or both.
- Send alerts to Power Automate for automation.

6. You can specify Governance **Actions** as below:

- **Office 365: Revoke App**

While Microsoft Defender for Cloud Apps allows you to create these powerful policies, there are few out-of-box anomaly detection policies that automatically review OAuth apps metadata to identify potential malicious applications. These detection policies are only available for OAuth apps that are authorized in Azure AD, and the severity of these anomaly detection policies cannot be modified. See the policies and descriptions in Table 3-18.

TABLE 3-18 Defender for Cloud Apps policies

Policy Name	Policy Description
Misleading OAuth app name	Scans OAuth apps connected to your environment and triggers an alert when an app with a misleading name is detected. Misleading names could indicate an attempt to disguise a malicious app as a known and trusted app.
Misleading publisher name for an OAuth app	Scans OAuth apps connected to your environment and triggers an alert when an app with a misleading publisher name is detected. Misleading publisher names, such as foreign letters that resemble Latin letters, could indicate an attempt to disguise a malicious app as an app coming from a known and trusted publisher.
Malicious OAuth app consent	Scans OAuth apps connected to your environment and triggers an alert when a potentially malicious app is authorized. Malicious OAuth apps may be used as part of a phishing campaign in an attempt to compromise users. This detection leverages Microsoft security research and threat intelligence expertise to identify malicious apps.
Suspicious OAuth app file download activities	Covers various things like IP Ranges/User Activities etc.

These out-of-box policies can help mitigate some of the risks that might arise from the OAuth apps being used in enterprises.

To view the OAuth apps detected by Microsoft Defender for Cloud Apps

- Go to **Investigate** > **OAuth Apps**.

You will see all the OAuth applications, along with details such as permissions level, authorized by, and ability to action them as Approved or Banned, as shown in Figure 3-83.

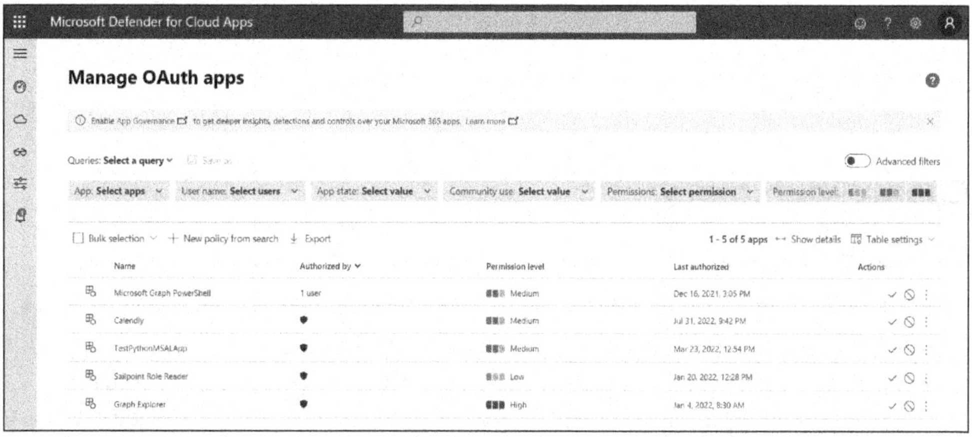

FIGURE 3-83 Manage OAuth apps console, showing permission levels for discovered OAuth apps.

It is possible that the admin might require more data for investigation to understand the applications permissions and other details like publishers and URLS. The administrators can click any of the applications to view more details, as shown in Figure 3-84 where the admin might be trying to investigate Microsoft Graph PowerShell details.

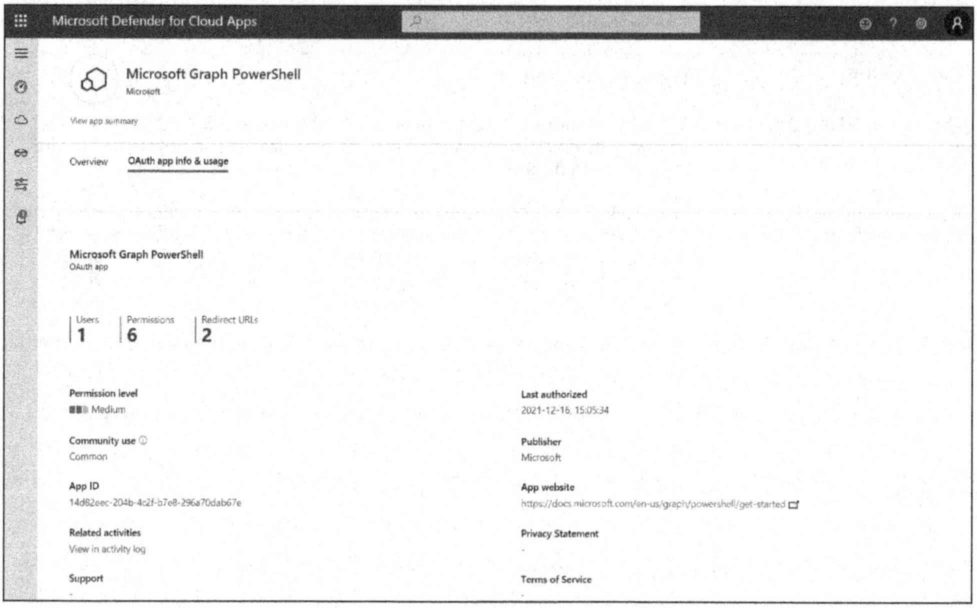

FIGURE 3-84 Manage OAuth apps console, showing permission details for specific apps.

Some of the key information that can be reviewed includes:

- Publisher
- Redirect URLs
- Permissions level
- Users
- Community use

Chapter summary

- The Cloud App discovery tool can help detect shadow IT applications.
- Cloud App discovery can add a lot of metadata, including application usage to help admins understand the usage and associated risk of the applications.
- ADFS Application activity reports can help you identify which applications can be migrated to Azure AD. It helps you prioritize the application based on the usage in the last 1, 7, and 30 days.
- The ADFS Application activity service automatically runs several tests to identify potential migration issues and provides recommendations on how those can be fixed.
- Administrators can configure consent settings to control the application creation behavior in the enterprise.

- Some consent settings can completely block users from consenting to apps, while some can allow users to request admin review for application consents instead of getting completely blocked. Consent settings can also be configured to approve consent for verified publisher applications.

- There are three built-in application management roles that can be assigned to users.

- Customer roles provide flexibility to scope certain permissions for a specified role.

- Azure AD Gallery supports thousands of applications. The application supports SAML, OIDC, Password, SSO, and Linked SSO options.

- Azure AD Administrator can control how end users interact with the application with application property settings.

- Application properties are different for SAML and OIDC applications; OIDC applications are app registrations.

- Access Management for an application can be configured using users or groups, but in production environments, access is generally controlled using groups.

- Azure AD Gallery supports thousands of applications that are preconfigured for ease of integration.

- You can also integrate any SAML/OIDC application as a non-gallery application.

- OAuth is an authorization protocol, while OIDC and SAML are authentication protocols.

- OIDC is generally used for apps that are purely in the cloud, such as mobile apps, websites, and web APIs.

- Azure AD supports automated provisioning for certain applications.

- SCIM is the modern approach to automated users and groups provisioning.

- SCIM makes the provisioning development faster, and the integration is standards based, avoiding the need to use custom API/schemas for every application.

- App Proxy supports secure remote access to multiple types of web applications running on-premises.

- App Proxy allows support for custom domain names. If you choose to use a custom domain, you will need a certificate matching the external hostname and DNS settings must be updated on the external DNS.

- App Proxy does not require any incoming ports to be opened to the application servers from the public internet because access is enabled using the App Proxy service.

- App Proxy is part of Azure AD Premium and requires at least a P1 License.

- Audit logs are considered sensitive information and allow access to certain privileged roles.

- Usage and insights reports can help understand Top failures and other information about the applications.

- Consent settings can be configured to reduce risk of overexposure to organizational data.

- Consent requests can take advantage of verified publishers. Admins should carefully review any consent request before approving.

- App Roles can be assigned to both Applications and Users/Groups.
- App Roles can be created using either the Azure AD console or the Manifest Editor.
- Microsoft Defender for Cloud Apps can be used as a powerful tool to manage and monitor SAML 2.0/OIDC applications.
- Defender for Cloud Apps can generate user risks/application usage/application risk patterns.
- Defender for Cloud Apps provides an integrated set of catalog apps that offer deeper integration and insights. It also offers powerful tools like access/session and OAuth policies.

Thought experiment

In this thought experiment, demonstrate your skills and knowledge of the topics covered in this chapter. You can find the answers in the section that follows.

WoodGrove Bank is a large-scale commercial bank that provides financial services to millions of users worldwide. WoodGrove Bank has thousands of full-time employees and part-time contractors spread across the globe. WoodGrove bank is in the process of modernizing their application strategy. They have a technical debt of legacy on-premises web applications and some SaaS applications that users need to access remotely from various field locations. They have had a number of breaches recently due to password exposure, and they're looking to block unauthorized access to the applications. They currently have an Azure Active Directory P1 subscription primarily being used for Office 365 integrations. They formed a planning committee that laid out certain key requirements, as follows:

- All Access must be logged.
- All Access must be protected using multifactor authentication.
- Access should be restricted from authorized healthy devices only.

You have been hired as a consultant to provide recommendations based on this scenario. Provide some of your top recommendations to the WoodGrove bank by answering the following questions:

1. You are the Global Administrator for the company, and you hire James to help the developers build and manage cloud applications. What role is best suited for James?

    A. Application Administrator

    B. Application Developer

    C. Cloud Application Administrator

    D. Global Administrator

2. You have been tasked to migrate 200 applications from ADFS to Azure Active Directory, and your organization uses ADFS Usage insights. What information is available for you to help with your planning (choose all that apply)?

   A. Application usage in last 30 days

   B. Potential issues with application migrations

   C. ADFS Certificate expiration

   D. Details on claims transform rules

   E. Number of users signed in using MFA

Thought experiment answers

This section contains the solution to the thought experiment. Each answer explains why the choice is correct.

Solution

There are several recommendations that align with the problem statement at hand:

- Ensure that all SaaS applications are tied to Azure Active Directory.

- Enforce Conditional Access Policy. For all applications, require Multifactor Authentication and/or Enforce Device Policy to require a complaint device to ensure that devices are healthy.

- For on-premises legacy web applications, you can recommend using the Azure AD Application Proxy, which can provide secure remote access without needing to create port openings in a firewall. You can also apply conditional policy.

- Azure AD sign-in logs can be used to track all user activity; for long-term retention, you might consider a SIEM system for storing logs.

- Block app consent for the end users. Although not directly related, this can block rogue applications from being registered and being able to steal user credentials.

Answers

1. You are the Global Administrator for the company, and you hire James to help the developers build and manage applications. What role is best suited for James?

   Consider the following:

   - Application Administrators can create and manage all aspects of app registrations and enterprise apps.

   - Application Developers can create application registrations independent of the "Users can register applications" setting.

   - Cloud Application Administrators can create and manage all aspects of app registrations and Enterprise apps except App Proxy.

   - Global Administrators can manage all aspects of Azure AD and Microsoft services that use Azure AD identities.

Based on the principle of least privilege, the correct response would be **C. Cloud Application Administrator**. Options A and D also would allow James to perform but do not follow the least-privilege principle. Option B might limit app types to just app registrations.

2. You have been tasked to migrate 200 applications from ADFS to Azure Active Directory, and your organization uses ADFS Usage insights. What information is available for you to help with your planning?

   You were asked to choose from the following information:

   ■ Application usage in the last 30 days. This data is available as part of the report and is helpful for understanding whether the application is being used and can potentially help with ranking the migration priority.

   ■ Potential issues with application migrations. This data is available as part of the report, and an application with no reported issues can be targeted first for the migration.

   ■ ADFS Certificate expiration. This information is not applicable to the application.

   ■ Details on claims transform rules. This is part of the potential migration issues report, but some of these could be difficult to resolve, hence affecting the migration planning and priority.

   ■ Number of users signed in using MFA. Not part of the report.

   The correct answer is **A**, **B**, and **D**.

CHAPTER 4

Plan and implement an Identity Governance strategy

Azure AD Identity Governance enables the capability to balance an organization's need for security and employee productivity with the right processes and visibility. It mitigates access risks by protecting, monitoring, and auditing access to critical organization assets while ensuring employee productivity. It also ensures that the right people have the right access to the right resources.

Identity Governance gives organizations the ability to perform identity lifecycle, access lifecycle, and privileged access for administration across employees, business partners, users outside of the organization, applications, and services. It helps address the following:

- Who has access to what resources?
- What are users doing with that access?
- What organization controls are in place for managing access?
- Can auditors verify that the controls are working?

> **NEED MORE REVIEW?** **IDENTITY LIFECYCLE**
>
> Read more about identity lifecycle, access lifecycle, and privileged access lifecycle at:
> *https://docs.microsoft.com/en-us/azure/active-directory/governance/identity-governance-overview.*

Skills covered in this chapter:

- Skill 4.1: Plan and implement entitlement management
- Skill 4.2: Plan, implement, and manage access reviews
- Skill 4.3: Plan and implement privileged access
- Skill 4.4: Monitor Azure AD

Skill 4.1: Plan and implement entitlement management

Employees need access to resources such as groups, applications, and SharePoint sites to perform their job. Managing access over time is challenging for the organization and becomes more complicated when new groups or applications are added or when users need additional access rights. It also becomes more complicated when organizations collaborate with users outside of their organization.

Azure AD entitlement management helps effectively manage access to groups, applications, and SharePoint sites for internal users as well as external users outside your organization.

An Azure AD P2 license is required to perform entitlement management.

> **This skill covers how to:**
> - Plan entitlements
> - Create and configure catalogs
> - Create and configure access packages
> - Manage access requests
> - Implement and manage Terms of Use
> - Manage the lifecycle of external users in Azure AD Identity Governance settings
> - Configure and manage connected organizations
> - Review per-user entitlements by using Azure AD entitlement management

Plan entitlements

When employees join organizations or switch teams, they need access to various resources. Managers need to identify what resources the employee needs access to and for how long. Granting access to resources one by one is a complicated task. It is also important to remove employee access when they move out of teams or organizations. The challenges will compound for users who need access from another organization.

Global administrators and Identity Governance administrators can create and manage entitlements. However, they might not know all the scenarios where access packages are required. Users from the respective departments know what resources are required to perform a job and for how long. You can identify non-administrators for these departments and delegate access governance. Delegating to non-administrators ensures that the right people are managing access.

It is important to understand the roles that are specific to entitlement management. Table 4-1 lists the tasks that the entitlement management roles can perform.

- **Catalog creator:** Creates and manages catalogs. Catalog creators own the catalog they created and can add more catalog owners. However, they can't manage or add resources to other catalogs that they don't own.

- **Catalog owner:** Can edit and manage existing catalogs.
- **Catalog reader:** Can view existing access packages within a catalog.
- **Access package manager:** Can edit and manage all existing access packages with a catalog.
- **Access package assignment manager:** Can edit and manage all existing access package assignments.
- **Approver:** Authorized by an access package policy to approve or deny requests to that access package. They don't have permission to change the access package.
- **Requestor:** Authorized by a policy of an access package policy to request that access package.

TABLE 4-1 Entitlement management roles and tasks

Task	Admin	Catalog creator	Catalog owner	Access package manager	Access package assignment manager
Delegate a catalog creator	x				
Add a connected organization	x				
Create a new catalog	x	x			
Add a resource to a catalog	x		x		
Add a catalog owner	x		x		
Edit a catalog	x		x		
Delete a catalog	x		x		
Delegate to an access package manager	x		x		
Remove an access package manager	x		x		
Create a new access package in a catalog	x		x	x	
Change resource roles in an access package	x		x	x	
Create and edit policies	x		x	x	
Directly assign a user to an access package	x		x	x	x
Directly remove a user from an access package	x		x	x	x
View who has an assignment to an access package	x		x	x	x
View an access package's requests	x		x	x	x

View a request's delivery errors	x		x	x	x
Reprocess a request	x		x	x	x
Cancel a pending request	x		x	x	x
Hide an access package	x		x	x	
Delete an access package	x		x	x	

Administrators create a catalog, create access packages, and add required resources. An access package must have at least one policy. The policy specifies who can request access, who can approve the request, whether the approval is a single-stage or a two-stage process, how long the assignment is valid, whether users can request an extension and use access reviews to enable planned reviews of the users' access. To see a list of access packages, users can sign in to the My Access portal (*https://myaccess.microsoft.com*).

Create and configure catalogs

A catalog is a container of resources and access packages. Administrators create a catalog, create access packages, and add required resources. To create a catalog, sign in to the Azure portal, select Identity Governance, and then select Catalogs. As shown in Figure 4-1, you can have a single catalog of all access packages or create separate catalogs. An administrator can add resources to any catalog, but a catalog owner can add resources to the catalog they own. A catalog owner can add catalog co-owners or access package managers.

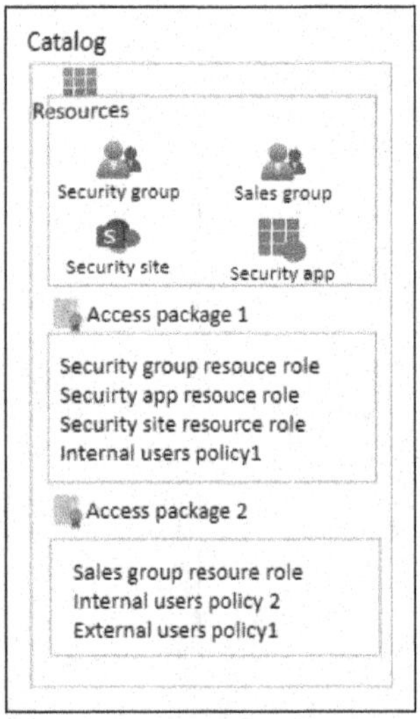

FIGURE 4-1 A catalog consists of resources and access packages.

Create a catalog: A Global administrator, Identity Governance administrator, or catalog creator can create a catalog. Sign in to the **Azure portal**, select **Identity Governance**, and select **Catalogs** from the left menu. As shown in Figure 4-2, select **New Catalog** and provide a name and description for the catalog. Choose options for **Enabled** and **Enabled for external users**, and then select **Create** to create the catalog.

- **Enabled**: Select **Yes** to enable the catalog for immediate use. Select **No** if you want the catalog to be unavailable until you intend to use it.

- **Enabled for external users**: Select **Yes** to allow users from the selected external directory to request access packages in this catalog. Select **No** for the catalog to be unavailable for users from an external directory.

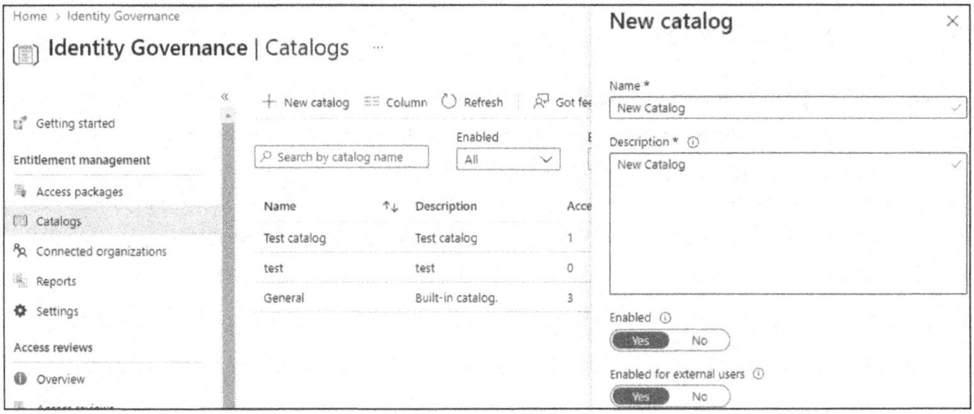

FIGURE 4-2 Create a new catalog.

Add resources to a catalog: You can include resources such as groups, applications, and SharePoint sites in a catalog, as shown in Figure 4-3. The resources must exist in a catalog to include them in an access package. Open **Catalog** and select **Resources**. As shown in Figure 4-3, **Add resources** provides options to select resources to add to the catalog.

- **Groups**: Groups can be Azure AD security groups or Microsoft 365 groups. Groups that originate in on-premises or Exchange online as distribution groups cannot be modified in the Azure AD.

- **Applications**: Azure AD enterprise applications that include both SaaS and LoB (Line-of-Business) applications integrated with Azure AD.

- **Sites**: SharePoint online sites or SharePoint online site collections.

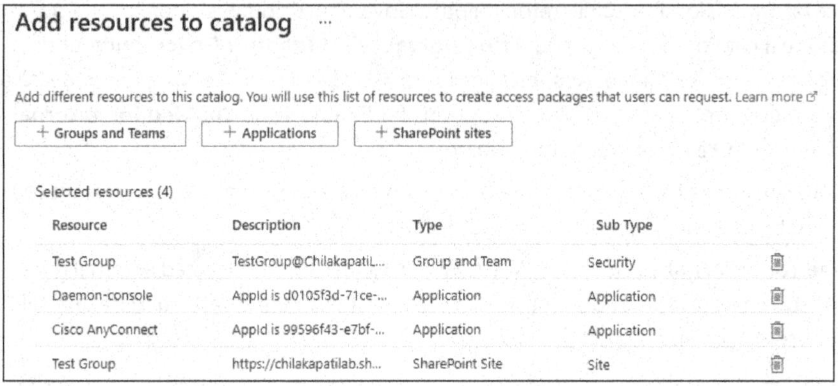

Add resources to catalog ...

Add different resources to this catalog. You will use this list of resources to create access packages that users can request. Learn more ☐

| + Groups and Teams | + Applications | + SharePoint sites |

Selected resources (4)

Resource	Description	Type	Sub Type	
Test Group	TestGroup@ChilakapatiL...	Group and Team	Security	🗑
Daemon-console	AppId is d0105f3d-71ce-...	Application	Application	🗑
Cisco AnyConnect	AppId is 99596f43-e7bf-...	Application	Application	🗑
Test Group	https://chilakapatilab.sh...	SharePoint Site	Site	🗑

FIGURE 4-3 Add resources to the catalog.

Add access package to a catalog: As shown in Figure 4-4, you can add access packages to the catalog (all access packages must be in a catalog). A catalog defines what resources can be added to the access package. The access package is placed in the General catalog if a catalog is not specified. All access packages must have at least one policy. The policy defines who can request the access packages, who can approve the request, and lifecycle settings.

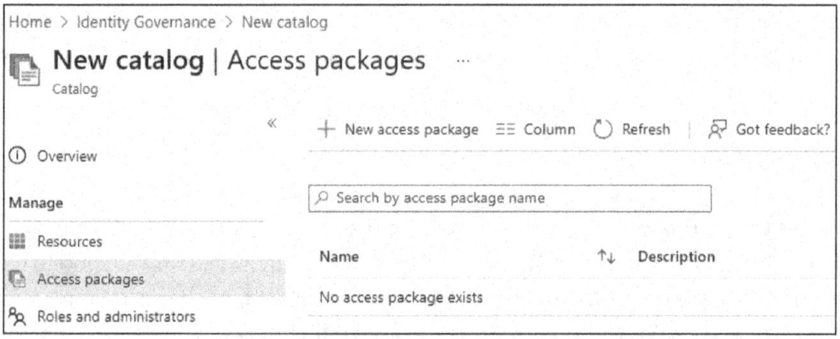

Home > Identity Governance > New catalog

New catalog | Access packages ...
Catalog

| « | + New access package   ≡≡ Column   ○ Refresh | 🗗 Got feedback? |

ⓘ Overview

Manage

▦ Resources

▢ Access packages

♟ Roles and administrators

🔍 Search by access package name

Name   ↑↓   Description

No access package exists

FIGURE 4-4 Add access packages to the catalog.

Create and configure access packages

Administrators create access packages. Access packages bundle the resources with the access that a user needs to perform the job. To create an access package, sign in to the **Azure portal**, select **Identity Governance**, and select **Access Packages**. Instead of granting access to individual resources, access packages help to grant or remove access in a more appropriate way for the following resource types:

- Membership of Azure AD security groups
- Membership of Microsoft 365 groups and Teams
- Assignment to Azure AD enterprise applications (including SaaS and custom apps)
- Membership of SharePoint online sites

Access packages are more appropriate when:

- Employees need limited access.
- Access that requires a manager or designated individual approval.
- Resources of a particular department are all grouped together.
- Users from one organization need access to another organization's resources.

Administrators can delegate non-administrators to create access packages with defined rules like who requests access, who approves access, and access expiration time.

Create an access package: Sign in to the **Azure portal**, select **Identity Governance**, open the catalog, and select **Access packages** to create an access package, as shown in Figure 4-5. You can also select Access packages from the left menu. Select **New access packages,** provide a name and description, and select a catalog for the access package. At the bottom of the page is an option to create a new catalog. Refer to Figure 4-2 to create a new catalog or add an existing catalog.

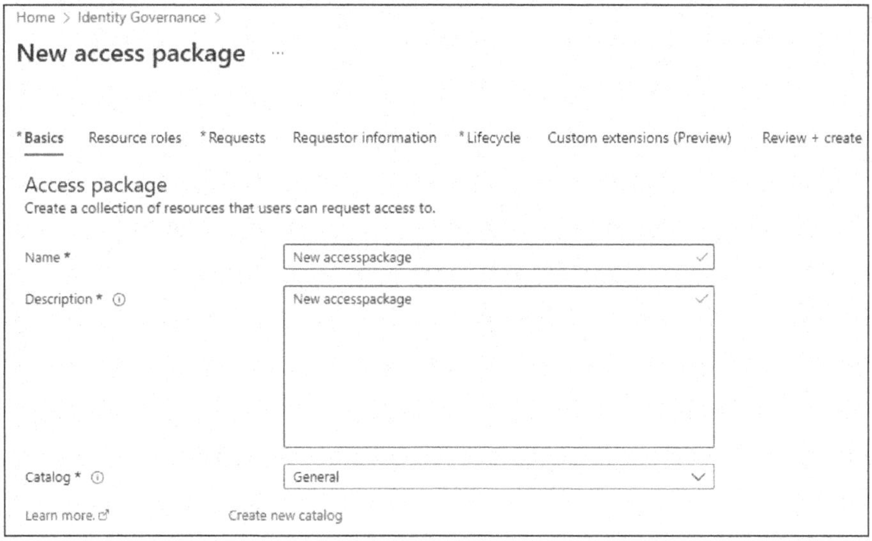

FIGURE 4-5 Create a new access package.

Resource roles provide options to add resources such as groups and Teams, applications, and SharePoint sites. If you create an access package in an existing catalog, you can select all the catalog resources without owning them. If you create an access package in a general catalog or a new catalog, you can select any resource from your own directory. You must be at least a Global administrator or catalog creator. After adding resources, select roles for these resources from the role list.

The **Requests** tab provides options to create the policy to specify who can request the access package and to configure approval settings. As shown in Figure 4-6, the Requests tab has three options:

- **For users in your directory:** This option allows users and groups in your directory to request the access package. You can select only specific users and groups in your directory or all users in your directory or all users and guest users in your directory request access to this access package.

- **For users not in your directory:** This option allows users in connected organizations to request this access package. You can select specific connected organizations or all connected organizations or all users from all connected organizations, and any new external users can request access to this access package.

- **None (administrator direct assignments only):** This option allows administrators to directly assign specific users to this access package.

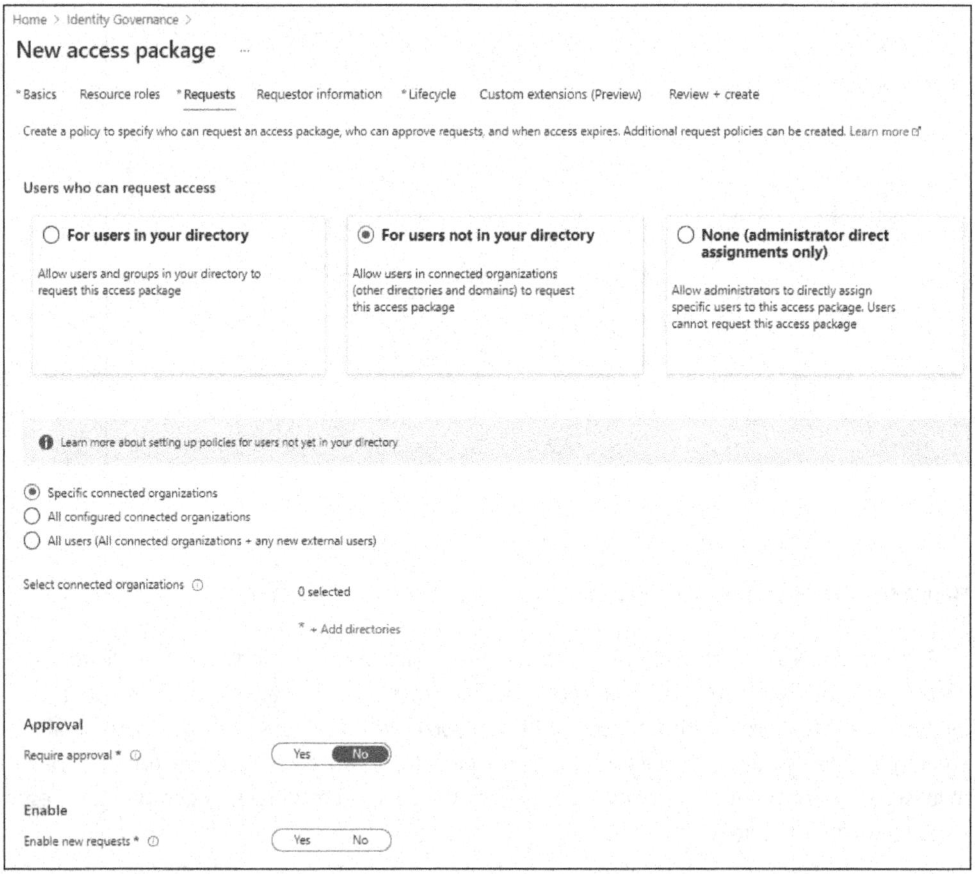

FIGURE 4-6 Users who can request the access package.

Figure 4-6 shows a configuration to enable new requests. Enabling new requests allows users to request the access package. When disabled, users are not allowed to request the access package.

Figure 4-7 shows the Requests tab approval section, where you can specify whether approval and requestor justification is required when users request this access package. The approval process has options to configure a single-stage or two-stage approval process. Single-stage approval has only one approver. The approver can be an internal or external sponsor or selected approvers. Selecting an internal or external sponsor gives the option to configure fallback approvers. For the two-stage approval, the selected approvers from each stage need to approve a request.

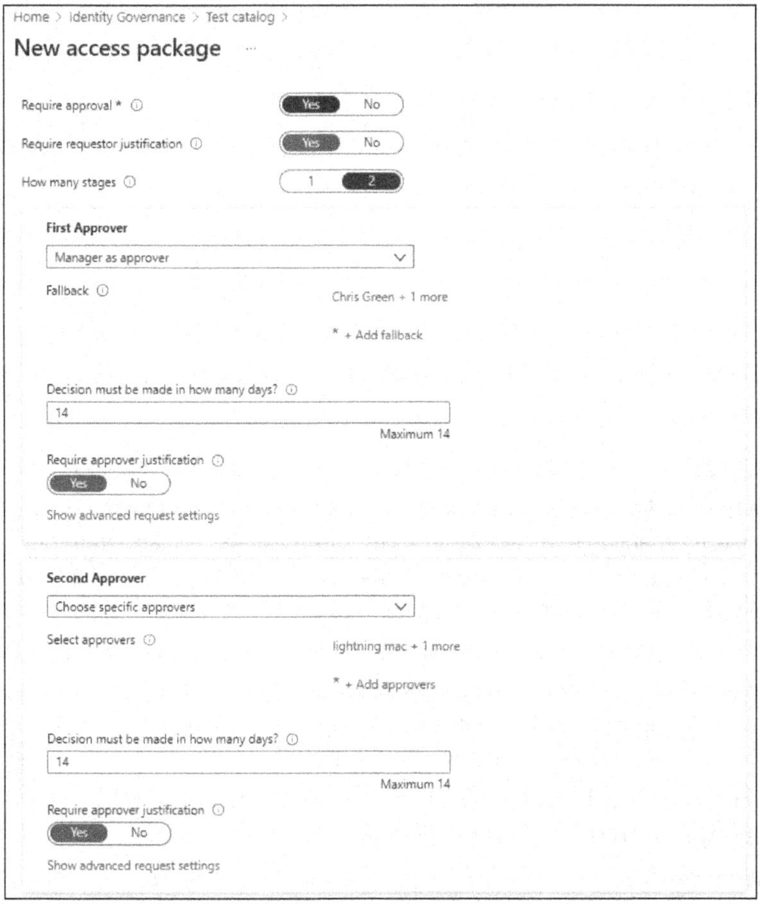

FIGURE 4-7 Approval configuration in an access package.

Configure **Requestor information** to collect information from the requestor. You can add questions and localization options. Enable **Require access reviews** to require answers when users request access to an access package.

Specify when the user's assignment expires and whether access reviews are required for the access package in the **Lifecycle section,** as shown in Figure-4-8.

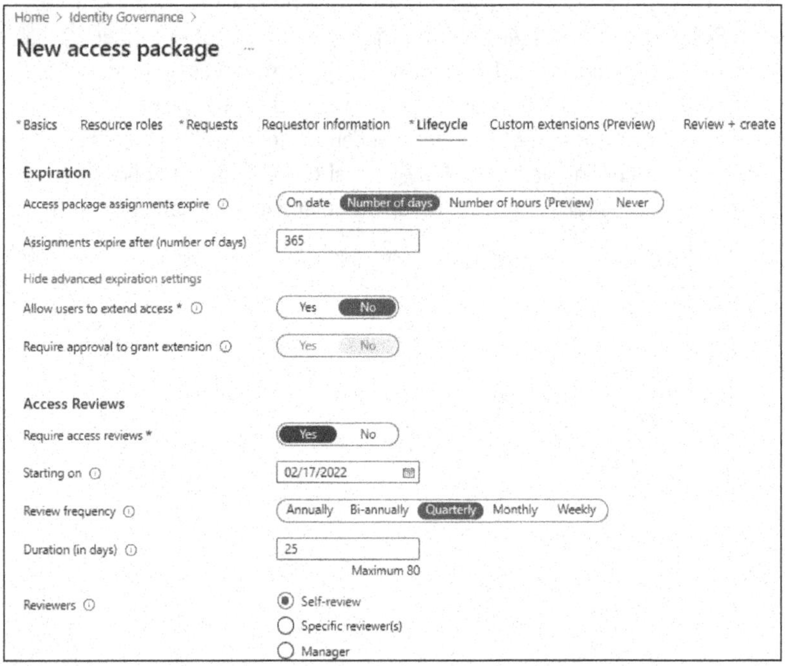

FIGURE 4-8 Access package Lifecyle configuration.

In the Lifecycle Expiration section, you can configure the user's assignment to the access package to expire on a specific date, a certain number of days or hours after the assignment is approved, or never expire. By enabling users to extend access, users can request an extension of their access to this package before their access expires. Specify whether approval is required when users extend the access by enabling **Require approval to grant extension**.

Enable access reviews for the access packages. Access reviews are the planned reviews of the users' access granted to the organizational resources to perform the required job. User access needs to be reviewed regularly to ensure that the right people have the right access to the right resources. You will learn access reviews in detail in Skill 4.2.

Configure custom attributes to enable automated custom workflows to trigger by access package. The use cases may support stages like the following:

- When the request is created
- When the request is approved
- When the assignment is granted
- When the assignment is about to expire in 14 days or a day or when the assignment is removed

You can use Azure Logic Apps to automate the custom workflows.

> ***NEED MORE REVIEW?*** **TRIGGER CUSTOM LOGIC APPS**
>
> **Read more about trigger custom Logic apps to automate the custom workflows at:** ***https://docs.microsoft.com/en-us/azure/active-directory/governance/entitlement-management-logic-apps-integration.***

In the **Review + create** tab, select **Create** to create the access package.

Manage access requests

Once the access package is created, administrators share the My Access portal link with the users, or users can request the access packages by signing in to the My Access portal. Figure 4-9 shows the My Access portal link in the access package overview page. When the administrator shares the My Access portal link with internal or external users, users can sign in to the My Access portal (*https://myaccess.microsoft.com*) to see a list of access packages they can request.

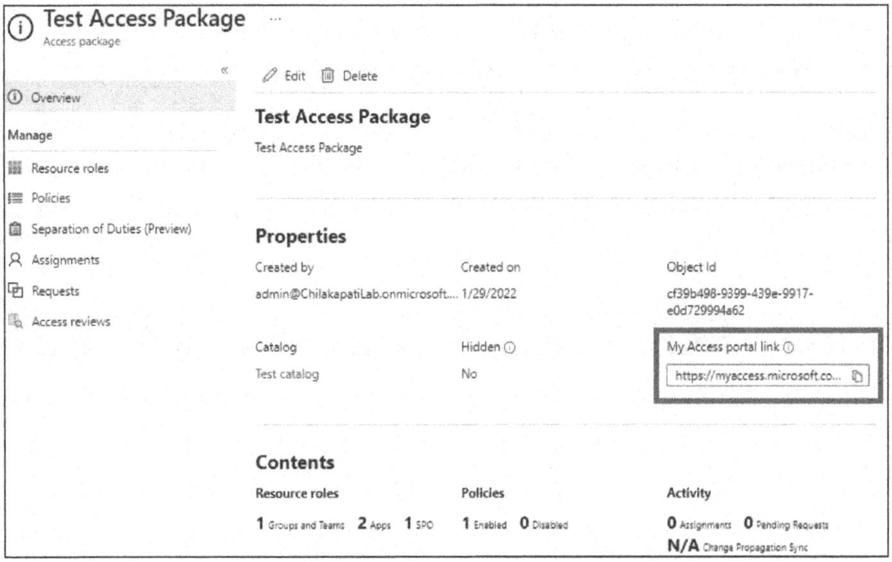

FIGURE 4-9 Access package My Access portal link.

Users request access to an access package. Administrators assign users to an access package. All users receive an email that includes a link to the access package, or they can sign in to the My Access portal (*https://myaccess.microsoft.com*) to see the list of access packages they can request, as shown in Figure-4-10.

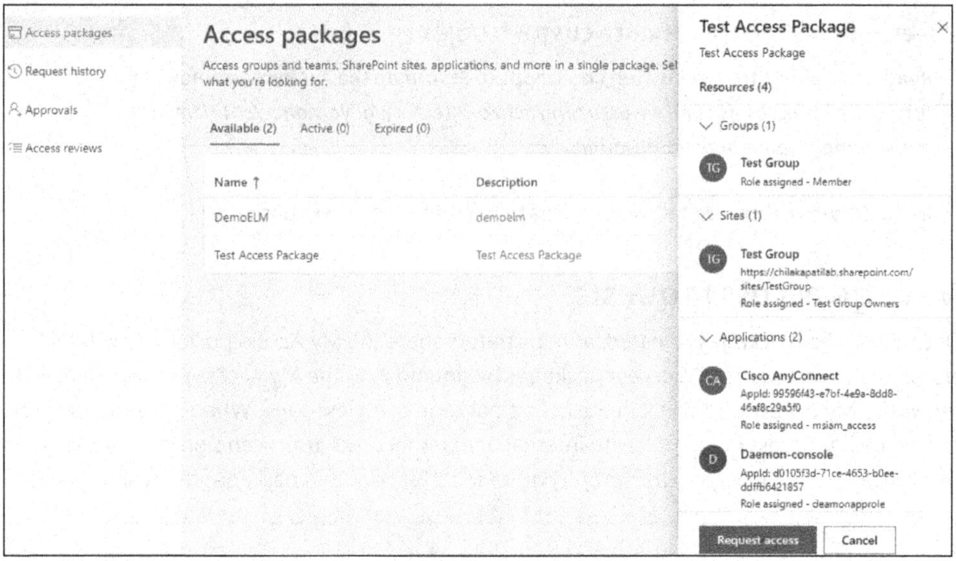

FIGURE 4-10 Users request access packages from the My Access portal.

Administrators assign approvers to an access package. **After users complete submitting requests for an access package,** approvers receive an email that includes a link to approve or deny the requests. The approver can either click the link to sign in to the My Access portal or sign in directly to the My Access portal (*https://myaccess.microsoft.com*) and navigate to the Approvals tab, as shown in Figure 4-11.

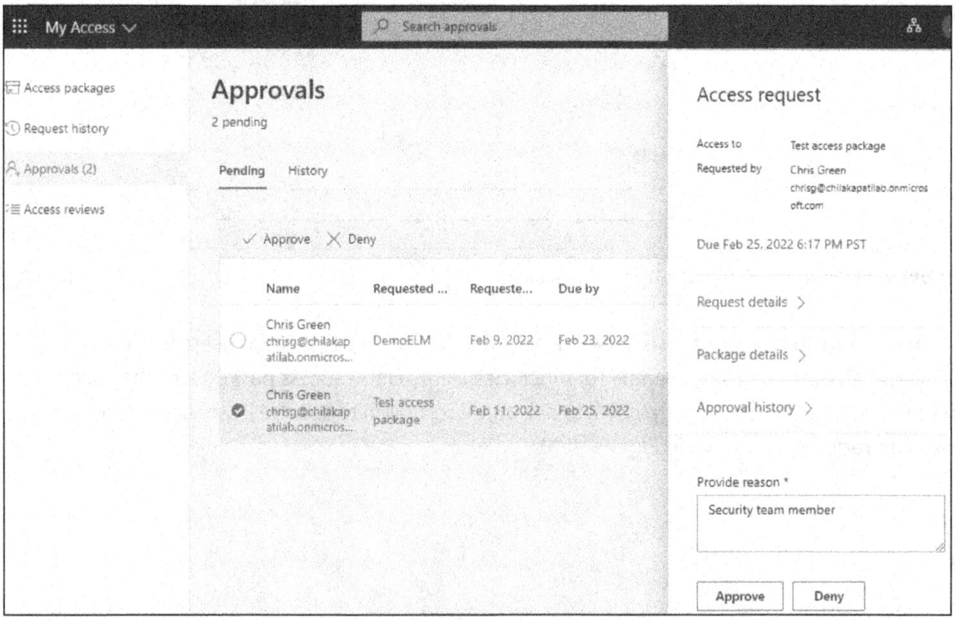

FIGURE 4-11 Approvers approve users, access package requests.

Implement and manage Terms of Use

Azure AD terms of use policies provide organizations with a simple way to present the information to their users. It requires users to accept and agree to the terms before accessing the organizations' sensitive resources. Terms of use policies ensure that users are aware of the organization's terms and conditions.

The terms of use policy can be a general policy or a specific policy. For example, a policy for a dynamic group or a policy for users accessing high-business-impact applications like Salesforce. Terms of use policies use the PDF format to present the content. To support users on mobile devices, the recommended font size in the PDF is 24 points.

A Global administrator, Security administrator, or Conditional Access administrator has permissions to create terms of use. Sign in to the **Azure portal** and navigate to **Identity Governance** to find the **Terms of use** in the left menu or navigate to **Conditional Access** under **Security** to find the **Terms of use**. Select **New terms of use** to create new terms of use. Figure 4-12 shows the "New terms of use" template. When the "New terms of use" template opens, give a name to the new terms of use. Upload a terms of use document, select a language, and enter a display name. Multiple terms of use policies can be uploaded, each with a different language.

Set **Require users to expand the terms of use** to **On** to require that users expand and view the terms of use policy before accepting them. To require users to accept the terms of use on every device, set **Require users to consent on every device** to **On**.

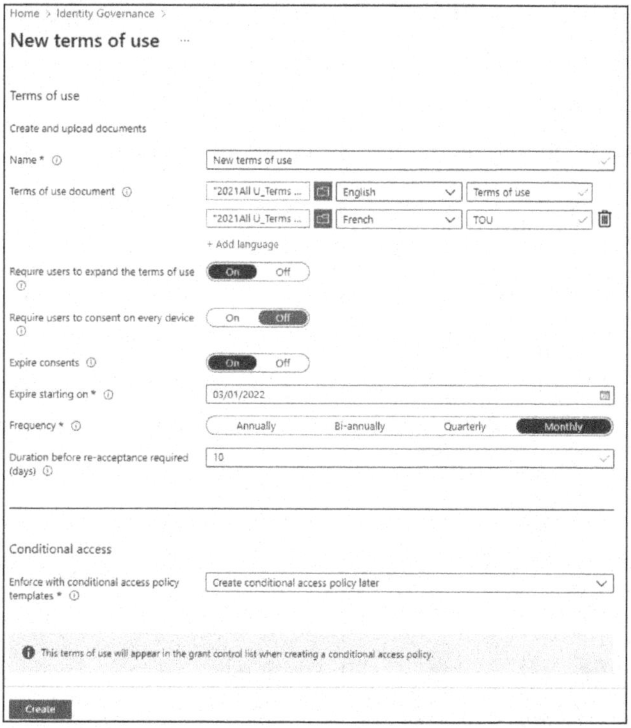

FIGURE 4-12 Create terms of use.

Admins can set an expiration date and frequency for terms of use policies using **Expire consents**. If **Expire starting on** is configured to today's date, and the frequency is monthly, users must accept the terms of use policy and reaccept it every month. For example, if Mike accepts the terms of use policy on Jan 1st, the first expiration date is Feb 1st and the second expiration date is March 1st. If Mike accepts the terms of use policy on Jan 15th, the first expiration date is Feb 1st, and the second expiration date is March 1st.

For the **Duration before re-acceptance required** field, specify the number of days before the user must reaccept the terms of use policy. Users may follow their own schedule. For example, if you set the duration to 30 days, if Mike accepts the terms of use policy on Jan 1st, the first expiration date is Feb 1st and the second expiration date is March 1st. If Mike accepts the terms of use policy on Jan 15th, the first expiration date is Feb 14th, and the second expiration date is March 16th.

It is possible to use constants and **Duration before re-acceptance required** settings together, but typically you use one or the other.

The **Enforce conditional access policy with templates** menu has options to create the conditional access policy later or create a custom policy. Selecting a custom policy opens a new conditional access template. As shown in Figure 4-13, you can find the new terms of use policy in the conditional access policy access controls.

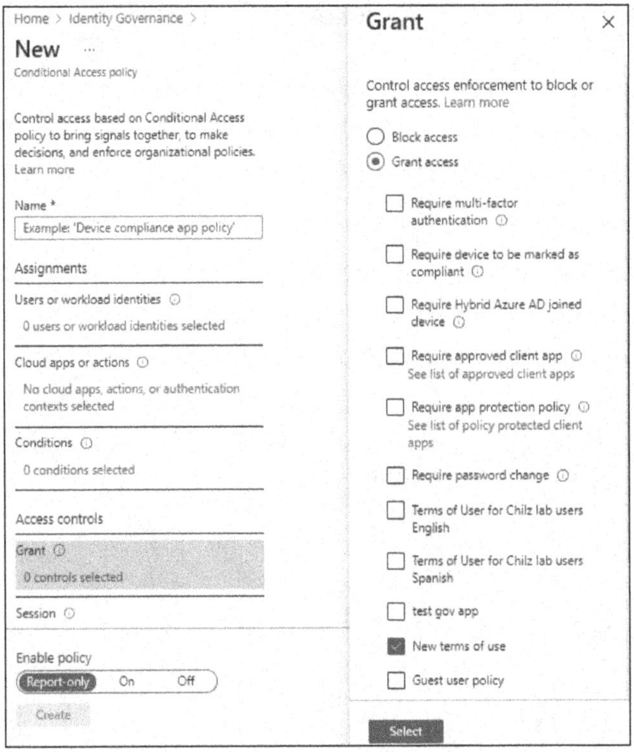

FIGURE 4-13 The Conditional Access policy shows terms of use.

When users accept or decline the terms of use policy, the number will be shown for each terms of use policy, as shown in Figure 4-14. Select the number to view the user activity, such as the number of users who have accepted or declined the terms of use.

To view the terms of use audit logs, select **View audit logs**.

Home > Identity Governance				
☑ **Identity Governance** | Terms of use 📌 ⋯				✕
	+ New terms ✎ Edit terms 🗑 Delete terms 📋 View audit logs 📋 View selected audit logs 🗨 Got feedback?			
🗒 Getting started	🔍 Search for a terms of use			
Entitlement management	Name ↑↓	Accepted ↑↓	Declined	↑↓
🏷 Access packages	Guest user policy	0	0	
📖 Catalogs	New terms of use	2	0	
🧑‍🤝‍🧑 Connected organizations	Terms of User for Chilz lab users English	1	0	
📰 Reports	Terms of User for Chilz lab users Spanish	0	0	
⚙ Settings				

FIGURE 4-14 Terms of use details.

EXAM TIP

Make sure you have a clear understanding of how the terms of use policy expiration date, duration, and frequency works.

Manage the lifecycle of external users in Azure AD Identity Governance settings

Granting access to external users and managing their access lifecycle is challenging. Since they are external users, you never know whether they continue in the same external organization or leave the organization. Keeping their access settings eventually ends up creating unused, stale accounts. Azure AD entitlement management can allow or block external users from signing in to the directory based on external users' sign-in activity.

A Global administrator, Identity Governance administrator, or User administrator can configure the entitlement management settings.

The Entitlement management setting **Block external users from signing in to this directory** blocks them from signing in if they lose their last assignment to any access package. If a user is blocked from signing in to your directory, the user will not be able to re-request the access package or request additional access.

As shown in Figure 4-15, set **Block external users from signing in to this directory** to **No** for external users to request access to other access packages.

To remove the guest user account from your directory for a user who has lost their last assignment to any access package, set **Remove external user** to **Yes**.

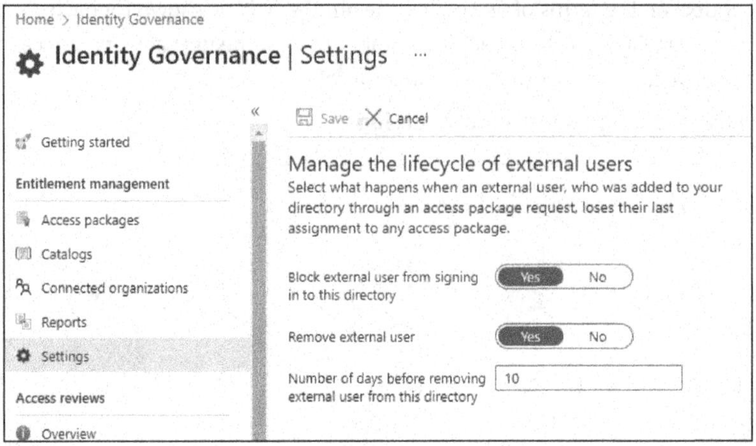

Identity Governance | Settings ···

Save ✕ Cancel

« Getting started

Entitlement management

Access packages

Catalogs

Connected organizations

Reports

Settings

Access reviews

Overview

Manage the lifecycle of external users

Select what happens when an external user, who was added to your directory through an access package request, loses their last assignment to any access package.

Block external user from signing in to this directory **[Yes | No]**

Remove external user **[Yes | No]**

Number of days before removing external user from this directory `10`

FIGURE 4-15 Entitlement management settings.

Configure and manage connected organizations

Entitlement management has the capability to select external organizations as connected organizations. Users from the connected organizations can request access, and if their access is approved, they are automatically invited to your organization. When their access expires, if they have no access package assignment, their account gets deleted automatically. There are three ways to specify the users from the connected organizations:

- Users in another Azure AD directory
- Users in another non-Azure AD directory, configured for direct federation
- Users in another non-Azure AD directory, whose email addresses have the same domain name

Figure 4-16 shows that Contoso has two connected organizations: Fabrikam and Woodgrove. Fabrikam uses Azure AD, and Woodgrove is a non-Azure AD directory. Users from the connected organizations are allowed to request access packages. Users with a user principal name that has a domain of woodgrove.com or fabrikam.com matches with Contoso connected organizations and are allowed to request access packages. Since Fabrikam uses Azure AD, users with a user principal name that matches with a verified domain added to a Fabrikam tenant, such as Fabrikam.in, can also request access packages by using the same policy. If email one-time passcode (OTP) authentication is turned on, users from these domains who do not yet have Azure AD accounts will authenticate using email OTP when accessing Contoso resources.

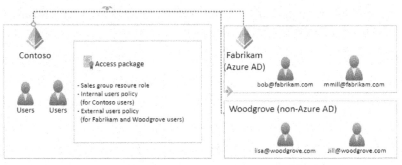

FIGURE 4-16 Access packages for users from connected organizations.

As shown in Figure 4-17, connected organizations have two states: configured and proposed. A configured connected organization is fully functional and allows users within that organization to request access packages. They will show up in the connected organizations picker and be in scope for any policies targeting **All configured connected organizations**. If a connected organization has a state of proposed, the administrator has not created or approved the connected organization. For example, if a user signs up for an access package outside of configured connected organizations, any automatically created connected organizations will be in the proposed state. Proposed connected organizations are not in scope for **All configured connected organizations**. Refer to Figure 4-17 to configure connected organizations.

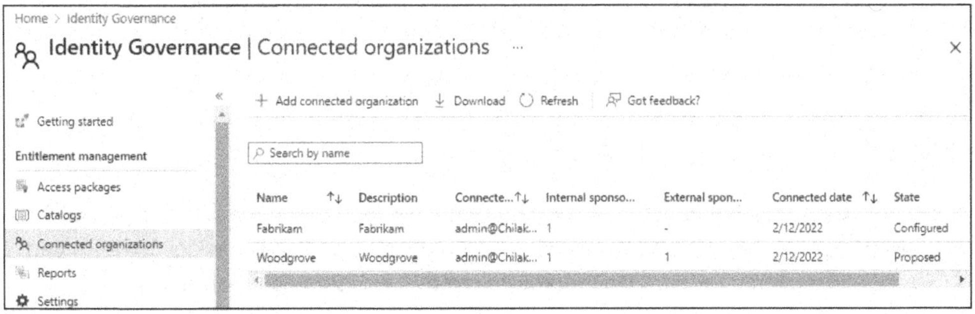

Home > Identity Governance

Identity Governance | Connected organizations ··· ✕

+ Add connected organization ↓ Download ○ Refresh ⊠ Got feedback?

🔍 Search by name

Name ↑↓	Description	Connecte...↑↓	Internal sponso...	External spon...	Connected date ↑↓	State
Fabrikam	Fabrikam	admin@Chilak... 1		-	2/12/2022	Configured
Woodgrove	Woodgrove	admin@Chilak... 1		1	2/12/2022	Proposed

Navigation (left pane): Getting started · Entitlement management · Access packages · Catalogs · Connected organizations · Reports · Settings

FIGURE 4-17 Connected organizations.

Review per-user entitlement by using Azure AD entitlement management

Entitlement management helps to view who has been assigned to access packages, policy, and status. If an access package has an appropriate policy, you can assign the user directly to the access package.

A Global administrator, Identity Governance administrator, User administrator, catalog owner, access package manager, or access package assignment manager can view, add, or remove assignment for access packages.

To view who has an assignment, sign in to the **Azure portal**, navigate to **Identity Governance**, select **Access Packages**, and open an access package. As shown in Figure 4-18, select **Assignments** in the left navigation to see a list of active assignments.

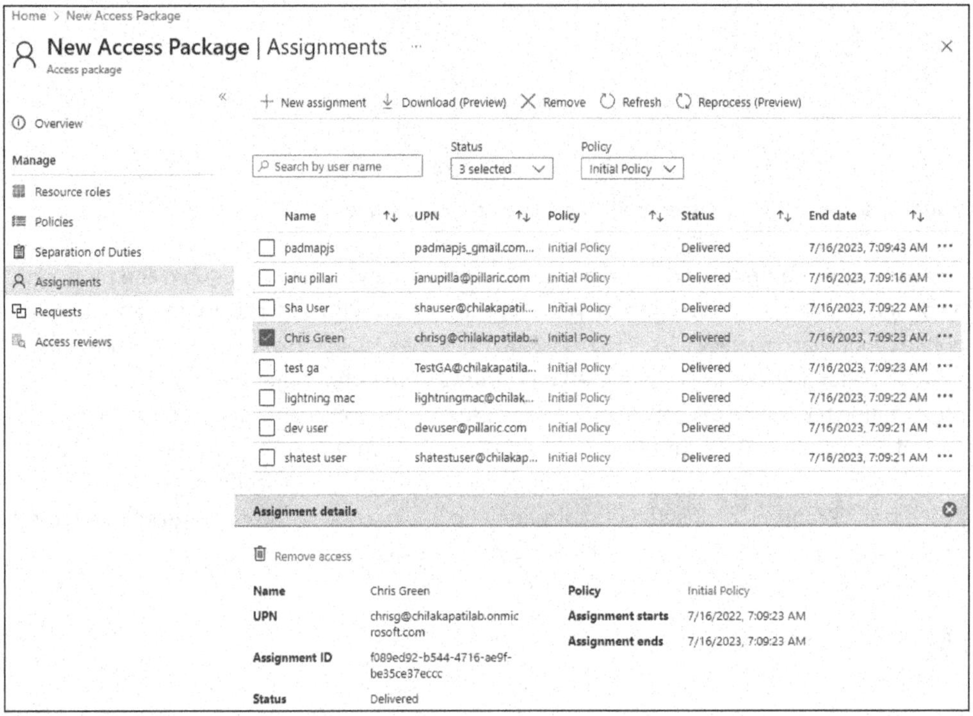

FIGURE 4-18   Assignments in an access package.

Select a specific assignment to view additional details. Select **Requests** on the Manage list on the left to see additional details regarding user requests and delivery errors. To download a CSV file of the filtered list, click **Download**. To remove an assignment, select a user and click **Remove access**.

Configure separation of duties checks for an access package

Users in an organization might have multiple policies with different settings, and sometimes users are granted excess permissions. Entitlement management separation of duties ensures only the amount of access to users needed to perform their jobs. Separation of duties helps configure that a user who is a member of a group or already has an assignment to an access package cannot request an additional access package.

For example, there are two access packages for sales and sales reports. The sales access package gives access to all the resources for the sales department, including reports. The sales report access package gives access only to sales reports. The admin can configure separation of duties for users from the sales department not to request access to the sales report access package. If a user from the sales department requests access to the sales report access package, it restricts the access.

A Global administrator, Identity Governance administrator, User administrator, catalog owner, or access package manager can create a separation of duties. As shown in Figure 4-19, sign in to the **Azure portal**, navigate to **Identity Governance**, select **Access Packages**, open an access package, and select **Separation of Duties**.

FIGURE 4-19 Create separation of duties.

Skill 4.2: Plan, implement, and manage access reviews

Azure AD access reviews are the planned reviews of the user access granted to the organization resources to perform the required job. Users' access needs to be reviewed regularly to ensure that the right people have access to the right resources at the right time. It helps mitigate access risk by protecting, monitoring, and auditing access to the resources while ensuring employee and guest user productivity.

An Azure AD P2 license is required to perform access reviews. The organization needs P2 licenses for users who are performing the following tasks:

- Users who are assigned as reviewers
- Users who perform a self-review
- Users as group owners who perform an access review
- Users as application owners who perform an access review

An Azure AD P2 license is not required for users with the Global Administrator or User Administrator roles to set up access reviews and configure settings.

Using access reviews, organizations can:

- Schedule regular or ad-hoc reviews to see who has access to what resources
- Delegate reviews to admins, business owners, or self-attest for continued access
- Automate review results, such as removing users' access to resources
- Track reviews for insights or compliance

This skill covers how to:

- Plan for access reviews
- Create and configure access reviews for groups and apps
- Create and configure access reviews for access packages
- Create and configure access reviews for Azure AD and Azure resource roles
- Create and configure access review programs
- Monitor access review activity
- Respond to access review activity, including automated and manual responses

---

Plan for access reviews

Planning access reviews before implementing them is essential for achieving a desired governance strategy for employees and guest users in your organization. To achieve a desired strategy:

- Engage the right stakeholders.
- Plan a pilot.
- List the resource types to be reviewed.
- Identify reviewers to review access.

Engage the right stakeholders

Engaging the right stakeholders is critical to achieve the desired impact, outcomes, and responsibilities. For access reviews, you would likely include representatives from the following teams:

- IT administrator – who manages your IT infrastructure, cloud investments, and Software as a Service (SaaS) apps
- Development teams – who build and maintain apps for your organization
- Business units – who manage projects and own applications
- Corporate governance – who ensures that the organization is following internal policy and complying with regulations

Plan a pilot

It is highly recommended to plan pilot access reviews with a targeted small group of non-critical resources. Based on the pilot results, you can adjust the processes and communication as needed.

Recommendations for planning a pilot include:

- Start with reviews where results are not automatically applied.
- Ensure that all users have a valid email address to receive email communications to take appropriate actions.
- Document any changes you made as part of the pilot, such as removing an access.
- Monitor audit logs to ensure all events are properly logged.

List of resource types to be reviewed

Resources such as users (both internal employees and external users), applications, and groups can be managed and reviewed through access reviews.

Typical targets for access reviews include:

- User access to applications – SaaS or line-of-business (LoB) applications that are integrated with Azure AD for single sign-on
- Group membership – groups that are synchronized to Azure AD or created in Azure AD or Microsoft 365, including teams
- Access packages – resources like groups, applications, and sites
- Azure AD roles and Azure resource roles – roles that are defined in Privileged Identity Management (PIM)

Table 4-2 lists the administrative roles required to create, manage, or read an access review.

TABLE 4-2 Administrative roles to create, manage, and read access reviews

Resource Type	Create and manage access reviews	Read access review results
Group or application	Global administrator User administrator Identity Governance administrator Privileged Role administrator (only performs reviews for Azure AD role-assignable groups) Group owners (if enabled by an admin)	Global administrator Global reader User administrator Identity Governance administrator Privileged role Security reader Group owners (if enabled by an admin)
Access packages	Global administrator User administrator Identity Governance administrator Catalog owner (for the access package) Access package manager (for the access package)	Global administrator Global reader User administrator Identity Governance administrator Catalog owner (for the access package) Access package manager (for the access package) Security reader

Azure AD roles	Global administrator Privileged role administrator	Global administrator Global reader User administrator Privileged role administrator Security reader
Azure resource roles	User access administrator (for the resource) Resource owner	User access administrator (for the resource) Resource owner Reader (for the resource)

Identify reviewers to review access

While creating access reviews, the creator decides who will perform the review. The access review creator can modify this setting at any time even once the review is started. Three people typically represent reviewers:

- Resource owners – business owner of a resource
- A set of individually selected delegates – selected by the access review creator
- An end user – self attests for continued access

Before implementing the access reviews, plan the types of reviews relevant for your organization. The following information is required to create an access review policy:

- What resources must be reviewed?
- Whose access is being reviewed?
- How often should the review occur?
- Who will perform the review?
- How will reviewer be notified to review?
- What are the timelines to be enforced for review?
- What happens if the reviewer doesn't respond in time?
- What automatic action should be enforced?
- What manual action will be taken based on review results?
- What communications should be sent based on actions taken?

Plan access reviews for groups

Assigning access to resources via groups, either Security groups or Microsoft 365 groups, and reviewing group membership effectively governs access. The group can be assigned to resources or to an access package that groups resources. With this you can review access to groups rather than users' access to each application. Consider the following while planning reviews for groups:

- Review group ownership
- Review membership of exclusion groups in conditional access policies
- Review guest users' group membership
- Review on-premises groups membership

Plan access reviews for applications

To perform a job, users and external users need access to the applications. It is a good governing process to have regular verifications for user access to the applications. This shows who has access to what specific applications instead of an access package or a group. Consider the following scenarios while planning reviews for applications:

- Users granted access to the application (not through a group or access package)
- Sensitive and critical applications
- Applications that have specific compliance requirements

To create access reviews for an application, in the application **Properties** set the **Assignment required?** option to **Yes**, as shown in Figure 4-20. If it is set to No, all users will be able to access the application, but you cannot review the access.

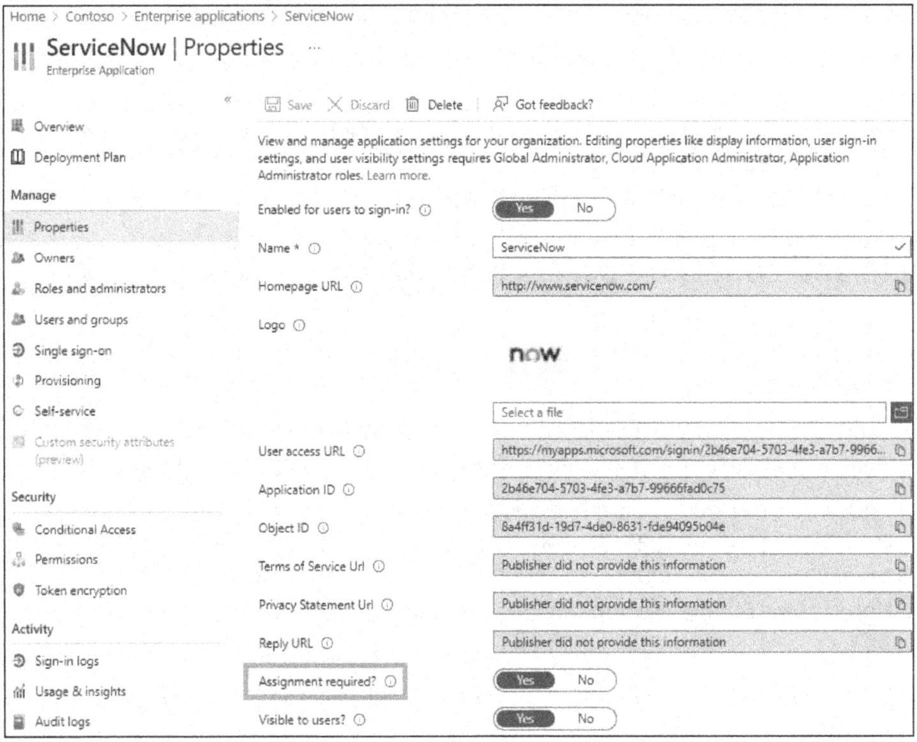

FIGURE 4-20   Set "Assignment required?" to Yes to create access reviews for an application.

Plan access reviews for access packages

An access package is a bundle of all the required resources (groups, applications, or SharePoint sites) for a user to perform the task. Enable access for access packages and perform periodic reviews to reduce the risk of stale (unused) access. Access reviews can be configured while creating a new access package or while editing an existing access package.

Plan access reviews for Azure AD roles and Azure resource roles

To increase the overall security posture of the organization, it is recommended to have privileged access to the resources. Privileged identity management (PIM) helps ensure privileged access with Azure AD roles and Azure resource roles. Access reviews are available to review user eligibility for these roles and attest which users need to be in a role. The following privileged roles are recommended to have access reviews regularly:

- Global administrator
- Use administrator
- Privileged authentication administrator
- Conditional access administrator
- Security administrator
- Microsoft 365 and Dynamics service administration roles

EXAM TIP

Remember the supported resource types and the required administrative roles to create, manage, and read access reviews.

Create and configure access reviews for groups and apps

When employees move teams or new applications are added, employee access to the groups and applications changes over time. Creating access reviews to review user access periodically reduces the risk of stale access assignments.

An Azure AD Premium P2 license is required to create access reviews. A user with a Global administrator, User administrator, or Identity Governance administrator role is required.

To create an access review, sign in to the **Azure portal** and select **Identity Governance**. Select **Access Reviews** from the left menu and create a new access review by selecting **New access review**. As shown in Figure 4-21, click the **Select what to review** dropdown menu to view the options for **Teams + Groups** and for **Applications**.

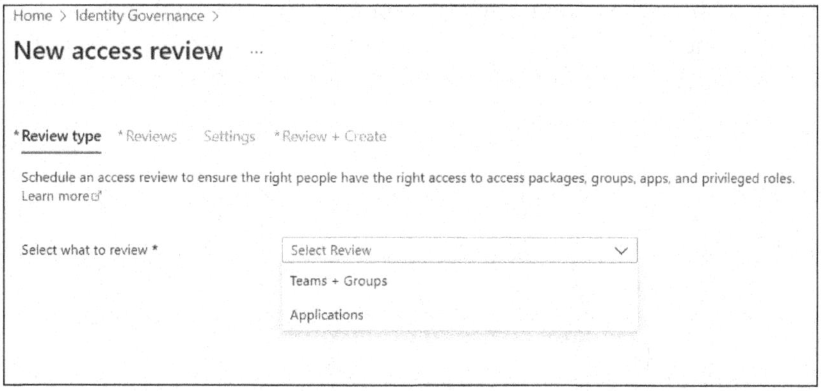

FIGURE 4-21 Access review showing options to select Teams + Groups or Applications.

Figure 4-22 shows that selecting **Teams + Groups** offers two additional options.

Select **All Microsoft 365 groups with guest users** to create reviews for all guest users across Microsoft Teams and Microsoft 365 groups in your organization. Dynamic groups and role-assignable groups are not included. You can exclude groups by selecting **Select group(s) to exclude**.

Select Teams + groups to create reviews for teams or groups.

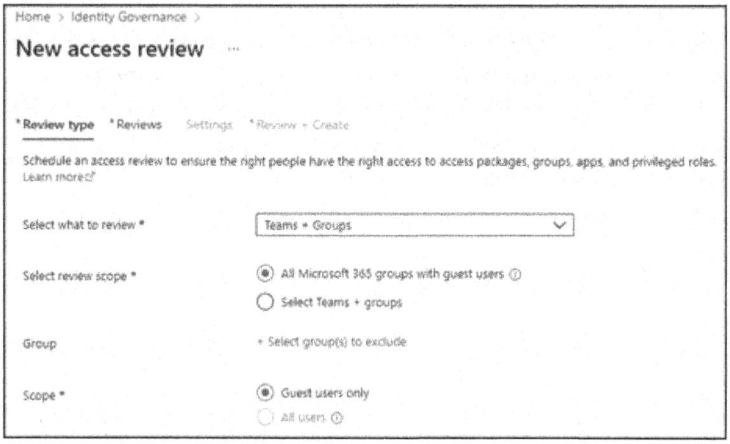

FIGURE 4-22 Configure teams and groups.

As shown in Figure 4-23, selecting **Applications** provides the option to select applications to review. Selecting multiple groups or applications creates multiple access reviews. For example, selecting three groups to review results in creating three different access reviews.

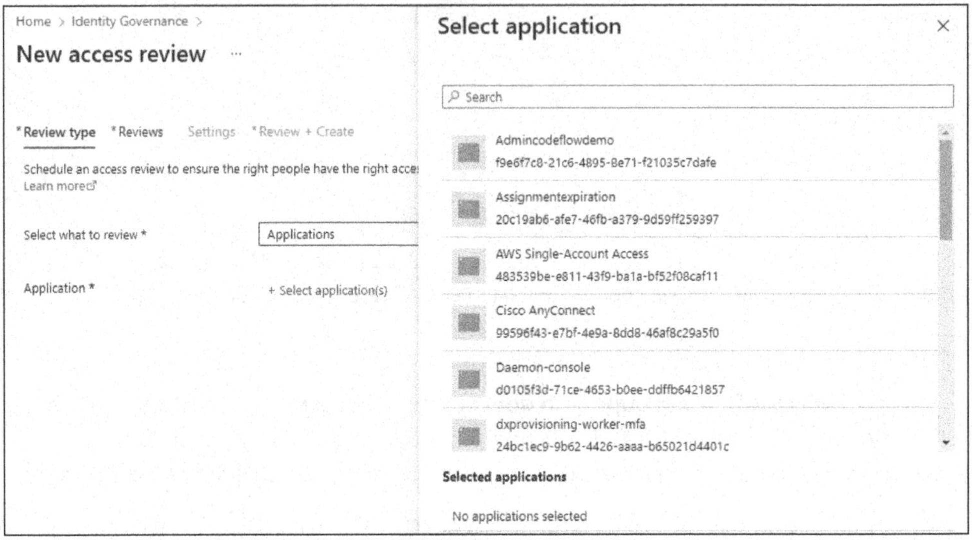

FIGURE 4-23 Configure application in an access review.

Figure 4-24 shows the Reviews tab options to select reviewers and timelines. You have options to select **Group owner(s)**, **Selected user(s) or groups(s)**, **Users review their own access**, or **Managers of users**. You will need to provide a fallback reviewer if you choose either Group owner(s) or Managers of users. Fallback reviewers perform access reviews when a group doesn't have an owner or a user has no manager.

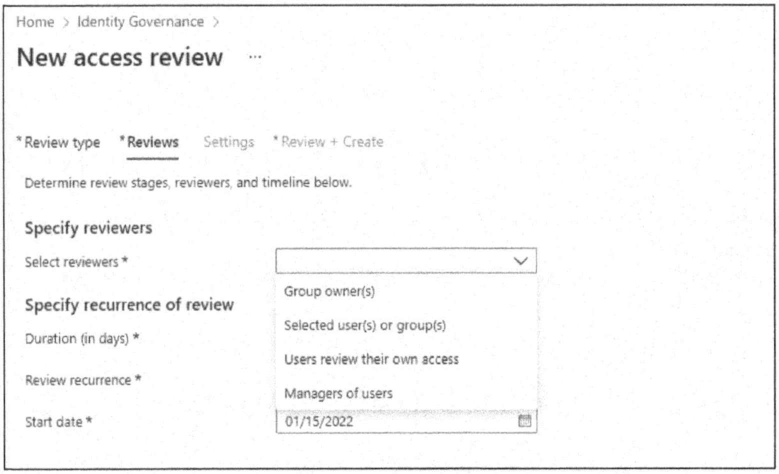

FIGURE 4-24 Configure reviewers in an access review.

Figure 4-25 shows a **Specify recurrence of review** section to configure review **Duration**, **Review recurrence**, and **Start date** and **End date** of an access review.

- Duration (in days) – Number of days a review is open for input from reviewers
- Review recurrence – This provides the option to specify review frequency, such as One time, Weekly, Monthly, Quarterly, Semi-Annually, and Annually.
- Start date – Specifies when the series of reviews begins
- End date- You can create an access review with no end date or end on a specific date or specify a number of occurrences.

Based on the duration, review recurrence options are available to avoid overlapping reviews. For example, the maximum duration that you can set for a monthly review is 27 days, and for a weekly review the maximum is 6 days.

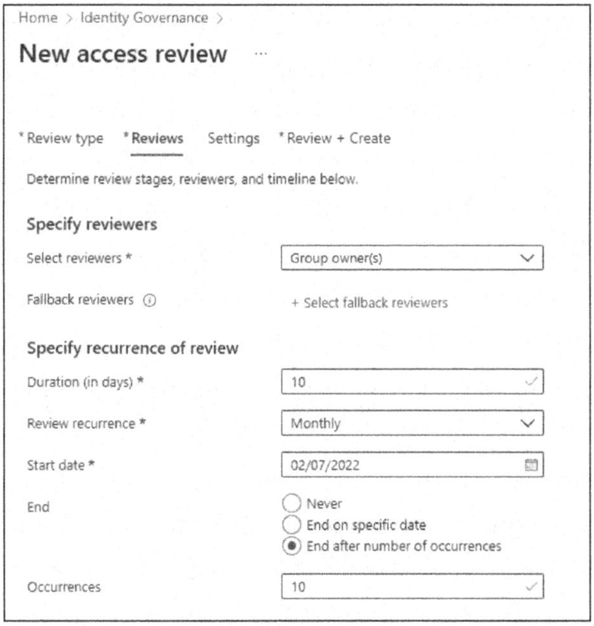

FIGURE 4-25 Configure access review duration.

The **Settings** tab (as shown in Figure 4-26) has information related to decision helpers, completion, and advanced settings.

Home > Identity Governance >

New access review ···

*Review type   *Reviews   Settings   *Review + Create

Set additional information regarding your access review such as decision helpers, completion and advanced settings.

Upon completion settings

Auto apply results to resource ⓘ   ☑

If reviewers don't respond ⓘ   Remove access   ⌄

Action to apply on denied guest users ⓘ   Remove user's membership from t... ⌄

At end of review, send notification to   System Administrator

Enable reviewer decision helpers

No sign-in within 30 days ⓘ   ☑

Advanced settings

Justification required ⓘ   ☑

Email notifications ⓘ   ☑

Reminders ⓘ   ☑

Additional content for reviewer email ⓘ   [   ]

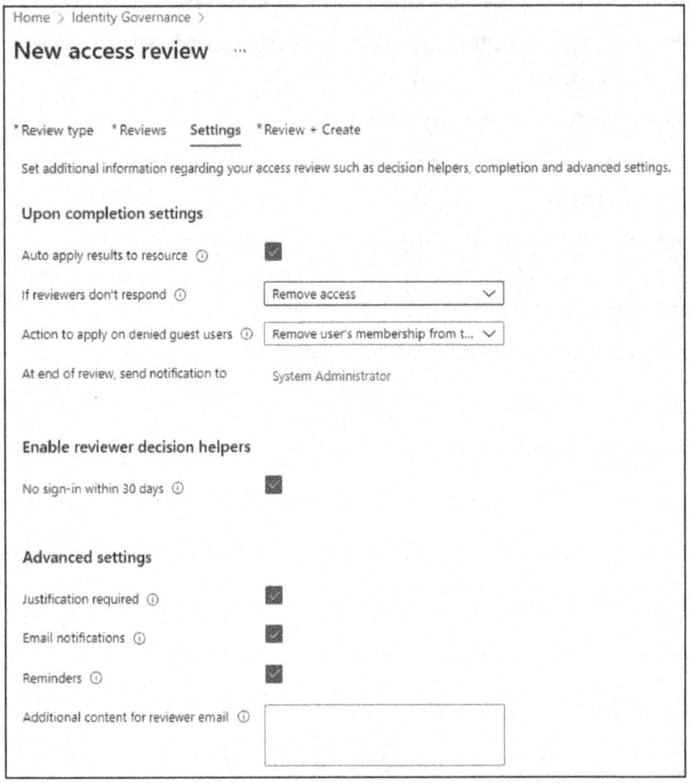

FIGURE 4-26 Configure access review settings.

Selecting the **Auto apply results to resource** checkbox automatically removes access of denied users after the review duration. If the checkbox is not selected, you will have to manually remove access of a denied user when the review finishes.

The **If reviewers don't respond** setting helps decide what would happen to the access of the user if the reviewer didn't complete the review within the review period. This setting doesn't apply to users for whom a reviewer completed the review. The available options are:

- No change: Leaves user's access unchanged
- Remove access: Removes user's access
- Approve access: Approves user's access
- Take recommendations: System recommends approving or denying user's access

The **Action to apply on denied guest users** setting provides options to specify what happens to guest users if the reviewer denies their access. The following options are available:

- Remove user's membership from the resource: removes denied guest user's access to the resource.

- Block user from signing in for 30 days, then remove user from the tenant: blocks denied guest users access from signing-in after the review ends. If the blocked guest users are not re-granted access within 30 days, they will be removed from the tenant.

Select the **No sign-in within 30 days** checkbox for reviewers to receive recommendations during the review process. When enabled, the system recommends that reviewers deny users who have not signed in within 30 days.

Select the **Justification required** checkbox if the reviewer is required to supply a reason for approval or denial.

Enable **Email notifications** to send reviewers email when an access review starts and send the review owners email when a review is completed.

Enable **Reminders** to send a reminder email to all reviewers at the midpoint of the review period. The content of the emails to reviewers is autogenerated based on review details, such as review date, resource, and due date; however, if you need to communicate additional information, you can specify the details in the **Additional content for the reviewer email** text box.

In the **Review + Create** section, provide a name to the access review, give a description, review the information, and create an access review.

After successfully creating an access review, you can see the new access review under the Access reviews section, as shown in Figure 4-27.

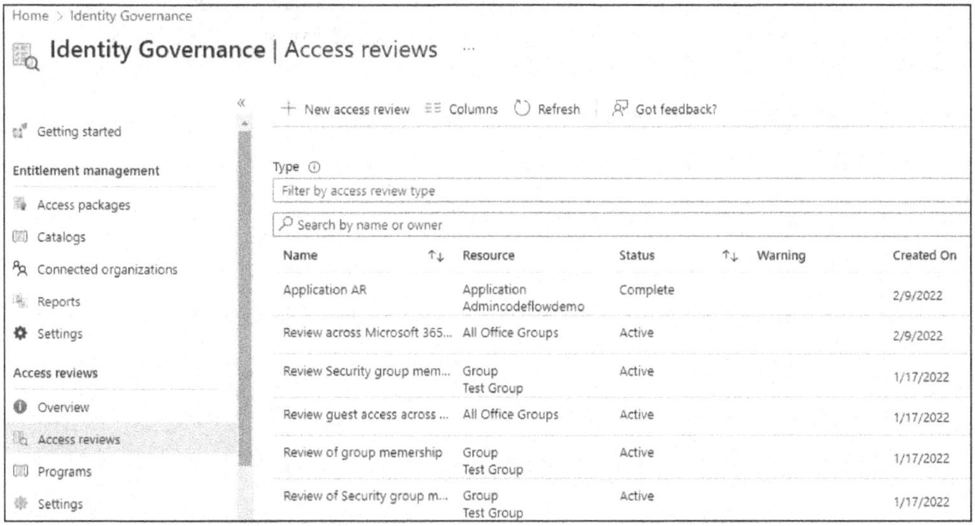

FIGURE 4-27   List of access reviews.

Create and configure access reviews for access packages

Skill 4.1 covered access packages in detail. Enabling access reviews for access packages is recommended to reduce the risk of stale access. Access reviews can be configured while creating a new access package or editing an existing access package.

A Global administrator, Identity Governance administrator, User administrator, catalog owner, or access package manager can create access reviews for the access packages.

As shown in Figure 4-28, use the access packages **Lifecycle** tab to configure access reviews. Set **Requires access reviews** to **Yes**. Specify the date the reviews will start next to **Starting on**. **Review frequency** has options to configure annually, bi-annually, quarterly, monthly, and weekly. Set the **Duration (in days)** to define how many days each review of the recurring series will be open for input from reviewers. For example, if the review frequency starts on March 1st and the duration is set to 30, the review will be open for reviewers to respond to until the end of the month.

Access reviewers can configure users to perform a self-review or select a specific reviewer to perform the review, or the user's manager can perform access reviews. The setting **If reviewers don't respond** helps decide what would happen to the user access if the reviewer didn't complete the review within the review period. This setting doesn't apply to users for whom a reviewer completed the review. The available options are:

- No change: leaves user's access unchanged
- Remove access: removes user's access
- Take recommendations: system recommends approving or denying user's access

Set **Show reviewers decision helpers** to **Yes** for reviewers to receive recommendations during the review process. When enabled, the system recommends reviewers deny users who have not signed in within 30 days. Set **Require reviewer justification** to **Yes** if the reviewer is required to supply a reason for approval or denial.

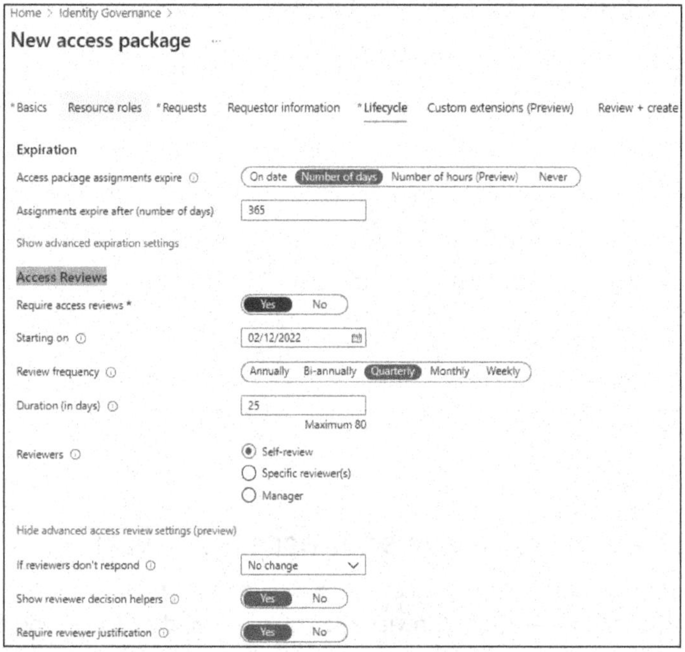

FIGURE 4-28 Configure access reviews for an access package.

Create and configure access reviews for Azure AD and Azure resource roles

You will learn Privileged Identity Management (PIM) for Azure AD and Azure resource roles in Skill 4.3. To reduce the risk associated with stale role assignments, it is recommended to regularly review access.

A Global administrator or a Privileged role administrator can create access reviews for Azure AD roles. A resource owner or user access administrator (for the role) can create access reviews for the Azure resource roles.

Select Azure AD roles or Azure resources under **Privileged Identity Management**. Select **Access Reviews** under the **Manage** section to create a new access review, as shown in Figure 4-29. Provide a name, description, start date, frequency, start date, end date, and scope.

- Start date - Specifies when the series of reviews begins.

- Frequency – This option specifies review frequency, such as One time, Weekly, Monthly, Quarterly, Semi-Annually, and Annually.

- Duration (in days) - Number of days a review is open for input from reviewers.

- End date- You can create an access review with no end date or end on a specific date or specify the number of occurrences.

- Scope – Determines whether Azure AD role users and role-assignable groups will be included. For Azure resource roles users and groups assigned to Azure, resource roles are in scope. It shows the option to select Service principals to review the machine account with direct access to either the Azure AD roles or Azure resources.

Select privileged roles and reviewers to create access reviews for Azure AD or Azure resources roles.

FIGURE 4-29 Configure access reviews for Azure AD roles.

Create and configure access review programs

The new access review appears in the access reviews list with the date created and status. After the review starts, Azure AD sends emails to reviewers.

You can modify or update access review settings after access reviews start. While updating access reviews, you can add or remove primary reviewers, but fallback reviewers are not removable. If you want to remind your reviewers at the review period midpoint, enable the **Reminders** option under **Advanced settings**, as shown in Figure 4-30.

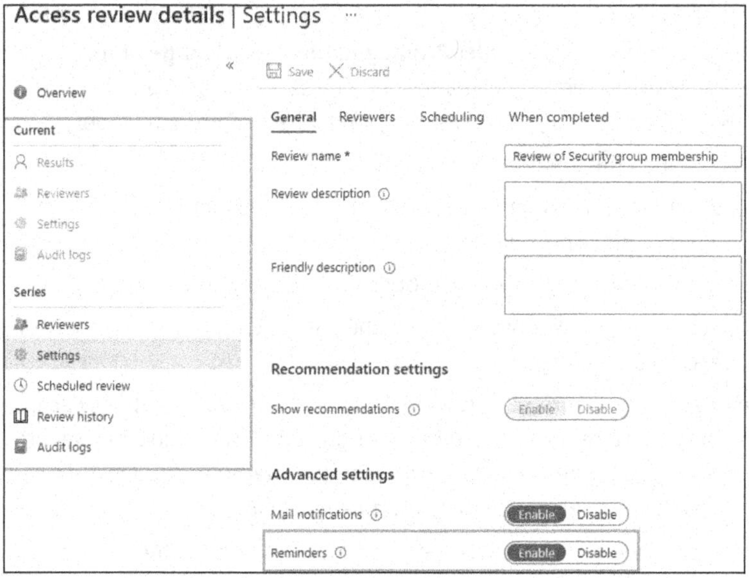

FIGURE 4-30 Update access review settings.

Access reviews can be implemented programmatically using the access review API in Microsoft Graph. The access review methods for both application and user contexts are available in Graph API. For an application context, the account must be granted the AccessReview.Read.All permission.

Access review tasks that can be automated using Graph API include:

- Create and start access review
- List all access reviews that are running and their status
- End an access review before its scheduled time
- Review access reviews history, decisions, and actions performed in each review
- Collect decisions from an access review

> **NEED MORE REVIEW?** **ACCESS REVIEW GRAPH APIS**
>
> Read more about access reviews Graph APIs at *https://docs.microsoft.com/en-us/graph/api/resources/accessreviewsv2-overview?view=graph-rest-1.0*.

Monitor access review activity

After the access review process starts, the designated reviewer performs an access review from the notification email or login to the My Apps or My Access portal.

Perform the access review

The reviewers can open access reviews from an email, the My Apps portal, or the My Access portal.

Open access review from email: Microsoft sends a notification email to the reviewer after creating and starting access reviews. As shown in Figure 4-31, the email consists of review details like review date, resource, due date, and a Start review link. The reviewer can select the **Start review** link to open the access review.

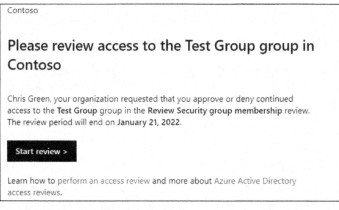

FIGURE 4-31   Email notification to reviewer.

Open access review from My Apps portal: The reviewer can sign in to the My Apps portal, *https://myapps.microsoft.com*, and click the user at the upper-right corner of the page to select the organization that requested an access review. As shown in Figure 4-32, at the upper-left corner, select the My Apps dropdown and select My Access to log in to open the My Access portal. Select Access reviews on the left side to open the access review.

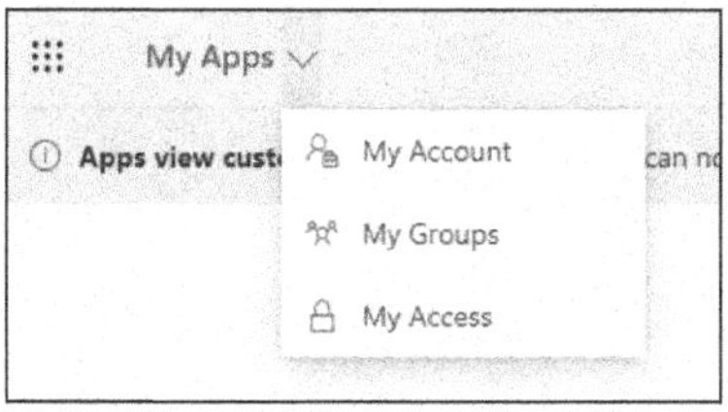

FIGURE 4-32   My Apps portal.

Open access review from My Access portal: The reviewer can sign in to the My Access portal, *http://myaccess.microsoft.com*, and select Access reviews on the left side to open the access review, as shown in Figure 4-33.

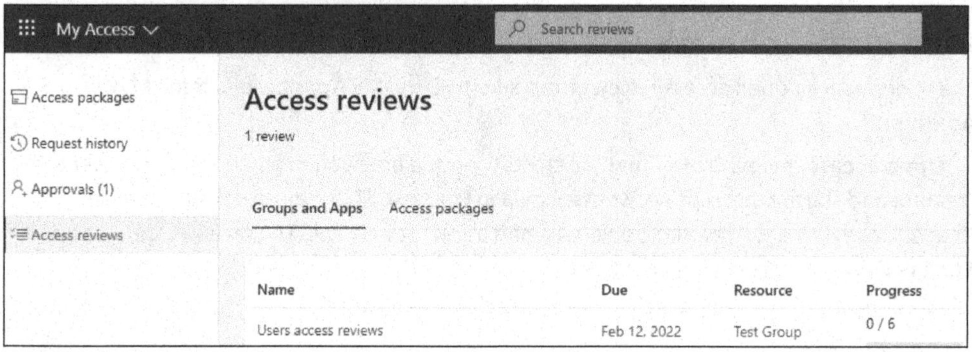

FIGURE 4-33 My Access portal.

Access review shows the review due date, the resource under review, and the progress of the number of users reviewed over the total number of users. Open an access review to see the list of users in scope.

There are two ways that a reviewer can approve or deny access:

- Manually approve or deny access
- Accept system recommendations

A reviewer reviews the list of users and decides whether to approve or deny users' access. If the reviewer selects **Don't know** for a user, the user gets to keep their access. The reviewer choice is recorded in the audit logs. The other reviewers will consider when they review the request. If the administrator requires a reason for the reviewer's decision, the reviewer must provide a reason in the **Reason** box. Until the access review ends, the reviewer can change their decision at any time.

Azure AD generates recommendations based on the user's sign-in activity to make access reviews easier and faster. As shown in Figure 4-34, reviewers can view these recommendations and accept them with a single click.

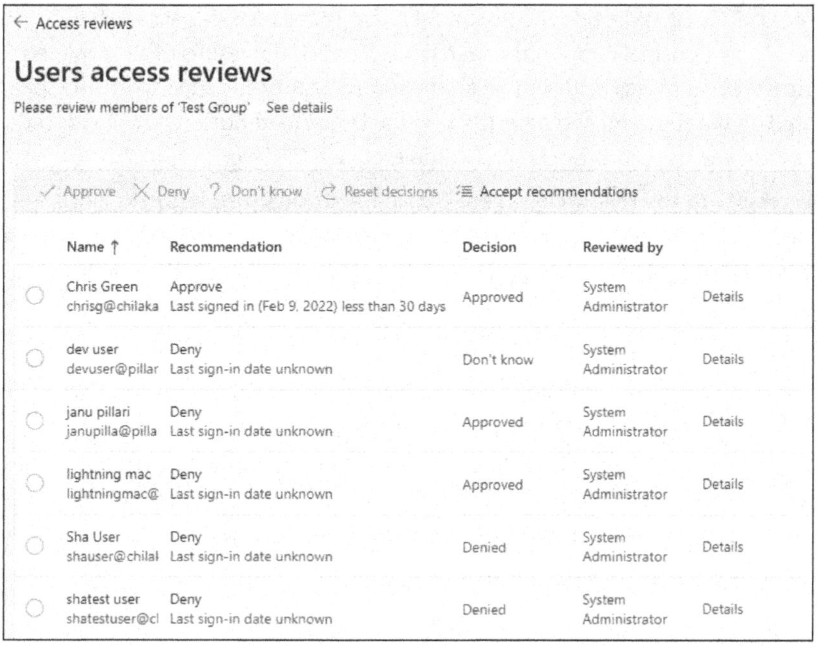

FIGURE 4-34 Reviewers can review access reviews in the My Access portal.

Complete an access review

Open the **Azure portal** access review **Overview** page to view the current instance of an access review, as shown in Figure 4-35. The information about reviews yet to take place will be shown under the Scheduled review section.

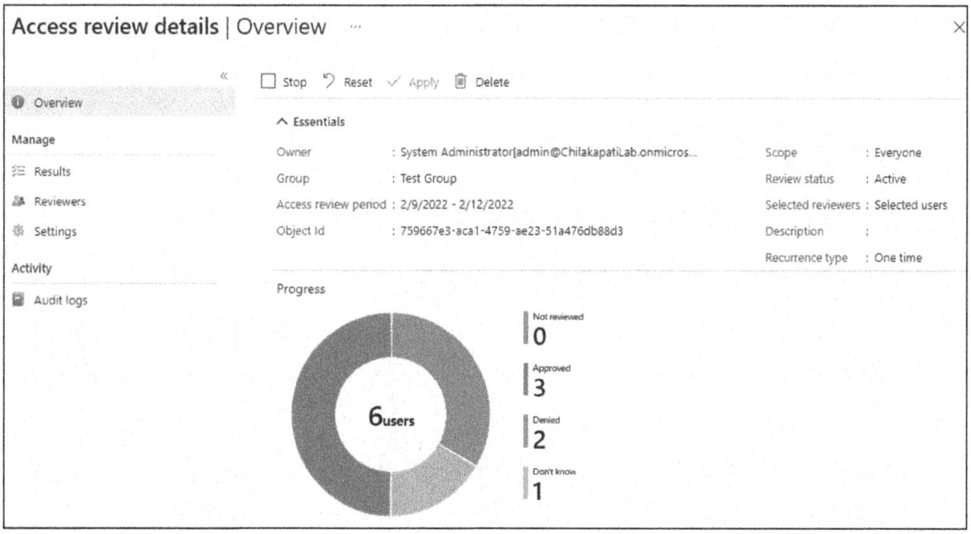

FIGURE 4-35 Access review overview.

To view the results for a review, open the **Results** section. To view a user's access, type the display name or user principal name in the search box. To view the results of a completed instance of an access review that is recurring, open the review history and then select the specific instance based on the start and end date. Clicking the **Download** button downloads the results of an access review, both in-progress and completed as a CSV file.

If **Auto apply results to the resource** was enabled in the **Upon Completion** settings, auto apply will be executed once a review completes or the administrator manually stops the review. If **Auto apply results to the resource** was not enabled for the review, navigate to **Review History** after the review duration ends and click the instance of the review that you would like to apply.

Manage licenses for access reviews

Access reviews need an Azure AD Premium P2 license. The Global administrator or User administrator roles who set up the access reviews configuration settings do not require an Azure AD P2 license. The P2 license is required for users who perform the following tasks:

- Users or guest users who are assigned as reviewers
- Users or guest users who perform a self-review
- Users or guest users as groups owners who perform an access review
- Users or guest users as application owners who perform an access review
- Azure AD guest user access is based on a monthly active users (MAU) billing model

Table 4-3 lists some example scenarios to help you determine the number of Azure AD P2 licenses required for users to perform an access review, assign reviewers, or self-review.

TABLE 4-3   Access review license model

Scenario	Number of licenses
Access review has 100 users and 1 group owner. The group owner is the reviewer.	1 (1 reviewer)
Access review has 100 users and 3 group owners. All group owners are reviewers	3 (3 reviewers)
Access review has 100 users, and users self-review their access	100 (each license for a self-review)
Access review has 100 users, and 50 guest users and users self-review their access	100 (each license for a self-review. Guest users are billed on a MAU basis)
Access review has 5 users, and 95 guest users and users self-review their access	5 (each license for a self-review. Guest users are billed on a MAU basis)

> **NEED MORE REVIEW?   ACCESS REVIEW LICENSE REQUIREMENTS**
>
> Read more about access review license requirements at: *https://docs.microsoft.com/en-us/ azure/active-directory/governance/access-reviews-overview#license-requirements*.

Respond to access review activity, including automated and manual responses

While creating access reviews, you can configure a few settings to automate actions based on access review management tasks.

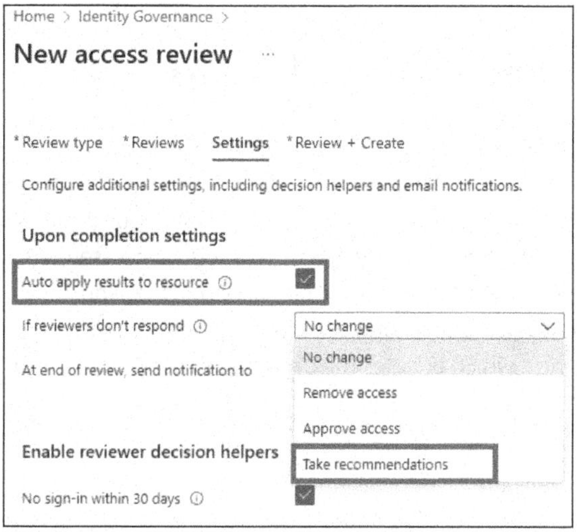

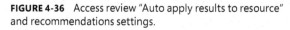

FIGURE 4-36 Access review "Auto apply results to resource" and recommendations settings.

Enabling the **Auto apply results to resource** setting automatically removes denied users access after the review duration. The **Don't respond** settings help determine what would happen to the user access if the reviewer didn't complete the review within the review period. Refer to Figure 4-36 for access review settings.

This setting doesn't apply to the users for whom a reviewer completed the review. The available options are:

- **No change:** Leaves the user's access unchanged
- **Remove access:** Removes the user's access
- **Approve access:** Approves the user's access
- **Take recommendations:** The system recommends approving or denying user's access

By enabling **Take recommendations**, the system recommends reviewers deny users who have not signed in within 30 days.

Access reviews help to review and clean up guest user access. While creating access reviews for groups and applications, you can choose to let the reviewer focus on **Guest users only** so that reviewers are given a focused list of external identities from Azure AD B2B that have access to the resource. Guest users can be granted access to different resources. They can be added to a group, invited to Teams, assigned to an enterprise app, assigned to an access package, or assigned to an Azure AD role and Azure resource. Refer to Figure 4-22 for guest user settings.

Skill 4.3: Plan and implement privileged access

Privileged Identity Management (PIM) improves the security posture of an organization by protecting, managing, and monitoring access to the critical resources within an organization. PIM can target resources residing within an Azure subscription, Azure AD, and various other Microsoft Online Services, such as Microsoft 365. PIM helps mitigate the risk of non-essential and excessive access assignments to the important organizational resources by enabling just-in-time and workflow-based access activation. It also logs the access requests and assignments to privileged resources in the audit logs, which enables the organization to monitor and analyze these assignments closely.

> **This skill covers how to:**
> - Plan and manage Azure roles in Privileged Identity Management (PIM), including settings and assignments
> - Plan and manage Azure resources in PIM, including settings and assignments
> - Plan and configure privileged access groups
> - Manage PIM requests and approval processes
> - Analyze PIM audit history and reports
> - Create and manage break-glass accounts

Plan and manage Azure roles in Privileged Identity Management (PIM), including settings and assignments

PIM enables you to manage both custom and built-in Azure roles, including but not limited to Owner, User Access Administrator, Contributor, Security Admin, and Security Manager.

To assign the Azure role:

1. Sign in to the **Azure portal** with an account that has User Access Administrator or Owner role permissions.

2. Locate the Azure AD **Privileged Identity Management** service and then select **Azure resources**, as shown in Figure 4-37.

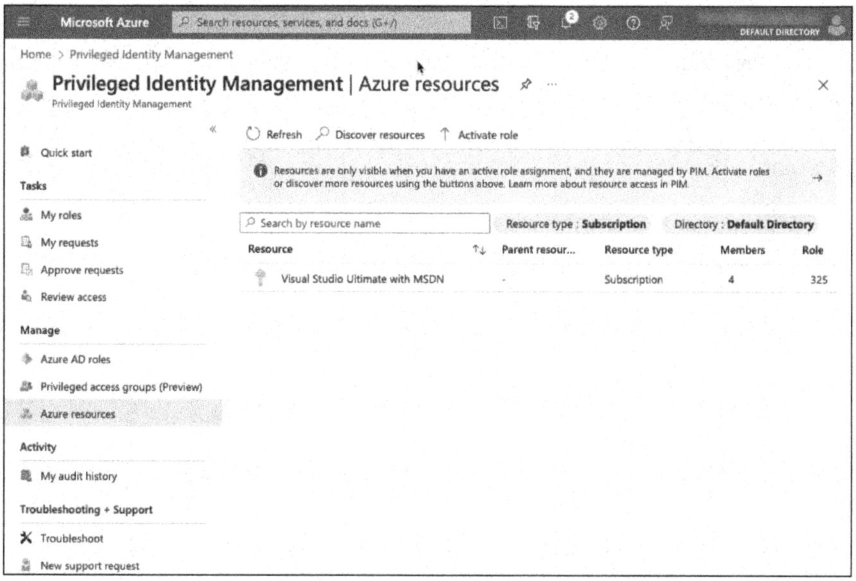

FIGURE 4-37 Azure resources management with Privileged Identity Management.

3. Select the resource you would like to be managed with PIM—for example, an Azure subscription.

4. Select **Roles**, as shown in Figure 4-38.

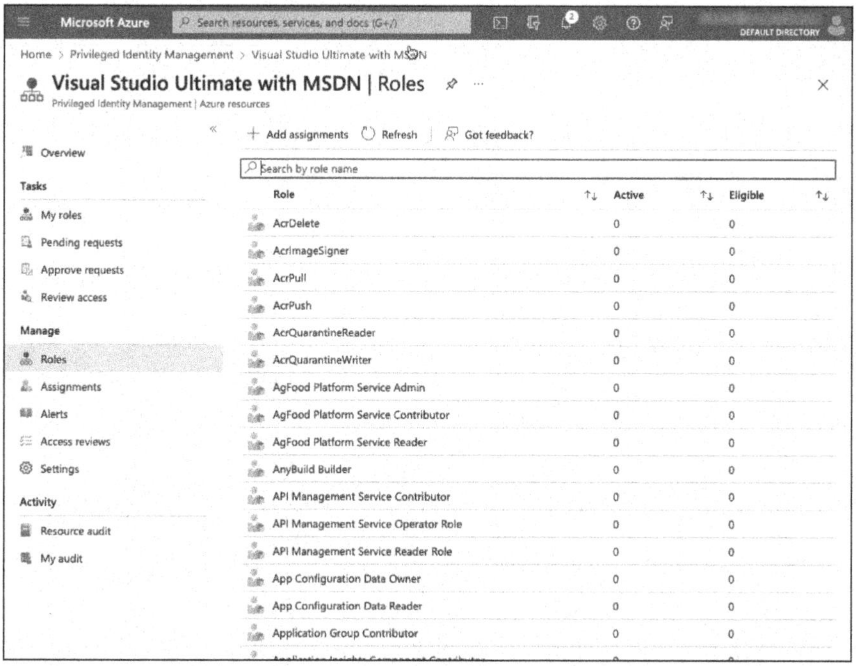

FIGURE 4-38 Azure roles management with PIM.

5. Select the **Add Assignments** button from the top row.

6. Select a role (for example, Security Admin) and then assign it to an individual user or a group, as shown in Figure 4-39.

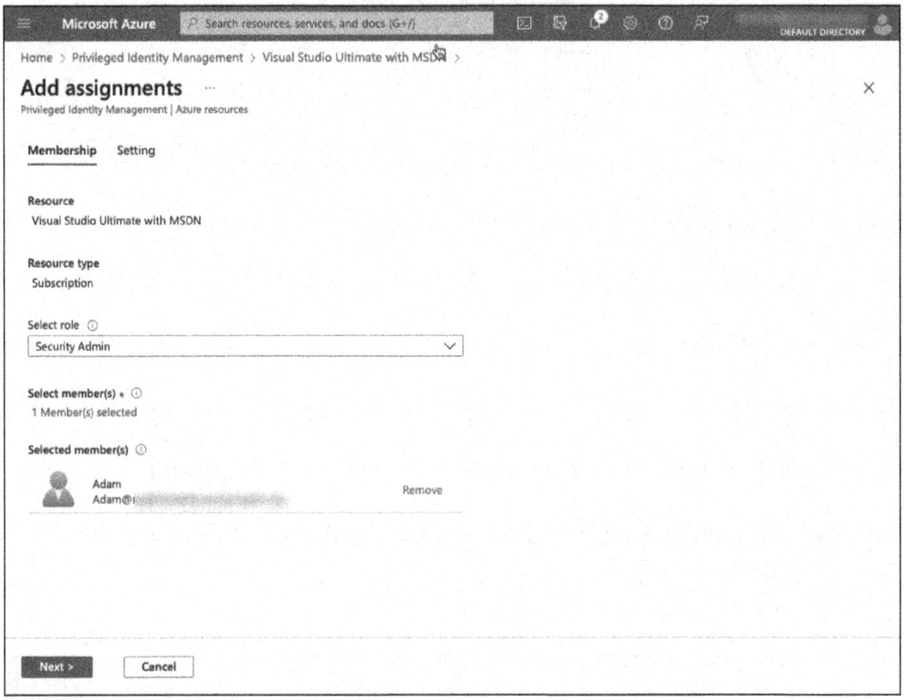

FIGURE 4-39 Assign membership to an Azure role.

7. Make this assignment either Eligible or Active, depending on the organization's needs, and set the start and end date for the assignment, as shown in Figure 4-40.

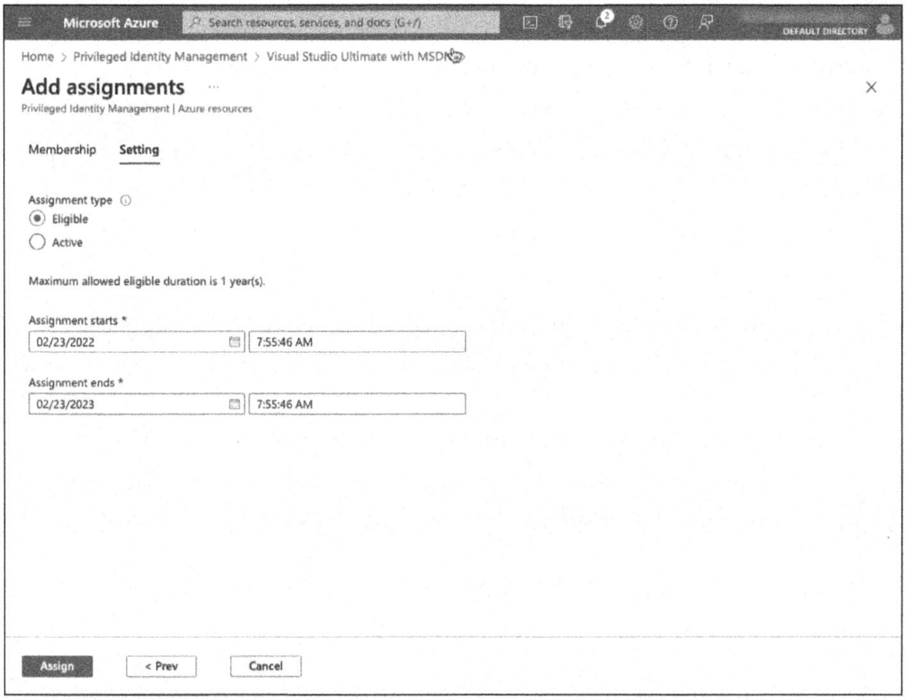

FIGURE 4-40 Azure Role assignment settings.

Real-world cost benefit analysis for PIM

Organizations planning to use PIM should perform cost–benefit analysis by comparing the overall cost of PIM against the security and governance benefits it provides. For example, consider a large corporate bank, which has geo-dispersed staff worldwide and its need for governance around privileged identities. In this case, features like built-in workflows and auditing are vital for governance. In contrast, for a small brick-and-mortar business with limited operations, the organization might want to balance out the overall cost associated with Azure AD. In these scenarios, it is better to approach cost–benefit analysis from a holistic viewpoint including damages that may incur to the business in the absence of PIM, such as potential data breaches, which may happen over time due to lack of access reviews.

You can use the Cost Analysis tool in Azure, which allows you to explore and analyze your organizational costs. It helps in understanding where costs occur over time and helps identify spending trends. More information on this subject can be found at *https://docs.microsoft.com/en-us/azure/cost-management-billing/costs/quick-acm-cost-analysis*.

PIM licensing

The organization needs P2 licenses for users who perform the following tasks:

- Users assigned as eligible to Azure AD or Azure roles managed using PIM
- Users who are assigned as eligible members or owners of privileged access groups
- Users who are able to approve or reject activation requests in PIM
- Users assigned to an access review
- Users who perform access reviews

An Azure AD P2 license is not required for users who perform following tasks:

- Users who set up PIM, configure policies, receive alerts, and set up access reviews

> **NEED MORE REVIEW?** **PIM LICENSING AND EXAMPLE SCENARIOS**
>
> Read more about PIM licensing and practical scenarios at: *https://docs.microsoft.com/en-us/azure/active-directory/privileged-identity-management/subscription-requirements*.

Table 4-4 describes a few example licensing scenarios related to PIM.

TABLE 4-4   PIM licensing scenarios example

Scenario	Licensing requirements	Total licenses needed
Contoso has 10 administrators for various departments, as well as 2 Global Administrators who configure and manage PIM. They made 5 administrators eligible.	5 licenses for the administrators who are eligible	5
Northwind Traders has 25 administrators, of which 14 are managed through PIM. Role activation requires approval, and there are 3 different users in the organization who can approve activations.	14 licenses for the eligible roles and 3 for approvers	17

Configure PIM for Azure AD roles

Privileged Identity Management (PIM) settings impact the user experience when they try to activate an Azure AD role. PIM configuration settings include MFA, activation duration, notification method, etc.

To configure an Azure AD role setting:

1. Sign in to the **Azure portal** with a user account that has **Privileged Role Administrator** role permissions.
2. Locate the Azure AD **Privileged Identity Management** using the top search bar.
3. Select the Azure AD roles located under the **Manage** section.
4. Next, select the **Settings** option, as shown in Figure 4-41.

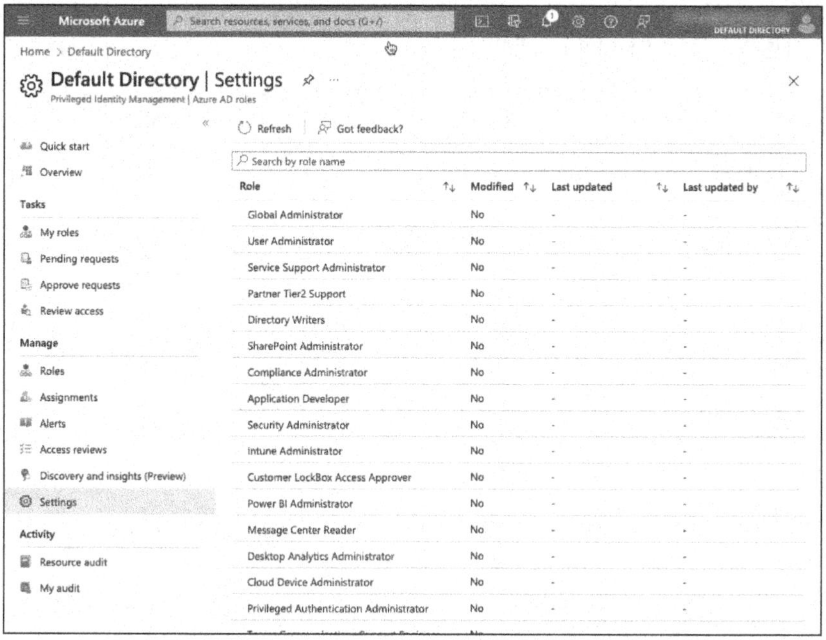

FIGURE 4-41 Configure Privileged Identity Management settings for Azure AD roles.

5. Select the Azure AD role for which you would like to configure the settings.

6. Next, select **Edit** to modify the role settings, as shown in Figure 4-42.

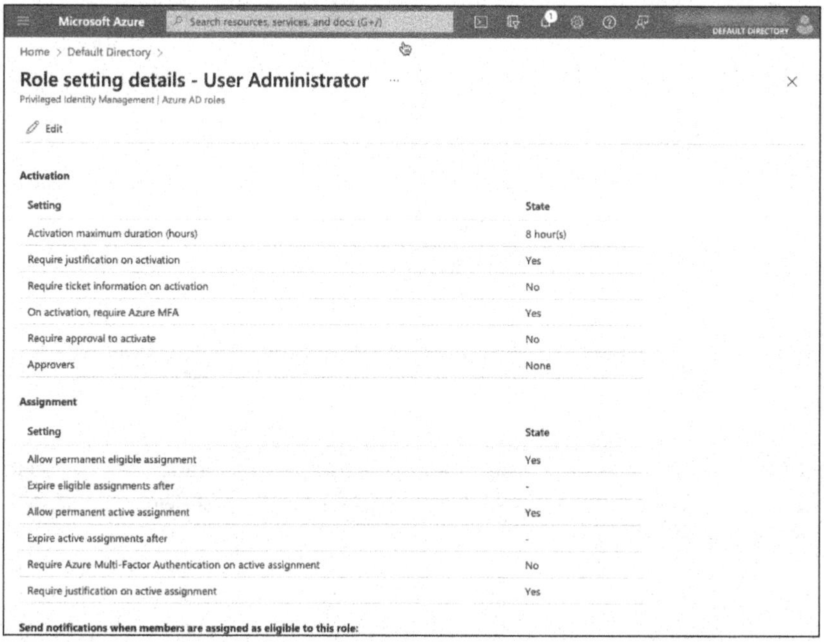

FIGURE 4-42 Edit role settings for Privileged Identity Management of Azure AD roles.

7. Review the **Activation** related settings, as shown in Figure 4-43. You can also review details about these settings in Table 4-5.

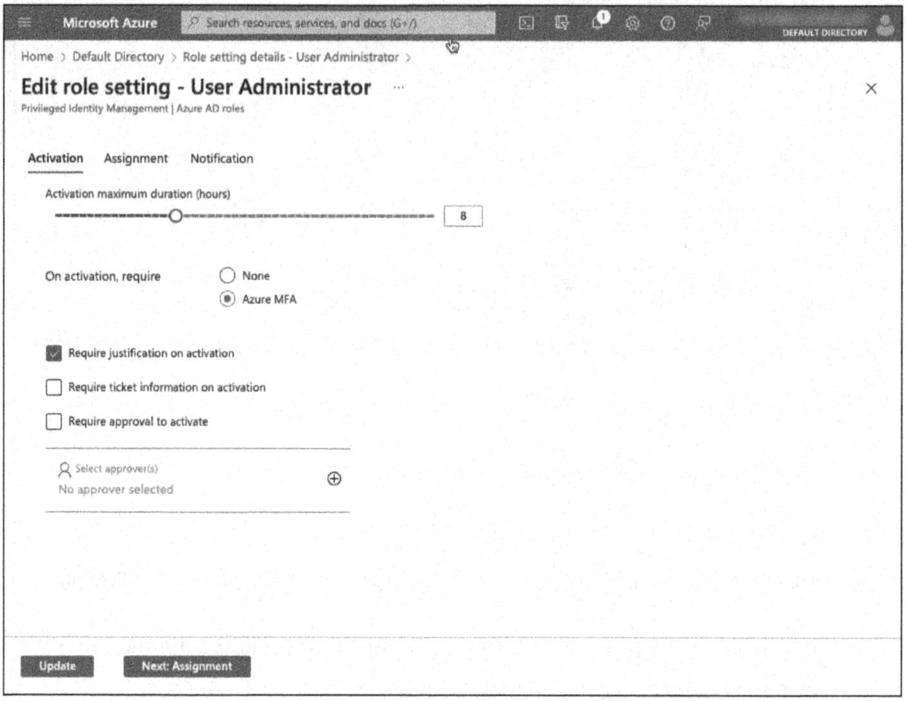

FIGURE 4-43 Activation settings for Privileged Identity Management of Azure AD roles.

TABLE 4-5 Activation settings

Name	Description
Maximum duration	This is the maximum duration for the activation. You can set it between 0.5 and 24 hours.
MFA	You can select either no MFA or Azure MFA.
Justification	Business justification for the role activation.
Ticket information	This is the ticket information—e.g., help desk or support—that led to the role activation.
Approval	This is the list of approvers who will be asked to approve the activation request. If no approvers are selected, Privileged role administrators or Global administrators will become the default approvers.

8. Keep the defaults and select **Assignment**. The assignment settings enable you to configure various options for active and eligible assignments, as shown in Figure 4-44 and explained in Table 4-6.

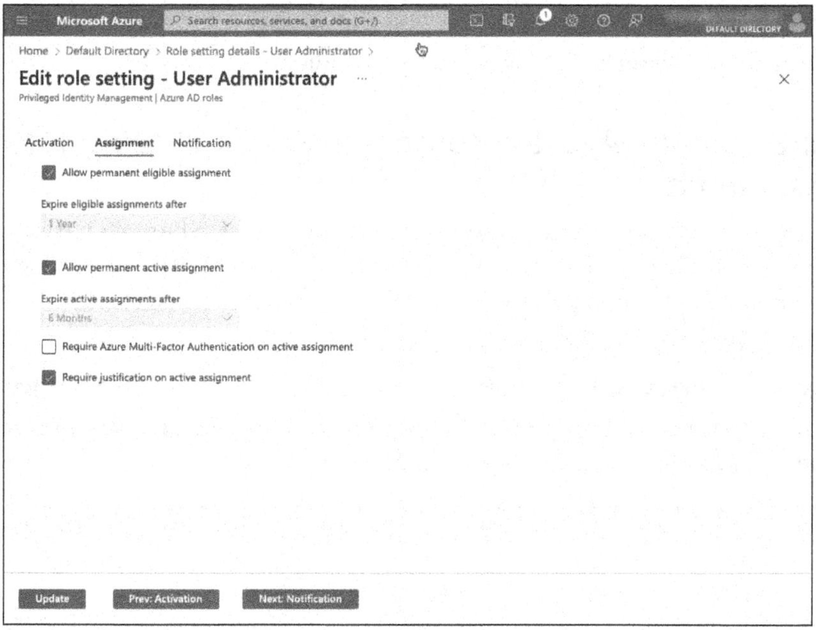

FIGURE 4-44 Assignment settings for Privileged Identity Management of Azure AD roles.

IMPORTANT **ACTIVE VERSUS ELIGIBLE ASSIGNMENT**

Make sure you have a clear understanding of eligible and active role assignments. Eligible assignments require an action to be performed by a user to use a particular role. The action might include requesting an approval, performing MFA, or providing a business justification. Active assignments, on the other hand, do not require a user to perform any action to use a particular role.

Table 4-6 provides a summary of assignment settings.

TABLE 4-6 Assignment settings

Name	Description
Allow permanent eligible assignment	Global administrators and Privileged role admins can assign permanent eligible assignments.
Expire eligible assignment after	Global admins and Privileged role admins can require that all eligible assignments have a specified start date and end date.
Allow permanent active assignment	Global admins and Privileged role admins can assign permanent active assignments.
Expire active assignment after	Global admins and Privileged role admins can require that all active assignments have a specified start date and end date.
Require multifactor authentication	This setting enables enforcement of Azure MFA on activation and on active assignment.

9. Select **Notification** and keep the default settings.

10. Finally, select **Update** to save the configuration settings.

Plan and manage Azure resources in PIM, including settings and assignments

In addition to Azure AD roles, you can also configure Azure resources to be protected with PIM. The process of configuring PIM for Azure resources starts with a discovery phase, where you first search the resources within an organization and then select them to be protected by PIM.

To begin the discovery process for Azure resources:

1. Sign in to the **Azure portal** and navigate to Azure AD **Privileged Identity Management**.

2. If this is the first time you are using PIM for Azure resources, the **Discover resources** button will be displayed on the top row, as shown in Figure 4-45.

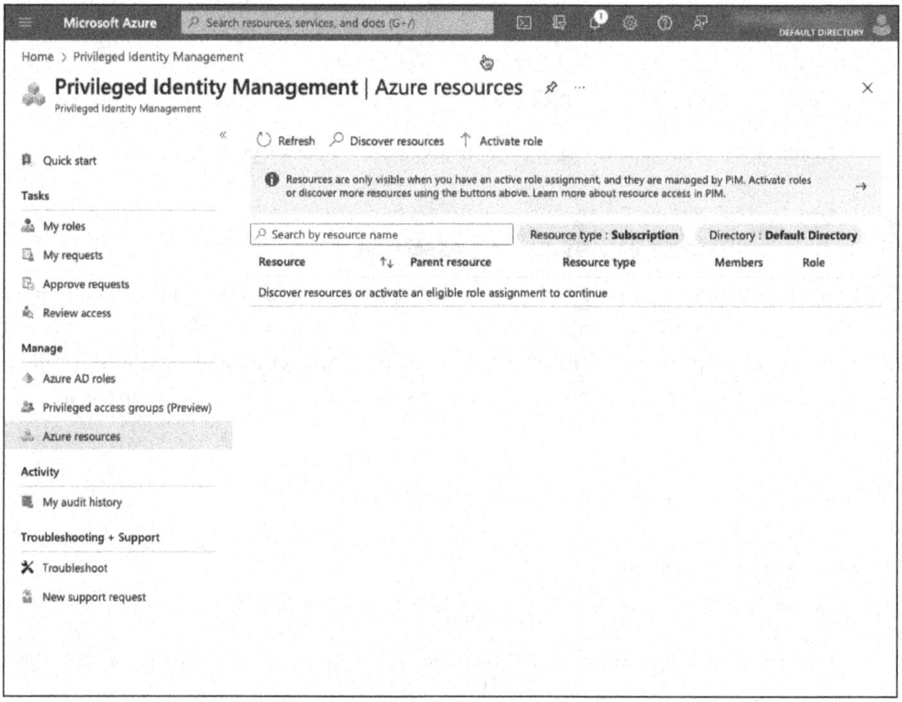

FIGURE 4-45 Discover Azure resources for Privileged Identity Management.

3. The **Discover resources** option enables you to bring either an Azure subscription or a management group, including its child resources, under PIM management. After you identify the resource—for example, the Azure subscription—select the **Managed resource** option. You can also decide to bring all child objects of the selected resource under PIM by selecting **OK**, as shown in Figure 4-46.

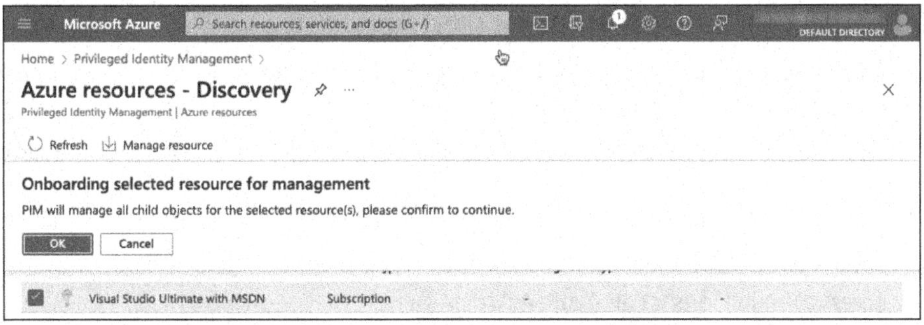

FIGURE 4-46 Manage Azure resources for Privileged Identity Management.

Plan and configure privileged access groups

You can give workload-specific administrators quick access to multiple roles with a single just-in-time request using the privileged access groups. You can assign eligibility for membership or ownership of privileged access groups in Privileged Identity Management (PIM). This is especially useful when working with Azure AD guest accounts. Instead of a single just-in-time policy for all privileged role assignments, you can create two separate privileged access groups with their own policies. Less stringent requirements can be imposed on employees, while stricter requirements, such as approval workflow, can be imposed on guest accounts when they request activation into their assigned role.

PIM allows you to manage the eligibility and activation of privileged access group assignments in Azure AD. Please refer to the documents available through the links below to learn more about privileged access groups configuration using PIM.

- Privileged access groups will be added to Privileged Identity Management: *https://learn.microsoft.com/en-us/azure/active-directory/privileged-identity-management/groups-discover-groups*

- Extend or renew privileged access group assignments (preview) in Privileged Identity Management: *https://learn.microsoft.com/en-us/azure/active-directory/privileged-identity-management/groups-renew-extend*

- Assigning eligibility for a privileged access group in PIM: *https://learn.microsoft.com/en-us/azure/active-directory/privileged-identity-management/groups-assign-member-owner*

- Approve activation requests for members of the privileged access group and owners: *https://learn.microsoft.com/en-us/azure/active-directory/privileged-identity-management/groups-approval-workflow*

- Activate my privileged access group roles in Privileged Identity Management: *https://learn.microsoft.com/en-us/azure/active-directory/privileged-identity-management/groups-activate-roles*

- Configure privileged access group settings (preview) in Privileged Identity Management: *https://learn.microsoft.com/en-us/azure/active-directory/privileged-identity-management/groups-role-settings*

Analyze PIM audit history and reports

PIM allows you to access complete audit history when activations and assignments are made against roles and resources under the management of PIM.

PIM also enables you to download the audit history on an ad-hoc basis in a standard CSV file for retention purposes.

Azure AD roles

To access the audit logs for an Azure AD role:

1. Sign in to the **Azure portal** and navigate to Azure AD **Privileged Identity Management**.

2. Select **Azure AD Roles**.

3. Select **Resource audit** to view the audit history associated with the Azure AD roles, as shown in Figure 4-47. By default, the last 24-hour (last day) audit logs are shown, but you can change the duration by using the **Time** span filter to last week, last month, or a custom time span.

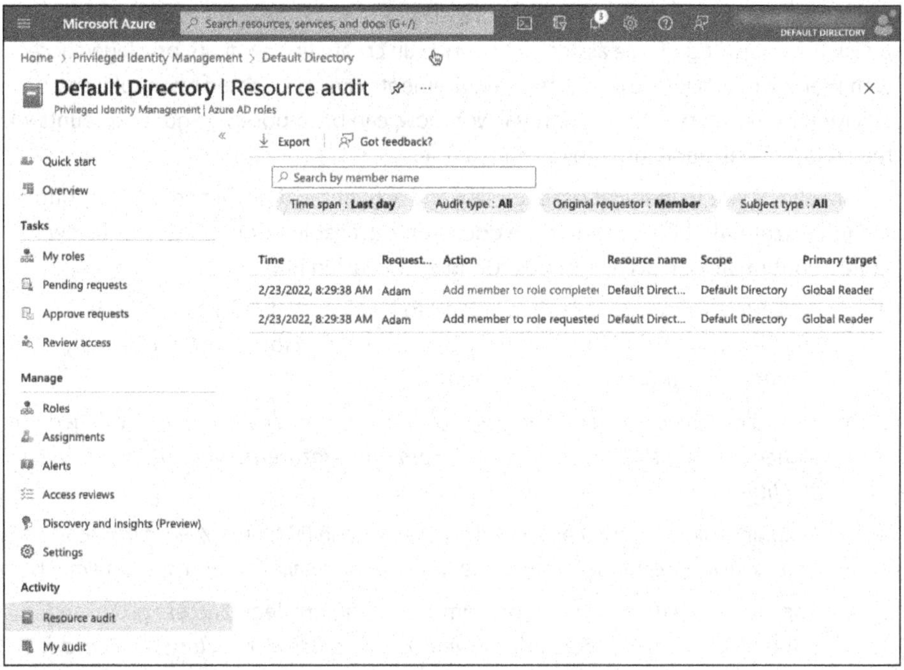

FIGURE 4-47 Resource audit history for Azure AD roles.

4. You can also export the audit history in a CSV file format by using the **Export** option located at the top row. The CSV file contains more holistic auditing data about the activities, including items like ticket information, ticket number, reason, etc.

The **My audit** option available under the Activity section is like the Resource audit but allows you to view your personal role activity.

Azure roles

PIM also enables you to view activity and activation history reports for Azure roles. To access audit history and reports for the Azure roles:

1. Sign in to the **Azure portal** and navigate to Azure AD **Privileged Identity Management**.

2. Select **Azure resources** and choose the Azure resource—for example, Azure subscription—for which you'd like to explore the audit report.

3. The **Overview** page for Azure resources, as shown in Figure 4-48, showcases a report with **Admin view** and **My view** tabs, containing critical data including **Role activations in last 7 days**, **Role assignment distribution**, **PIM activities in last 30 days**, and **Roles by assignment**.

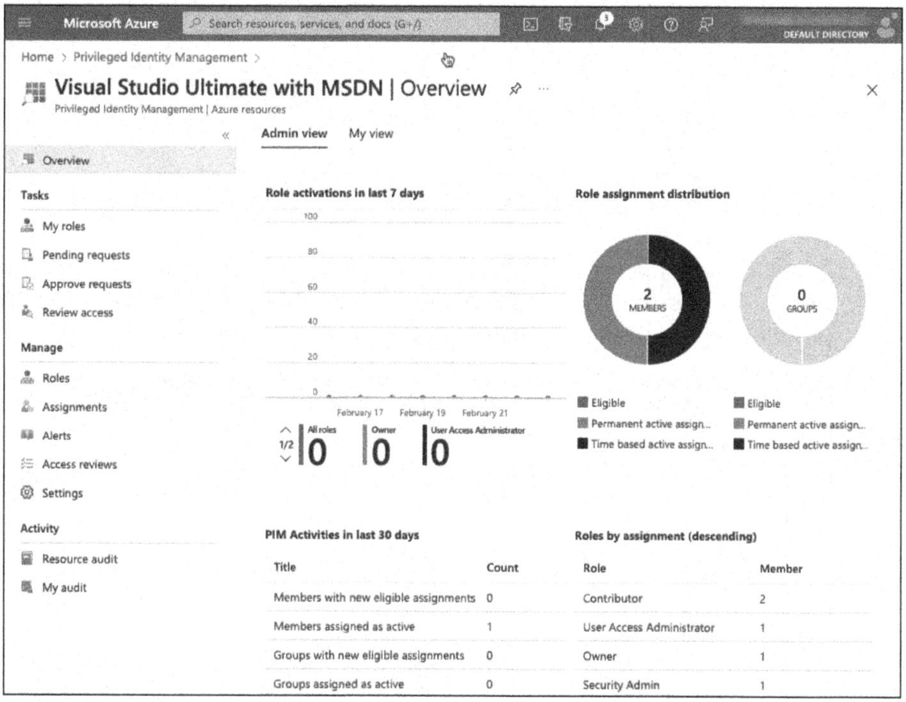

FIGURE 4-48 Azure resources report with Azure role activation and assignments.

4. Select **Resource audit** under the Activity section, as shown in Figure 4-49, to view the audit logs against the Azure resources including Azure role assignments and requests for administrative purposes.

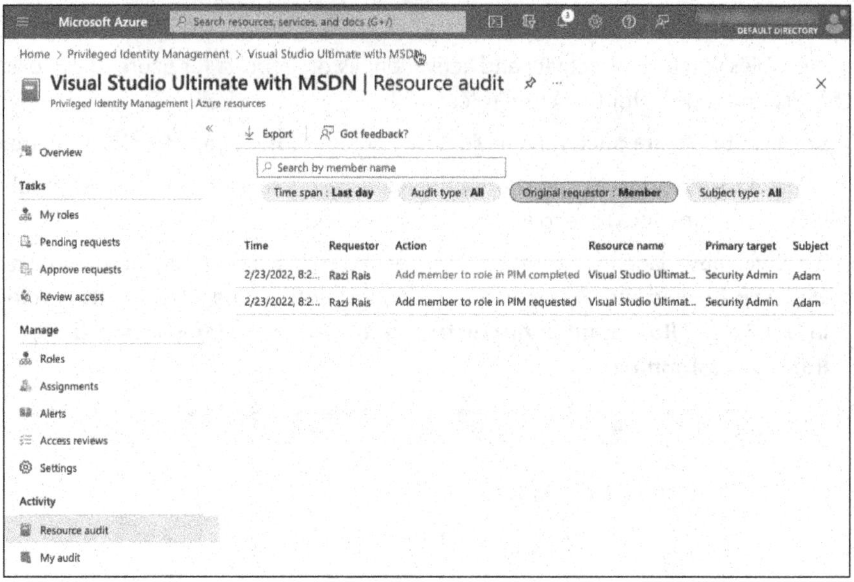

FIGURE 4-49 Resource audit for Azure resources.

5. To gather more insights about the action of a particular user, select **Role** or **Assignments**, and then select a user. The **Activity details** page, as shown in Figure 4-50, provides a resource activity summary associated with the user account.

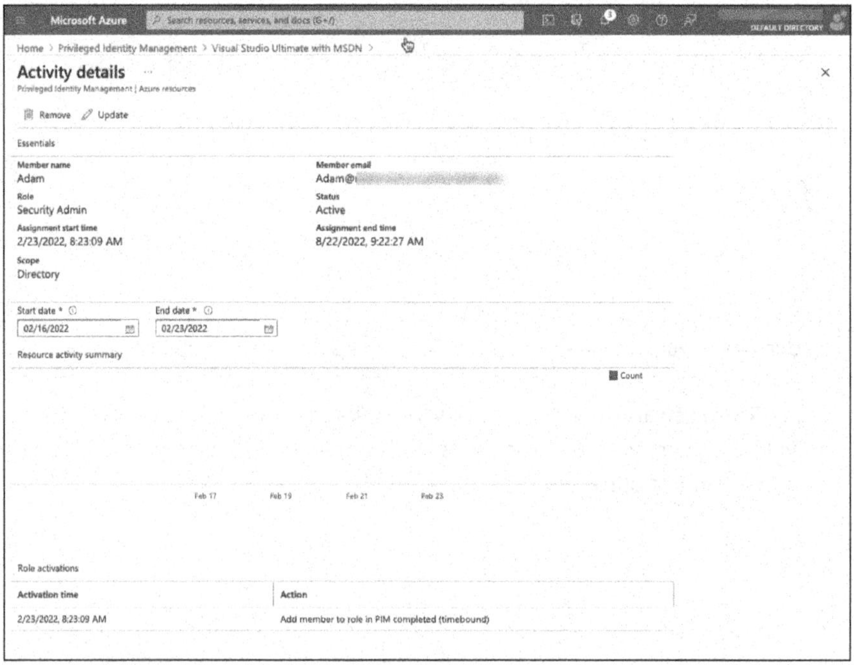

FIGURE 4-50 Role assignment activity details for a specific user.

PIM also allows you to export a complete list of role assignments, along with all its child resources for a particular Azure resource, as shown in Figure 4-51. This is particularly useful for compliance reasons since auditors within an organization are often required to capture all resource assignments, including the parent resource all the way down to child resources.

To export the complete list of role assignments:

1. Sign in to the **Azure portal** and navigate to Azure AD **Privileged Identity Management**.

2. Select **Azure resources** and choose the Azure resource—for example, an Azure subscription—for which you would like to explore the audit history.

3. Select **Assignment** and then select **Export**.

4. The **Export membership** blade provides you with an option to either export all members, including those under child resources, or export only members under the currently selected Azure resource, such as an Azure subscription.

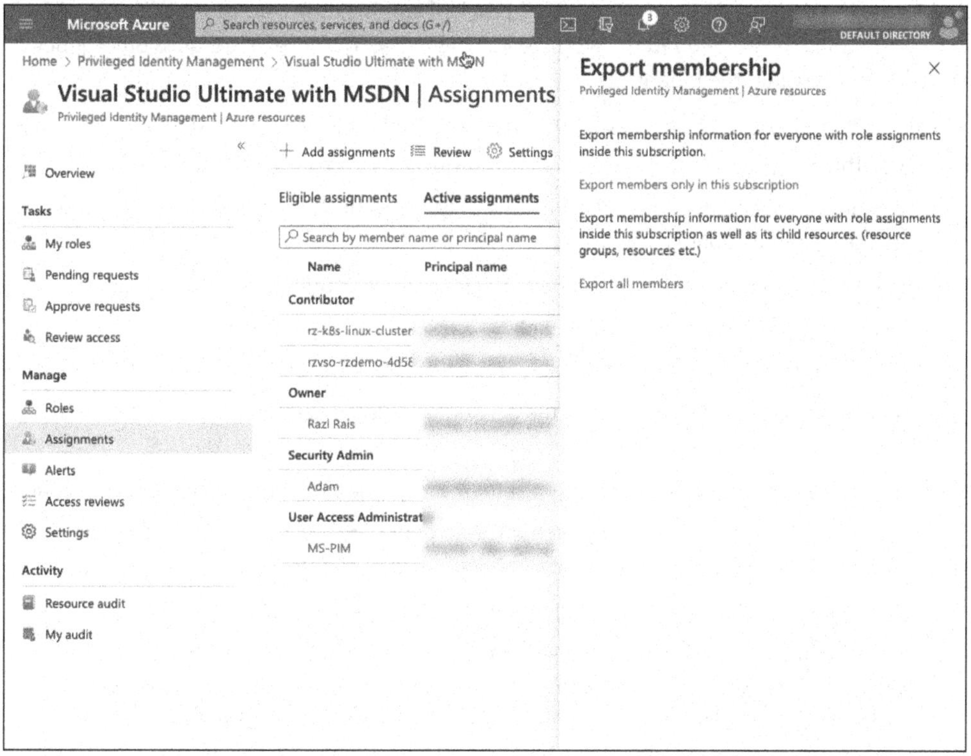

FIGURE 4-51 Export membership information for everyone with a role assignment.

Create and manage break-glass accounts

Break-glass accounts are highly privileged accounts that are intended to be used only under emergency situations where regular administrative accounts cannot be used. Emergency situations that may warrant the use of break-glass accounts include but are not limited to:

- When an administrator account has lost the ability to perform Azure AD MFA either due to network failure or lack of access to the device, which is required to successfully perform the MFA.

- For authentication, an administrator account relies on the federated identity provider (Idp) that is experiencing an outage and as a result the account cannot complete the sign-in operation.

- The last user with Global Administrator permissions is no longer available or is no longer a part of the organization.

- To mitigate the risks associated with the lack of administrative access to the Azure AD, it is highly recommended that you create at least two or more break-glass emergency accounts within the tenant.

When creating the break-glass accounts, use the following recommendations:

- Use the Azure AD cloud-only account with the *.onmicrosoft.com* domain.

- Assign Global administrative permissions to the emergency account and make sure the assignment is permanent.

- Do not use federated or on-premises synchronized accounts.

- Account credentials should never expire.

- The account should not be associated with an individual user.

- Any device required for accessing the account should be kept in a well-documented secure location with multiple communication channels with Azure AD.

- For resiliency purposes, use a different authentication method for each emergency account.

- Exclude at least one emergency account from conditional access policies to ensure its access to Azure AD is not blocked due to a misconfigured policy.

- Automate the creation and management of all emergency accounts.

- Continuously monitor activity associated with emergency accounts. Azure Monitor provides the capability to generate alerts whenever emergency accounts are used. Also, reports can be created to capture the usage of emergency accounts over time.

- Document details about emergency accounts in a clear step-by-step fashion and make them available to relevant employees.

- Validate the emergency accounts periodically—at a minimum, every 90 days or sooner. Also, validate the accounts whenever there is a significant change in an organization, such as when a new employee with administrative privileges joins the team.

Skill 4.4: Monitor Azure AD

Monitoring is a critical aspect of the Azure AD governance process. It also plays a vital role in meeting compliance and security requirements of an organization.

Azure AD sign-in and audit logs contains useful information that provides valuable insights into users, applications, and various system directory-level activities.

Administrators and business stakeholders can use monitoring:

- To generate reports that provide actionable insights to business and IT operations. For example, peak and off-peak hours when a particular Azure AD application is used by the users, usage telemetry showing the adoption of SaaS application within an organization, number of times in a week a password reset has been performed by the user using the self-service password reset (SSPR) feature, etc.

- To generate custom alert notifications when there is a sudden drop or influx in the number of sign-in requests. These types of custom notifications are particularly useful for smooth IT operations.

- To meet organizational compliance requirements that require tracking and reporting of administrative operations on an Azure AD tenant.

- To meet state or local regulatory requirements that require archival of user and administrative activities for a specified duration and to provide reporting on these activities.

This skill covers how to:

- Design a strategy for monitoring Azure AD
- Review and analyze sign-in, audit, and provisioning logs by using the Azure Active Directory admin center
- Configure diagnostic settings, including Log Analytics, storage accounts, and Event Hub
- Monitor Azure AD by using Log Analytics, including KQL queries
- Analyze Azure AD by using workbooks and reporting in the Azure Active Directory admin center
- Monitor and improve the security posture by using the Identity Secure Score

---

Design a strategy for monitoring Azure AD

Legal, security, and operational requirements, as well as existing organizational processes, all influence the design of an Azure AD monitoring solution. A successful monitoring strategy is a combination of various aspects, some of which are described below.

Engage the appropriate stakeholders

Technology projects frequently fail because of misaligned expectations regarding their influence, results, and roles. Make sure you're involving the appropriate stakeholders if you want to prevent these issues. Documenting the stakeholders, their project input, and their accountability obligations will also help to ensure that their responsibilities in the project are fully understood.

Create a thorough communication plan

For any new service to be successful, communication is essential. Inform your users in advance of any changes that will affect their experience, as well as when and how they can contact you for assistance. Because monitoring is a component of many organizations' broader Security Information and Event Management (SIEM) capabilities, it is critical to ensure that any changes to processes are clearly documented and communicated to avoid last-minute delays.

Define Azure AD monitoring capabilities

Administrators and business stakeholders can use Azure AD monitoring:

- To generate reports that provide actionable insights to business and IT operations. For example, peak and off-peak hours when a particular Azure AD application is used by the users, usage telemetry showing the adoption of SaaS application within an organization, number of times in a week the password reset has been performed by the user using the self-service password reset (SSPR) feature, etc.

- To generate custom alert notifications when there is sudden drop or influx in the number of sign-in requests. These types of custom notifications are particularly useful for smooth IT operations.

- To meet organizational compliance requirements that require tracking and reporting of administrative operations on an Azure AD tenant.

- To meet state or local regulatory requirements that require archival of user and administrative activities for a specified duration and to provide reporting on these activities.

Review and analyze sign-in, audit, and provisioning logs by using the Azure AD admin center

Azure AD sign-in logs provide detailed information about user activities, which can be useful for troubleshooting access-related issues. For example, too many sign-in failures from a user may indicate a permission-related issue or can be a result of a cyberattack against a user account.

Table 4-7 summarizes the subset of fields available within the sign-in log, which are particularly relevant to troubleshoot access-related issues.

TABLE 4-7   Azure AD sign-in logs schema (abridged)

Name	Description
Time	The datetime, in UTC.
CallerIpAddress	The IP address associated with the client that made the sign-in request.
Location	The location of the sign-in activity. For example, "US."
Identity	The identity that was presented during the sign-in request. It can be a user account, system account, or service principal—for example, "John Doe."
OperationName	For the user sign-in operation, the value is always "Sign-in activity."
TenantId	This is the GUID that corresponds to the Azure AD tenant's unique identifier.
ResultType	The result of the sign-in operation. This is "0" when the result of the sign-in operation is a success or contains a detailed error code for failure. See the section on the sign-in error codes for more details.
ResultDescription	The description of the error during the sign-in operation.
RiskDetail	The reason associated with the risk behind a specific state of a risky user, sign-in, or a risk detection. Possible values include none, adminGeneratedTemporaryPassword, userPerformedSecuredPasswordChange, userPerformedSecuredPasswordReset, adminConfirmedSigninSafe, aiConfirmedSigninSafe, userPassedMFADrivenByRisk-BasedPolicy, adminDismissedAllRiskForUser, adminConfirmedSigninCompromised, and unknownFutureValue. This field requires an Azure AD P2 license; otherwise, the value "hidden" is returned.
RiskEventTypes	The risk detection types associated with the sign-in. Possible values include unlikelyTravel, anonymizedIPAddress, maliciousIPAddress, unfamiliarFeatures, malwareInfectedIPAddress, suspiciousIPAddress, leakedCredentials, investigationsThreatIntelligence, generic, and unknownFutureValue. This field requires an Azure AD P2 license; otherwise, the value "hidden" is returned.
RiskLevelAggregated	The aggregated risk level associate with the user. Possible values include none, low, medium, high, and unknownFutureValue. This field requires an Azure AD P2 license; otherwise, the value "hidden" is returned.
RiskLevelDuringSignIn	The risk level associated with the user sign-in. Possible values include none, low, medium, high, hidden, and unknownFutureValue. This field requires an Azure AD P2 license; otherwise, the value "hidden" is returned.
RiskState	The state of the risk associated with the user sign-in. Possible values include none, confirmedSafe, remediated, dismissed, atRisk, confirmedCompromised, and unknownFutureValue.

Working with real-world PII data during troubleshooting

Azure AD sign-in logs contain Personally Identifiable Information (PII), which includes sensitive information about user identity such as unique identifier number, IP address, location, etc. Handling PII carefully is critical to avoid legal and regulatory fines that may be imposed if data is shared broadly without proper user consent. For example, an IT administrator working for a financial services company, Contoso, may want to download the sign-in logs and share them for troubleshooting purposes with an IT support engineer who is working for a contract company, Fabrikam. By default, data in sign-in logs are not redacted or even encrypted, which may lead to data leakage. This is why when working with logs that contain PII data, it is critical to first review organizational guidelines regarding the sharing of logs with a broader audience, even for troubleshooting purposes. It is highly recommended that you always ask users for their consent before reading their PII data. Also, redacting PII attributes from the logs, which may not be required during troubleshooting, is generally a good idea since it prevents accidental data breaches. You can read more about working with personal data in logs at *https://docs.microsoft.com/en-us/azure/azure-monitor/logs/personal-data-mgmt*.

To gain access to the sign-in logs using the Azure portal, sign in to the portal with a user account with Global administrator permissions or with one of the following permissions:

- Security administrator
- Security reader
- Global reader
- Reports reader

IMPORTANT **ACCESSING YOUR SIGN-IN ACTIVITY**

Individual users can always access their own sign-in activity by navigating to the link *https://mysignins.microsoft.com*.

To access sign-in logs:

1. Sign in to the **Azure portal** and navigate to **Azure Active Directory**.

   The sign-in logs are available under the **Monitoring** section of the Azure AD blade, as shown in Figure 4-52.

Monitoring
⊃ Sign-in logs

   FIGURE 4-52
   Azure AD sign-in logs.

2. The **Activity Details: Sign-ins** blade appears when you select a particular sign-in activity, as shown in Figure 4-53. This blade contains sign-in information for a particular sign-in event in a tabular format.

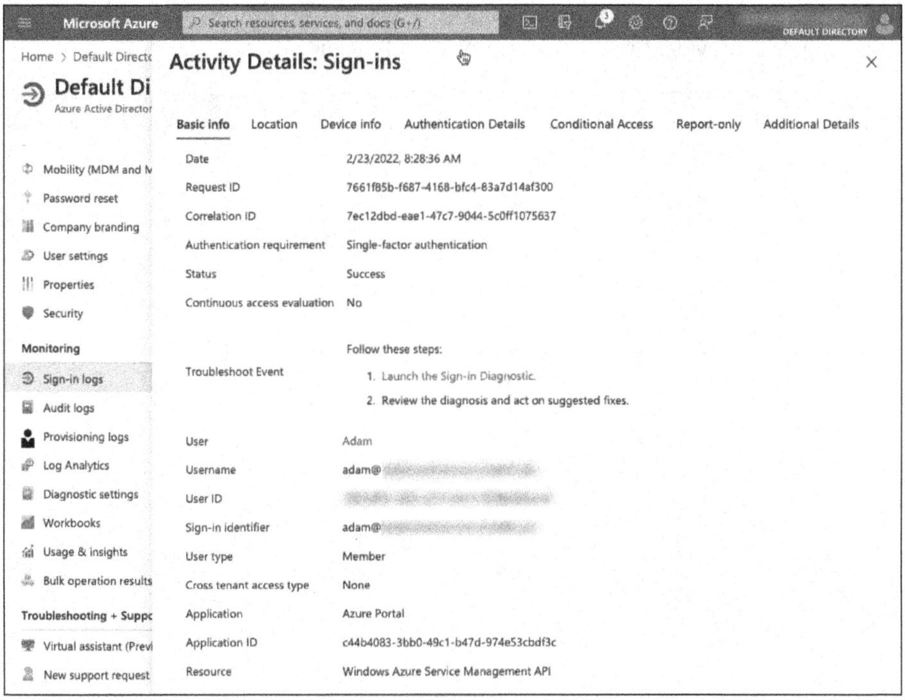

FIGURE 4-53 Activity details for a user sign-in.

IMPORTANT **AZURE AD PREMIUM LICENSE**

Azure AD licensing plays an important role when it comes to the level of detail available within sign-in logs. For example, an Azure AD Premium P2 license is required to log information related to Azure Identity Protection features such as the risk associated with a particular sign-in operation. In the absence of an Azure AD P2 license, the sign-in log may only provide generic values labeled "hidden" instead of actual risk details such as the risk level or risk detection type of a particular sign-in.

Analyzing error codes for troubleshooting

When a sign-in event results in a failure, Azure AD logs the relevant details in the sign-in logs, including an error code along with a failure reason. Figure 4-54 shows the **Sign-in error code** and the **Failure reason** due to unsuccessful user sign-in. Also, notice the **Additional Details** property, which provides further information about the failure.

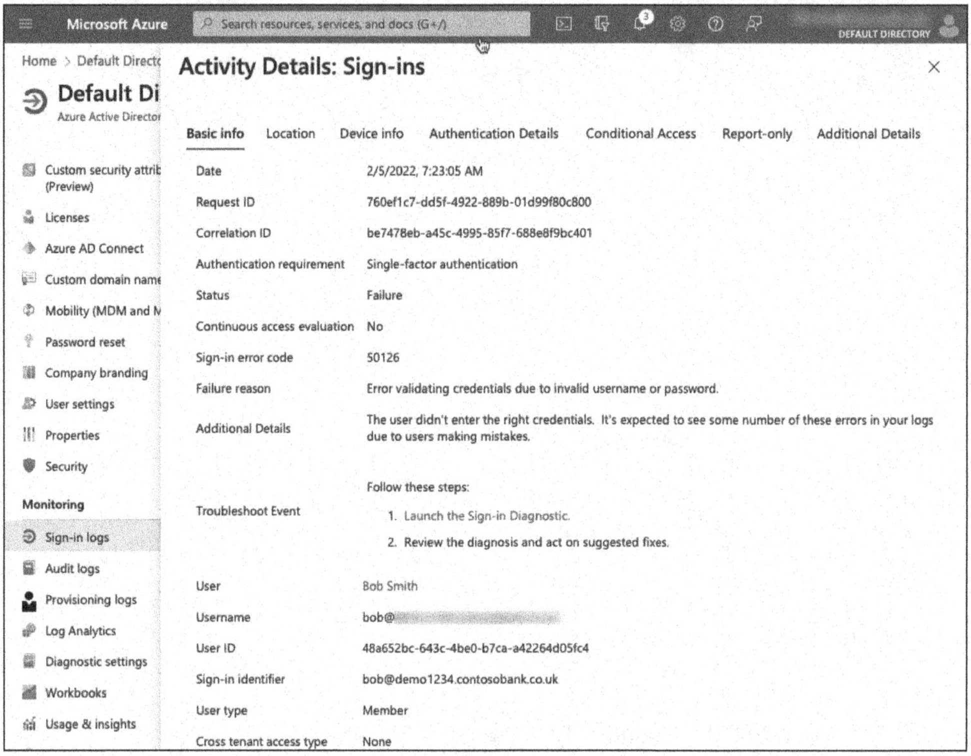

FIGURE 4-54 Sign-in failure error code and description.

> **IMPORTANT ERROR CODES LOOKUP**
>
> Microsoft provides an online error code lookup tool that provides a list of possible remediation steps if they are available against a particular error code. You can access this tool by visiting the link *https://login.microsoftonline.com/error*.

Review and monitor Azure AD audit logs

Organizations can use the Azure AD audit logs to track and monitor system activities across the Azure AD tenant for compliance and regularity reasons. Audit logs track activities on various objects including users, groups, applications, and others. Table 4-8 summarizes the most common activities against different Azure AD objects found in the audit logs.

TABLE 4-8 Summary of activities tracked in the Azure AD audit logs

Azure AD Object	Activity
User	All create, update, and delete operations on the user object.
	Administrative actions including but not limited to resetting of users' passwords, license assignments, etc.
Group	All create, update, and delete operations on the group object.
	Administrative actions including but not limited to adding/removing users from/to the group, changing group ownership, assigning licenses to groups, etc.
Application	All create, update, and delete operations on the application object.
Other	Various Azure AD features log activities related to create, read, update, delete (CRUD) operations in the audit log. For example, when Azure AD conditional access policies are created, updated, or deleted, details about such activity will be available in the audit log for compliance.

To access Azure AD audit logs:

1. Sign in to the **Azure portal** and navigate to **Azure Active Directory**.

2. Select **Audit logs**, as shown in Figure 4-55.

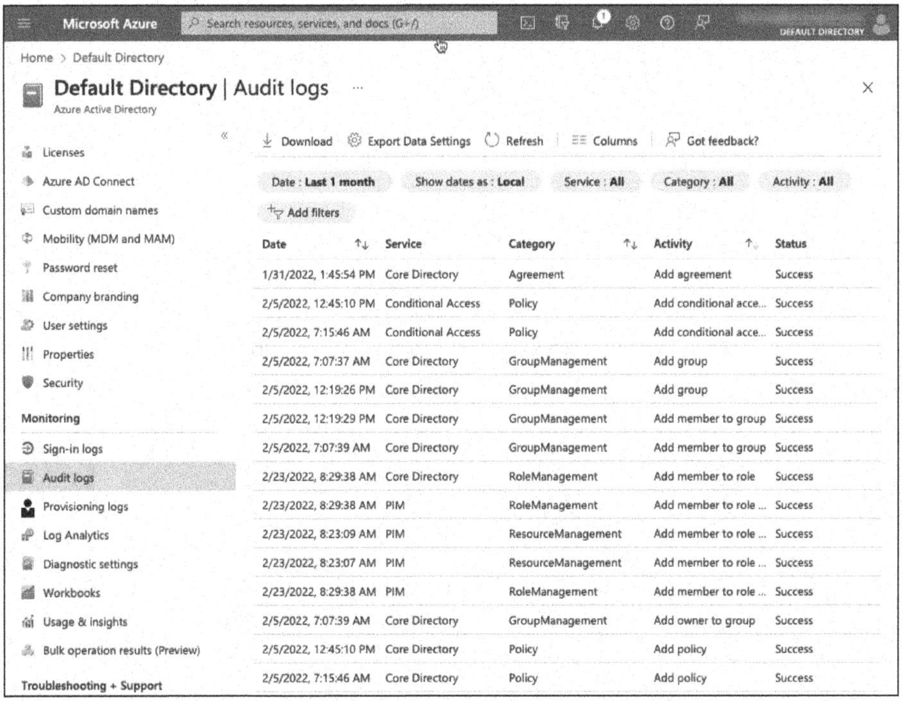

FIGURE 4-55 Azure AD audit logs.

3. The **Audit Log Details** blade, as shown in Figure 4-56, appears when you select a particular audit log entry. This blade contains comprehensive details about the activity performed on a particular Azure AD object.

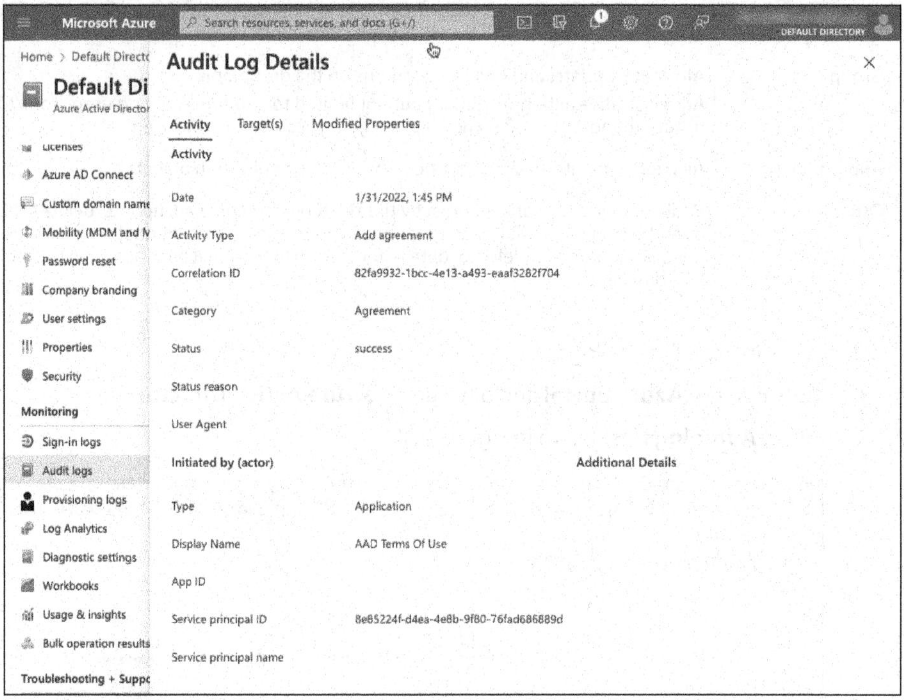

FIGURE 4-56 Audit log entry showing a detailed log with an Activity Type of Add agreement.

At times, you might want to filter the activities in the audit log based on datetime span, category, etc. Table 4-9 summarizes the commonly used filtering options available for audit logs activities.

TABLE 4-9 Commonly used filtering options for Azure AD audit logs

Filter type	Filter target	
Category	All	ExternalUserProfile
	AdministrativeUnit	GroupManagement
	Agreement	IdentityProtection
	ApplicationManagement	KerberosDomain
	AttributeManagement	KeyManagement
	Authentication	Label
	Authorization	Other
	AuthorizationPolicy	PendingExternalUserProfile
	CertificateBasedAuthConfiguration	PermissionGrantPolicy
	Contact	Policy
	CrossTenantAccessSettings	PolicyManagement
	Device	PrivateEndpoint
	DeviceConfiguration	PrivateLinkResource
	DeviceManagement	ProvisioningManagement
	DeviceTemplate	ResourceManagement
	DirectoryManagement	RoleManagement
	EntitlementManagement	UserManagement
Service	All	Entitlement Management
	AAD Management UX	Hybrid Authentication
	Access Reviews	Identity Protection
	Account Provisioning	Invited Users
	Application Proxy	MIM Service
	Authentication Methods	Mobility Management
	Azure AD Recommendations	My Apps
	Azure MFA	PIM
	B2C	Self-Service Group Management
	Conditional Access	Self-Service Password Management
	Core Directory	Terms of Use
	Device Registration Service	
	Administrative actions including but not limited to adding/removing users from/to the group, changing group ownership, assigning licenses to groups, etc.	
Date	Last 1 month	
	Last 7 days	
	Last 24 hours	
	Custom time interval	
Status	All	
	Success	
	Failure	

Audit logs download

To download the Azure AD audit logs:

1. Sign in to the **Azure portal** and navigate to **Azure Active Directory**.

2. Select **Audit logs**.

3. Select **Download** from the top row. This allows you to save the logs in CSV or JSON format, as shown in Figure 4-57.

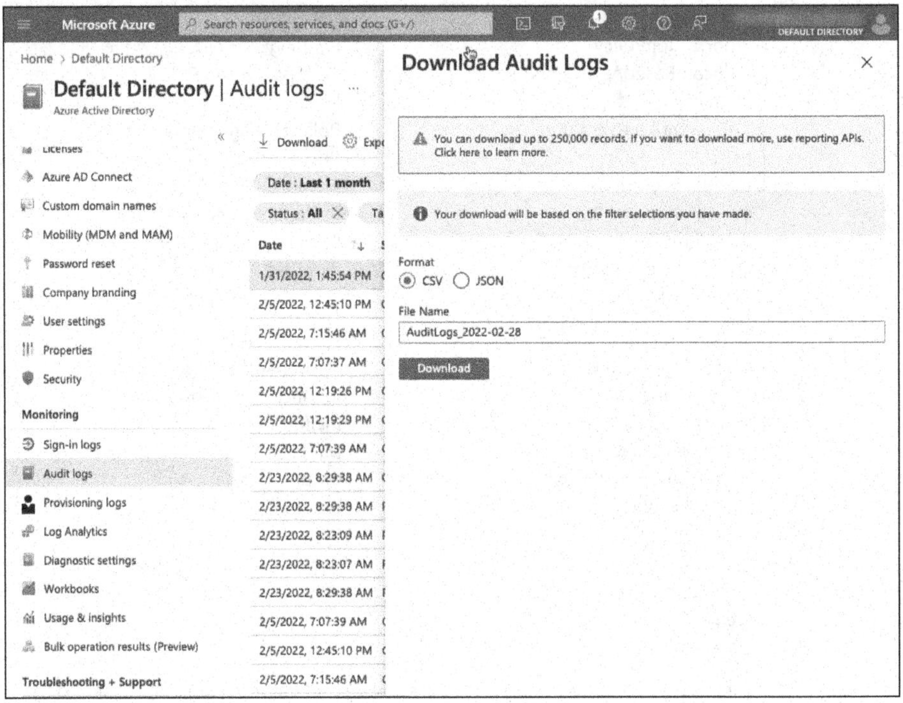

FIGURE 4-57 Download Azure AD audit logs.

Audit logs retention

The audit logs retention period depends on the Azure AD license. For the Azure AD Free license, the retention period is 7 days, while for Azure AD Premium P1 and P2 licenses, the retention duration is 30 days. If your scenario requires you to retain the audit logs for a longer duration, Azure Monitor can be used to push the audit logs to different Azure services including Log Analytics, Azure Storage, or Azure Event Hub. Each of these services enables you to persist logs for an extended duration based on your needs.

Configure diagnostic settings, including Log Analytics, storage accounts, and Event Hub

Tracking activity within the Azure AD tenant, such as sign-in attempts and other administrative operations on the tenant, is a routine task for an IT team. The information required to track activities throughout the Azure AD tenant is available in the diagnostic logs for Azure AD.

Azure AD provides a variety of diagnostic logs that can be ingested into various Azure services or third-party/partner solutions. Review Table 4-10, which lists various Azure AD diagnostics logs.

TABLE 4-10 Azure AD diagnostic logs

Log	Description
Sign-in	This log contains information about interactive user sign-ins to Azure AD.
Non-interactive sign-in (PREVIEW)	This log contains information about non-interactive user sign-ins to Azure AD. This includes sign-ins performed by a client on behalf of a user without any interaction from the user.
Service principal sign-in (PREVIEW)	This log contains information about sign-ins by Azure resources that use secrets managed by Azure to authenticate against Azure AD.
Provisioning logs (PREVIEW)	This log contains information about users, groups, and roles provisioned by the Azure AD provisioning service.
Audit Logs	This log contains information about system activities related to the management of users, groups, applications, and other directory objects.

License requirements

An Azure Active Directory Premium P1 or P2 license is required for ingesting sign-in logs. Any other Azure AD license, including Azure AD Free, is sufficient to ingest other types of Azure AD diagnostic logs.

> **IMPORTANT COST ASSOCIATED WITH LOGS INGESTION**
>
> When configuring Azure AD diagnostics logs for ingestion, keep in mind the cost association with data ingestion on Azure Monitor. It is highly recommended that you estimate the overall cost before starting the logs ingestion. For more information on this topic, refer to this document: *https://learn.microsoft.com/en-us/azure/azure-monitor/usage-estimated-costs*.

The Diagnostic settings option for Azure AD is shown in Figure 4-58, while Azure services that can ingest the diagnostic logs are shown in Figure 4-59. Please see the links below for step-by-step instructions on configuring diagnostic logs ingestion to Log Analytics, Azure Storage accounts, and Azure Event Hub.

- **Log Analytics:** *https://learn.microsoft.com/en-us/azure/active-directory/reports-monitoring/howto-integrate-activity-logs-with-log-analytics*

- **Azure Storage account:** *https://learn.microsoft.com/en-us/azure/active-directory/reports-monitoring/quickstart-azure-monitor-route-logs-to-storage-account*

- **Azure Event Hub:** *https://learn.microsoft.com/en-us/azure/active-directory/reports-monitoring/tutorial-azure-monitor-stream-logs-to-event-hub*

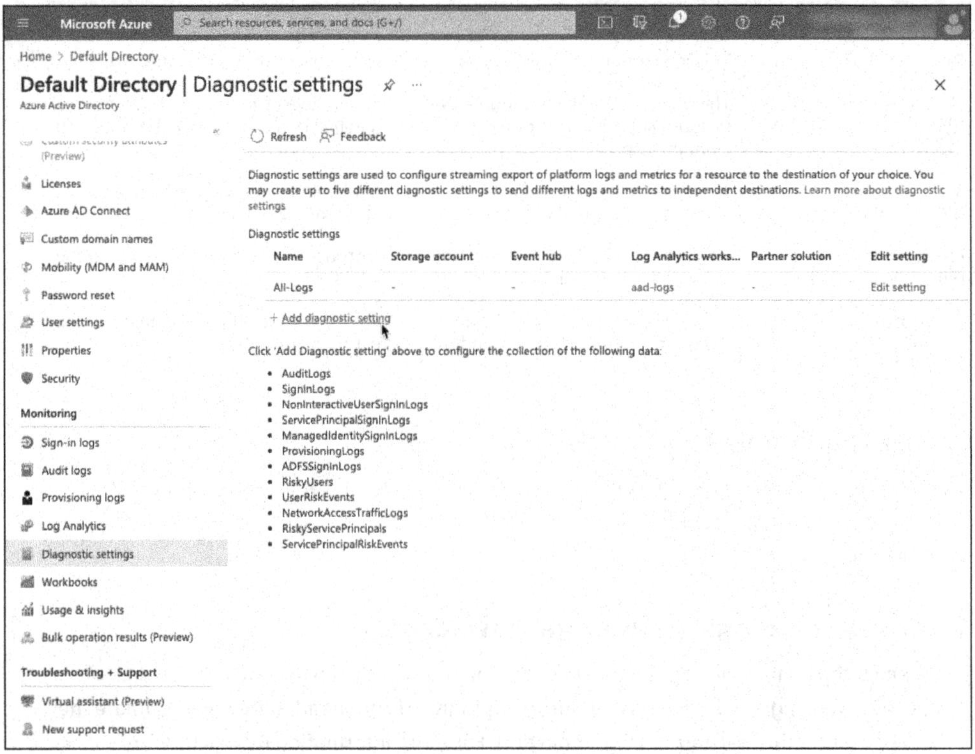

FIGURE 4-58 Azure Active Directory Diagnostic settings.

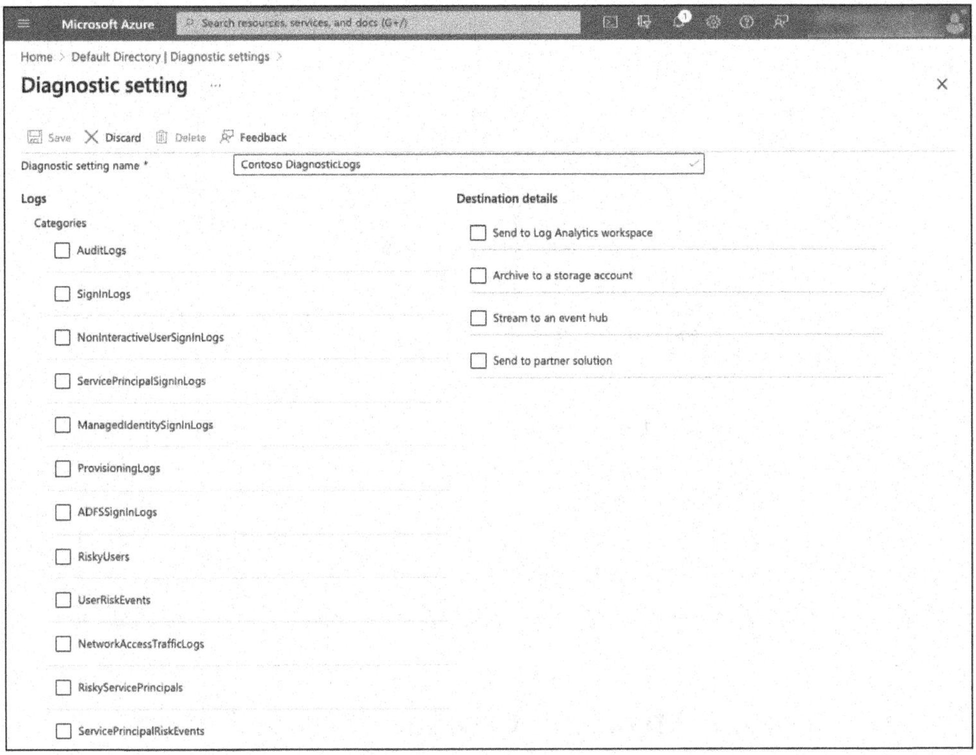

FIGURE 4-59 Azure Active Directory Diagnostic setting logs and destinations.

> ***EXAM TIP***
>
> **When preparing for the exam, pay attention to the fact that Azure AD activity logs may have different retention periods, even when the same Azure AD license is used. To get up-to-date retention duration for the logs, visit *https://docs.microsoft.com/en-us/azure/active-directory/reports-monitoring/reference-reports-data-retention*.**

Export sign-in and audit logs to a third-party SIEM

Azure AD diagnostic logs, including sign-in and audit logs, can be routed to third-party SIEM tools and services. Azure supports sending the logs to Azure Event Hub by using Azure Monitor, and the logs are then read by SIEM tools for further processing. Table 4-11 summarizes some third-party SIEM tools that can access the sign-in and audit logs through Azure Event Hub.

TABLE 4-11   Third-party SIEM tools

Tool	description
Splunk	Splunk provides a range of security features including SIEM and SOAR capabilities. For more details, please review *https://docs.microsoft.com/en-us/azure/active-directory/reports-monitoring/howto-integrate-activity-logs-with-splunk*.
ArcSight	ArcSight is a SIEM tool that enables detection and response for a range of security threats. For more details, please review *https://docs.microsoft.com/en-us/azure/active-directory/reports-monitoring/howto-integrate-activity-logs-with-arcsight*.
Sumo Logic	Sumo Logic provides visual dashboards and real-time analysis of data. It can also be used to conduct real-time forensics and log management. For more details, please review *https://docs.microsoft.com/en-us/azure/active-directory/reports-monitoring/howto-integrate-activity-logs-with-sumologic*.

If your scenario requires working with a third-party SIEM tool, which may not have native capability to read data from Azure Event Hub, then building a custom connector using Event Hubs API might provide a better solution.

> ***NEED MORE REVIEW?***   **AZURE EVENT HUB API**
>
> Read more about Azure Event Hub API at *https://docs.microsoft.com/en-us/rest/api/eventhub/*.

Monitor Azure AD by using Log Analytics, including KQL queries

Log Analytics enables you to monitor and review a range of Azure AD activities based on various diagnostics logs using workbooks and Kusto Query Language (KQL) queries.

Commonly used workbook use-cases include:

- Get shareable, at-a-glance summary reports about your Azure AD tenant, as well as the ability to create your own custom reports.

- Find and diagnose sign-in failures, as well as see a trending picture of your organization's sign-in health.

- In a flexible, customizable format, monitor Azure AD logs for sign-ins, tenant administrator actions, provisioning, and risk.

- Keep an eye on trends in your tenant's use of Azure AD features like conditional access, self-service password reset, and others.

   - Understand who is using legacy authentication to access your environment.

   - Understand the impact of your conditional access policies on the sign-in experience of your users.

For more information on Azure AD monitoring with Log Analytics, visit *https://learn.microsoft.com/en-us/azure/active-directory/reports-monitoring/how-to-use-azure-monitor-workbooks*.

Permission requirements

You must have access to the underlying Log Analytics workspace and be assigned to one of the following roles to access workbooks in Azure Active Directory:

- Global Reader
- Reports Reader
- Security Reader
- Application Administrator
- Cloud Application Administrator
- Company Administrator
- Security Administrator

Logs Schema

Log Analytics can use a variety of logs provided by Azure AD. The list of commonly used Azure AD diagnostic logs, along with their schema definitions, is provided below.

- **AuditLog:** *https://learn.microsoft.com/en-us/azure/azure-monitor/reference/tables/auditlogs*

- **SignInLogs:** *https://learn.microsoft.com/en-us/azure/active-directory/reports-monitoring/reference-azure-monitor-sign-ins-log-schema#field-descriptions*

- **NonInteractiveUserSignInLogs:** *https://learn.microsoft.com/en-us/azure/azure-monitor/reference/tables/aadnoninteractiveusersigninlogs*

- **ServicePrincipalSignInLogs:** *https://learn.microsoft.com/en-us/azure/azure-monitor/reference/tables/aadserviceprincipalsigninlogs*

- **ManagedIdentitySignInLogs:** *https://learn.microsoft.com/en-us/azure/azure-monitor/reference/tables/aadmanagedidentitysigninlogs*

- **ProvisioningLogs:** *https://learn.microsoft.com/en-us/azure/azure-monitor/reference/tables/aadprovisioninglogs*

- **ADFSSignInLogs:** *https://learn.microsoft.com/en-us/azure/azure-monitor/reference/tables/adfssigninlogs*

- **RiskyUsers:** *https://learn.microsoft.com/en-us/azure/azure-monitor/reference/tables/aadriskyusers*

- **UserRiskEvents:** *https://learn.microsoft.com/en-us/azure/azure-monitor/reference/tables/aaduserriskevents*

Log Analytics displays Azure AD logs as tables, as shown in Figure 4-60, with the Audit logs table selected. Figure 4-61 shows the Audit logs table's fields and the data types associated with them.

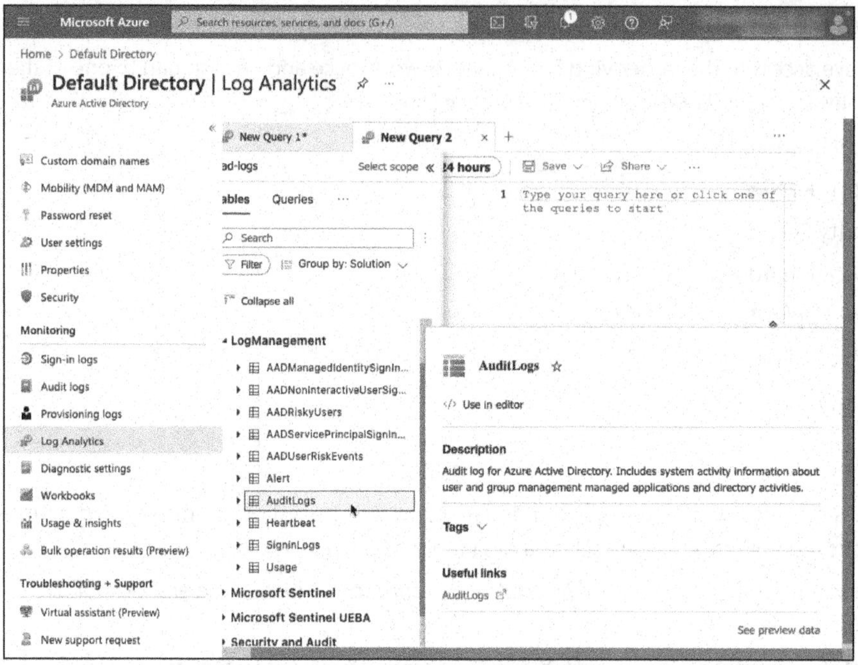

FIGURE 4-60 Log Analytics showing Azure AD a Audit logs and other logs as tables.

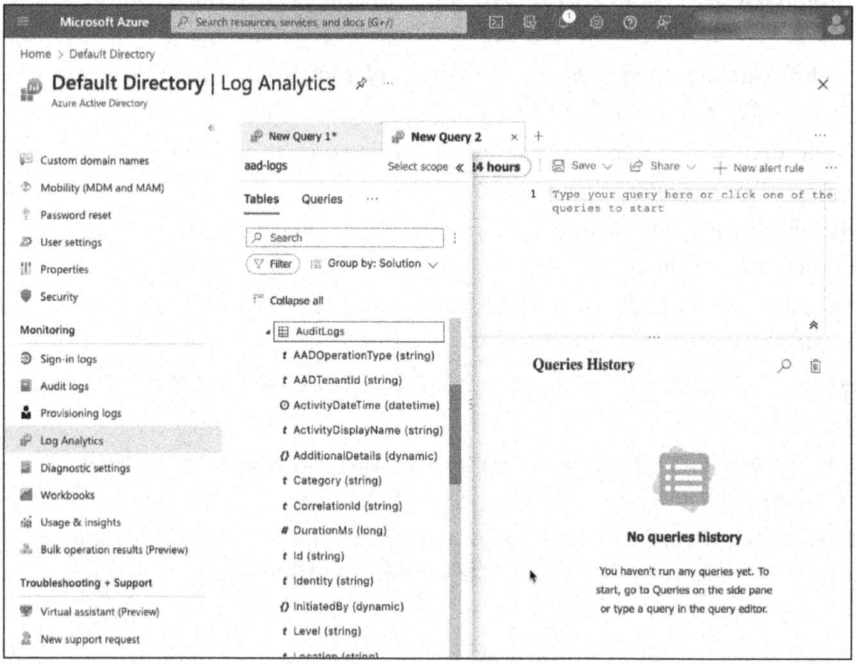

FIGURE 4-61 Azure AD Audit logs fields along with data types.

Working with KQL Queries

The Kusto Query Language (KQL) allows you to explore data and identify useful patterns and anomalies, as well as perform basic and advanced statistical analysis. KQL queries use schema entities organized in a hierarchy, like SQL databases, tables, and columns, making them easier to learn.

The majority of KQL queries are driven by scenarios. For example, the KQL query shown in Figure 4-62 will return the top ten Azure AD applications used in the last 14 days.

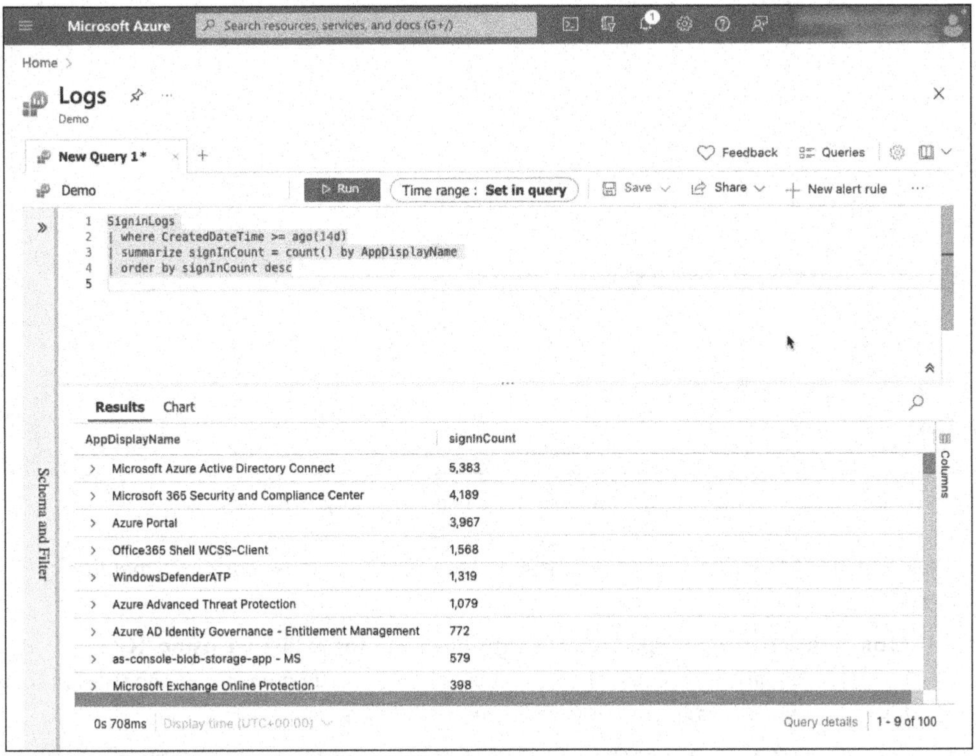

FIGURE 4-62 KQL query to list the top ten Azure AD applications used in the last 14 days.

Another useful KQL query is shown in Figure 4-63, which displays a chart of successful sign-ins per city during the last 24 hours.

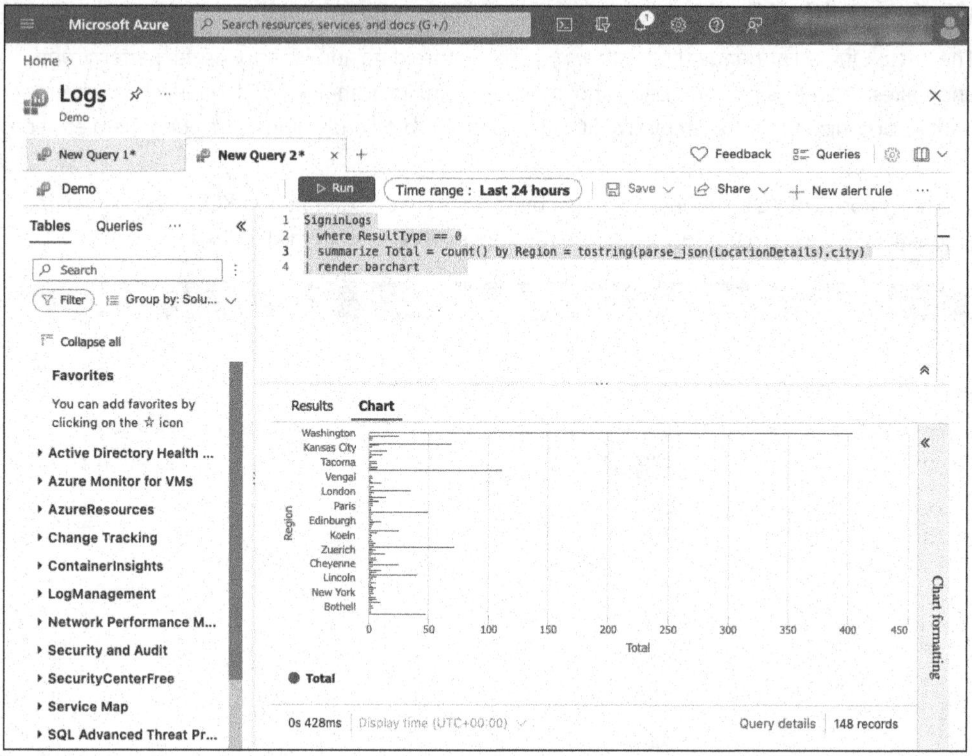

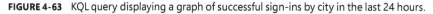

FIGURE 4-63 KQL query displaying a graph of successful sign-ins by city in the last 24 hours.

Please use the links below to learn more about KQL queries and their usage to monitor Azure AD.

- **Monitoring Azure AD applications sign-in health for resilience using KQL:** *https://learn.microsoft.com/en-us/azure/active-directory/fundamentals/monitor-sign-in-health-for-resilience#kusto-query-for-increase-in-failure-rate*

- **Sample for KQL queries:** *https://learn.microsoft.com/en-us/azure/data-explorer/kusto/query/samples?pivots=azuremonitor*

- **KQL query best practices:** *https://learn.microsoft.com/en-us/azure/data-explorer/kusto/query/best-practices*

Analyze Azure AD by using workbooks and reporting in the Azure Active Directory admin center

Azure AD usage and insights reports provide useful information about application-related sign-in activity with a focus on:

- **Azure AD Application Activity (Preview):** This dashboard helps you analyze various application usage patterns including most-used applications, successful and failed sign-ins, and success rate of sign-ins.

- **Authentication methods activity:** Provides insights about various authentication methods that are registered within an Azure AD tenant and how they're being used.
- **AD FS application activity:** This report provides details about applications using AD FS and may be a potential candidate for migration to Azure AD.

Permission requirements

A user must be in the one of the following roles to view usage and insights reports:

- Global administrator
- Security administrator
- Security reader,
- Report reader

To view the usage and insights:

1. Sign in to the **Azure portal** and select **Azure Active Directory**.
2. Select **Usage & insights**, as shown in Figure 4-64.

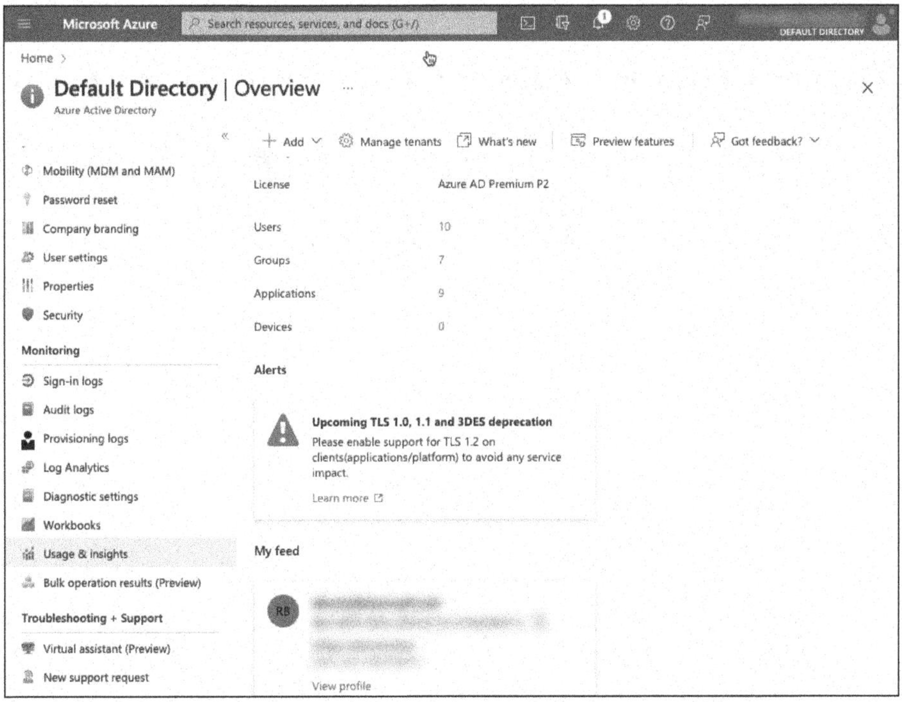

FIGURE 4-64   Azure Active Directory Usage & insights.

3. From the list of application activity reports, select **Azure AD application activity (Preview)**, as shown in Figure 4-65. This report provides details about sign-in activities against various Enterprise applications within Azure AD.

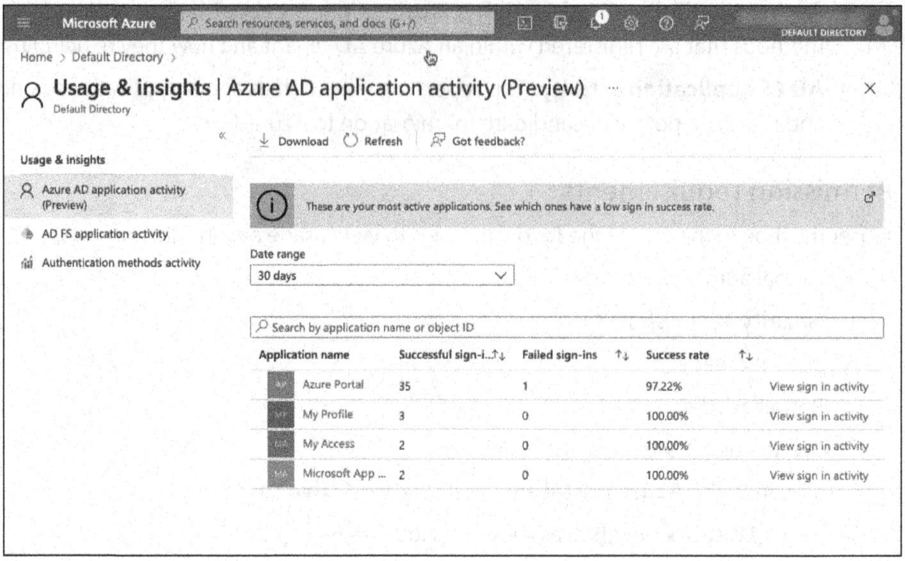

FIGURE 4-65 List of Usage & insights reports.

4. Select **View sign-in activity for Azure portal** to navigate to the **Usage & insights** dashboard, as shown in Figure 4-66.

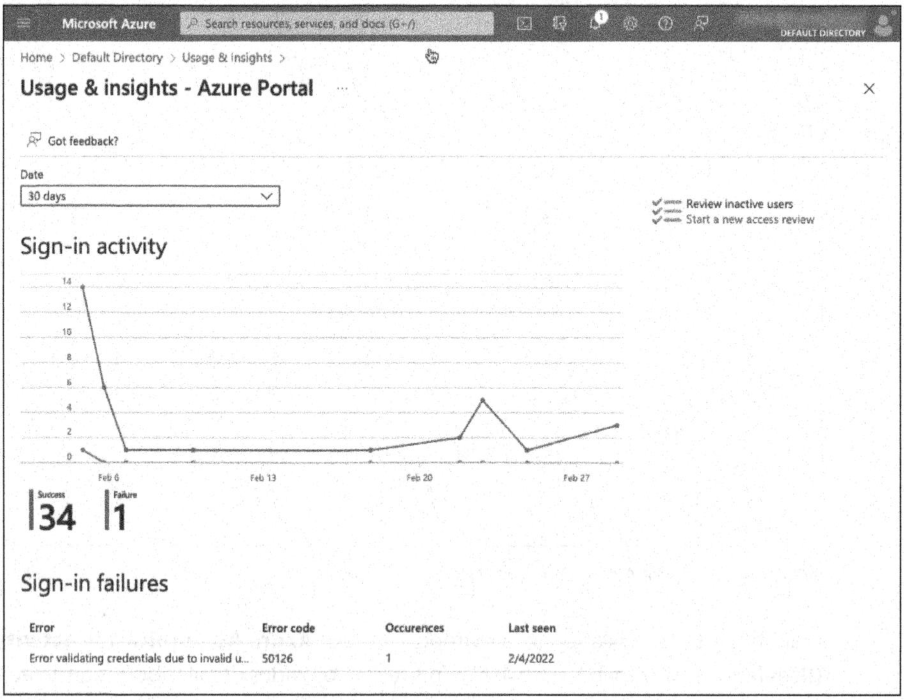

FIGURE 4-66 Usage & insights dashboard for Azure portal.

5. Close the dashboard and select **Authentication method activity** to view the dashboard, as shown in Figure 4-67, which provides telemetry related to registration and usage of various authentication methods.

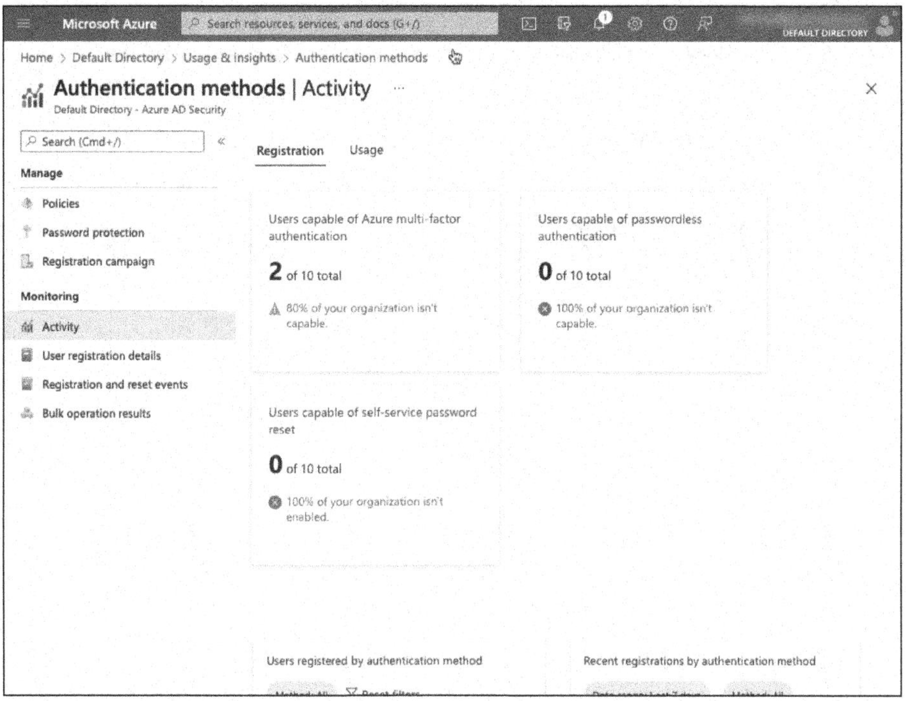

FIGURE 4-67 Usage & insights dashboard for Authentication methods.

Configure notifications

Email notifications can be configured for Azure Active Directory managed domains, which will send alerts whenever health-related issues are detected. Follow the steps below to configure email notifications:

1. Sign in to the **Azure portal** and select **Azure Active Domain Services**.
2. Select the managed domain—for example, identity.contoso.com.
3. Select the **Notification settings** located under the Settings pane.
4. You can add or remove existing email recipients, as shown in Figure 4-68.

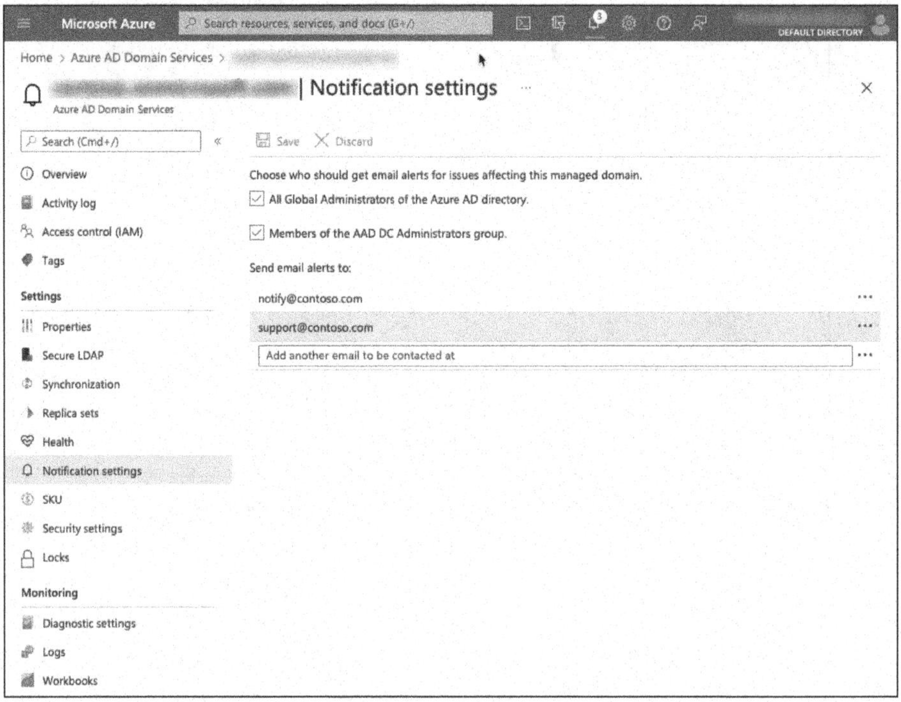

FIGURE 4-68 Notification settings for Azure AD Domain Services.

In addition to configuring individual email addresses, you can also select an option to send email notifications to all members of Global Administrators and AAD DC Administrators.

> **NOTE MAXIMUM NUMBER OF EMAIL ADDRESSES**
>
> Azure AD DS allows up to five individual email addresses to be added for email notifications. Also, when AD DS sends a notification, it will cap it up to the total of 100 email addresses, including the email addresses of members within Global Administrators and AAD DC Administrators group.

Monitor and improve the security posture by using the Identity Secure Score

The Identity Secure Score, as shown in Figure 4-69, allows you to objectively assess the identity security posture of an Azure AD tenant, plan security improvements, and finally assess the success of those improvements. The Identity Secure Score is a percentage that indicates how well an Azure AD tenant configuration is aligned with Microsoft's best practice security recommendations. Each Identity Secure Score improvement action is tailored to a specific configuration within the Azure AD tenant.

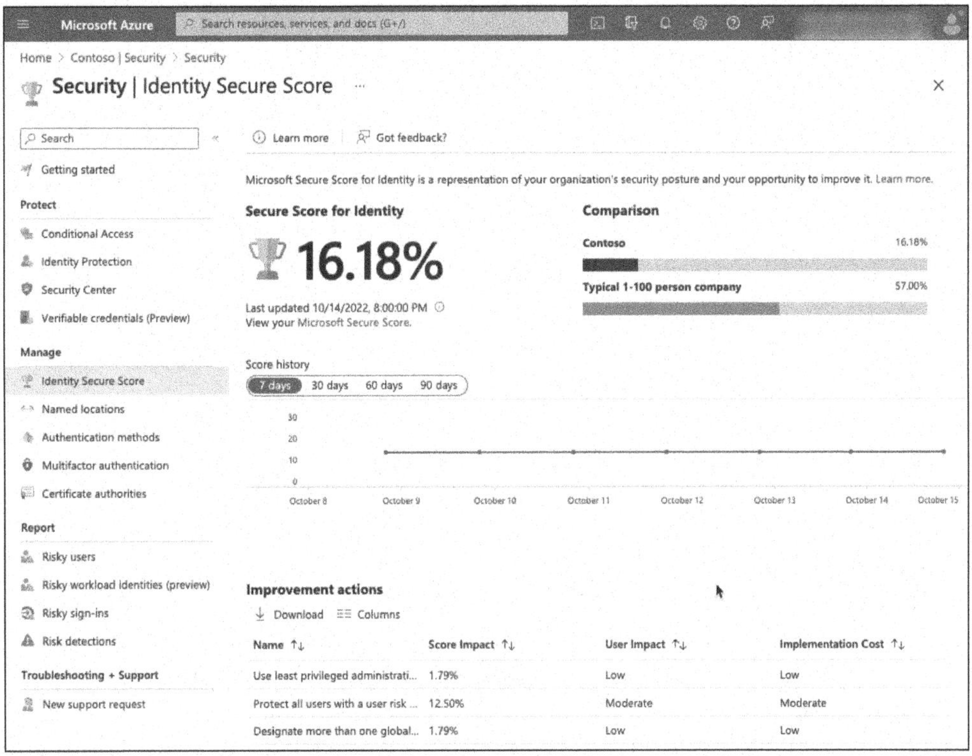

FIGURE 4-69 Identity Secure Score.

Azure examines the security settings for the Azure AD tenant every 48 hours and compares them to the advised best practices. A new score is determined for the Azure AD tenant based on the results of this assessment. You can also choose the recommended improvement action and then act on it. Figure 4-70 shows the improvement action "Use least privileged administrative roles," and the status dropdown displays the most recent status of the improvement action. To learn more about improvement actions please visit *https://learn.microsoft.com/en-us/azure/active-directory/fundamentals/identity-secure-score*.

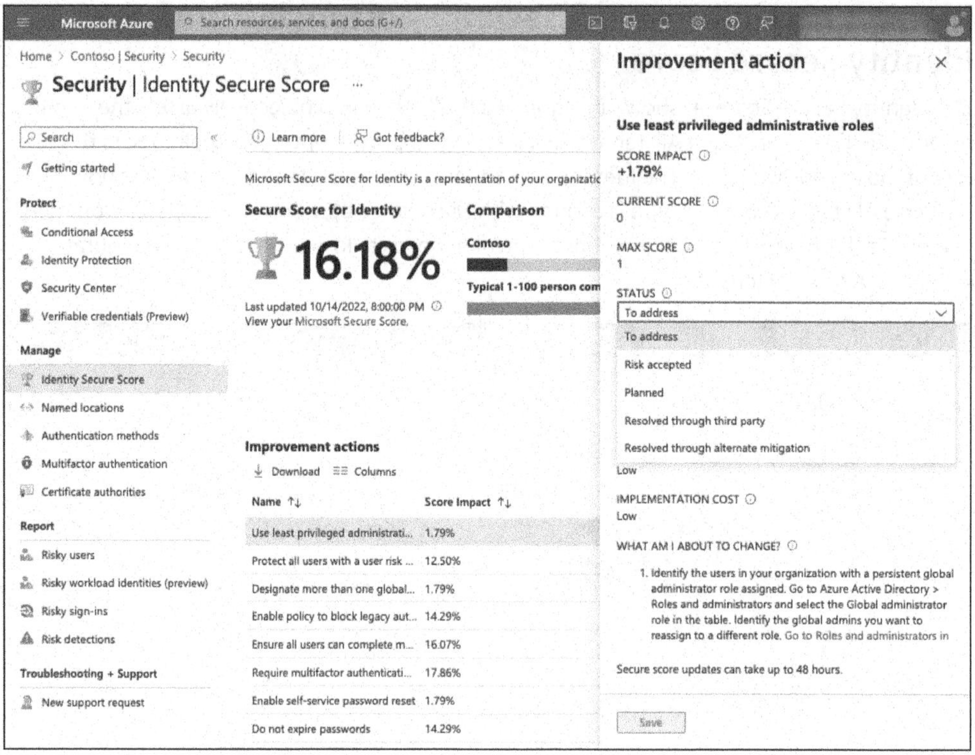

FIGURE 4-70 Identity Secure Score with an Improvement action.

Chapter summary

- Identity Governance features in Azure AD enable organizations to perform entitlement management, access reviews, and Privileged Identity Management (PIM) in a streamline fashion.

- Entitlement management enables organizations to provide just-enough access to the users with the ability to track all their activity though Azure AD audit and sign-in logs.

- An Azure AD Premium P2 license is required to perform access review but not to create and configure its settings.

- PIM can include resources within the Azure subscription, Azure AD, and various other Microsoft Online Services, such as Microsoft 365.

- Emergency accounts in Azure AD play a critical role in making sure that administrative tasks against Azure AD can be performed without disruption even when regular user accounts with administrative permissions are no longer available.

- Azure AD audit logs help organizations to track system activities across the Azure AD tenant for compliance and regularity reasons.

- Azure AD sign-in logs provide information about user sign-ins, including authentication details, failures during sign-in, device details, location, etc.

- Azure Sentinel provides security information and event management (SIEM) capabilities to Azure AD by ingesting its diagnostic logs.

- Sign-in logs can be ingested by Microsoft Sentinel, but an Azure AD Premium (P1 or P2) license is required.

- Azure AD Usage & Insights reports provide useful information about application-related sign-in activity in the form of visual dashboards.

- Identity Secure Score enables you to objectively assess your identity security posture, plan security improvements, and, finally, assess the success of those improvements.

Thought experiment

In this thought experiment, demonstrate your skills and knowledge of the topics covered in this chapter. You can find answers to this thought experiment in the next section.

You work as an Azure AD administrator for Woodgrove Bank, a large-scale commercial bank that provides financial services to millions of users worldwide. Woodgrove Bank has thousands of full-time employees and part-time contractors spread across the globe. Due to cybersecurity challenges, the Woodgrove CISO has put forward a high-level plan to improve the overall security posture of the organization by implementing just-enough access, just-in-time access, and security information and event management (SIEM) capabilities on an urgent basis.

You are assigned to plan and implement these capabilities.

Woodgrove Bank employees and external contractors use SharePoint Online and Microsoft Teams for document sharing and collaboration purposes. Due to the geo-dispersed nature of the teams within the bank, it is hard to assign correct access to new employees and to revoke access when they switch teams. Also, external contracts find it hard to request access to the resources. This creates overhead for administrators who need to grant access to the external contractors on an ad-hoc basis without proper workflow. This is identified as a security risk that needs to be remediated.

Woodgrove bank currently does not have any monitoring in place, which makes it very hard to track what is happening in the environment. Administrators manually download activity logs (particularly sign-in logs) on an ad-hoc basis, but they don't have the ability to view reports in the form of dashboards that can provide a comprehensive breakdown of sign-ins and system-wide activity within the Azure AD tenant.

Finally, Woodgrove Bank has a regularity requirement to track and archive system activities including creation, updating, and deletion of user accounts up to 365 days. It is also required to export sign-in logs to various third-party SIEM providers.

With this information in mind, answer the following questions:

1. What is needed to be implemented to automate the access request process to the required resources by employees and external contractors?

2. What type of Azure AD diagnostic log appropriately tracks the creation, updating, and deletion of the user accounts?

3. How should SIEM capabilities to monitor and analyze activities within the environment be achieved?

4. Which Azure service should sign-in logs be sent to so that third-party SIEM providers can access them?

Thought experiment answers

This section contains the solution to the thought experiment. Each answer explains why the answer choice is correct.

1. Access package. With an access package, an administrator can bundle the resources such as SharePoint Online, Teams, etc. with the correct access that a user needs to perform the job. Instead of granting access to individual resources, access packages help to grant or remove access in a more streamlined fashion.

2. Azure AD audit logs. The Azure AD audit logs provide records of system activities, including creation, updating, and deletion of user accounts.

3. Azure Sentinel. Azure Sentinel has built-in security information and event management (SIEM) capabilities, which include features like workbooks that provide reporting through visual dashboards, which can be used for monitoring and analytics.

4. Azure Event Hub. Azure supports sending sign-in logs to Azure Event Hub, which can be read by SIEM tools for further processing.

Index

A

AADIP (Azure AD Identity Protection)
and B2B, 174–175
exporting risk data, 185–186
group emails, 185
notifications, 184–185
Risk Detections report, 182
risk remediation, 183–184
risk reports, 176
Risky Sign-ins report, 179–181
Risky Users report, 177–179
security for workload identities, 187–190
SIEM integrations, 185
sign-in risk policies, 172–174
user risk policies, 168–172
access management. *See also* apps
Azure AD (Active Directory), 22
Azure resources, 190–198
conditional access app control, 266–270
connectors to apps, 264–265
custom Azure roles, 191
implementing, 216–220
implementing restrictions, 261–264
Key Vault RBAC and policies, 196–198
managed identities, 193–195
access packages
access reviews, 311–312
assignments, 300
entitlement management, 288–293, 300–301
planning access reviews for, 305
separation of duties checks, 300–301
using, 286

Access Panel
group properties, 30
Join groups, 32
access policies, Microsoft Defender for Cloud Apps,
270–272
access requests, entitlement management, 293–294
access reviews
access packages, 311–312
Azure AD, 313
Azure resource roles, 313
completing, 317–318
Graph APIs, 314
groups and apps, 306–311
licenses, 301, 318
monitoring activity, 315–317
performing, 315–317
planning for, 301–306
programs, 314
resource types, 306
responding to activity, 319
access/sign-ons, monitoring and auditing, 234–237
accessToken, 249
Account lockout, MFA service settings, 119
accounts, locking and locking, 143–144
active and eligible assignments, 327
activity logs, retention periods, 347
ADDS (Active Directory Domain Services), 11, 56
and Azure AD Connect Health, 98
ADFS (Active Directory Federation Services), 56, 205–208
Application Activity report, 207–208
and Azure AD Connect, 84–91
and Azure AD Connect Health, 96–97
SSO (Single Sign-On), 205–206
usage and insights, 207–208

ADFS deployment, hybrid identity, 82–91

ADFSSignInLogs, Log Analytics, 349

admin consent, granting via URL, 255. *See also* consent settings

administrative roles. *See also* application admin roles; roles
access packages, 299
access reviews, 303–304
entitlement management, 297
separation of duties, 301
terms of use, 295–297

administrative units, Azure AD (Active Directory), 11–14

API permissions, configuring, 254–255. *See also* permissions

app consent, blocking users, 209

app management roles, 208–212. *See also* roles

App passwords, MFA service settings, 118

app provisioning, 225–228

app registrations, 240–250

app roles, creating, 257–260. *See also* roles

Application Activity report, ADFS (Active Directory Federation Services), 207–208

application admin roles, 245. *See also* roles

application authorization, 250–260

application behavior controls, 218

Application ID URI, 250

application management, built-in roles, 212–215

Application Objects, 241–244

application ownership, 211–212

application permissions, 250–260

Application Proxy, 229–234

application registrations, implementing, 244–250

application user provisioning, 225–229

apps. *See also* access management; Azure AD Application Proxy
access reviews, 306–311
discovering, 202–208
planning access reviews for, 305
publishing in gallery, 225

ArcSight tool for SIEM, 348

assignments
access packages, 300
eligible and active, 327

audit, Azure AD admin center, 336–344

audit history and reports, PIM (Privileged Identity Management), 330–333

audit logs
downloading, 344
exporting to SIEM, 347–348
retention, 344, 347
reviewing and monitoring, 340–343
using, 234–236

AuditLog, Log Analytics, 349

authentication. *See also* CBA (certificate-based authentication); PTA (Pass-Through Authentication); user authentication
methods, 125–132
planning for, 124–125
SSPR (self-service password reset), 110–112

authorization. *See* application authorization

Azure AD (Active Directory). *See also* monitoring Azure AD
access management, 22
access reviews, 313
administrative units, 11–14
analyzing, 352–355
app registration control, 209
application gallery, 216–219
Application Object key properties, 241
application properties, 219
audit logs, 234–236
CBA (certificate-based authentication), 144–146
conditional access app control, 266–270
configuring delegation, 11–14
configuring notifications, 356
Cost Analysis tool, 323
custom domains, 16–20
data location, 21
design strategy for monitoring, 336
diagnostic logs, 349
dynamic groups, 29
email one-time passcodes, 52–54
emergency accounts, 5
external user accounts, 51–54
features, 1
Group Expiration policy, 33
group nesting, 28
Identity Governance, 153
identity providers, 54–56
IdFix tool, 61
integrating SaaS applications, 220–225
inviting users, 45–50

LinkedIn accounts, 22
Password Protection, 140–142
privacy information, 20
Privileged Identity Management, 5
resending invitation emails, 51
sign-in logs schema, 337
smart lockout, 143–144
SSO (Single Sign-On), 36
tenancy, 260
tenant setup, 1
tenant-wide settings, 20–22
usage insights, 236–237
What If tool, 148–149
Azure AD admin center. *See also* monitoring Azure AD
    audit, 336–344
    provisioning logs, 336–344
    sign-in, 336–344
    workbooks and reporting, 352–355
Azure AD Application Proxy, 229–234. *See also* apps
Azure AD B2B, 40–42, 44
    federation, 54–56
    guests invite, 50
    user credentials, 52
Azure AD Connect
    and ADFS (Active Directory Federation Services),
        84–91
    installation prerequisites, 83
    troubleshooting synchronization, 99–101
Azure AD Connect cloud sync, hybrid identity, 66–74
Azure AD Connect Health, hybrid identity, 91–98
Azure AD Connect, hybrid identity, 57–66
Azure AD DS, email addresses, 356
Azure AD identities
    device joins and registrations, 33–37
    device writeback, 37
    groups, 26–33
    licenses, 37–40
    SAML, 54–56
    users, 23–25
    writeback, 33–37
    WS-Fed, 54–56
Azure AD Identity Governance
    connected organizations, 298–299
    lifecycle of external users, 297–298
    overview, 283

Azure AD Join, 34
Azure AD logs, integrating with Azure Monitor, 186
Azure AD P2 license, 301–302, 320
Azure AD Registration, 34
Azure AD roles. *See also* administrative roles: app roles;
    application admin roles; Azure AD roles; custom roles
    for application management, 212–213
    assigning, 190–191
    assigning membership, 322–323
    assigning to applications, 258–259
    assigning to groups, 259–260
    assigning to users, 259–260
    configuring, 191–192
    configuring and managing, 3–11
    documentation, 11
    Graph API, 11
    permissions, 14–16
    PIM (Privileged Identity Management), 320–328
    planning access reviews for, 306
    resources about, 4
Azure AD user authentication
    Linux virtual machines, 146–147
    planning for, 124–125
    Windows virtual machines, 146–147
Azure MFA
    access management, 108
    enforcing, 160
    evaluating, 125
    licensing requirements, 107–108
    planning deployment, 106–108
    registration policy, 175–176
    rollout strategy, 107
    supported devices, 123
Azure monitor, 344–349. *See also* monitoring Azure AD
Azure portal
    Azure AD roles, 5–7
    bulk inviting guests, 49–50
    creating groups, 27–28
    creating users, 23–25
Azure resource management, PIM (Privileged Identity
    Management), 328–329
Azure resource roles
    access reviews, 313
    planning access reviews for, 306

B

banned passwords, 135–140. *See also* passwords

Block User, Risky Users report, 179

Block/unblock users, MFA service settings, 119

break-glass accounts, PIM (Privileged Identity Management), 334

BYOD (Bring Your Own Device), 34

C

CAE (Continuous Access Evaluation), 167

CallerIPAddress, sign-in log schema, 337

CASB (Cloud Access Security Broker), 202

catalogs, entitlement management, 286–288

Category filter, audit logs, 343

CBA (certificate-based authentication), 144–146. *See also* authentication

certificate, App Registration, 248–249

claims and token types, 249

ClaimsXray app

   custom SSO integration, 221–225

   role claim, 256

Client Secret, App Registration, 248–249

cloud apps. *See* MCAS (Microsoft Cloud App Security); Microsoft Defender for Cloud Apps

Collaboration restrictions, Azure AD, 44. *See also* external collaboration

combined registration feature, 125

conditional access

   app control, 266–270

   CAE (Continuous Access Evaluation), 167

   deployment planning, 151

   device-enforcement restrictions, 165–166

   enforce MFA, 160

   evaluation, 167

   licensing requirements, 149–150

   policies, 262

   security defaults, 152

   session management, 165

   ToU (Terms of Use), 153–159

   Windows Hello for Business, 134

conditional access policies

   assignments, 152–153

   controls, 159

   creating from templates, 167

   deployment planning, 151

   planning, 147–148

   and Sign-in risk signal, 160

   terms of use, 296

   testing, 161–162

   troubleshooting, 163–164

connected organizations, configuring and managing, 298–299

connectors to apps, configuring, 264–265

consent settings, implementing and configuring, 238–240. *See also* admin consent

Cost Analysis tool, 323

custom app integration, 220–225

custom domains, Azure AD, 16–20

custom roles, 213–215. *See also* roles

CustomApp, 241–242

D

data location, Azure AD (Active Directory), 21

Date filter, audit logs, 343

delegated permissions, 251

delegation, Azure AD (Active Directory), 11–14

device joins and registrations, Azure AD identities, 33–37

Device writeback, Azure AD identities, 37

diagnostic logs, Azure AD, 349

diagnostic settings, configuring, 345–347

DNS names, adding, 19

domains, Azure AD (Active Directory), 16–20

Dual Enrollment, Windows Hello for Business, 133

dynamic groups, Azure AD (Active Directory), 29

Dynamic Lock, Windows Hello for Business, 133

E

effective permissions, 251

eligible and active assignments, 327

email addresses, Azure AD DS, 356

email one-time passcodes, Azure AD, 52–54

Enterprise application, 234–237

entitlement management

   access packages, 288–293, 300–301

   access requests, 293–294

   catalogs, 286–288

   per-user entitlement, 299–300

   planning entitlements, 284–286

roles and tasks, 285–286

ToU (Terms of Use), 295–297

error codes, analyzing for troubleshooting, 340

Event Hub, 345–347

Exchange Online, 262

external collaboration, Azure AD, 41–44. *See also* Collaboration restrictions

external users. *See also* users

accounts, 45–50

lifecycle in Identity Governance, 297–298

F

Federated Credentials, App Registration, 248–249

Federation, hybrid identity, 82–91

FIDO2 security key authentication, 124–132

Fraud alert, MFA service settings, 119

G

Global Administrator, Azure AD, 21

Graph API

access reviews, 314

Azure AD roles, 11

Group Expiration policy, Azure AD, 33

group nesting, Azure AD (Active Directory), 28

groups

access reviews, 306–311

assigning to roles, 259–260

Azure AD identities, 26–33

planning access reviews for, 304

privileged access, 329

groups and apps, access reviews, 306–311

guest permissions, Azure AD, 43–44. *See also* permissions

guest user account, removing, 297

guests, bulk inviting in Azure AD, 49–50

H

Hybrid Azure AD Join, 34–36

hybrid identity. *See also* Identity

ADFS deployment, 82–91

Azure AD Connect, 57–66

Azure AD Connect cloud sync, 66–74

Azure AD Connect Health, 91–98

Federation, 82–91

PHS (Password Hash Synchronization), 74–77

PTA (Pass-Through Authentication), 77–81

SSO (Single Sign-On), 81–82

synchronization errors, 99–101

I

Identity, sign-in log schema, 337. *See also* hybrid identity

Identity Governance, Azure AD, 153

identity lifecycle, 283

Identity platform, protocols, 221

Identity Protection. *See* AADIP (Azure AD Identity Protection)

identity providers, Azure AD (Active Directory), 54–56

Identity Secure Score, 357–358

IdFix tool, Azure AD (Active Directory), 61

idToken, 249

invitation email, resending in Azure AD, 51

J

Join

Hybrid Azure AD, 34-36

Workplace, 34

K

KDC (Key Distribution Service), 140

Key Vault RBAC and policies, 196–198. *See also* RBAC (role-based access control)

KQL (Kusto Query Language), 348–352

L

licenses

access reviews, 301, 318

Azure AD identities, 37–40

Azure AD P2, 301–302, 320

external identities, 44

PIM (Privileged Identity Management), 324

sign-in logs, 339, 345

Linked application, Azure AD gallery, 216

LinkedIn accounts, Azure AD (Active Directory), 22

Linux virtual machines, user authentication, 146–147

LOB (line-of-business) applications, 240–244

Location, sign-in log schema, 337

locked accounts, 143–144

Log Analytics, 345–352

Logic Apps, 293

M

malicious applications, dealing with, 255
ManagedIdentitySignInLogs, Log Analytics, 349
MCAS (Microsoft Cloud App Security), 202–205
MFA (Multifactor Authentication)
  access management, 108
  enforcing, 160
  evaluating, 125
  licensing requirements, 107–108
  planning deployment, 106–108
  registration policy, 175–176
  rollout strategy, 107
  supported devices, 123
MFA registration policy, 175–176
MFA settings
  activity monitoring, 123
  implementing and managing, 115–119
  third-party and on-premises devices, 122–123
  for users, 119–122
Microsoft Authenticator app, 124
Microsoft Defender for Cloud Apps
  access policies, 270–274
  architecture, 203
  cloud discovery, 203–204
  conditional access, 266–270
  configuring connectors, 264–265
  connectors to apps, 264–265
  implementing restrictions, 261–264
  limiting SharePoint sites, 263–264
  policies for OAuth apps, 275–278
  sanctioned apps, 205
  session policies, 270–274
  using, 202–208
Microsoft Identity, protocols, 221
monitoring Azure AD. *See also* Azure AD admin center;
  Azure monitor
  designing a strategy, 336
  KQL queries, 348–352
  Log Analytics, 348–352
  notifications, 356
  using, 335
Multifactor Unlock, Windows Hello for Business, 133
multi-tenant apps, 260. *See also* tenant-wide settings
My Access portal, 286, 293, 315–316

N

NonInteractiveUserSignInLogs, Log Analytics, 349
Notifications, MFA service settings, 119

O

OATH tokens, MFA service settings, 119, 125
OAuth apps, policies, 275–278
OAuth authorization, 221
OAuth2 protocol, 251, 253
OIDC (OpenID Connect) authentication, 221, 225
  scope, 252
  tokens, 253
on-premises apps, integrating, 229–234
OpenID Connect application, Azure AD gallery, 216
OperationName, sign-in log schema, 337
organizations. *See* connected organizations
OTP (one-time passcode), 298

P

password protection, 135–142. *See also* SSPR (self-service
  password reset)
passwordless authentication, 125
passwords. *See also* banned passwords
  authentication, 124
  banned list, 135
permissions. *See also* API permissions; application
  permissions; guest permissions; role permissions
  Azure AD roles, 8–11
  and scopes, 250–254
  users and guests, 43
per-user entitlement, reviewing, 299–300. *See also* users
Phone call settings, MFA service settings, 119
PHS (Password Hash Synchronization), 61, 74–77, 81
PII (Personally Identifiable Information), 338
PIM (Privileged Identity Management)
  assignment settings, 327–328
  audit history and reports, 330–333
  Azure resource management, 328–329
  Azure roles, 320–323
  break-glass accounts, 334
  configuring for Azure AD roles, 324–328
  cost benefit analysis, 323
  licensing, 324
PIN Reset, Windows Hello for Business, 134

privacy information, Azure AD (Active Directory), 20

privileged access

    break-glass accounts, 334

    groups, 329

    overview, 320

provisioning, support for, 225–228

provisioning logs, Azure AD admin center, 336–344

ProvisioningLogs, Log Analytics, 349

PRT (Primary Refresh Token), 81

PTA (Pass-Through Authentication), 61, 77–81. *See also* authentication

R

RBAC (role-based access control), 190. *See also* Key Vault RBAC and policies

registration. *See* app registrations

Remember MFA on trusted device, MFA service settings, 118

Remote Desktop, Windows Hello for Business, 133

reporting and workbooks, Azure AD admin center, 352–355

resource identifier, 250

resource roles

    access reviews, 313

    planning access reviews for, 306

REST APIs, SCIM standards, 229

restrictions, implementing, 261–264

ResultDescription, sign-in log schema, 337

ResultType, sign-in log schema, 337

Risk Detections report, AADIP (Azure AD Identity Protection), 182

risk remediation, AADIP (Azure AD Identity Protection), 183–184

risk reports, AADIP (Azure AD Identity Protection), 176

RiskDetail, sign-in log schema, 337

RiskEventTypes, sign-in log schema, 337

RiskLevelAggregated, sign-in log schema, 337

RiskLevelDuringSignIn, sign-in log schema, 337

RiskState, sign-in log schema, 337

Risky Sign-ins report, AADIP (Azure AD Identity Protection), 179–181

Risky Users report, AADIP (Azure AD Identity Protection), 177–179

RiskyUsers, Log Analytics, 349

role permissions, analyzing, 195. *See also* permissions

Role-Based Access Control, 11

roles. *See also* administrative roles: app roles; application admin roles; Azure AD roles; custom roles

    for application management, 212–213

    assigning, 190–191

    assigning membership, 322–323

    assigning to applications, 258–259

    assigning to groups, 259–260

    assigning to users, 259–260

    configuring, 191–192

    configuring and managing, 3–11

    documentation, 11

    Graph API, 11

    permissions, 14–16

    PIM (Privileged Identity Management), 320–328

    planning access reviews for, 306

    resources about, 4

S

SaaS (Software as a Service), 202, 225

SaaS apps

    integrating with Azure AD, 219–225

    for SSO, 220–225

SAML (Security Assertions Markup Language), 225

SAML application, Azure AD gallery, 216

SAML authentication, 221

SAML claims, 221

saml2Token, 249

SCIM (System for Cross-Domain Identity Management), 226, 229

scopes and permissions, 250–254

SCP (Service Connection Point), 35

security posture, improving, 357–358

separation of duties checks, access packages, 300–301

Service filter, audit logs, 343

Service Principal Objects, 241–244

ServicePrincipalSignInLogs, Log Analytics, 349

session management, implementing, 165

session policies, Microsoft Defender for Cloud Apps, 272–274

SharePoint online, 262

SharePoint sites, limiting, 263–264

SIEM (Security Information and Event Management), 176

    sign-in and audit logs, 347–348

SIEM integrations, AADIP (Azure AD Identity Protection), 185

sign-in
   Azure AD admin center, 336–344
   event details, 237
   troubleshooting, 181
sign-in activity, accessing, 338–339
sign-in logs
   exporting to SIEM, 347–348
   ingesting, 345
   schema, 337
sign-in risk policies, AADIP (Azure AD Identity Protection), 172–174
Sign-in risk signal, and conditional access policies, 160
SignInLogs, Log Analytics, 349
smart lockout and password protection, 135–144
Splunk tool for SIEM, 348
SSO (Single Sign-On), 225
   ADFS (Active Directory Federation Services), 205–206
   Azure AD (Active Directory), 36
   hybrid identity, 81–82
SSPR (self-service password reset), 108–115. See also password protection
Status filter, audit logs, 343
storage accounts, 345–347
Sumo Logic tool for SIEM, 348
synchronization errors, hybrid identity, 99–101

T

teams, configuring for access reviews, 307
tenant setup, Azure AD (Active Directory), 2
TenantId, sign-in log schema, 337
tenant-wide settings, Azure AD (Active Directory), 20–22. See also multi-tenant apps
text messages authentication, 124
threat scenarios, 261
Time, sign-in log schema, 337
token configuration, app registration, 249
tokens, OAuth2.0/OIDC, 253
ToU (Terms of Use)
   conditional access policies, 153–159, 161
   entitlement management, 295–297
trigger custom Logic Apps, 293
troubleshooting
   analyzing error codes for, 340
   working with PII data, 338
Trusted IPs, MFA service settings, 118

U

unlocking accounts, 144
UPN (User Principal Name), 16
usage insights, 236–237
UsageLocation, licenses, 38
user accounts. See external users
user authentication. See also authentication
   Linux virtual machines, 146–147
   planning for, 124–125
   Windows virtual machines, 146–147
user consent settings, 238–240
user risk policies, AADIP (Azure AD Identity Protection), 168–172
UserRiskEvents, Log Analytics, 349
users. See also external users; per-user entitlement
   assigning to roles, 259–260
   Azure AD identities, 23–25
   blocking for app consent, 209
   and guest permissions, 43
   inviting in Azure AD, 45–50
   MFA settings, 119–122

V

Verification Options, MFA service settings, 118
VMs (virtual machines), 146–147
voice call authentication, 124

W

What If tool, Azure AD (Active Directory), 148–149
Windows Hello for Business authentication, 124, 132–135
Windows virtual machines, user authentication, 146–147
workbooks and reporting, Azure AD admin center, 352–355
Workplace Join, 34
writeback, Azure AD identities, 33–37
WS-Fed, Azure AD identities, 54–56